INFORMATION SYSTEMS FOR BUSINESS: AN EXPERIENTIAL APPROACH

France Bélanger, Ph. D.
Virginia Tech

Craig Van Slyke, Ph. D.
Saint Louis University

WILEY

John Wiley & Sons, Inc.

VP AND EXECUTIVE PUBLISHER	Don Fowley
EXECUTIVE EDITOR	Beth Lang Golub
EDITORIAL ASSISTANT	Elizabeth Mills
MARKETING MANAGER	Christopher Ruel
CREATIVE DIRECTOR	Harry Nolan
COVER PHOTO	©Blend Images/SuperStock
SENIOR PRODUCTION EDITOR	Sujin Hong
PRODUCTION MANAGEMENT SERVICES	Furino Production
PHOTO RESEARCHER	Sheena Goldstein

This book was set in 10/12 pt. Times Roman by Thomson Digital and printed and bound by Courier Westford. The cover was printed by Courier Westford.

This book is printed on acid free paper. ∞

Founded in 1807, John Wiley & Sons, Inc. has been a valued source of knowledge and understanding for more than 200 years, helping people around the world meet their needs and fulfill their aspirations. Our company is built on a foundation of principles that include responsibility to the communities we serve and where we live and work. In 2008, we launched a Corporate Citizenship Initiative, a global effort to address the environmental, social, economic, and ethical challenges we face in our business. Among the issues we are addressing are carbon impact, paper specifications and procurement, ethical conduct within our business and among our vendors, and community and charitable support. For more information, please visit our website: www.wiley.com/go/citizenship.

ISBN: 978-0-470-90372-8

Printed in the United States of America
10 9 8 7 6 5 4 3 2 1

To all of the students who have inspired us.
FB & CVS

To Pierre, who continues to challenge and inspire me, and to my friends and family for their encouragements during the process of writing this book.
FB

To Tracy, you brought life to my existence.
CVS

About the Authors

Dr. France Bélanger, Virginia Tech France Bélanger is Byrd Senior Faculty Fellow and Professor in the department of Accounting and Information Systems at Virginia Tech. Dr. Bélanger has been teaching information systems for close to 20 years in the United States, as well as in Canada, Ethiopea, Portugal, and New Zealand. She has published two books and several articles on IS education-related topics, including a highly cited book on distance learning. Dr. Bélanger is a proponent of learner-centered approaches to IS education, and has developed a number of tools and materials to facilitate such learning. She currently teaches introductory classes on information systems to undergraduates and master's-level students, as well as executive MBA students, in addition to teaching information systems research seminars to Ph.D. students.

Dr. Craig Van Slyke, Saint Louis University Craig Van Slyke is Associate Dean for Academic Programs and Professor of IT Management at Saint Louis University. Dr. Van Slyke has over 15 years of university teaching experience, primarily in the area of information systems. He has published extensively on information systems education and has co-authored several IS textbooks. Dr. Van Slyke is on the editorial review board of the *Journal of IS Education*, and has held leadership positions in Southern AIS and AIS SIG:ED. In addition, he has applied the principles of learner-centered education to a variety of courses, including the introduction to IS course for undergraduates and the core IT course for MBA students.

Contents

SECTION II MANAGING INFORMATION

5 Storing and Organizing Information   75

6 Analyzing Information for Business Decision-Making   91

| 7 | Transmitting Information | 113 |

11   Information-Based Business Process   235

| **12** | Enterprise Information Systems | 251 |

Online In-Depth Guides (posted at the Instructor and Student Companion Sites: www.wiley.com/college/belanger)

1. Hardware

2. Software

3. Networking Basics

4. Advanced database concepts

5. Spreadsheets

6. Funding information systems

7. Managing projects

8. Advanced security, privacy, and risk management

Preface

MISSION/PURPOSE

An interesting paradox often exists in introductory information systems courses. Information systems touch almost every aspect of students' lives, yet students are often detached and uninterested in the introductory course. Often they do not see the point of taking such a class, unless they are information systems majors. This book is meant to generate an interest in information systems for everyone by taking a learner-centered approach, which provides experiential learning activities and reflection questions throughout the book. In addition to being effective in terms of learning outcomes, learner-centered education is also more satisfying for the learner. The focus of a learner-centered class is on a learner-teacher partnership with shared responsibility for learning. The method not only introduces important concepts, but also deepens the learning through active application of the concepts, and reflection upon what has been learned. The learner-centered approach fits well with the characteristics of "Millennial" generation students, who are team-oriented, value continuous learning, and seek frequent feedback. They may find the learner-centered approach particularly satisfying.

The purpose of the book is to engage students while helping them become intelligent consumers of information. The book puts information center stage to allow the relevance of information systems to be put into context, thus increasing student interest. Our goal is to help students understand that they will be using information throughout their personal and professional lives. Information systems not only produce information, but they also help us make better use of information. By focusing on information, rather than systems, students are grounded in the end goal, and are better able to understand why knowledge of information systems is important. This translates into greater engagement; everyone is more engaged when they understand the relevance of what they are learning.

TARGET AUDIENCES AND APPROACH

The book is primarily directed at students who are taking the Introduction to IS course as juniors or seniors, or even first time non-IS master's-level students. Those who are not IS/IT majors often fail to see the value in the course, especially if the course is traditionally structured and focused on conceptual knowledge. Our approach to this text is based on our experience in reaching these students. Allow us to describe two experiences that have helped shape our approach.

I (Van Slyke) was asked to teach a junior-level Intro to IS course in a large-section format (200+ students per section). The first semester was somewhat of a disaster. It was the first time I had ever received evaluations below the mean. For the next semester, two changes were made. One change was to add a third exam. The more meaningful change was to have an activity in every class meeting. Instead of a 75-minute lecture, each meeting had an activity approximately halfway through the class. The activities typically lasted 5 or 10 minutes. After the activity, I led a discussion based on the activity. For example, during the supply chain management class, students were asked to get into groups of two or three and come up with three ways in which SCM systems and ERP systems are similar, and three ways in which they differ. During the activity, my fellow instructor and I (the course was team taught, although I was primarily responsible for the lectures) would wander around the auditorium answering student questions. We knew we had a winner when we saw many students flipping back through their notes on ERP, which had been covered a few weeks earlier. After the activity, I would ask students to share their findings. The findings were insightful and showed a solid grasp of the basic concepts of BOTH SCM and ERP systems. The results of the more active, learner-centered class sessions were remarkable. Not only did students perform better on the exams, but also our evaluations went up almost a full point on a five-point scale. A nice side benefit was that class sessions were much more enjoyable for the students and the instructors.

On a different level, I (Bélanger) was asked to take over and improve our Introduction to Information Systems master's-level course targeted at Masters of Accountancy (and a few MBA) students. For years, the students had been complaining about the course, which is a requirement for completion of their degree. When I first taught the class, I quickly realized that the students did not want to be there and did not care about the content. I did bring in cases as I had used the case approach in most of my master's classes. I quickly realized that the case discussion went well, but that the remainder of the "lecture" material was pretty much lost on them. In redesigning the class for the second semester, I decided to include "practice" slides for every subtopic, resulting in shorter lectures and "practice" elements throughout. The most obvious impact is that students really wanted to know why certain things happened when they acted on some technology-related issue, be it developing a privacy policy, testing their computer's security, or finding information about an emerging technology. The resulting discussions were animated, and the students came to class, even though I made attendance non-mandatory! The most blatant example of the impact of practice on student interest is the first exercise of the semester (Chapter 1) where students have to spend 5 or 6 hours without using any information technology, and then blog about it. I am surprised every time to see the depth of their realization about the importance of IT in their lives . . . and in their future careers. It starts the semester on a very different foot than what I had experienced with the traditional lecture (and case) approach.

These experiences led us to embrace a learner-centered, active approach in all of our classes (both graduate and undergraduate). Such an approach seems to be especially effective for today's students. They seem to appreciate being an active participant, rather than a passive vessel, in the learning process.

KEY FEATURES OF THE BOOK

The book is designed to support an active, learner-centered approach, with the guiding model of "praxis," putting learning into practice. Students learn best when they actively apply their learning, rather than simply learning to parrot facts and concepts. The book facilitates a learning cycle of "learn-do-reflect," which follows closely the ideas of experiential learning.

To ensure continued relevance, the book will be updated on a frequent basis since information technologies and the use of information in business will continue to evolve. An important feature of the book is that it is concise, but complemented with substantial online material. The conciseness of the book helps students who today are used to receiving information in small chunks; they live in a world of Facebook wall postings, tweets, and text messages. Forty- and 50-page chapters, filled with details, are incongruent with their world. As a result, we offer tightly focused, concise chapters that provide the necessary information without bogging down students in unnecessary detail. Students will actually fill in many of the details themselves through the active learning exercises and online materials. Our goal is to help students understand how to utilize information systems rather than being able to regurgitate facts. As such, the chapters are not meant to give every detail on every topic, but rather to provide broad guidelines for students to explore the topics of interest.

The activities and content of the text consider a constructivist perspective to learning. We try to connect the new information to what most students will already know, either from general life experience or material covered earlier in the course. For example, the SCM/ERP activity described in the examples above connected the new SCM concepts to the ERP concepts covered earlier.

In the text, we implement the concepts of experiential learning in the following ways:

- **Concise, focused chapters**—Textbooks often try to cover all possible aspects of a topic. While this is appropriate for many courses, in the introductory course, we believe it is better to focus on key information. Because of this, our chapters are concise and focused.

- **Focusing stories**—Each chapter opens with a focusing story accompanied by focusing questions that ask students to reflect on the story. This approach helps students ground the content in a concrete example. It also demonstrates the relevance of the material, which increases student engagement. The topics are specifically chosen to be relevant and understandable to most students.

- **Designed for active learning**—For each major topic, we provide activities that are designed to help students deepen their learning through application.

- **Reinforcing end-of-chapter materials**—Each chapter provides end-of-chapter activities and reflection questions that help students synthesize the various concepts in the chapter. There are three types of reinforcing elements. Review questions are straightforward questions designed to help students check their declarative knowledge of the material. Reflection questions require deeper thinking. Many of these questions require synthesis of multiple concepts. Additional learning activities are active-learning exercises that reinforce the material in the chapter through application and synthesis.

- **Detailed instructor manual**—An important element of this book is the instructor manual, which provides guidance to instructors on how to use the book in various settings and on how to apply the learning-centered approach to the material provided in the chapter. The IM provides detailed teaching notes and suggestions regarding the duration of each section and learning activity.

- **Online in-depth guides**—One of the challenges of writing a text for an introductory class is that there are many opinions on what should be covered. To accommodate this, we provide several in-depth guides that are available online. These guides take advantage of the capabilities of the online environment.

- **Online resources for active learning**—The book's website provides resources for extending and enhancing learning material from the text. Resources include links to demonstrations, simulations, interactive activities, videos, and podcasts.

- **Cases**—Recommended cases from sources such as the Ivey Business School or the Harvard Business School are provided for some of the chapters so that instructors can also use this book in a case-based class.

SUPPLEMENTAL MATERIALS

As noted above, the Instructor's Manual is an important element of this book. We developed each chapter's instructors manual while we were writing the manuscript. The publisher reviewed the chapter and its instructor's manual together to get reviewers' input on how to make the instructors material most useful. The goal is to help instructors who may be new to a learning-centered approach become more comfortable and effective in using these techniques in the classroom.

Each chapter of the Instructor's Manual includes a detailed chapter outline, an introduction to how to use the Learning-Centered Approach for this chapter, suggestions on "Pre-chapter Assignments," suggested time schedules, detailed teaching suggestions for each section of the chapter and how and when to incorporate the Learning Activities, detailed notes on how to lead the Learning Activities, answers to Review Questions, suggestions for grading the Reflection Questions, and additional Learning Activities.

Also available are comprehensive Test Banks and Slide Decks. These resources are specifically designed to support the active learning approach. In addition, there are test questions that are constructed to assess deeper levels of learning beyond simple declarative knowledge.

The Instructor's Manual, Test Banks and Slide Decks are available at the Instructor's Companion Site at www.wiley.com/college/belanger. The companion site also includes links to various resources relevant to the class, including additional exercises, articles, and learning activities developed by other instructors.

OVERVIEW OF THE CONTENT AND ORGANIZATION

The book is organized around three main sections of content. Section I provides introductory material, Section II focuses on topics related to managing information, while Section III discusses various uses of information. In-Depth Guides provided on the book website supplement these contents. Each chapter starts with a focusing story and includes learning activities for each major topic. The chapters all end with summaries of the chapter, review questions, reflection questions, additional learning activities, references, bibliography and further readings, and a glossary.

A brief summary of the chapters follows:

Section I – Introduction

Chapter 1 – The Value of Information Chapter 1 sets the stage for the rest of the book by discussing information and its role in business. The focus here is on understanding what information is and how it is used both personally and by businesses. We classify information use into three areas: communication, process support, and decision-making. This provides the framework that is used throughout the book. We also discuss the wisdom hierarchy (data, information, knowledge, wisdom), which provides further grounding for students.

Chapter 2 – Introduction to Information Systems This chapter gives a high-level view of information systems. A brief overview of key systems concepts is also provided. This overview gives students the foundation knowledge necessary to better understand information systems. In addition, the chapter provides an overview of how information systems can facilitate organizational change. The chapter also builds a case for the importance of understanding information systems, even if one is not an information systems professional.

Chapter 3 – Evaluating Information With the tremendous amount of information available today, it is especially important to be able to evaluate information. This chapter provides an overview of information quality and presents a methodology for evaluating information. Also, it discusses how to deal with information overload, information quality, and source credibility.

Chapter 4 – Gaining Strategic Value from Information The material in this chapter expands the concepts introduced in Chapter 1 to explore the strategic value of information. The chapter provides an overview of the key frameworks and concepts related to the role of information and information systems in the creation and maintenance of competitive advantage. The chapter includes popular frameworks that can be used to identify strategic initiatives and others that can be used to evaluate such initiatives. It also includes a discussion of whether competitive advantage can be sustained or not.

Section II – Managing Information

Chapter 5 – Storing and Organizing Information Databases are the core of information systems. Many business students have considerable experience with using information systems, but few have any understanding of the databases that sit at the core of these systems. This chapter serves two purposes. First, it introduces and provides a high-level overview of relational databases, database management systems, and data warehousing. The intent is to provide foundational knowledge that is useful for users rather than the in-depth knowledge necessary for IS professionals. Second, the chapter discusses how to retrieve information from databases and online resources. (Note that more detail regarding databases and database management systems is available in the online in-depth guides.)

Chapter 6 – Analyzing Information for Business Decision-making Making good decisions requires information, but that is not enough. Students must also be able to analyze information. In this chapter we help students understand the basics of business-oriented decisions and the process by which they are made. In Chapter 14 students learn about systems specifically designed to support decision-making. Here the focus is on understanding more about the decision-making process and tools that can retrieve and analyze information as part of that process.

Chapter 7 – Transmitting Information This chapter covers basic networking concepts, including the Internet and web. To demonstrate the relevance of the topics covered, the chapter opens with a discussion of cloud computing. The chapter concludes with considerations and tools for collaboration, which have become very important to business with their increasingly globally distributed workforce.

Chapter 8 – Securing Information This chapter provides an overview of information security concepts and issues, and the technologies used to handle information security. This includes discussions of personal information security, security threats, security technologies, and approaches.

Chapter 9 – Protecting the Confidentiality and Privacy of Information This chapter gives an overview of information privacy and the technologies and techniques used to help protect information privacy. The ethics of privacy are also discussed. Issues are discussed from both the individual and organizational perspectives.

Section III – Using Information

Chapter 10 – Developing Information Systems In this chapter, we provide a high-level view of the information systems development process. We focus on the perspective of an end user who may be involved in the development process. We achieve this by helping students understand the goals, processes, and roles involved with systems development.

Chapter 11 – Information-based Business Processes This chapter discusses how information supports business processes. The concept of a process is introduced, along with some familiar examples. Emphasis is placed on how information and its flow are critical to the successful completion of processes. In addition, the idea of redesigning processes to make use of information technology is discussed.

Chapter 12 – Enterprise Information Systems This chapter includes a general overview of Enterprise Information Systems. ERP, supply chain management systems, and customer relationship management systems are discussed. The chapter makes the point that virtually all business professionals interact with one or more of these systems.

Chapter 13 – Information for Electronic Business Because of its importance to individuals and businesses, we devote an entire chapter to e-business. Common e-business models and other e-business trends such as mobile commerce and global e-commerce are discussed. The chapter also includes a brief discussion of e-government.

Chapter 14 – Information and Knowledge for Decision Making Making good decisions requires good information and good decision-making processes, skills, and tools. This chapter ties together various elements of the book by showing how information is central to the decision-making process. The chapter provides students with an understanding of what is necessary for good decision making and introduces a decision-making methodology. Because ultimately an organization's only sustainable competitive advantage lies in how its employees apply knowledge to business problems, we discuss in this chapter the concept of knowledge and various approaches to knowledge management.

ACKNOWLEDGMENTS

Writing a book is always a major undertaking, and we are fortunate to have received the help of several individuals. First, we want to thank Lindsey Angle for her help testing some of the Learning Activities and to the publishing teams at Wiley and at Furino Production. We also wish to thank the reviewers of the preliminary and final versions of the chapters for insightful comments about the book:

Mary Granger, George Washington University

Derrick Huang, Florida Atlantic University

Jerry Flatto, University of Indianapolis

Amita G. Chin, Virginia Commonwealth University

Chen-Huei Chou, College of Charleston

Nathan Stout, University of Oklahoma

Gladys Simpson, Florida International University

Judith Gebauer, University of North Carolina at Wilmington

Brian West, University of Louisiana at Lafayette

Jennifer Pitts, Columbus State University

Mary Carole Hollingsworth, Georgia Perimeter College

Nenad Jukic, Loyola University, Chicago

Gary Hackbarth, Northern Kentucky University

Fred Roddamer, Michigan State University

Jun He, University of Michigan, Dearborn

Bernard Han, Western Michigan University

Lauren Eder, Rider University

David Croasdell, University of Nevada, Reno

Joan Lumpkin, Wright State University

Dan Kim, University of Houston, Clear Lake

The Value of Information

CHAPTER 1

LEARNING OBJECTIVES

By reading and completing the activities in this chapter, you will be able to:

- Compare and contrast data, information, and knowledge
- Explain the concepts of connectedness and usefulness as they relate to information
- Name the skills required for information literacy
- Discuss the importance of information literacy in a business career
- Name and describe the three main uses of information in businesses
- Compare and contrast information systems careers and information analysis careers

CHAPTER OUTLINE

- Focusing story: How information cost me (a lot of) money
- Learning Activity 1.1: A day in my technology-free life blog
- Data, information, knowledge, and wisdom
- Information literacy
- Learning Activity 1.2: How I use information
- Uses of information
- Learning Activity 1.3: How businesses use information
- Information and your career

This book is about information systems. Although it seems obvious it is worth noting that there are two parts to "information systems": information and systems. All too often people tend to get caught up in the "systems" part (the technology) and do not pay enough attention to the "information" part. But the information is really the critical part. If the information is not valuable, there is not much need

1

for the system. Because of this, we begin the book by focusing on the value of information.

However, it is also important to understand that knowing about technology can help you better deal with information. Information technology helps us organize, locate, and use information. So, while we start the book by focusing on information, much of the book helps you understand the technologies and systems that can help you deal with information.

FOCUSING STORY: HOW INFORMATION COST ME (A LOT OF) MONEY

Here's a personal story that illustrates the value of good information, or more accurately the consequences of *not* having the right information. After running my own business for several years, I decided that it was time to try something different. One of my clients wanted to expand their use of computers to a new department and needed someone with my capabilities. Since they were one of my long-term clients, I knew the company and its employees quite well. The company and its needs were a good match for me, so I discussed the possibilities with the president of the company. He was very enthusiastic about my coming to work for him. At the end of our discussion, he asked me my salary requirements. I knew what salary I needed to meet my living expenses and I gave him a figure. He immediately agreed; I instantly knew I'd make a mistake, one that would cost me quite a bit of money. My mistake was in not gathering information on the market salaries for that particular type of job. Had I been armed with this simple bit of information, I could have increased my salary by at least 20%. That's quite a bit of money to leave on the table! The thing to remember about this little tale is that better information usually results in better outcomes.

While this might seem like a simple example, it illustrates how being "information deficient" can have serious consequences. The decisions that business professionals face every day often have significant impacts. Making good decisions requires having good information. With the rapid pace of today's business world, being successful in a business career requires being able to understand what information is required, and being able to efficiently and effectively gather, evaluate, and analyze that information. Because of this, the theme of this book is information. We will help you understand information and the systems businesses use to deal with the vast quantity of information they generate and use. Our goal is for you to build the knowledge and skills you'll need to be successful in your career.

FOCUSING QUESTIONS:

1. What were the consequences of not having competitive salary information?

2. Suppose I did have information on competitive salaries, but that information was inaccurate. What are the possible consequences of having poor quality information?

LEARNING ACTIVITY 1.1	A DAY IN MY TECHNOLOGY-FREE LIFE BLOG

Most of us interact with information technology (IT) throughout our day, although we may not always be aware of it. Some uses of IT are relatively obvious, such as using email or surfing the Web. Others are not readily apparent, such texting a friend or using a debit card. Your assignment is to go one-half day without using any information technology and then write a short paper reflecting on the experience. Here are a few of the things you *won't* be able to use:

- Facebook, email, or the Web (don't even turn on your computer)
- Texts to your friends
- Debit or credit cards (unless the merchant uses an old-fashioned imprint machine)
- Smart phone applications (apps)
- And many, many others

You need to time this so that you will not have any issues with completing assignments from this or other classes. Also, if there is an emergency that requires your use of IT, disregard this assignment and deal with the emergency.

At the end of the half-day, prepare a one- to two-page reflection paper that addresses the following questions:

- What did you learn from your experience?
- What technology was the most difficult to live without?
- What kinds of tasks were the most difficult to complete without technology?

Data, Information, Knowledge, and Wisdom

Consider the following question. Is 62 good or bad? Of course, this is a meaningless question, but why is this so? The number 62 is an item of **data** (or datum), but it lacks any real meaning. Let's combine 62 with some other bits of data. Maybe 62 is the number of computers your company sold this month, which is 10 more than last month and 15 more than the same month last year. When we combine the original data with other related data, we now have **information** that helps us interpret whether 62 is good or bad. Once we have the meaningful information, we need to interpret it in order to determine what actions should be taken. (In our example, we might decide to keep doing what we've been doing, since it seems to be going well.) When we apply information to some decision or action, we have **knowledge**. **Wisdom** involves using knowledge for the greater good. Because of this, wisdom is deeper and more uniquely human. It requires a sense of good and bad, right and wrong, ethical and unethical.

One way to think about this is to consider how data, information, and knowledge form a hierarchy. Data are raw symbols (unconnected facts), information is data that has been processed so that it is useful, and knowledge is when information is applied to some decision or action. Russell Ackoff popularized this concept, although the root of the idea goes back to a T.S. Elliot's poem, "The Rock":

> . . . *Where is the Life we have lost in living?*
> *Where is the wisdom we have lost in knowledge?*
> *Where is the knowledge we have lost in information?*

There are two reasons we bring up this hierarchy. First, it gives us a way to think about different kinds of systems and how they have evolved. Data processing is relatively straightforward. Handling information is messier. You need the capability to do ad hoc (specific, customized) queries to allow different views and combinations of data. Managing knowledge is messier still.

The hierarchy also parallels how businesses have applied **information technology**. In the early days, the focus was on processing data for relatively straightforward tasks, such as tracking payrolls or bookkeeping. This evolved into **information systems**, which enabled users to connect and process data to help with management decision-making. More recently there has been movement toward being able to manage knowledge. Although it is hard to imagine, it is possible that we may see a day when technology helps us manage wisdom. This is debatable since many consider wisdom to be uniquely human.

A second, and perhaps more important, reason to understand the hierarchy is that it helps frame two important concepts: connectedness and usefulness. The shift from data to information requires connecting data elements. Combining bits of data gives the data some context and meaning. This meaning may or may not be useful, though. To be useful, information is interpreted and applied (in other words, is used), leading to knowledge.

One last thought on the hierarchy is that when we reach the knowledge level, we often realize that we need more data and information. This creates a sort of cycle, as illustrated in Figure 1.1.

While it is useful to understand the relationships among data, information, and knowledge, it is more important to know how to deal with the tremendous amount of information available today. In other words, it is important to be information literate, which is the topic of the next section.

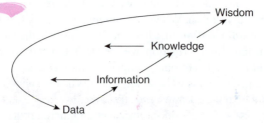

FIGURE 1.1 Data, Information, Knowledge, Wisdom Hierarchy

Information Literacy

What does it mean to be information literate? While there are a number of definitions of **information literacy**, it boils down to the ability to efficiently and effectively determine what information is needed, then access, evaluate, use, and manage that information in an ethical manner.

It may be hard to believe, but not that long ago, we had access to a much more limited amount of information. Then along came the Web and today we're faced with a tremendous amount of information every day. While it is great to have access to almost unlimited information, this comes at a price; we must learn how to deal with this information. Think about it this way. If you do not have any money, understanding investments and money management is not very important. But once you start to make a good living, you need to pay a lot more attention to these matters. It's great to have money, but the price is that you have to pay more attention to using it effectively. We are faced with a similar situation with respect to information; we're information rich, which has many advantages, but requires more skill and effort if we want to use that information effectively.

Let's look at an example. In the "old days" (before the Web), if you wanted to buy a car, you might look at a couple of magazines for reviews, then go to two or three dealers to check their prices. You would also need to get quotes on your trade-in. This was all very time consuming and inefficient, and the information you gathered was incomplete. Today the situation is very different. You can access multiple automobile reviews, get a good estimate of the value of your current car, and see the pricing of dozens of dealers—all without leaving home. There's a catch, though—you have to know what you're doing. You have to know what information you need, where to get that information, and whether that information is trustworthy. Then, since you will have so much information, you need to be able to manage and use it effectively. In other words, you need to be information literate.

Understanding how to deal with information may well have serious benefits as you move through your business career. There are many who believe that information literacy is *THE* critical skill for the future. Ilene Rockman, a leading authority on information literacy put it well:

> *Individuals who are knowledgeable about finding, evaluating, analyzing, integrating, managing, and conveying information to others efficiently and effectively are held in high esteem. These are the students, workers, and citizens who are most successful at solving problems, providing solutions, and producing new ideas and directions for the future.*
>
> (Source: http://media.wiley.com/product_data/excerpt/78/07879652/0787965278.pdf)

Uses of Information

All businesses, regardless of their size, use information for three main purposes; communication, process support, and decision-making. When properly applied, information technology enhances all of these.

LEARNING ACTIVITY 1.2   HOW I USE INFORMATION

You might be surprised at the variety of different ways in which you use information every day. Take a few minutes to identify five ways in which you use information. For example, when deciding what to buy for lunch you might use information about the restaurant's offerings such as the descriptions and prices of the items. Try to come up with a range of decisions from simple to more complex. Then, for each one, rate the impact of having bad information as being a large, moderate, or small impact. After you have done this, compare your lists with another student. For each item, discuss why you rated the impact of bad information the way you did.

The *Merriam-Webster Dictionary* defines communication as "a process by which information is exchanged between individuals through a common system of symbols, signs, or behavior." This definition clearly shows that one use of information is to communicate. Organizations must exchange information for a variety of reasons including sharing ideas, coordinating actions, and transmitting information to stakeholders. Chapters 8–10 deal with technologies that help with business communications.

Businesses also use information to support processes. A **business process** is a set of coordinated activities that lead to a specific goal or outcome. (Chapter 11 goes into much more depth regarding business processes.) Many business processes are quite complex and involve various parts of a business. For example, a customer order process might look something like Figure 1.2. (Note that this is a greatly simplified view.)

Information is used at each stage in the process. We need to know what products were ordered, who the customer is, where to ship the order, how much the products cost, and so on. This information must be communicated and properly processed throughout the process. Without information, the process simply cannot be completed. Information systems can help streamline and improve the quality of business processes.

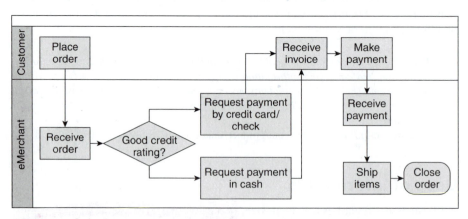

FIGURE 1.2 Order Process

(*Adapted from:* http://media.visual-paradigm.com/media/documents/bpva20ug/pdf/bpva_user_guide_ch6.pdf)

Businesses (and individuals) also use information for **decision-making**. Decision-making involves choosing among alternatives. Making this choice requires information about the alternatives (as well as other information). Put simply, you can't make decisions without information. For most of you, this is the main way in which you will use information. Because of this, quite a bit of this book is related to using information for decision-making, including Chapters 6, 7, and 13.

Two other aspects of business information use are worth mentioning. First, some businesses actually use information as a product. For example, the Nielsen Company (http://www.nielsen.com/) gathers information on television viewing habits and sells this information to various clients who use the information for decision-making. While all businesses use information for communication, process support and decision-making, only some businesses use information as a product. Second, information can be used to gain strategic value; this is the topic of Chapter 4.

LEARNING ACTIVITY 1.3	HOW BUSINESSES USE INFORMATION

As we've discussed, businesses ~~~~ with another student and think about a busine~~~~ quent, or one assigned by your instructor). Iden~~~~ related to the business. Identify key pieces of inf~~~~ on or process. Write these down and be prepared ~~~~

Communication
Process support
decision-making.

BUSINESS BOX	PROMISING INFORMATION CAREERS

Careers related to information systems and information analysis are in high demand. They also tend to pay well. The table below shows a few examples.

	Median Salary	Growth
Information Systems Careers		
Systems analyst	$75,500	20%
Information systems manager	$112,200	17%
Information systems support	$43,450	14%
Software engineer		
Database administrator	$69,740	20%
Information Analysis Careers		
Financial analyst	$73,150	20%
Auditor	$59,430	22%
Compensation analyst	$53,860	24%

Notes: Median salaries in May 2008, growth projections are from 2008–2018
Source: Bureau of Labor Statistics 2010–2011 *Occupational Outlook Handbook*, http://www.bls.gov/oco/

Knowing how to successfully deal with the incredible and growing amount of information available to us is a key life and professional skill. Businesses use information in several important ways, including for communication, to support processes, and for decision-making. Some businesses also use information as a product. They gather and perhaps analyze information, then sell that information to other businesses that use it for a variety of purposes. Understanding information and how it is used and having good information literacy skills will help you be more successful professionally and personally.

Information and Your Career

Information systems and technologies are key elements of business. Because of this, knowledge of the systems and technologies you will learn about in this book can help you in your future career.

Individuals in information systems careers design, build, support, or manage information systems. These are the jobs that typically require a major in information systems or a related field. People in information analysis careers use these systems to retrieve, report on, and analyze the information contained in the systems. The results of the analyses are passed along to information consumers, who use the results to carry out transactions and make decisions. Information systems and information analysis offer a surprising variety of interesting, rewarding careers, as illustrated in Tables 1.1 and 1.2. Information consuming careers include almost any business career, so we do not provide a table of examples.

Table 1.1 Information Systems Careers

System analyst	Works with users to understand and document system requirements
Business process analyst	Analyzes business processes in order to find ways to improve efficiency and/or effectiveness (which often involves applying information systems)
Software developer	Writes the computer programs that make up part of an information system
IT project manager	Organizes and controls projects related to information systems
Information security specialist	Ensures that the information contained in information systems is properly protected
Chief information officer	Oversees all information and information systems–related activities of an organization
System architect	Develops high-level designs of information systems, including the overall structure and essential design features.
Database administrator	Manages systems that store and organize data used in information systems
Information system trainer	Designs or delivers educational programs that help users utilize information systems

Table 1.2 Information Analysis Careers

Marketing analyst	Analyzes information related to the marketing activities of an organization
Business intelligence professional	Uses various reporting and statistical tools to help organizations gain value from their informational assets
Economic analyst	Develops economic models that help organizations predict economic conditions and outcomes
IT auditor	Ensures that an organization's information systems are operating properly and producing accurate information
Compensation analyst	Analyzes information related to the costs of paying employees
Financial analyst	Provides guidance in how to best utilize financial assets
Forensic accountant	Analyzes accounting and financial information to determine whether an activity is illegal or fraudulent

CHAPTER SUMMARY

The overall goal of this chapter is to help you understand why information is valuable in business and your personal life. Understanding the value of information is important to understanding the importance of the various information systems presented in this book. The main points of the chapter are provided below:

- Data are raw symbols or unconnected facts.

- Information is processed data that is useful.

- Knowledge is information that is applied to a decision or action.

- Information literacy is an important professional and personal skill.

- Being information literate requires being able to efficiently and effectively determine information needs, then acquire, evaluate, use, and manage that information ethically.

- Businesses use information for communication, process support, and decision-making.

- Information-related knowledge is important to virtually all careers.

- There are many careers that involve designing, building, supporting, managing, and analyzing information.

REVIEW QUESTIONS

1. Contrast data, information, and knowledge.
2. Apply the data, information, and knowledge (DIK) hierarchy to the evolution of how information technology has been applied in businesses.

3. Describe the concepts of connectedness and usefulness as they relate to the DIK hierarchy.
4. Describe how the DIK hierarchy can be thought of as a cycle.
5. What are the key abilities related to information literacy?
6. Why is it important to be information literate?
7. Name three general ways in which businesses use information.
8. Name and briefly describe three information systems careers.
9. Name and briefly describe three information analysis careers.

REFLECTION QUESTIONS

1. What is the most important thing you learned in this chapter? Why do you think it's important?
2. Why is it important for business professionals to be information literate?
3. How does better information help businesses?
4. What impact do you think improving your information literacy skills will have on your career?
5. When did bad information or incomplete information lead to bad outcomes in your life? If you were facing that situation again, what would you do differently?

ADDITIONAL LEARNING ACTIVITIES

1. Think about a common situation that a business professional (such as one in marketing, accounting, etc.) might face. For example, a finance professional might be analyzing an investment opportunity. Identify five pieces of information that would be useful in that situation. For each, discuss how bad or incomplete information might lead to negative outcomes.
2. Share your findings from #1 with two other students who are in different majors. Compare your answers. How are the answers similar? How are they different?
3. Consider one of the following major decisions: a) where to go to grad school b) what car to buy, c) which apartment to move to, d) which job offer to accept. Identify five important pieces of information that you would need to make a good decision.
   a. For each, discuss why you think that information is important. Focus on consequences.
   b. Where would you find the information you need?
   c. How will you know whether or not to trust the information you gather?
4. Consider the order process shown in Figure 1.2. For each stage in the process, what information is needed? What might be the consequences of bad information at that stage?
5. Use a job hunting website (e.g. monster.com, careers.com, or your school's career website) to find job postings for two of the information systems and two of the information analysis careers discussed in the chapter. Be prepared to share your results.

REFERENCES

Ackoff, R. L. "From Data to Wisdom." *Journal of Applied Systems Analysis* 16 (1989): 3–9.

Rockman, I. F. "The Importance of Information Literacy." *Exchanges: The On-Line Journal of Teaching and Learning in the California State University,* 2002. http://www.exchangesjournal.org/viewpoints/1100_Rockman_pg1.html.

GLOSSARY

Business process: set of coordinated activities that lead to a specific goal or outcome.

Data: raw symbols (unconnected facts).

Decision-making: process of choosing among alternative courses of action.

Information: data that has been processed so that it is useful.

Information literacy: the ability to know when information is needed, and to be able to locate, evaluate, and effectively use that information.

Information system: an organized combination of hardware, software, infrastructure, data, and people that is used to accomplish a specified organizational or personal objective.

Information technology: the hardware, software, and media used to store, organize, retrieve, and communicate information.

Knowledge: information that is applied to a decision or action.

Wisdom: the use of knowledge for the greater good.

Introduction to Information Systems

CHAPTER 2

LEARNING OBJECTIVES

By reading and completing the activities in this chapter, you will be able to:

- Describe the major functions of an information system
- Explain why it is important for business professionals to understand information systems
- Explain key concepts related to systems
- Describe the information processing cycle
- Describe the critical elements of an information system
- Explain how information systems help managers deal with information
- Give examples of business rules
- Discuss how information systems facilitate organizational change
- Compare and contrast common information systems

CHAPTER OUTLINE

- Focusing story: Registering for classes in 1981
- Learning Activity 2.1: Identifying my information systems
- Why all business professionals need to be information systems managers
- Learning Activity 2.2: Components of a system
- Overview of systems
- Learning Activity 2.3: Components of a business information system
- Foundations of information systems
- How information systems help us deal with information
- Learning Activity 2.4: Information systems and change

- How information systems facilitate organizational change
- Common information systems
- Chapter summary
- Review questions
- Reflection questions
- Additional learning activities
- References
- Glossary

FOCUSING STORY: REGISTERING FOR CLASSES IN 1981

When you registered for this class, you probably did so over the Web. Registration was very different in the 1980s. Let us describe how one of us registered for classes in 1981. First, you get a copy of the printed schedule of classes. After spending quite a bit of time studying the course offerings you finally come up with an ideal schedule. But wait . . . the chances of getting all of your "first choice" classes is pretty slim (some things haven't changed!). So, you come up with some backup plans—alternative courses and sections that are less than ideal, but will still work. Fortunately you have a good registration appointment time this semester. A little before your appointment time, you head to the student union and join the very long line for registration. While you're waiting in line, you keep an eye on the bank of television screens that are scrolling through the classes and their status. You're constantly checking to see if any of your ideal classes have closed out. When this happens, you start turning to your backup plans. You finally make it into the registration room, which is just a big multipurpose room filled with computer terminals and people. As you stand in line, you keep a sharp eye on the screens displaying the most up-to-date class status. These screens are showing the transparencies of the entire class schedule. As you watch, a person with a transparency marker walks around, crossing off classes that have recently filled. Of course, if one of your classes closes, you turn to your backup, backup plan. You finally make your way to one of the computer terminals, which is operated by trained university staff. The staff person takes your desired schedule, enters the code numbers into the system, and in a minute or two you find out if you're successfully registered. If one of your classes happens to close between the time you checked out the overheads and your data actually got entered, you're sent to the "problem table" where someone will work with you to finally get a schedule. Once your schedule is successfully entered, you stand in another line, waiting for your printed schedule and tuition bill. Congratulations, after a couple of hours (if you're lucky), you're registered!

FOCUSING QUESTIONS:

Compare the scenario above to your course registration process.

1. Name four ways the current process is better for students.

2. Name four ways the current process is better for universities.

LEARNING ACTIVITY 2.1	IDENTIFYING MY INFORMATION SYSTEMS

An **information system (IS)** is a combination of technology, data, people, and processes that is directed toward the collection, manipulation, storage, organization, retrieval, and communication of information. The system you use to register for classes is an example of an information system. Identify three information systems that you use frequently. What do you accomplish using these systems? How would your life be affected if these systems did not exist?

Why All Business Professionals Need to Be IS Managers

Information systems, such as the registration system in the opening story, are an ingrained part of our daily lives. Each of us interacts with many information systems throughout our day. In fact, information systems are so prevalent that we often do not even notice them. Most of you probably use these systems as consumers. You use your credit card to pay for a purchase, buy a song on the Web, and check your course grades online. However, in the future, most of you will use information systems as part of your profession. Because of this, it is useful to start to think like an information systems manager.

Today, everyone in business needs to be an information systems manager to some extent. Let's be blunt about this; regardless of your major or your career path, you're going to be using information systems. Learning how to effectively use these systems can help you be more effective and successful in your career. Sales representatives who know how to use customer relationship management systems well, accountants who know the ins-and-outs of a company's enterprise system, finance managers who know how to use a spreadsheet to analyze different investment scenarios will all be more successful than those who lack knowledge of these systems. To utilize these (and other) systems, it is helpful to know something about how they work. In this chapter, we lay the foundation by helping you understand concepts that are the basis of all information systems.

One reason that it is useful to think like an IS manager is that information systems are increasingly ingrained in our business and professional lives. As you may have learned in the last chapter, it is pretty hard to get through the day without interacting with an information system. How much of a pain would it be if you could not use these systems? To top it off, information systems are likely to become even more pervasive. So, it is going to become even more important to understand and know how to use information systems. A big part of career success is in knowing how to use important tools of the trade. Just as a carpenter needs to be skilled in using a hammer and saw, a businessperson needs to be skilled in using information systems. Our goal throughout this chapter and the entire book is to help you gain the knowledge you will need to make the best use of information systems in your career.

LEARNING ACTIVITY 2.2	COMPONENTS OF A SYSTEM

Part 1: Consider one of the following systems:

- Video game system

- Personal computer

- Home entertainment system

Sketch the different components (pieces) of the system. (For example, a television might be a component of a home entertainment system.) Draw lines to indicate which components interact.

Part 2: Repeat Part 1 using your school's course registration system (or another system assigned by your instructor).

Be prepared to share your diagrams.

Overview of Systems

A **system** is a set of interacting components, working together to form a complex, integrated whole in order to achieve some goal by taking inputs and processing them to produce outputs. Figure 2.1 shows a simple system and its key elements. Let's break down this definition to understand the key ideas related to systems.

- A system is made up of different pieces, called components. Components can take many different forms ranging from human organs to computer software.

- These components work together; they are interrelated.

- A system has some purpose or goal.

- The goal is achieved by taking inputs and processing them to produce outputs.

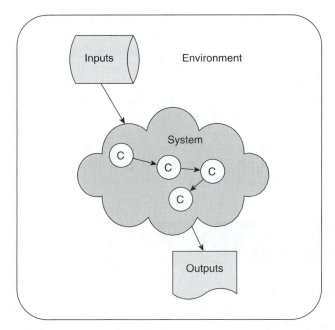

FIGURE 2.1 A System and Its Environment (Note: Components are labeled "C")

There are a few systems-related concepts that are not apparent from the definition. First, a system is separated from its environment by the system's boundary. Most systems are **open systems,** which means that they interact with their environments (closed systems, in contrast, do not). For example, your body reacts to hot weather (an element of the environment) by sweating. This is also an example of **feedback**. Your body senses its temperature rising, so the brain sends a signal to your sweat glands to activate. It is also important to note that systems are often made up of **subsystems**. A subsystem is a system that is part of a larger system. Your respiratory system is an example; it is a complete system in its own right, but is also part of the larger system of your body. Finally, **equifinality** is the idea that in an open system there are many different potential paths to the final outcome. In other words, there are different ways to end up in the same place.

One way to think about systems is to consider the components as a set of transformation processes. In this view, systems follow an input-process-output sequence. Consider a manufacturing system. Raw materials are the inputs, which are processed by various machines to produce the final product (the output). Of course, this is a greatly simplified view of a manufacturing system. Information systems work similarly. They take data as the raw material and transform it in various ways to produce usable information.

This brings us to our final general systems concept, feedback and **control:** set of functions intended to ensure the proper operation of a system. Systems often have a feedback loop, where information from the environment is sensed by the system, which may change its behavior based on the feedback. Feedback is closely linked to the concept of system control. Many systems include a control element. Think about a thermostat, which is a subsystem of a heating and air-condition system. The thermostat receives data (the current temperature) as feedback from its environment. When the temperature reaches a certain level the thermostat sends a signal to the air conditioner or heater to begin operation (the control). Then, when the temperature reaches the desired level, the thermostat signals the air conditioner or heater to turn off.

Now that you have some basic understanding of systems in general, let's turn our attention to information systems. In the next section, we cover some important concepts regarding systems designed to deal with information.

LEARNING ACTIVITY 2.3	COMPONENTS OF A BUSINESS INFORMATION SYSTEM

Pick one of the business information systems below (or another system assigned by your instructor). Identify at least five components of the system. Briefly describe the purpose of each component.

- Online ordering system (for example ordering something from Amazon.com)

- Membership tracking system for a health club

- Hotel reservation system

Foundations of Information Systems

Earlier we defined an information system as a combination of technology, data, people, and processes that is directed towards the collection, manipulation, storage, retrieval, and communication of information. The goal of this section is to help you understand some fundamental ideas related to information systems. Keeping these in mind will help you better understand the material in the rest of this book.

Before going further it is important to realize that an information system does *not* require a computer. Information systems existed for hundreds of years before the invention of the electronic computer. In this book we are primarily concerned with *computerized* information systems, which, of course, *do* require computers. Throughout this book when we say "information system" we are referring to computerized systems. Non-computerized systems will be called manual information systems.

One final note before we get into the details. People are the most important component of any information system. We will discuss the role of people in an

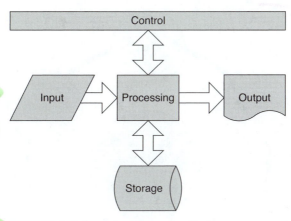

FIGURE 2.2 Information Processing Cycle

information system in more detail later. However, we want to make sure that you understand that people are critical to the success of any information system.

Information systems include the following operations, as shown in Figure 2.2. This is sometimes called the information processing cycle. (Note that some versions of this cycle do not include control as a separate operation.)

1. Input: Collection of data and its conversion into a form that allows processing.

2. Processing: Manipulation and transformation of data.

3. Storage: Holding place for data so that it can be retrieved at a later time.

4. Output: Transformation of processed data into a form that can be understood by its eventual user.

5. Control: Enforcement of correct processing procedures.

These operations are carried out by the various components of the information system. For example, the screen on your laptop computer may perform output operations. As is the case with any system, these components interact with one another in an organized manner. For instance, when you drag your mouse to select some text, the mouse provides input to the system, which processes the input and highlights the text on your screen (an output device). Your computer's central processing unit (CPU) carries out much of the processing and control activities, while your hard drive performs storage activities.

Information systems have six critical elements, as shown in Figure 2.3:

• Data: raw facts, text, numbers, images, and the like that serve as the inputs for producing information.

• Hardware: physical devices such as the processor, storage media, and peripheral devices (such as printers and displays).

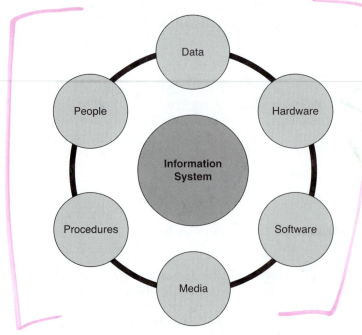

FIGURE 2.3 Elements of an Information System

- Software: set of instructions that govern the operation of an information system.

- Communication media: set of devices and protocols (rules) that enable computers to communicate with each other.

- Procedures: instructions for the proper use of the information system.

- People: individuals who use the information system.

You might be a little surprised to see people included in this list, but they are critical to any information system. People are necessary to use and interpret the output of the information system. Even in information systems that seem like they are totally automated, people still need to monitor the system to make sure it is working correctly. Of course, people also build and maintain the system. Procedures for using the system are also necessary. Basically, the procedures tell the users how to properly utilize the system to support their tasks.

Before moving on, let's talk a little more about hardware and software. (There is more detail about this in the In-Depth Guides.) Software provides the instructions that govern the operation of a computerized system. Broadly speaking, there are two types of software: systems software and application software. Systems software includes operating systems, such as Windows and Linux, and utilities such as antivirus and data-compression software. This is a little confusing because when you install an operating system a number of utility programs are often installed at the same time. For our purposes, it is enough to just think of system software as a "necessary evil." Most people would not buy a computer just to run the system software, but you have to have the system software in order for the computer to operate.

People buy computers to run application software, which lets you do what you really want to do with the computer. Examples include word processors, spreadsheets, accounting packages, games, and media players. One of the exciting aspects of today's information systems landscape is the dizzying array of applications that are available. As more and more applications are developed, our computers become more and more useful (and more fun!).

There are also different types of hardware involved in an information system. In addition to the computers involved, there are storage devices (such as hard disks), printers, keyboards, and communication devices. You can learn more about hardware in the In-Depth Guide.

To understand how the elements of an information system fit together, let's consider a simplified view of an information system for hotel reservations. (To keep this discussion from being too long, we are omitting some details of the system.) The goal of this system is to allow reservation agents at a hotel to reserve rooms for guests. Let's take a look at the specific roles involved in this information system.

- Data: The data serve as the facts that are manipulated by the system to produce information that is used by the reservation agent and hotel management.
  - a list of rooms, their status (available or reserved), prices, payments, customer information, and name of reservation clerk.

- Hardware: The hardware performs computations, stores the data and software used by the system, displays information, and provides the platform for users to interact with this system.
  - reservation agent's personal computer, a computer that has the software for the system, hard drives that have the database that stores the data for the system, and printers for reports.

- Software: The software controls the operation of the computer, including how the data are retrieved, manipulated, and communicated.
  - the operating system of the various system computers, and one or more applications specific to the task of making room reservations.

- Communication media: This allows the various hardware components to communicate with each other.
  - the network cabling and other devices that facilitate communication such as routers.

- Procedures: The procedures govern how the reservation agent and hotel managers should interact with the system.
  - instructions for how to get into the system, which data has to be entered, how to retrieve information, and how to generate reports.

- People: In this system, people provide input for the system, control how the system is used, and interpret the information from the system.
  - customer, reservation agent, and hotel managers.

Now that you know the basics of information systems, let us turn our attention to how information systems help businesses deal with the tremendous volume of information they must cope with every day.

STATS BOX: GROWTH OF APPLICATIONS IN APPLE'S APP STORE

By any measure, Apple's iPhone has been very successful. One reason for its success is the large and growing number of applications, or "apps" available in Apple's App Store. These applications make the phone more useful to its owners, whether the app is work-related or just a fun game. The chart below shows the steady growth of the number of available apps. Google's Android has a similar store, called the Android Marketplace.

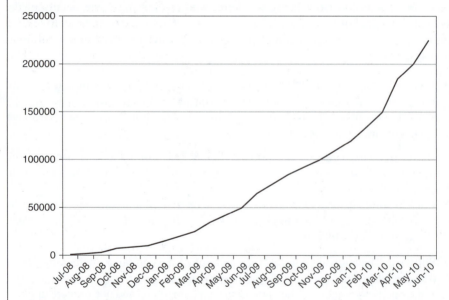

FIGURE 2.4 Available Apps in Apple's App Store

Source: http://en.wikipedia.org/wiki/App_Store

How Information Systems Help Us Deal with Information

Businesses face an ever-increasing amount of information. Given the increasing complexity of today's business environment, this is unlikely to change anytime soon.

We are fortunate to have information systems to help us cope with this tsunami of information. Let's look at how information systems accomplish this.

First, information systems let us gather large amounts of data quickly, easily, and reliably. Think about your last trip to the grocery store. Today most stores have electronic scanners that read a bar code (called the Universal Product Code, or UPC) that is printed on most products. The checkout clerk runs each product across this scanner, which reads the UPC and electronically enters the fact that the product is being purchased into the system that facilitates the checkout process. (Eventually, this data also goes into other systems, such as the inventory control system.) The system retrieves the item's price from a database, and the amount is added to the order's total. (This is an example of a point-of-sale information system.) All of this happens in a fraction of a second, and many different clerks can be performing the same basic operation at one time. In addition, the data are entered very accurately. A large grocery store has tens of thousands of transactions per day, so being able to gather this data quickly and accurately is important.

Second, information systems allow businesses to store and organize very large amounts of data. Databases of over one terabyte (approximately one trillion characters of data) are not uncommon. Information systems allow businesses to store volumes of data in an organized manner that allows for rapid retrieval. This simply would not be possible with manual systems.

Third, information systems perform their data manipulations quickly, accurately, and consistently. As long as the hardware is operating correctly and the software is designed and implemented correctly, an information system is very consistent in its manipulations. Using our grocery store example, the checkout system will retrieve the same price for a given item every time that item is scanned (unless the price changes). It will also correctly calculate any necessary sales tax and will correctly total the customer's order. Again, this degree of speed, accuracy, and consistency simply cannot be matched with manual systems.

Finally, information systems let us retrieve and output information in a variety of forms, depending on what is useful to the user. The same information can be displayed on a screen, printed, or graphed. Different purposes may require different forms of displaying data; charts and graphs are good for showing large amounts of data at a glance, while printed reports are often better for showing details.

One important function of many business information systems is to enforce **business rules**. A business rule is a statement that defines or constrains an aspect of a business with the intent of controlling behaviors within the business. All businesses have rules that govern the operation of the business. Some examples include:

- A hotel reservation system that will not allow assigning a room that is already occupied.

- A course registration system that does not allow registering for a course that is full.

- An order entry system that automatically calculates the proper sales tax and adds it to the customer's invoice.

Information systems enforce business rules by not allowing violations to occur. Let's look at an example. Suppose your company had a business rule that said you could not accept an order from any customer who is more than 30 days past due on their bill. Only a supervisor can override this rule. The business' order entry system enforces this rule by not allowing sales representatives to enter orders from past-due customers. When such customers want to place orders, the system refuses to accept the order until a supervisor gives approval. Later we will tell you about how information systems are analyzed and designed. One critical aspect of systems analysis and design is to properly understand business rules, which are then carefully built into the design of the system.

BUSINESS BOX   **HOW SOUTHWEST AIRLINES FLIES HIGH WITH INFORMATION SYSTEMS**

Southwest Airlines has grown from a small, three-city commuter airline to become one of the major players in the United States domestic air travel market. One reason for Southwest's success is its ability to maintain low fares while still being profitable. The company prides itself on offering a positive "end-to-end" customer experience while being highly efficient. Information systems help Southwest achieve these goals. Millions of customers and potential customers visit Southwest's website each month. While using Southwest.com is fairly simple from the customer's perspective, the process of buying tickets is actually very complex. Highly sophisticated information systems handle the tasks of finding and pricing available flights. International code sharing with other airlines further complicates things. Southwest's systems must make it easy for customers while properly communicating with its own internal systems as well as those of partner airlines.

Southwest is an innovator in the use of information technology. For example, it was the first airline to use barcode scanning on boarding passes. (Formerly magnetic strips on the back of cardstock were used; a much more expensive product.) In addition, Southwest.com allows customers to book other travel-related services, such as rental cars and hotel rooms. All of this is accomplished by a sophisticated, complex set of information systems that must interact smoothly and seamlessly.

Gary Kelly, CEO of Southwest, summarized Southwest's view on information systems:

"I think in many cases, we've got the best of both worlds, where we've enhanced customer service through automation, and we've also lowered our costs through automation. And that's just a grand slam homerun."

(Source: Ross & Beath, 2007)

LEARNING ACTIVITY 2.4   **INFORMATION SYSTEMS AND CHANGE**

Research a process that has been substantially improved by information systems. (Registering for classes is one example.) Briefly describe the before and after processes. Describe how the process was improved. Was the process more efficient/effective for both the organization and its customers? How?

Here are some Web resources that might help you with your research:

- *CIO Magazine*: http://www.cio.com/magazine
- Technology section of the *New York Times*: http://www.nytimes.com/pages/technology/index.html
- *Computer World* online: http://www.computerworld.com/
- *Information Week*: http://www.informationweek.com/index.jhtml

(Note: Your instructor may give you a specific example to research.)

How Information Systems Facilitate Organizational Change

There are many ways in which information systems help managers bring about organizational change. To help you understand how this occurs, we break down these ways into four categories: process improvements, automation, control, and information flow.

Process Improvements

The increasing use of information systems was partially responsible for the business process redesign movement that started in the 1990s and continues today. Information systems can help organizations improve both the efficiency and effectiveness of processes. For example, many companies use information to enable customer self-service, which means that individual customers interact with systems to perform their own customer-service activities. A classic example of this is the automated teller machine (ATM). In the past, when you needed cash you would go into your bank and either cash a check or make a withdrawal. Now, you simply find a convenient ATM, put in your card, push a few buttons, and get your cash. The old process was less efficient from the bank's perspective because of the need for the teller's time. The ATM illustrates how information systems can bring about process improvements and control. Not only is the process more efficient, it is also more effective due to the reduced number of errors and the increased convenience for the customer. Of course, there are many other such examples of information systems improving efficiency and effectiveness, including the course registration example at the beginning of the chapter.

Automation

Some processes have been totally automated. A good example of this is online ordering. Prior to the popularity of the Web, ordering something from a company typically involved either calling the company and placing the order with a sales representative or filling out and mailing in an order form, which was then entered into the company's order system by a clerk. Today, you simply go to the company's website, fill out an online form, and the order is directly entered into the order system. Even something as simple as buying gasoline is often fully automated. When you pull up to the pump all you need to do is slide your credit or debit card through the slot, fill your tank, take your receipt, and go on your way. In this past, an attendant would make an imprint of your card on a special form, and would then fill out the relevant information. This form would go to the bank, which would do additional processing so that the gas station could be paid for your purchase.

Control

Information systems also enable organizational change by improving process controls. When properly designed and implemented, an information system can ensure that business rules are followed throughout a process. For example, an order entry system might refuse to accept an order for a customer whose account is past due. Returning to our gas station example, prior to automation the station attendant was required to check a "hot list" of stolen or suspended credit cards before accepting a card as payment. As you might imagine, this business rule was often violated, especially when the station was busy. Today, the information system checks the status of the account before allowing the customer to pump any gas. The course registration system from the chapter opening is another example of enforcing rules. Under the less-automated system it was relatively easy to register for a class even if you did not have the necessary prerequisites. (Don't ask us how we know this!) Today's systems typically check prerequisites before allowing a student to register for a course. (This assumes that the prerequisites have been properly entered into the system.)

Information Flow

Finally, information systems improve communication and information flow in organizations. Workflow systems facilitate information flow throughout a work task. Consider a simple example of a grade change. The professor enters the grade change into the information system. The system generates an email notifying the appropriate administrator that a grade change is pending her or his approval. The administrator reviews and approves or denies the request. If the request is approved, the system notifies the professor and student, and the grade change is recorded and made permanent. Throughout the process, the system manages the flow of information and controls the process. Information systems also facilitate information sharing. Examples include document repositories and communication systems, such as electronic mail.

BUSINESS BOX	COOPERS BREWERY: USING INFORMATION SYSTEMS FOR QUALITY AND SUSTAINABILITY

Coopers Brewery, Australia's largest family-owned brewery, uses information systems to improve the quality of their beer while at the same time minimizing waste and maximizing energy efficiency. Coopers uses s supervisory control and data acquisition (SCADA) system to ensure the quality and consistency of their beer. The system uses electronic monitors and regulators to control and monitor brewing conditions throughout the brewing and fermentation process. This is an example of how information systems can improve process control. The data captured from the large brewing tanks are stored in a database and are analyzed by brewers. In addition, an enterprise system helps Coopers determine the quantity that should be brewed for each type of beer, making sure that supply is sufficient to satisfy demand without overproducing.

Information systems also help Coopers in its quest to be a more environmentally friendly company. For example, fluid waste products are monitored to make sure that they meet certain environmental standards. Also, the enterprise system allows Coopers to optimize their packaging and distribution processes, resulting in less waste and lower fuel consumption. Information systems also control product movement throughout the manufacturing process, which further reduces waste by reducing packaging losses due to manufacturing errors. The manufacturing system also lets Coopers track the amount of waste materials sent to landfills and the ratio of recyclable to nonrecyclable materials used in the manufacturing process.

Compiled from: http://www.coopers.com.au/corporate/
environment, http://www.cio.com/article/print/596252,
http://www.packagingcovenant.org.au/documents/File/
Coopers_Brewery_AP_07_10.pdf

The ways in which information systems enable change combine to allow for changing organizational forms. To help you understand this, we discuss virtual teams and the role of middle managers. Members of virtual teams are not necessarily located in the same place; they may literally be spread across the globe. Information systems allow these teams to work together by providing communication functions such as email and video conferencing, which allow the members to interact even though they are not co-located (in the same location). Other tools such as shared calendars and document repositories also help virtual teams function.

On a larger scale, information systems help companies flatten their organizational structure. In the past, many mid-level managers existed to monitor the activities of lower level workers and to facilitate communication between lower and upper levels of the organization. Today, information systems can serve some of these same functions by enforcing business rules and facilitating communication throughout various processes. In addition, communication technologies such as email and websites improve communication flow across organizational levels and provide employees with information that previously only existed at higher levels of the organization. As a result, many companies have flattened their organizational structures.

Our goal up to this point in the chapter has been to help you understand information systems and their role in organizations. In the next section, we provide brief overviews of some common information systems. Many of these are discussed in greater detail later in the book.

Common Information Systems

There are numerous different types of information systems in modern organizations; we will cover many of these in the rest of this book. For now, it is useful to get a flavor of the range of information systems used by organizations. A useful way to do this is to classify information systems according to the impact or "reach" of the system, as shown in Figure 2.5. At the bottom of this triangle are personal productivity systems, which are typically used by one person or a small group. At the top are global systems, the use of which spans multiple organizations across the world.

To further help you understand the range of information systems available today, below we provide some brief examples of systems at each level of our triangle.

- Personal applications: These systems serve to help make individuals' daily work more efficient and effective. Office automation systems (such as office suites like Microsoft Office) are included in this category. Other examples include are note-taking systems such as Evernote or OneNote, to-do list systems, personal information managers, personal calendars, and drawing programs.

- **Transaction processing systems** (TPS): collect, monitor, process, reports, and store large volumes of data that are created by business processes. The grocery store point-of-sale system we mentioned earlier is an example. Many organizations have a large number of TPS. Other examples include payroll processing

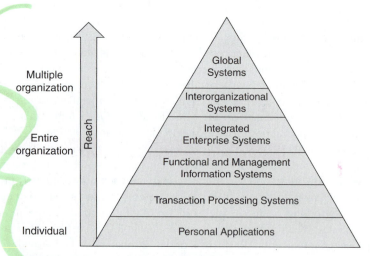

FIGURE 2.5 Levels of Information Systems
Source: Adapted from: Turban & Volonino (2009), p. 43

systems, invoicing systems, and inventory control systems. (Note that many of these stand-alone TPS have been replaced by integrated enterprise systems, which we discuss later.) In the earlier days of information systems, most TPS operated in batch mode, which means that they gathered all of the data to be processed, then processed the data in one batch. The modern trend is towards online transaction processing (OLTP) systems, which process the data as soon as it is gathered.

- Functional and management information systems: monitor, control, and analyze the operation of functional areas. Examples include financial management systems, sales force automation systems, materials requirements planning (MRP) systems, and benefits administration systems. As was the case with TPS, integrated enterprise systems have replaced many of these stand-alone systems.

- Integrated enterprise systems: Today, many organizations (particularly large organizations) have replaced many of their stand-alone TPS and functional systems with integrated, enterprise-wide systems that impact multiple functional areas. A stand-alone system is primarily used in isolation from other systems. An integrated system has multiple applications in a cohesive interrelated system. For example, enterprise resource planning systems provide an integrated set of modules that carry out the information processing and reporting systems for the entire organization. Enterprise systems are very important; we devote an entire chapter (Chapter 12) to them.

- Interorganizational systems: span organizational boundaries to connect companies to suppliers and customers. **Electronic data interchange** (EDI) is at the heart of many of these systems. EDI allows the systems in one organization to directly interact with those in a partner organization. Many electronic business systems enable partner organizations to interact seamlessly and thus are considered interorganizational systems.

- Global systems are simply interorganizational systems that cross national boundaries. These systems are often more complex than other systems due to cross-national differences in language, currency, and culture.

Stand-alone systems are often integrated so that they can exchange data. For example, an accounting application may pull data from a transaction processing system. Such integration is very important to the smooth operation of an organization.

CHAPTER SUMMARY

This chapter helped you learn how information systems help organizations operate effectively. This knowledge gives you a foundation that will be helpful in understanding the rest of the book. Here are the main points discussed in the chapter.

- Information systems combine technology, data, people, and processes to help collect, manipulate, store, organize, retrieve, and communicate information.

- In today's information-rich business environment, business professionals must be skilled at dealing with a variety of information systems.

- Systems are made up of components that work together to achieve a goal by taking inputs and processing them into outputs.

- The information processing cycle consists of input, processing, storage, output, and control.

- Information systems are made up of six critical elements: data, hardware, software, communication media, procedures, and people.

- Information systems help managers deal with information by improving how data are collected, organized, manipulated, and output.

- Information systems can help enforce business rules.

- Information systems facilitate organizational change through improving, automating, and controlling processes and improving information flow.

- Categories of common information systems include personal applications, transaction processing systems, functional and management information systems, integrated enterprise systems, and global information systems.

REVIEW QUESTIONS

1. Explain why business professionals need to understand information systems.
2. Define the term "system."
3. Name the key system concepts discussed in this chapter.
4. Describe the information processing cycle.
5. Name and describe the six critical elements of an information system.
6. Why are people a critical element of an information system?
7. Contrast system and application software.
8. Name four ways in which information systems help managers deal with large volumes of information.
9. What is a business rule? How do information systems relate to business rules?
10. Name five ways in which information systems can facilitate organizational change.
11. Name and briefly describe six types of common information systems.

REFLECTION QUESTIONS

1. What is the most important thing you learned in this chapter? Why is it important?
2. What topics are unclear? What about them is unclear?
3. What relationships do you see between what you learned in this chapter and what you learned in Chapter 1?

4. How do information systems impact your life? Pick one information system and discuss how your life would change if it did not exist in a computerized form.

5. Think about your future career. How do you think you will use information systems? In what ways will better understanding information systems help advance your career?

6. In the text, we said that people are key components of information systems. How can people cause an information system to fail? Provide specific examples to back up your claims.

ADDITIONAL LEARNING ACTIVITIES

1. Relate the information processing cycle to the class registration system described at the beginning of the chapter. Provide examples of the inputs required, the processing that occurs, outputs produced, data that are stored, and controls that should be in place.

2. Use the information processing cycle to discuss a system that allows consumers to make purchases from an online store. (Your instructor may give you a different information system example to use.)

3. Consider an information system that processes a company's payroll. Give specific examples of each of the critical elements involved in this information system. (The critical elements are data, hardware, software, communication media, procedures, and people.)

4. Identify three business rules that you have encountered. For each rule, briefly discuss how information systems enforce the rule. (For example, a course registration system would block a student from registering for a course if s/he did not have the necessary prerequisites.)

5. Find an example of how information systems facilitated organizational change. Using the categories presented in the chapter, discuss how the information system helped facilitate the change.

6. Describe two examples of how an information system improved the efficiency or effectiveness of a business process. Be specific: What elements of the process were improved? How? Did the improvement benefit both the organization and its customers or suppliers?

7. Find a specific example of an information system for each of the six types of common information systems described in the chapter. For instance, Microsoft Excel would be an example of a personal productivity information system. (Note: Do not use the examples provided in the chapter!)

REFERENCES

Ross, J.W. and C. Beath. "Building Business Agility at Southwest Airlines." MIT Sloan Research Paper No. 4664-07; CISR Working Paper No. 369 (2007). Available at SSRN: http://ssrn.com/abstract=102096; http://www.cio.com/article/print/504370)

Turban, E. and Volonino, L. *IT for Management: Improving Performance in the Digital Economy.* New York: John Wiley & Sons, 2009.

GLOSSARY

Business rule: statement that defines or constrains an aspect of a business with the intent of controlling behaviors within the business.

Control: set of functions intended to ensure the proper operation of a system.

Electronic data interchange: structured, electronic transmission of data between organizations.

Equifinality: the idea that in an open system, there are many different potential paths to the final outcome.

Feedback: process by which a system regulates itself.

Information system: combination of technology, data, people, and processes that is directed towards the collection, manipulation, storage, retrieval, and communication of information.

Open system: a system that interacts with its environment.

Subsystem: a system that is part of a larger system.

System: set of interacting components that work together to form a complex whole by taking inputs and processing them to produce outputs.

Transaction processing system: system that collects, monitors, processes, reports, and stores data generated by an organization's transactions.

CHAPTER 3

Evaluating Information

LEARNING OBJECTIVES

By reading and completing the activities in this chapter, you will be able to:

- Discuss why it is important both personally and professionally to be an informed information consumer
- Describe information overload, its consequences and approaches for dealing with information overload
- Discuss the relationship between information overload and information evaluation
- List and describe the dimensions of information quality
- List and describe the elements of an information evaluation framework
- Given an information-related task, evaluate information for its usefulness and believability

CHAPTER OUTLINE

- Focusing story: Biased information in a trusted outlet
- Learning Activity 3.1: How good is this information?
- Being a smart information consumer
- Learning Activity 3.2: My online life and information overload
- Information overload and the need to evaluate information
- Learning Activity 3.3: Dimensions of information quality
- Information quality
- Learning Activity 3.4: Evaluating information sources
- Evaluating information
- Chapter summary
- Review questions

- Reflection questions

- Additional learning activities

- References

- Bibliography and further readings

- Glossary

With the tremendous amount of information available today, information evaluation is an important skill. The goal of this chapter is to help you gain the knowledge and skills necessary for effective information evaluation.

FOCUSING STORY: BIASED INFORMATION IN A TRUSTED OUTLET

Information is often biased, sometimes intentionally, sometimes unintentionally. This point was driven home to me personally many years ago. I was reading an article in a trade magazine that I read frequently. Generally I found the magazine informative and useful. This particular article was about an output device called a plotter. A plotter is used to produce large-format drawings, such as architectural and engineering plans. I was quite knowledgeable about plotters having sold and used them extensively. This particular article was about a special kind of plotter that used pencils rather than pens, inkjet, or laser technologies. To say the article was positive about pencil plotters would be a gross understatement. The author went on and on about how much better the pencil technology was than any of the others. This was puzzling to me, as I knew that other technologies had many advantages that were not mentioned in the article. For example, inkjet and laser-like plotters were much faster than pencil plotters. They were also more versatile with respect to the kinds of images they could produce. To be blunt, I questioned the sanity and knowledge of the author. After coming to the end of the article, I saw in small print a short "about the author" note. The author was the national marketing manager for the only company that manufactured pencil plotters (at that time). The reason for the article's glowing opinion of pencil plotters became quite clear. The author had a heavy bias for pencil plotters; the information in the article reflected this bias. I often wondered how many companies purchased pencil plotters because of that article; hopefully not many.

This story illustrates the importance of taking a critical view of information, especially when making important decisions. Being able to evaluate and understand information quality are important skills for business professionals. You will face many situations that will require you to gather information in order to make important decisions. Making these decisions based on biased or otherwise low-quality information can lead to serious consequences, such as spending thousands of dollars on an inferior plotter.

FOCUSING QUESTIONS:

1. Give two examples of instances where you encountered biased information. What made you think the information was biased?

2. What are some of the consequences of relying on biased information?

LEARNING ACTIVITY 3.1   HOW GOOD IS THIS INFORMATION?

The Focusing story related a situation in which bad information led to unfortunate outcomes. But what do we mean by "bad information" ? In small groups, discuss the meaning of information quality. Develop a list of characteristics of "good" information.

After your discussion your instructor will give you an information source, such as a blog or wiki. Evaluate the information contained in the source using the characteristics you developed as a guide.

Being a Smart Information Consumer

Being successful in today's knowledge society requires being a good information consumer. We are faced with an ever increasing array of information and being able to deal with that information is a key life skill. In Chapter 1 we discussed the concept of information literacy. You may recall that being able to effectively evaluate information is an element of information literacy. The goal of this chapter is to help you improve your information evaluation skills.

As is often the case, the amount of readily accessible information available online has both advantages and disadvantages. The obvious advantage is that we now have easy access to information that would have been quite time consuming and difficult to track down just a few years ago. Unfortunately, there are also a few downsides as well. One of the great things about the Internet is that there are almost no "gatekeepers" who determine what can be posted. However, this also means that there is no quality control. Almost anyone can post information about almost any topic. In more traditional media, the responsibility for evaluating the quality and correctness of information was the job of editors and publishers. Today, with respect to much of the information on the Internet, that responsibility shifts to the information consumer (in other words, you). So, the ability to evaluate information is an important skill.

Often when we deal with something routinely, we tend to go into an autopilot mode; we act without really thinking. Being faced with so much information, we run the risk of using the information without thinking critically about it. When we are making small decisions, this is usually fine. However, when making higher-impact decisions, it is worthwhile to be a more discerning information consumer, especially by critically evaluating the quality of the information.

Information evaluation is the systematic determination of the merit and worth of information. Information evaluation skills will be important to you both personally and in your business career. Personally you need to be able to sift through and evaluate many kinds of information. As you go through life you will have to make many decisions, some big and some small. When facing a big decision, such as choosing a job or making a major purchase, the consequences of relying on bad information can be quite severe. As you saw in the Focusing Story, acting on bad information can lead to bad outcomes.

STATS BOX

Poor quality information is costly. One study estimated that on average bad information costs businesses up to 10% of their revenue. (Kerr et al., 2007). Another study, conducted by the Data Warehousing Institute, estimates that poor quality data costs organizations in the United States over $600 billion per year.

(http://www.crmbuyer.com/story/44711.html?wlc=1278446605)

The need to intelligently deal with information is also important to your career. As is the case with your personal life, you will face many decisions throughout your career. Knowing how to evaluate the information you must deal with is particularly important. Much of your reputation and thus career success depends on the outcomes of the decisions you make. Making decisions based on better information usually leads to better outcomes.

In business, we often use information to reduce uncertainty. The more uncertainty there is surrounding a decision, the more we seek information in order to reduce that uncertainty. This makes intuitive sense, but there is an underlying assumption that the information is of good quality. Poor-quality information is ineffective at reducing decision uncertainty.

Consider the example of hiring a new employee. When a manager is evaluating potential new employees, s/he gathers information about the person in order to increase the odds of making a good hiring decision. Information on the applicant's experience, education, and character all come into play. If this information is accurate, then the manager is better able to hire the right person. But what if the information on the applicant's resume is false? In this case, the likelihood of hiring the right person decreases.

The bottom line here is that it is important to be able to intelligently evaluate all sorts of information. In this chapter we help you understand information quality and provide some approaches to evaluating information.

BUSINESS BOX   **RESUME FRAUD**

Although resume fraud has been around for many years, instances of fraud often increase in times of high unemployment. Such fraud ranges from small embellishments to outright lies. Here are a few of the more common resume lies:

- False or exaggerated education, such as listing degrees that were not completed

- Omitting past employment

- False military record

- Enhancing job responsibilities or titles

- Falsifying credentials, such as certifications

- Exaggerating skills and accomplishments

What does this have to do with information evaluation? First, evaluating a job candidate's resume requires a critical eye in much the same way as evaluating any information source. Second, as is the case with all information evaluation, the amount of effort you should put into evaluation depends on the consequences of making a bad decision. For example, more effort should go into evaluating the resume of a potential executive than those of entry-level, part-time workers.

Here are a few tips for evaluating resumes:

- Ask the applicant for specific dates of employment and verify these dates.

- Seek out additional references through contacts within the organization or profession.

- Perform a Web search of the candidate, but allow the candidate to respond to any negative information. (Remember that it is easy to post false information about someone.)

- Look for inconsistencies, such as missing dates and employment gaps.

- Actually check with references to verify employment dates, job titles, and responsibilities.

As a job applicant, you should be sure to not fall into the trap of inflating your resume. Any short-term gains will be more than erased when the fraud is uncovered. More and more organizations are taking very hard lines on resume fraud, in part because it displays a commitment to ethical business practices. The bottom line is that resume fraud is not only unethical, it is also unprofitable in the long run.

Sources: http://online.wsj.com/article/SB122653695797922735.html; http://www.marquetinternational.com/pdf/Resume%20Fraud-Top%20Ten%20Lies.pdf

---

LEARNING ACTIVITY 3.2　　**MY ONLINE LIFE AND INFORMATION OVERLOAD**

We all face a daily torrent of information. The more "connected" you are, the more information you face. As you go throughout tomorrow, pay attention to how you deal with the information you face. Prepare a one- or two-page report that addresses the following questions:

- What strategies do you use to determine what information is important and to reduce the amount of information you deal with?

- How successful are these strategies?

- How could you improve your approach to information filtering?

Information Overload and the Need to Evaluate Information

Herbert Simon, the Nobel Prize–winning psychologist and economist, stated in 1971:

> ... in an information-rich world, the wealth of information means a dearth of something else: a scarcity of whatever it is that information consumes. What information consumes is rather obvious: it consumes the attention of its recipients. Hence a wealth of information creates a poverty of attention and a need to allocate that attention efficiently among the overabundance of information sources that might consume it.

Although he did not use the words "**information overload**" this is basically what he is talking about: being faced with more information than we can effectively process. The more information we have to sift through, the less attention we have to devote to other tasks. Information overload is a very real problem, both in terms of our business and personal lives. It reduces productivity, increases stress, and can actually lead to physical health problems.

Business managers bring some of this on themselves. Managers know the value of information and gather information for many different reasons (Butcher, 1998):

- To improve decision making

- To justify decisions

- To verify previously-acquired information

- To "play it safe" by making sure they do not miss any relevant information

- To use the information later

Add to this the amount of unsolicited information that managers face and you can see why information overload is a problem for many managers.

To better understand this, we will use the example of an IT manager named Pat. Pat's company is getting ready to purchase a large number of laptop computers and Pat has to decide which brand of computers to buy. (The company has already decided on the specifications needed.) Pat could easily become overloaded with information for this decision. She may begin reading reviews of the various brands, checking prices and specifications, and so on. She may reach out to her colleagues to see what their experiences have been with the brands being considered. While this is a big decision, Pat could easily become bogged down with more and more information. Being able to deal with these situations is important to being a successful manager.

Two major strategies for dealing with information overload are filtering and withdrawal (Savolainen, 2007). Withdrawal essentially involves disconnecting from sources of information; not checking email, turning off the television, not surfing the Web, and so on. This may not always be a viable option for business professionals, so filtering may be a better choice for many of us.

Filtering information involves knowing what information we need and what information merits attention and use, which makes knowing how to evaluate information a critical skill in today's information-rich world. Most of us evaluate information almost constantly, but without really paying attention to how we do so. For example, we scan our email inboxes and choose which messages to open, which to save for later reading, and which to delete or ignore. We make these decisions, in part, based on an evaluation of the information we think is contained within the message. In most cases, we evaluate the information in email messages based on its relevance to whatever we are working on at the time. Relevance is one aspect of information quality, which we discuss later in the chapter.

If we dig a little deeper, we see that relevance is only one piece of the puzzle. Whether consciously or unconsciously, we evaluate other aspects of information when we decide what to do with it. If the information is too old, untrustworthy, or is otherwise of questionable quality, we essentially ignore the information and do not use it (at least that is what we should do). As you can see, improving your information evaluation skills will help you better deal with information overload.

Sidebar – Dealing with Information Overload

How can you deal with the torrent of information you face every day? Fortunately, there are a number of techniques you can use to help avoid information overload. First, understand and identify your information priorities and needs. Once you have determined these, try to focus on the most relevant information. This can be difficult, especially when you see information that is not really relevant at the moment, but may be later. To deal with these situations, it is a good idea to develop some organizational structure for this "may need later" information. There are some good technology solutions for this. If the information is mostly Web-based, an application such as "Read it Later" (http://readitlaterlist.com/) provides an easy means of saving items for later reading. You can also use a note-taking application such as Evernote (www.evernote.com/) to make a quick note about an item that you may want later. Evernote lets you tag notes and organize them in notebooks, which can make recalling information easier. You can also use something like Google Docs to make a quick note or record a link for later use. Be sure to put something meaningful in the document so you can find it later. Finally, think about what information sources are the most useful and highest quality. Be sure to consider these sources first when faced with relevant information needs. This can save quite a bit of searching time.

LEARNING ACTIVITY 3.3   DIMENSIONS OF INFORMATION QUALITY

Information quality is an important, complicated topic. Because of this, there are many views on what constitutes "high quality" information. Search the Web to discover different views on the dimensions of information quality. What, in your opinion, are the three most important dimensions of information quality? Why do you think these are the most important?

Information Quality

Garbage in, garbage out. This old saying succinctly sums up the importance of information quality. As we mentioned in previous chapters, businesses rely on information to carry out business processes and for decision-making, both of which require good information. If you use bad information as the basis for a decision, you are probably going to make a bad decision. But just what does "good information" mean?

The issue of information quality is surprising complex. As you may have noticed when doing your research for Learning Activity 3.3, there are many different opinions regarding the meaning of information quality. We like the definition of **information quality** as information that is fit for its intended use. In other words, the information is useful toward the achievement of whatever task is at hand. While we like this definition, it is not particularly useful in helping us understand information quality. A more useful approach is to think about the dimensions of information quality; the characteristics of information that make it useful or not useful.

Dozens of studies have investigated the issue of the dimensions of information quality. As a result there are many different lists of information quality dimensions. (Some of these studies are listed in the References and Further Reading section at the end of the chapter.) Richard Wang and Diane Strong (1996) developed a framework that is useful for understanding and evaluating information quality. (They used the term "data quality" but the concepts apply to information quality.)

Wang and Strong put quality dimensions into four categories:

- Intrinsic quality includes dimensions of quality that are important regardless of the context or how the information is represented.

- Contextual quality includes the dimensions that may be viewed differently depending on the task at hand.

- Representational quality concerns how the information is provided to the user.

- Accessibility quality has to do with whether authorized users can easily access the information.

In this chapter we focus on the first two categories. Figure 3.1 shows the dimensions in these categories, and Table 3.1 provides definitions for each dimension.

We need to make a few points regarding the information in Figure 3.1 and Table 3.1. First, there is considerable disagreement regarding the dimensions of information quality. It is possible (even likely) that your instructor will have a different perspective on which dimensions are most important. If you want to know more about this topic, we recommend that you read some of the articles in the Bibliography and Further Reading section of this chapter. The Lee et al. (2002) and Knight and Burn (2005) papers both give nice overviews of prior research on information quality.

Second, we want to reemphasize the importance of considering context when thinking about information quality. Consider the example of stock price information. It is common for free information services (such as Yahoo! Finance) to delay stock

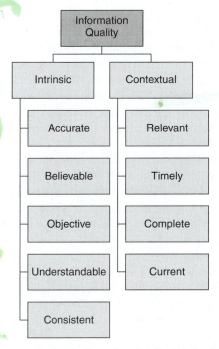

FIGURE 3.1 Information Quality Dimensions

price information by 15 minutes. If you are a casual investor this usually is fine; the delayed information is acceptably current for keeping track of the value of your portfolio. However if you are a professional stock day-trader, a 15-minute delay is unacceptable (even a 15-second delay could be a problem), and would be considered poor-quality information.

Table 3.1   Information quality dimension definitions

Intrinsic Dimension	Definition: Extent to which the information is:
Accurate	Correct, free from error, and reliable
Believable	Regarded as true and credible
Objective	Free from bias
Understandable	Easily comprehended
Consistent	Compatible with previous information
Contextual Dimension	
Relevant	Applicable and useful for the task at hand
Timely	Available in time to perform the task at hand
Complete	Of sufficient depth and breadth for the task at hand
Current	Sufficiently up-to-date for the task at hand

(*Sources:* Adapted from U.S. Department of Justice (2010) and Knight & Burn (2005))

Finally, information quality costs. On the surface, it may seem like we should want the highest quality information possible. However, this typically is not true. Few individuals or organizations are willing to invest the resources necessary to ensure the highest possible information quality. More commonly, we want information that is of sufficient quality to carry out tasks effectively. In other words, we want "good enough" information quality. This is not to say that information quality is not important; quite the opposite is true. Information quality is critical to business success. However, it is also important to consider the costs of information quality and what level of cost is justified.

At a more micro level, a good way to think about the costs of information quality is to consider the possible consequences of poor-quality information. For more important, higher-impact decisions, it is worthwhile to pay much more attention to information quality than for lower-consequence decisions. If you are buying a house, you want very high-quality information. If you are buying a pack of notebook paper, lower-quality information is probably fine. We will talk more about this in Chapter 6, which covers decision-making.

It is easy to see how poor-quality information can negatively impact a business. Consider when you order a product from an online store. If the description of the product is inaccurate, you may end up with a product that does not meet your needs. If the inventory information is not current, you may not receive the product when expected. Biased reviews may lead you to order a poor-quality product. We could go on, but you probably have the idea. In almost any business situation you can easily see the impact of poor-quality information.

Let's return to Pat, the IT manager who needs to pick a laptop brand. She needs to pay careful attention to the quality of the information she is using to make this decision. She clearly needs to have accurate information, but she also needs to get the information in a timely manner. Objective information is very important in this case. Pat probably would not want to rely on a vendor's sales representative for information on the durability of the laptops. One thorny issue in this situation is the completeness of the information. Pat needs to have enough information to make the decision while avoiding information overload. It is also important to have current information. Specifications and pricing information changes often in the computer industry, so Pat needs to ensure that she has current information.

Now that you have some understanding of information quality, it is useful to gain a better understanding of how to evaluate information, which is the topic of the next section.

BUSINESS BOX	**INFORMATION QUALITY AS AN ETHICAL ISSUE**

In 1986, the journal *MIS Quarterly* published Richard Mason's important article, "Four Ethical Issues of the Information Age." One of these four issues was information accuracy. In the article, Mason relates the story of the March family who were the victims of information inaccuracy. Despite the fact that for years the Marches had faithfully made their mortgage payments on time, the computerized system used by the bank for some reason failed to record one of the payments. This ultimately led to a foreclosure proceeding. Unfortunately, Mrs. March learned of the foreclosure while recovering from a heart attack. The news was such a shock that she suffered a stroke that almost took her life. The good news is that after considerable time and effort, the Marches were able to keep their home and actually won a substantial settlement from the bank.

Because of the degree to which our lives depend on information, Mason points out that the organizations responsible for the information have a special ethical obligation to ensure and maintain the accuracy of the information.

We have personal experience with this; one of us was once denied a loan due to incorrect information in a credit report. One of the negative entries in the credit report was a default on a credit card that occurred at the age of twelve, which was clearly inaccurate. It took quite a bit of time and effort to eventually clean up the credit report. The loan was to make a substantial retail purchase, so in this case the merchant also lost a sale. There are many other examples of inaccurate information causing everything from minor inconveniences to death. We agree with Mason that information accuracy is an ethical issue and an obligation for organizations that store and provide information.

Source: http://www.misq.org/archivist/vol/no10/issue1/vol10no1mason.html

LEARNING ACTIVITY 3.4	EVALUATING INFORMATION SOURCES

You are thinking about investing in real estate. While doing some initial research you obtained the following sources of information:

- A 2004 book on investing in residential real estate

- A local real estate broker

- A database of historical sales prices from your local tax collector

Rank these three sources based on how willing you would be to rely on the information from the source. Briefly justify your rankings.

Evaluating Information

Now that you understand a bit about information quality, the question of how to evaluate information comes into play. There are some elaborate methodologies for examining information that is internal to an organization's information systems. A full discussion of that topic is beyond our scope in this chapter, but is discussed in more detail in Chapter 14. So we focus on how to evaluate information obtained from third parties, such as websites and published articles. Although we frame the discussion around external sources, the basic principles can also be applied to internal information.

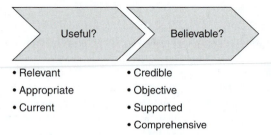

FIGURE 3.2 Information Evaluation Framework.

A quick Web search for information evaluation strategies reveals many different approaches to evaluation. There are common themes that run through most of these strategies. Basically, there are two questions you need to answer: 1) Is the information useful? and 2) Is the information believable? In the next few paragraphs we discuss the various "questions within questions" that you need to answer in order to evaluate information. Figure 3.2 illustrates our information evaluation framework.

As we noted earlier, filtering is one strategy for dealing with information overload. The ability to effectively evaluate information is important to being able to effectively filter information. Being able to quickly disregard poor-quality information is a big help to dealing with information overload.

Before getting into the details, it is important to understand that the information evaluation is highly context-dependent. You can only evaluate information within the context of your information needs. Consider Wikipedia as an information source. Anyone can add information to Wikipedia regardless of his or her credentials. If you are researching a topic for pleasure, Wikipedia is often a fine source of information. However, if you are researching a topic for a work task, we would caution against relying exclusively on Wikipedia. In the first situation, it really does not matter much if the information is slightly inaccurate, incomplete, or out of date. For a work-related task, however, inaccurate, incomplete, or old information may be completely unacceptable.

Evaluating Usefulness

Before taking the time to assess the believability of information, you should determine whether the information is useful for the task at hand. If the information is not useful, then there is no need to assess its believability. To determine whether information is useful, evaluate whether the information is relevant, appropriate, and sufficiently current. Each of these is a "go, no-go" assessment. At any point if you evaluate the information as not passing the test, there is no need to go further. For example, if the information is not relevant, you do not need to determine whether it is appropriate or sufficiently current.

Information relevance is the degree to which the information is pertinent to the task at hand. You can determine the relevance of information by asking yourself a simple question: Will this information help me accomplish my task? The answer

to this question is often not a simple yes or no. There are varying degrees of relevance. Some information is highly relevant while other information may only be
tangentially relevant. With experience you will be able to determine what degree
of relevance merits further evaluation. To complicate matters further, relevance is
context-dependent. In some cases information that does not seem relevant early in
a task may become relevant as you move towards a solution. All this being said,
relevance really does come down to figuring out whether the information helps you
accomplish your task.

If the information seems relevant then you should evaluate whether the information is appropriate: Is the information suitable for your purpose? For example,
if you are researching a new technology when preparing a report for your manager,
the information contained in a high school student's report may not be appropriate for your use. You will need to assess the level of detail and the depth of the
information in light of your information needs. Again, this is a context-dependent
question.

Currency is the final evaluation criteria related to usefulness. Assessing
whether information is sufficiently current requires thinking about how current you
need the information to be. If you are seeking information related to rapidly evolving topics, such as information technology, you may need information that is very
up-to-date. For less volatile topics, older information may be fine. Unfortunately,
determining the currency of Web-based information is often difficult. Many websites do not clearly indicate when the information was last updated. We caution
you against relying too much on undated websites when you need up-to-date
information.

Evaluating Believability

Once you establish that the information is sufficiently useful, you need to determine
whether the information is believable. This requires assessing whether the information comes from a credible, objective source, is well supported, and sufficiently
comprehensive.

Evaluating the credibility of an information source can be tricky in many cases
and relatively straightforward in others. For example, more formal publications, such
as peer-reviewed journals, often include short author biographies, which can be helpful in assessing credibility. Often a quick search of the author can further help you
evaluate credibility. If the author has written widely on the topic in reputable sources,
s/he probably has sufficient expertise to merit using the information. In some cases,
however, it is almost impossible to determine who wrote the information. We would
be reluctant to trust information from such sources, unless it is provided by an organization with a solid reputation. If the information is provided by a respected organization you can usually trust that the individual who created or compiled the information
is knowledgeable on the topic.

The next step is to evaluate whether the information is objective. To determine
whether information is objective, first consider the source of the information. An
organization or individual who is credible may still have a bias or some agenda that

makes the information less objective. Our opening story provides a good example of this. The author of that article undoubtedly had considerable expertise in plotters, but he also had a bias toward his own company's products, which tainted the information he provided. Another example is when an organization provides information on its own product or service. Using factual information from Dell's website is fine, but relying on Dell to provide an unbiased comparison of their computers to Hewlett-Packard's is a bad idea. You should also pay attention to the language used. If much of the information is presented using persuasive or emotional language the information probably is not entirely objective. Language that is more fact-based and neutral is more likely to be objective. Finally, if the topic is controversial, consider whether all sides of the issue are presented. If only one side is presented, the information is probably not entirely objective.

Evaluating the support for claims is also important. Begin by determining whether or not any support is offered. Claims without support should not be trusted. For example, we might say that this is the greatest information systems book ever written, but unless we present some evidence to back this claim, it is not believable. When support is offered, you should evaluate the quality of the support. Claims that are supported by credible sources, such as peer-reviewed journals, are usually believable. Also consider the reasonableness of the claim. There is a saying that states extraordinary claims require extraordinary evidence. If a claim seems unreasonable or is widely different from other views of the topic, you should require more supporting evidence before believing the claim. Finally, think about whether the claim is testable. This does not mean that you have to actually test the claim, but if you can see no reasonable way to do so, be reluctant to rely on the information.

Our final evaluation criterion is whether the information is sufficiently comprehensive. Assessing comprehensiveness requires assessing the depth and breadth of the information. Breadth concerns whether all aspects of a topic are covered while depth concerns the level of detail provided. When evaluating comprehensiveness look for obvious gaps in the information. If it seems like something is missing, it probably is. Finally, consider whether there are unanswered questions. If there are you will need to gather more information. Throughout your evaluation, keep in mind the context of your particular task; information that is sufficiently comprehensive for one task may be lacking for another.

All of this probably seems like a lot of work. Keep in mind that the more information you evaluate, the more some of this will become second nature. Also, match the level of effort you put into evaluation against the importance of the task. The more important the task, the more worthwhile the effort put into evaluating the information.

CHAPTER SUMMARY

In this chapter you learned about information quality and information evaluation. The intent of the chapter was to give you an appreciation for the importance of information evaluation from both a personal and professional perspective, and to help you gain the knowledge necessary to effectively evaluation information. The main points from the chapter are given below:

- Being able to evaluate information is a key element of information literacy, which is an important skill for both our professional and personal lives.

- Career and personal success depends, in part, on the outcomes of the decisions we make. Our ability to evaluate the information we use to make these decisions affects the quality of our decisions.

- Information overload occurs when we are faced with more information than we can effectively process.

- Increasing our information evaluation skills helps us deal with information overload by reducing the amount of attention and time we devote to low-quality or nonuseful information.

- Intrinsic dimensions of information quality include accuracy, believability, objectivity, understandability, and consistency.

- Contextual dimensions of information quality include relevance, timeliness, completeness, and currency.

- Evaluating information concerns determining whether the information is useful and believable.

- Useful information is relevant, appropriate, and sufficiently current for the task at hand.

- Believable information is credible, objective, well-supported, and comprehensive.

REVIEW QUESTIONS

1. Briefly explain why information evaluation skills are important personally and professionally.
2. Explain the relationship between information and uncertainty in decision-making. Use a decision-making example to illustrate your answer.
3. What is information overload? How is information evaluation related to information overload?
4. Briefly describe five reasons managers gather information.
5. Name and briefly describe two major strategies for dealing with information overload.
6. Explain the phrase "garbage in, garbage out" as it relates to information quality and decision-making.
7. Name and briefly describe the four categories of information quality dimensions discussed in the chapter.
8. Contrast intrinsic and contextual information quality.
9. Name and briefly describe the information quality dimensions discussed in the chapter.
10. What are the two main questions that must be addressed when evaluating information?
11. Name and describe the elements of the Information Evaluation Framework.

REFLECTION QUESTIONS

1. What is the most important thing you learned in this chapter? Why is it important?
2. What topics are unclear? What about them is unclear?
3. What relationships do you see between what you learned in this chapter and what you have learned in earlier chapters?
4. How does information evaluation relate to information systems?
5. How do you think information evaluation skills will be helpful in your future career?
6. Describe a situation where, looking back on it, you spent more time gathering information than you should have. How do you know when you've gathered enough information?
7. Why is information quality an ethical issue?
8. How do you decide how much effort to put into information quality/evaluation?
9. Why is context important to information quality and evaluation?

ADDITIONAL LEARNING ACTIVITIES

1. Think about a situation in which you relied on poor-quality information. Briefly describe the situation and what poor-quality information you relied on. Identify the dimension(s) of information quality where the information was not of adequate quality. (For example, you might have taken a course that you thought was required, but you were looking at out-of-date requirements and the course was no longer required. This information was poor on the accuracy and timeliness dimensions of information quality.)
2. A rubric is a set of rules for assessing something. For example, many professors use rubrics for grading assignments. Develop a rubric for judging information quality. (For a rubric template see: http://edweb.sdsu.edu/triton/july/rubrics/Rubric_Template.html).
3. Many of you may have graduate school in your future. Choosing the right graduate school is a major decision-making task. Suppose you want to attend a full-time MBA program. Use the information evaluation framework to evaluate the information you would find in each of the following sources. For each information source, rate each dimension on a scale of 1 (lowest) to 5 (highest). Give a brief explanation of each of your ratings:
   - Princeton Review's Graduate Business Schools website (http://www.princetonreview.com/business-schools-programs.aspx)
   - A university's website about their MBA program
   - A friend who recently got his MBA
   - The admissions councilor for an MBA program
4. For each of the following tasks, one a scale of 1 (very little) to 10 (a significant amount of time) indicate how long you would spend evaluating the information you would use in completing the task. Briefly justify each of your ratings.
   a. Deciding where to go for a celebration dinner
   b. Deciding what pair of running shoes to buy
   c. Deciding what laptop to buy
   d. Deciding which of two post-graduation job offers to accept
5. For each of the following tasks, one a scale of 1 (very little) to 10 (a significant amount of time) indicate how long you would spend evaluating the information you would use in completing the task. Briefly justify each of your ratings.

a. Deciding which item to make the "daily special" for a restaurant
b. Deciding what employee to hire for a part-time, temporary job
c. Deciding what employee to hire for a management-level job
d. Deciding which outlets to use for a national marketing campaign
6. In this chapter, you learned about information quality and information evaluation. Create a diagram that links the information quality dimensions to the information evaluation criteria.

REFERENCES

Butcher, H. *Meeting Managers' Information Needs*, London: Aslib, 1998.

Kerr, K., T. Norris and R. Stockdale, "Data Quality Information and Decision Making: A Healthcare Case Study", *Proceedings of the 18th Australiasian Conference on Information Systems*, Toowoomba, (5–7 December 2007) 1017–1026.

Knight, S., and J. Burn. "Developing a Framework for Assessing Information Quality on the World Wide Web." *Informing Science* 8. (2005) 159–172. http://inform.nu/Articles/Vol8/v8p159-172Knig.pdf.

Savolainen, R. "Filtering and Withdrawing: Strategies for Coping with Information Overload in Everyday Contexts." *Journal of Information Science*, 33(5) (2007): 611–621.

Simon, H. "Designing Organizations for an Information-rich World," in *Computers, Communications and the Public Interest.* Martin Greenberger, ed. Baltimore: Johns Hopkins Press, 1971, 40–41.

United States Department of Justice. *Information Quality: The Foundation for Justice Decision Making*, 2010. http://www.it.ojp.gov/documents/IQ_Fact_Sheet_Final.pdf.

Wang, R. and D. Strong. "Beyond Accuracy: What Data Quality Means to Consumers." *Journal of Management Information Systems* 12(4) (1996): 5–34.

(http://jis.sagepub.com/content/33/5/611.short).

BIBLIOGRAPHY AND FURTHER READINGS

Lee, Y., D. Strong, B. Kahn, and R. Wang. "AIMQ: A Methodology for Information Quality Assessment." *Information & Management* 40 (2002): 133–146.

GLOSSARY

Accurate (information): The degree to which information is correct and free from error.

Believable (information): The degree to which information is regarded as true and credible.

Comprehensive (information): The degree to which information is of sufficient depth and breadth for the task at hand.

Consistent (information): The degree to which information is compatible with previous information.

Current (information): The degree to which information is sufficiently up-to-date for the task at hand.

Information evaluation: The systematic determination of the merit and worth of information.

Information overload: Being faced with more information than one can effectively process.

Information quality: The degree to which information is suitable for a particular purpose.

Objective (information): The degree to which information is free from bias.

Understandable (information): The degree to which information is easily comprehended.

Relevant (information): The degree to which information is applicable and useful for the task at hand.

Timely (information): The degree to which information is available in time to perform the task at hand.

Gaining Strategic Value from Information

LEARNING OBJECTIVES

By reading and completing the activities in this chapter, students should be able to:

- Present the main steps in the strategic planning process.
- Identify competitive advantage frameworks and discuss their purposes.
- Discuss methods for evaluating strategic initiatives.
- Explain the concept of hyper-competition.

CHAPTER OUTLINE

- Evaluating Strategic Initiatives

  Critical Success Factors

- Learning Activity 4.1: What does Yahoo! need for success?

  Priority Matrix

- Learning Activity 4.2: Competitive Advantage at Outrigger Hotels and Resorts

- Hyper-competition: Sustainability of Competitive Advantage

- Learning Activity 4.3: Google vs. Yahoo!

- Chapter Summary

- Review Questions

- Reflection Questions

- Additional Learning Activities

- References

- Bibliography and Further Readings

- Glossary

FOCUSING STORY: HEALTHCARE ON MY CELL PHONE

In the business world, a key goal for many companies is to achieve some form of competitive advantage over rivals. Of course, creating a new product that no one has ever thought of before, or a product that is so much better than previous ones, definitely gives an organization a competitive advantage (think of the Apple iPod, for example). However, it is often possible to also get competitive advantages from creative uses of existing technologies. One of these exciting newer trends in the world of medicine is mobile health, also called mHealth.

mHealth offers healthcare services delivered via mobile technology, such as cellular or smart phones, tablets, or personal digital assistants (PDA). Mobile healthcare services can include compliance (ensuring that patients follow their medication plan), information dissemination (providing caloric information for obese patients or sugar content for diabetics), or monitoring (measuring hypertension, cholesterol, etc.). Surveys conducted in 2010 suggest that there are actually over 200 million mHealth applications available today, and that 70% of individuals around the world would be willing to pay for using at least one such application. Another survey by PricewaterhouseCoopers suggests that 40% of Americans would be willing to pay for a device that would monitor their health remotely and send the information to their doctor.

The idea of mHealth is to provide healthcare services where they are needed, and often to those who cannot access them. One application called text4baby from Voxiva helps prevent infant mortality by sending weekly text messages to young women about their babies' health. There are also mobile health screening programs at home for executives in Pakistan and at truck stops for truck drivers in Canada. mHealth smoking applications have been shown to help smokers quit smoking. Another company called Avacta is developing a handheld device to detect dangerous flu diseases in the field, without having to bring samples to laboratories for tests. In China and Malaysia, doctor offices have started using less expensive text messaging instead of phone calls to remind patients of appointments; results include improved attendance by 7% in China and reduced nonattendance rates of 40% in Malaysia. An even more exciting potential for mHealth is in providing health services to remote regions of developing countries, which are facing constant growth of life-threatening chronic diseases (hypertension, obesity, heart disease, and diabetes) and other communicable diseases. In developing countries, there are limited healthcare infrastructures, hospital resources, and not enough healthcare workers, particularly in remote regions. This is where mHealth can make a difference because even in remote regions of developing countries, mobile phones are often available. There was a 56% penetration rate of mobile phones in developing countries as a whole in 2009, with countries like South Africa and Gabon achieving 88% (in 2007).

FOCUSING QUESTIONS:

1. Identify other potential applications of mHealth.

2. Would you be more likely to follow a health program if it was offered on your mobile device?

3. What are the benefits of mHealth for existing healthcare organizations?

Sources: "Case Study: Organizations, Technology and PR Unite to Deliver Mobile Health Service Targeted at Moms and Moms-to-Be," *PR News* 66 (45) (Nov 22, 2010): 45; Contant, Jason. "Mobile Health Unit Rolls into Truck Stop," *OH & S Canada* 24 (7) (Oct/Nov 2008): 21; "Dow University Launches Mobile Health Screening Program," *Financial Post* (Oct 15, 2010); Kahn, James G., Joshua S Yang, & James S Kahn. "Mobile Health Needs and Opportunities in Developing Countries," *Health Affairs* 29 (2) (Feb 2010): 252–58; McNamara, Paul. "Would 40% Pay for Mobile Health Services?" *Network World* 27 (17) (Sep 13, 2010): 42; "Mobile Health Apps to Triple by 2011." *Informationweek – Online,www.informationweek.com,* (Jan 5, 2011); "NEWS: Mobile Health Check," *The Engineer* (Jul 16, 2007): 9.

Strategic Information Systems

Today, organizations need a wide variety of information systems for conducting their day-to-day business. For example, some information systems can be used for basic accounting services, such as payroll systems, or for communication support services, like electronic mail. In this chapter, we are interested in those information systems that are more specifically meant to provide organizations with competitive advantages. We call those business initiatives **strategic information systems**. Importantly, it is not necessary to have unique and proprietary information technology to make an initiative strategic; it is how the information systems are used that can provide the added value or strategic advantage organizations seek by implementing such initiatives.

Strategic Planning Process

The identification of strategic information systems should follow a structured set of steps, or **strategic planning process**. Of course, there are situations when some techno-oriented individuals start using a new technology and believe everyone should have access to it to increase productivity of the workforce. When the Blackberry and iPhone devices came out, many managers believed they needed them, even though they had no real idea why. Some companies gained real advantages from increased mobility, while others realized the devices did not really help their employees beyond being more accessible. Most large organizations, however, do have a strategic planning process in place. The goal of the strategic planning effort is to identify how the organization will use and manage their resources for strategic purposes (think competitive advantage). It provides a roadmap for decision-making related to information systems. Figure 4.1 shows an example of the steps involved in a typical information systems strategic planning process. Notice how the process is iterative, with later steps in the process requiring managers to revisit earlier steps. In addition, there may be several phases involved within each of the stages (rectangles).

Step 1: Strategic Business Planning

Before an organization can decide what IT initiatives can be used to gain competitive advantage, it has to clearly identify what the mission of the organization is, and how it is going to achieve this mission. The strategic business planning phase is often referred to as "Know Who You Are." Executives or leaders of the organization should perform strategic business planning on a regular basis (which varies substantially between companies as to how often this is). The outcomes of the strategic business planning sessions should include the mission and vision of the organization, its goals for the future, and the strategies that will be used to achieve those goals.

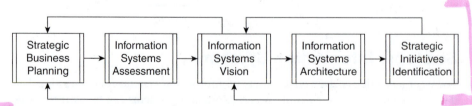

FIGURE 4.1 Sample Information Systems Strategic Planning Process

While strategic business planning is not specifically focused on information systems, it is essential to the IS strategic planning process because the organization needs to know what it is trying to achieve before it can identify how information systems are going to help achieve those strategic objectives. The goal is to achieve a high level of alignment between the business side of the organization and its information systems. With high alignment, there will be a high level of fit between the priorities and activities of the IS function and the strategic goals of the organization.

STATISTICS BOX

The alignment of business and information systems objectives is a key concern for top managers. Every year a survey is conducted among members of the Society for Information Management (SIM) about the top concerns of senior managers about information technology. As can be seen in the table below, the most recent survey continues to highlight IT and business alignment as one of the top priorities.

Top IT Management Concerns, 2003-2010*

Concern	2010	2009	2008	2007	2006	2005	2004	2003
Business productivity and cost reduction	1	1	7	4				
Business agility and speed to market	2	3	13	17	7		5	7
IT and business alignment	3	2	1	2	1	1	1	1
IT reliability and efficiency	4	6						
Business process re-engineering	5	4	18	15	11	5	10	10
IT strategic planning	6	7	3	8	4	4	4	2
Revenue-generating IT innovations	6	8						
IT cost reduction	8	5	7	4				
Security and privacy	9	9	8	6	3	2	3	3
Globalization	10	15						

*Cells with blanks represent an issue that the survey did not ask about in that year.
Source: Jerry Luftman and Tal Ben-Zvi. "Key Issues for IT Executives 2010: Judicious IT Investments Continue Post-Recession," *MIS Quarterly Executive* 9 (4) (Dec 2010): 263–273.

Step 2: Information Systems Assessment

Once managers know the main strategic goals of the organization, they need to identify the current state of information systems resources in the organization. This phase is sometimes referred to as "Know Where You Start." It is important to conduct a proper assessment of resources because these resources could enable information systems managers to meet or surpass some strategic objectives, or conversely constrain the organization regarding what it can do. For example, if the organization has been collecting data about their customers for a very long time but never used that data, there might be some great potential for new systems that will make use of this data (we will discuss Customer Relationship Management Systems (CRM) in Chapter 12). On the other hand, lack of certain resources may also constrain what an organization can achieve. For example, if all individuals in the IT group are trained on a particular system, replacing the system with technology that is completely different may create a very disruptive situation for the organization, which may even impact profits for some time. The outcome of the **information systems assessment** is a picture of the current state of information systems resources in the organization. Depending on the assessment, it may be necessary for the organization to revise their strategic goals.

As you can see, information systems resources are not limited to just technology. There are three categories of resources: technical resources, which include hardware, software, and networks; data and information resources, such as databases; and human resources, which would include the skills and personal characteristics of the information systems employees, the user community, and the management, as well as the structure of the organization and its incentive systems.

Step 3: Information Systems Vision

In the first step, the executives of the organization developed mission and vision statements for the organization as a whole. Given those statements and the information systems resources identified in the second phase, information systems managers must now develop a vision specifically for information systems. For this and the following steps, the senior information systems person in the organization must gather not only employees of the information systems group, including individuals with technical skills, but also functional managers. Functional managers work in other areas of the organization, such as accounting or marketing, and are likely to be the end user of the information systems initiatives that will be identified later. They therefore need to be part of the information systems strategic planning process from the start.

The **information systems vision** should be a broad statement of how the organization should use and manage its information systems for strategic purposes. It basically suggests that organizations need to "Know Where They Want To Go." Clearly, the information systems vision has to be aligned with the organization's mission, vision, and strategies, which may require revisiting the organization's strategies. An example of an IS vision statement could be: "We will strive to offer leading-edge but tested technologies to our functional areas, provide leadership in managing external and internal data, and promote technologies that will enhance the competitive advantages of our firm." Of course, each organization is unique and the statements will be more specific to each company. Nevertheless, the statement should define what role information systems should play for the organization.

Step 4: Information Systems Architecture

In most organizations, an information systems vision is likely to already exist. Therefore, the previous phase involves modifying it if needed. Similarly, most large organizations will already have selected an information systems architecture.

Information systems architecture specifies how information systems resources should be used and how they should work together. It is the "Know How You Are Going To Get There" phase. We will discuss information systems architectures more in depth in Chapter 7 (Transmitting Information). The development of an architecture may require managers to revisit the information systems vision if, for example, the architecture cannot support the vision that was established.

The selected information systems architecture will provide some guidelines for future uses, acquisitions, and the management of information resources. It is therefore general enough to provide guidelines for several years, but specific enough to offer actionable guidelines. Consider the following architectural statement: "We will strive to provide a technology environment that will allow a variety of vendors to interact with our systems independently of their technology platforms." The statement clearly points to the need for interoperability of technology, which is the ability of heterogeneous systems to communicate with one another. Therefore, acquisition of software or hardware that limits interoperability is not consistent with the selected architecture. Architectural guidelines could include statements about all information resources, including hardware, software, and networks; as well as the way data is stored, protected, and managed; and how information systems human resources are managed, such as whether information systems work can be outsourced.

Step 5: Strategic Initiatives Identification

The ultimate goal of the information systems strategic planning process is to identify **strategic information systems initiatives** that will provide competitive advantages to the organization. These initiatives tend to be longer term (two to five years), although some strategic initiatives can be launched rapidly. It should be noted that strategic initiatives can be about systems, but most of the time involve much more than technology, which may result in a new strategic direction for the organization. For example, when an organization decides to implement a Customer Relationship Management System, installing software and hardware is not enough, and employees must be trained to be highly customer-oriented if the implementation is to succeed.

There are many frameworks that can be used to identify strategic information systems initiatives, and we will discuss several of them in the next section of this chapter. As you learn how to use the frameworks to identify initiatives, however, keep in mind that the initiatives that are identified need to be aligned with the IS vision, and the strategic goals of the organization.

Advantages of IS Strategic Planning Process

The identification of strategic initiatives is in itself an important goal of the information systems strategic planning process. There are, however, several other benefits from using a structured approach to identify strategic initiatives.

- *Improved communication:* Having stakeholders involved in the planning process allows everyone to provide their input into initiatives that will potentially affect individuals in different areas of the organization. By providing documented discussions of the advantages and disadvantages of each initiative, overall communication inside the organization is improved.

- *Improved coordination;* Since various stakeholders are involved in the planning process, they develop a shared mental image of the initiatives, their purposes, and their advantages and disadvantages. Furthermore, each member of the planning team gets a clear picture of everyone's responsibility. This improves overall coordination of the efforts related to the initiative, both before and during the implementation.

- *Improved decision making:* When a structured approach is used for identifying strategic initiatives, a clear set of guidelines and criteria for selection of initiatives is established. For example, initiatives have to be aligned with the goals of the organization. The result is that decision-making is more consistent over time with respect to which strategic initiatives are supported and more importantly, why.

Frameworks for Strategic Information Systems

The last phase of the strategic planning process is the identification of strategic initiatives. As previously discussed, each phase is actually composed of several steps. In this section, we look more specifically at a number of frameworks or tools that can be used to identify strategic information systems initiatives.

Information Systems SWOT Analysis

Most students will have discussed SWOT (Strengths, Weaknesses, Opportunities, and Threats) analyses in one of their management or marketing classes. SWOT analyses can be used for strategic information systems planning, just like for other areas of the organization. While the technique of SWOT analysis has existed for some time now, the basic concepts remain. Table 4.1 summarizes the components of a SWOT analysis, with some example statements that could be applied to Amazon.com.

When considering the use of a SWOT analysis for the purpose of identifying potential strategic information systems initiatives, it is important to consider factors beyond technology in the strengths, weaknesses, opportunities, and threats. Say for example, a firm has a great idea for implementing an information system to improve the sales cycle by providing mobile devices to sales representatives. If one of their weaknesses is that their customer base is limited to military agencies where mobile devices may not be allowed on the facilities for security reasons, then this may not be a good initiative for the organization. On the other hand, if one of their opportunities is to have more physical presence with customers (which may seem contradictory to use of electronic media), it may be that changes in technologies available at home can free up more time for sales representatives to visit their clients. The important point is that you should not limit yourself to thinking only about technology when you perform a SWOT analysis.

Table 4.1   SWOT Analysis Components

Component	Description	Example for Amazon.com
Strengths	What gives the organization advantages over others in their industry?	Leadership position in online retailing
Weaknesses	What creates disadvantages for the organization relative to others in their industry?	Increased size of the company requires more investments
Opportunities	What activities or factors could help the organization get new advantages over others in their industry?	Expand to services instead of just retailing
Threats	What activities or factors could create disadvantages or troubles for the organization relative to others in their industry?	Increasing global competition from online retailers

How do you identify information systems strategic initiatives from a SWOT analysis? Of course, you can look at the opportunities and see which ones can be achieved with the implementation of information systems. However, you can also look at weaknesses, and see if you can remove or reduce those weaknesses via better use of information systems. Similarly, ask yourself: How can the organization reduce the external threats by making better use of information systems? How it can make better use of its strengths through new information systems? All of these ways to look at the SWOT elements can allow managers to identify a number of initiatives. Not all of them will be viable, but at this point we are only focused on identifying them.

SWOT ANALYSIS OF A PERSON?

Does a SWOT analysis seems too basic to you? While it is true that SWOT analyses are more often discussed in academia, they sometimes find their way into the real world. One interesting use of a SWOT analysis is to focus on the SWOT of a person as opposed to an organization. For example, to study the leadership style of a successful executive named Gordon Lankton as he created the Museum of Russian Icons, Sheila Puffer and Elitsa Banalieva (2010) used a SWOT analysis to discuss why he was successful. The strengths identified include his transformational leadership style, his ability to appear trustworthy to others and maintain honest relationships, his ability to inspire others by creating a vision for his work, and the fact that he serves as a role model for others. The weaknesses included "no formal training in art history, painting, iconography, or appraisal methods" (p. 629). Opportunities were identified as his relationship with a painter knowledgeable about this domain, his hiring of an experienced curator, and the potential for improved inter-cultural understanding of art by Russians and Americans. Finally, threats identified included attracting a sufficient number of visitors, and dealing with politically sensitive issues.

Source: Puffer, Sheila M. and Elitsa R Banalieva. "From Iconic Business Leader to Russian Icon Museum Founder: Bridging Business and the Arts across Cultures," *Thunderbird International Business Review* 52 (6) (Nov/Dec 2010): 617.

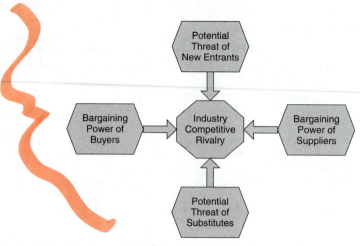

FIGURE 4.2 Porter's Five Competitive Forces Model

Source: (Adapted from Porter, 1979)

Porter's Five Competitive Forces Model

Porter's Five Competitive Forces Model is one of the most popular frameworks for analyzing a firm's competitive position by looking at the major forces that shape an organization's competitive environment. An adaptation of the framework is presented in Figure 4.2. The original purpose of the model is to analyze how competitive an industry is and therefore determine if a particular market (product, service, geography, etc.) could be attractive for an organization to consider. It could also be used to reevaluate a company's competitive position if one of the competitive forces changes, for example if a major merger changes the level of rivalry in a particular industry.

Porter's Five Competitive Forces Model could also be used to identify strategic information systems initiatives. Table 4.2 shows how each of the forces could be examined from a strategic information systems point of view.

Porter's Value Chain Analysis

Porter proposed another framework that could be useful in identifying strategic information systems initiatives. In a **Value Chain analysis,** managers identify all of the activities that the organization must perform to conduct its business (Porter, 1996). As each activity is performed, the organization adds value to the product or service it delivers. Clearly, all industries and organizations are likely to have their own value chain. Porter identified two broad categories of activities in the value chain: primary and support. Primary activities are directly related to the creation, processing, or delivery of the product or service. Support activities are those overall tasks that make it possible for the organization to function, but that are not directly involved in the product or service. Figure 4.3 shows a typical value chain in a manufacturing firm. Note that many organizations today are in the service industry and their value chain would be completely different. We will discuss service industry firms in the next section.

Table 4.2 Porter's Five Competitive Forces Model and Strategic Information Systems

Competitive Force	Description	Desired Level	Strategic Information Systems	Examples
Potential Threat of New Entrants	How easy is it for new companies to enter the market in which the organization operates?	Low—no new companies can enter the market.	How could you use information systems to increase barriers to entry in the organization's market?	Create barriers to entry—leverage data about customers that others cannot access, creating information asymmetry.
Bargaining Power of Buyers	What is the ability (or market power) of the organization's buyers (customers) to reduce its competitive position (e.g., by bringing prices down)?	Low—customers cannot dictate lower prices or better conditions.	How could you use information systems to reduce the power of negotiation of buyers?	Create switching costs—give customers value-added services such as personalization or lower costs (through economies of scale) that will make them loyal to the organization.
Bargaining Power of Suppliers	What is the ability (or market power) of the organization's suppliers to reduce its competitive position (e.g., by bringing prices up)?	Low—suppliers cannot dictate higher prices or better conditions.	How could you use information systems to reduce the power of negotiation of suppliers?	When there are few suppliers, this tends to be a high barrier. Use information systems to aggregate buying power with others (for example, online exchanges) or reduce the cost of buying (electronic procurement).
Potential Threat of Substitutes	What is the likelihood that other products of equal of superior value will be available?	Low—no products can substitute for the organization's products (or services).	How could you use information systems to make your products unique or make customers unwilling to use substitutes?	Create switching costs so customers will not be willing to use substitutes (personalization, lower costs, etc.) or use information systems to create unique or patented products such as proprietary systems (like Google applications or Apple products).
Industry Competitive Rivalry	What is the current level of competition in the industry?	Low—there is limited competition.	How could you use information systems to ensure that competition is limited in the industry?	Use information systems to differentiate the organization's products so that there are few or no competitors.

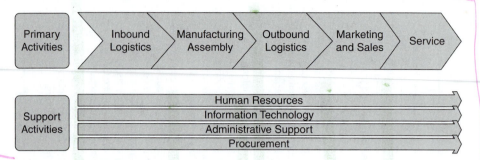

FIGURE 4.3 Sample Value Chain in Manufacturing Firm

Source: (Adapted from Porter, 1996)

How could you use a value chain analysis to identify strategic information systems initiatives? Porter identified two major ways to create competitive advantages in the value chain: lower the costs of performing an activity, or add more value to the final products and services in an activity. Therefore, managers can ask themselves for every activity in their value chain: How can I use information systems to perform this activity at a lower cost? How can I use information systems to improve the value added from this activity to the final product or service? If we take the example of marketing a product, in what ways can information systems reduce marketing costs? The organization could use electronic marketing through social networks or electronic mailings. What about adding value to the product? Well, the organization could make their products more personalized. For example, instead of selling cute teddy bears, the organization could create online profiles for the teddy bears that would have their own online lives, making the product more attractive than the other teddy bears that do not have an online "life."

There are a lot of opportunities for managers to examine the activities of their organization in order to identify potential strategic uses of information systems. But now think of extending this outside of the organization's value chain to their suppliers and customers. With more and more organizations linked electronically, are there possibilities for the activities of members of an organization's value system (upstream and downstream value chains) to be improved via technology? That is what the giant retailer Wal-Mart is doing when they manage their inventory not only within their organization, but at their suppliers as well (see Chapter 12 Enterprise Systems, for a story on this).

Virtual Value Chain

As discussed in the previous section, many firms today are mainly information-based organizations. Think about what Google offers as a product. The company creates and offers software tools to individuals and companies. In addition, the company offers information to individuals through its search engine, as well as information to organizations via its analytical software that provides analysis of traffic on organizations' websites.

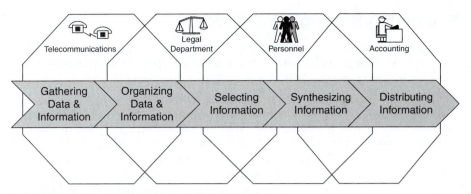

FIGURE 4.4 Virtual Value Chain: Handling Information

Source: (Adapted from Piccoli, 2008)

Instead of looking at activities that turn raw materials into a final product, as in manufacturing organizations, the **Virtual Value Chain** looks at activities that turn raw data into useful information (Piccoli, 2008). An example of an information-based business is consulting. Consulting firms' main outputs are information and knowledge-based reports and documents they provide to their clients about specific questions of interest, specific analyses regarding their own business or certain markets they are considering, or even reports about general industry trends. In the business of consulting, professionals regularly gather substantial amounts of data and information and then organize and store them in some useful way (retrievable, indexed, etc.). When the organization is asked to provide consulting on a specific topic, the professionals in the firm identify and retrieve the relevant information from a repository (where it is stored), synthesize the information (rendering it useful), and then distribute it to the client. Figure 4.4 shows an example of a Virtual Value Chain.

Similar to the other frameworks we discussed so far, an analysis of the Virtual Value Chain can help identify strategic information systems initiatives. Managers can ask themselves in what ways can information systems make gathering, organizing, selecting, synthesizing, and distributing information less expensive, adding value to the firm. For example, within the human resources (personnel) department, information could be distributed more rapidly to employees using an intranet (discussed in Chapter 7, Transmitting Information). Are there better ways to gather information and data for the human resources department? One could imagine, for example, collecting work hours (time sheets) for remote employees via website applications as opposed to paper forms. Similarly, are there better ways to organize and select information within the human resources department? It may be that a new system could be implemented for identifying information requirements for employees who travel internationally. As you can see, different questions can lead managers to the identification of potential strategic information systems. And, we only discussed the human resources department! This can be extended to all departments that require gathering, organizing, selecting, synthesizing, and distributing information.

Evaluating Strategic Initiatives

In the previous section of this chapter, we used a variety of frameworks to identify potential strategic information system initiatives that the organization should consider. In theory, we should at this point have a significant number of initiatives identified. Not all of them are doable, e.g., some simply cannot be done (for example, requiring technology that does not exist yet), and others are not worth doing (for example, they may be too costly with only limited benefits). We therefore need to rank the initiatives, or at least eliminate those that cannot or should not be considered. There are several tools that can be used for doing this analysis, and we will discuss two: the Critical Success Factors method and the Priority Matrix. Both methods can be used for evaluating the viability of the strategic information systems initiatives, although the priority matrix provides a more in-depth analysis.

Critical Success Factors

Critical success factors (CSF) are those few important considerations that must be achieved for the organization to survive and be successful (achieve its mission). These are not about technology (in general), but more about business objectives. In other words, CSFs must be in line with the organization's vision and mission. Organizations usually have just a few critical success factors, and top management typically identifies these.

Identification of CSFs is a process in itself that resembles brainstorming sessions where top managers sit together with a moderator who helps them develop a short list of the main factors necessary for the company's success. The key questions asked to start the discussion are similar to these: What needs to happen for our organization to increase its revenues? What are the most important actions we need to take to be more competitive? What is needed for us to be more successful? These questions just help start the discussion, which subsequently involves deliberations among the executives, identification of potential obstacles, and mostly the development of priorities among the most important factors for the organization's success.

Imagine that you are an executive at your school involved in developing strategies for the future of the school. Your group of school executives would have to ask themselves what is needed for the school to be a leader in education? The group would probably identify factors like 1. Having the highest quality students possible (no students is not a good idea; having poor quality students does not help the school to be successful); 2. Having the best possible faculty; and 3. Providing close link to the community.

Once the critical success factors are identified for the organization, managers can map their proposed strategic information systems initiatives to the CSFs. Initiatives that do not support the CSFs of the organization should not be considered as top priorities. This ensures that the organization achieves the business and IT alignment discussed earlier in the chapter, and that the planning team is able to prioritize initiatives in a consistent way.

CSFS FOR IMPLEMENTING WEB PORTALS IN SAUDI ARABIA

Critical Success Factors can be used for the organization as a whole, like we described in this chapter, but also sometimes for specific projects. In this example, researchers explored the Critical Success Factors (CSF) for the implementation of Web portals in two Saudi organizations: the Saudi Food and Drug Authority (SFDA) and the Saudi Stock Exchange. A Web portal usually provides a point of access to integrated information and services. Both organizations had launched portals that provided several services to their constituents. In the table below, the researchers identified 21 CSFs based on rankings where 1 = critical, 2 = very high importance, 3 = high importance, 4 = moderate importance, and 5 = low importance. The researchers who developed this list interviewed a large number of managers and looked for factors that emerged as the most commonly mentioned for success.

Ranking	Critical Success Factor	Mean Value
1	Strong communication inwards and outwards	1.00
2	User acceptance	1.00
3	Top management support	1.33
4	Clear goals and objectives	1.33
5	Project monitoring and controlling	1.33
6	Requirements analysis	1.33
7	Defining the portal architecture	1.67
8	Dedicated resources	1.67
9	Selection of the appropriate portal package	2.00
10	Process and application integration	2.00
11	Prototyping	2.00
12	Flexible project structure	2.00
13	Project management	2.00
14	Portal design	2.33
15	Change management	2.33
16	Team competencies and skills	2.67
17	Portal strategy	2.67
18	User training and education	2.67
19	Business process reengineering	2.67
20	Organizational culture	3.00
21	Portal engineering roadmap	3.00

Recall that in the chapter we suggest there should be only a few CSFs in an organization (three to five). Having 21 items to worry about is unlikely to be very productive. Since critical success factors should focus on the "critical" ones, managers might consider only items 1 to 8. Alternatively, they can merge some items together, as recommended by the researchers who developed this list. For example, they suggest merging five factors into one called project management (project monitoring and controlling, change management, project management, team competencies and skills, and user training and education).

Source: Abdullah S Al-Mudimigh, Ullah Zahid,andAbdullah Alsubaie Talal. "A Framework for Portal Implementation: A Case for Saudi Organizations," *International Journal of Information Management* 31 (1) (Feb 2011): 38–43.

LEARNING ACTIVITY 4.1   WHAT DOES YAHOO! NEED FOR SUCCESS?

The purpose of the activity is to get some practice identifying critical success factors. Your instructor will assign you to groups, and each group of student will act as a top management team from the company Yahoo! Your job is to brainstorm critical success factors for the company.

Priority Matrix

The **Priority Matrix** allows managers to evaluate potential initiatives and prioritize them along two key dimensions: the ease of implementation and the potential returns. The ease of implementation includes several factors such as costs, time required, efforts required, or the actual complexity of the system. The potential returns can be in terms of revenues, market shares, savings, reputation, etc. Figure 4.5 shows a sample Priority Matrix.

Looking at Figure 4.5, you can easily identify which strategic information systems initiatives should be given higher priority by managers. **Imperatives** are initiatives that should be relatively easy to implement, for example, because they cost little or the technology is already implemented, and they have the potential to bring high returns to the organization. **Quick Wins** represent initiatives that do not have much upside potential but are easy to implement (low or no cost, low or no difficulties involved, limited effort, etc.). They are called Quick Wins because the organization can get some visible impacts without much effort. The initiatives may not be the top priorities, but since they can be implemented rapidly and easily, it is worth considering them. The initiatives in the **Evaluate** quadrant need to be discussed and evaluated thoroughly by managers. Some of them will be implemented and others will not. In the end, it may depend how many initiatives are on the table and what resources are available to the organization to implement these initiatives. Finally, the **Stay Away** quadrant includes what many say are lost causes, initiatives that would be difficult to implement and would have limited potential returns.

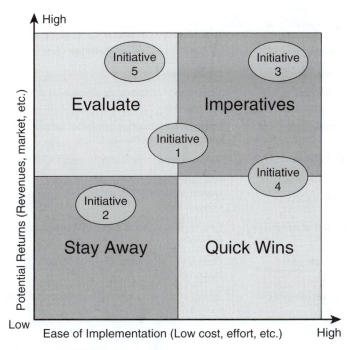

FIGURE 4.5 Sample Priority Matrix

LEARNING ACTIVITY 4.2	COMPETITIVE ADVANTAGE AT OUTRIGGER HOTELS AND RESORTS

This activity requires you to complete a competitive analysis of Outrigger Hotels and Resorts (Piccoli, 2005). The case may be accessed through the book's website, or may be provided to you by your instructor. Use one of the frameworks we discussed to 1. Identify the competitive position of Outrigger Hotels and Resorts, and 2. Identify three strategic information systems initiatives you believe the company should consider.

Hyper-competition: Sustainability of Competitive Advantage

Most of the frameworks we discussed previously to help us identify potential strategic information systems initiatives were developed with the idea that firms can create competitive advantages that would differentiate them from other organizations over time. Today, however, the pace of change in information technologies and other innovations is faster than ever. This has led some individuals to question the sustainability

Table 4.3 D'Avenis' 7S's

D'Avenis' 7S's	Definition
Strategic Move	**Description**
Superior stakeholder satisfaction	Maximizing customer satisfaction by adding value strategically.
Strategic soothsaying	Using new knowledge to predict or create new windows of opportunity.
Positioning for speed	Preparing the organization to react as fast as possible.
Positioning for surprise	Preparing the organization to respond to the marketplace in a manner that will surprise competitors.
Shifting the rules of competition	Finding new ways to serve customers, transforming the industry.
Signaling strategic intent	Communicating intentions in order to stall responses by competitors.
Simultaneous and sequential strategic thrusts	Taking steps to stun and confuse competitors in order to disrupt or block their efforts.

Source: (D'Aveni, 1994)

of any competitive advantage a firm obtains through its initiatives. This is the concept of **hyper-competition**.

In his 1994 book *Hyper-competition,* Richard D'Aveni suggests that any competitive advantage an organization has will be rapidly eroded by competitors, and that focusing on trying to sustain competitive advantages could be a deadly distraction for organizations. Instead, he suggests that organizations should seek to create disruptions in the market through a series of initiatives. He identifies seven strategic moves that organizations should consider to compete in hyper-competitive markets; these are called D'Avenis' 7S's, which are summarized in Table 4.3.

While not many companies have adopted the 7's framework of hyper-competition, it can still be used to identify strategic information systems initiatives. Think about new ways that an organization can try to maximize customer satisfaction (superior stakeholder satisfaction) using information systems. For example, a new Customer Relationship Management System (Chapter 12, Enterprise Systems) can be used to know what customers prefer in their interactions with the organization. Similarly, new Web 2.0 technologies (Chapter 7, Transmitting Information) can be used to seek new knowledge directly from potential customers (strategic soothsaying). As you learn about the various technologies and information systems available today and in the near future in the next chapters, remember how they can be used for strategic purposes.

| LEARNING ACTIVITY 4.3 | GOOGLE VS. YAHOO! |

The purpose of this activity is to practice some of the concepts discussed in this chapter. Your instructor will assign you to groups, ideally the same groups used for Learning Activity 4.1. Each group represents a senior management team at Yahoo! Your team is tasked with selecting one of the 7S's from the D'Aveni's framework, specifically targeted at finding a way for Yahoo! to better compete with Google. The team must then identify a specific strategic initiative that will be used to implement the selected strategy.

Once this activity is completed, all initiatives proposed by the groups in the class should be prioritized using the Critical Success Factors identified in Learning Activity 4.1.

CHAPTER SUMMARY

In this chapter, we discussed how organizations can obtain competitive advantages by implementing strategic information systems. We started by discussing the strategic planning process, which involves more than planning about information technology, and then explored various frameworks that can help managers identify strategic information systems initiatives. We then discussed how managers can evaluate which strategic initiatives to implement, and concluded with a discussion of hyper-competition, or the idea that competitive advantage cannot be sustained but that organizations should try to achieve market disruptions instead.

Here are the main points discussed in the chapter:

- There are five main steps in the strategic planning process: Step 1: Strategic Business Planning; Step 2: Information Systems Assessment; Step 3: Information Systems Vision; Step 4: Information Systems Architecture; and Step 5: Strategic Initiatives Identification.

- We discussed four frameworks that can be used to identify strategic information systems initiatives. The SWOT analysis is used for managers to identify Strengths, Weaknesses, Opportunities, and Threats for the organization. Porter's Five Competitive Forces Model helps managers analyze the organization's competitive position by looking at five major forces in the firms' competitive environment: threats of new entrants, threats of substitutes, bargaining power of buyers, bargaining power of suppliers, and industry rivalry. Porter's Value Chain helps managers identify all of the activities that the organization must perform to conduct its business. Finally, the Virtual Value Chain looks at activities that turn raw data into useful information instead of looking at activities that turn raw materials into a final product like in manufacturing organizations.

- We discussed two methods for evaluating strategic initiatives: the Critical Success Factors method, and the Priority Matrix. Critical success factors (CSF) are those few important considerations that must be achieved for the organization to survive and be successful (achieve its mission). The Priority Matrix allows managers to evaluate potential initiatives and prioritize them along two key dimensions: the ease of implementation and the potential returns.

- Hyper-competition is when competitors rapidly erode competitive advantages so that organizations should focus on market disruptions instead of trying to sustain competitive advantages.

REVIEW QUESTIONS

1. What is a strategic information system? How is it different from a strategic information system initiative?
2. What is the purpose of the strategic planning process and what are its main steps?
3. What are the main advantages of using an information systems strategic planning process?
4. What do the SWOT, Porter's Five Forces Competitive Model, and Porter's Value Chain Model have in common?
5. What are the key differences between the traditional Value Chain model and the Virtual Value Chain?
6. How can a SWOT analysis be used for identifying strategic information systems initiatives?
7. What is the purpose of the Porter's Five Competitive Forces Model and how can it be used for information systems strategic planning?
8. What are Critical Success Factors (CSF) and how should they be used to evaluate strategic initiatives?
9. What is the Priority Matrix and how should it be used to evaluate strategic initiatives?
10. What is Hyper-competition and how can D'Avenis's 7S's framework be used in that context?

REFLECTION QUESTIONS

1. What is the most important thing you learned in this chapter? Why is it important?
2. What topics are unclear? What about them is unclear?
3. What relationships do you see between what you learned in this chapter and what you have learned in earlier chapters?
4. Why do you think the information systems strategic planning process is iterative?
5. If the strategic planning process has the benefits of improved communication, coordination, and decision-making, could it be used or applied by students for group projects? How?
6. In what situations in your personal life could you apply a SWOT analysis (not for a specific course)?
7. How are the Virtual Value Chain and the traditional Value Chain similar and different?
8. How does the Priority Matrix relate to Critical Success Factors?
9. Do you believe that Hyper-competition exists today? If so, do you think it will continue to happen in the future?
10. Looking back over the content of the chapter, why do you think it is important to discuss strategic initiatives in the context of introducing information systems?

ADDITIONAL LEARNING ACTIVITIES

1. Use the Priority Matrix to rank initiatives identified in Learning Activity 4.3. Compare the results of your analysis with the results of the analyses conducted in Learning Activity 4.3. Be prepared to discuss the differences.

2. This activity requires you to complete a competitive analysis of Carnival Cruise Lines. The case may be accessed through your university website, the Ivey School business case website (http://cases.ivey.uwo.ca), the Harvard Business school cases website (http://cb.hbsp. harvard.edu/cb/web), or may be provided to you by your instructor. **Note**: please do not perform a complete case analysis, but focus on the competitive analysis. What is Carnival Cruise Line's competitive position?

    CASE: *Carnival Cruise Lines*, by Lynda M. Applegate, Robert J. Kwortnik, and Gabriele Piccoli, Harvard Business Case, Product Number: #9-806-015, rev. April 2006.

3. Find the mission statement for the Amazon.com company and your school. Compare the two statements and identify similarities and differences. Why are there differences?

4. Complete Table 4.1 with at least five new statements for each of the SWOT components for Amazon.com.

5. Conduct a Virtual Value Chain analysis to identify potential strategic information systems in the hotel industry.

REFERENCES

D'Aveni, Richard. *Hyper-competition*. New York: Free Press, 1994.

Piccoli, Gabriele. *Information Systems for Managers*. Hoboken, NJ: Wiley, 2008.

Piccoli, Gabriele. "Outrigger Hotels and Resorts: A Case Study," *Communications of the Association for Information Systems* 15 (no.1, art. 5), 2005.

Porter, M.E. "How Competitive Forces Shape Strategy," *Harvard Business Review* 57 (no 2), (March/April), 1979: 137–145.

Porter, M. E. "Wha*t Is Strategy?" *Harvard Business Review* 74 (no 6), (November–December 1996): 61–78.

BIBLIOGRAPHY AND FURTHER READINGS

Porter, M.E. *Competitive Strategy*. New York: Free Press, 1980.

Porter, M.E. "The Five Competitive Forces That Shape Strategy," *Harvard Business Review*, 86 (no. 1), (January 2008): 78–93.

Value Chain Development. Washington, D.C.: USAID. (2009) http://apps.develebridge.net/amap/index.php/Value_Chain_Development

GLOSSARY

Bargaining Power of Buyers: in Porter's Five Competitive Forces Model, asks what is the ability of the organization's buyers (customers) to reduce the organization's competitive position?

Bargaining Power of Suppliers: in Porter's Five Competitive Forces Model, asks what is the ability of the organization's suppliers to reduce its competitive position?

Critical Success Factors (CSF): the few important considerations that must be achieved for the organization to survive and be successful (achieve its mission).

Evaluate: in priority matrix, initiatives that need to be discussed and evaluated thoroughly by managers.

Hyper-competition: when competitive advantages are rapidly eroded by competitors of that organizations should focus on market disruptions instead of trying to sustain competitive advantages.

Imperatives: in priority matrix, initiatives that should be relatively easy to implement and have the potential to bring high returns to the organization.

Industry competitive rivalry: in Porter's Five Competitive Forces Model, asks what is the current level of competition in the industry?

Information systems architecture: specifies how information systems resources should be used and how they should work together.

Information systems assessment: step of planning process where the organization identifies the current state of information systems resources in the organization.

Information systems vision: a broad statement of how the organization should use and manage its information systems for strategic purposes.

Opportunities: in SWOT analysis, asks what activities or factors could help the organization get new advantages over others in their industry?

Porter's Five Competitive Forces model: framework to help managers analyze the organization's competitive position by looking at five major forces in the firms' competitive environment: threats of new entrants, threats of substitutes, bargaining power of buyers, bargaining power of suppliers, and industry rivalry.

Porter's Value Chain analysis: framework to help managers identify all of the activities that the organization must perform to conduct its business.

Positioning for Speed: in D'Avenis's 7S's framework, strategy about preparing the organization to react as fast as possible.

Positioning for Surprise: in D'Avenis's 7S's framework, strategy about preparing the organization to respond to the marketplace in a manner that will surprise competitors.

Potential Threat of New Entrants: in Porter's Five Competitive Forces Model, asks how easy is it for new companies to enter the market in which the organization operates?

Potential Threat of Substitutes: in Porter's Five Competitive Forces Model, asks what is the likelihood that other products of equal of superior value be available?

Priority Matrix: framework that allows managers to evaluate potential initiatives and prioritize them along two key dimensions: the ease of implementation and the potential returns.

Quick Wins: in priority matrix, initiatives that do not have much upside potential but are easy to implement.

Shifting the Rules of Competition: in D'Avenis's 7S's framework, strategy about finding new ways to serve customers, transforming the industry.

Signaling Strategic Intent: in D'Avenis's 7S's framework, strategy about communicating intentions in order to stall responses by competitors.

Simultaneous and Sequential Strategic Thrusts: in D'Avenis's 7S's framework, strategy about taking steps to stun and confuse competitors in order to disrupt or block their efforts.

Stay Away: in priority matrix, initiatives would be difficult to implement and would have limited potential returns.

Strategic information systems: information systems specifically meant to provide organizations with competitive advantages.

Strategic information systems initiatives: detailed (usually two- to five-year) plans for implementation of systems that may result in a new strategic direction for the organization.

Strategic planning process: structured set of steps to identify strategic information systems.

Strategic Soothsaying: in D'Avenis's 7S's framework, strategy about using new knowledge to predict or create new windows of opportunity.

Strengths: in SWOT analysis, asks what gives the organization advantages over others in their industry?

Superior Stakeholder Satisfaction: in D'Avenis's 7S's framework, strategy about maximizing customer satisfaction by adding value strategically.

SWOT analysis: framework used for managers to identify Strengths, Weaknesses, Opportunities, and Threats for the organization.

Threats: in SWOT analysis, asks what activities or factors could create disadvantages or troubles for the organization relative to others in their industry?

Virtual Value Chain: framework that looks at activities that turn raw data into useful information instead of looking at activities that turn raw materials into a final product like in manufacturing organizations.

Weaknesses: in SWOT analysis, asks what creates disadvantages for the organization relative to others in their industry?

Storing and Organizing Information

CHAPTER 5

LEARNING OBJECTIVES

By reading and completing the activities in this chapter, you will be able to:

- Discuss the purpose of a database management system

- Decide whether it is better to store data using a database management system or a spreadsheet.

- Explain the basic structure and components of relational databases

- Describe the purpose of foreign keys in a relational database

- Discuss the purpose of a relational database schema and explain its notation

- List and describe a number of online databases

CHAPTER OUTLINE

- Focusing story: The database behind Facebook

- Learning Activity 5.1: Data for an Amazon order

- Database management systems

- Learning Activity 5.2: Connecting data elements

- Spreadsheets versus databases (when to use a DBMS)

- Relational databases

- Database diagrams

- Learning Activity 5.3: Finding business databases online

- Online databases

- Chapter Summary

- Review Questions

- Reflection Questions

- Additional Learning Activities

- Bibliography and Further Readings

- Glossary

Throughout this book, our focus has been on information. Much of the information used by businesses is stored in databases. While there are different schemes for storing data, much of the data you will deal with is stored in relational databases. Databases may seem pretty mysterious, but they are actually not hard to understand at a basic level. In this chapter we will help you learn about how relational databases store data. We will help you learn how to construct, populate, and retrieve data from databases using Microsoft Access in the In-Depth Guides.

FOCUSING STORY: THE DATABASE BEHIND FACEBOOK

Odds are you are one of the over 500 million active users of Facebook. If so, you probably know how to "friend" people and post photos, videos, and status updates. What you may not know is that there is a giant database that keeps track of all of this information. Here is a partial list of what Facebook's database must track:

- Almost 1 billion objects, such as pages, groups, events, and communities

- Over 30 billion pieces of content, including links, posts, photos, notes, videos, and new stories.

- Friend connections among the over 500 million active users. The average user has well over 100 friends.

Keeping track of all of this information requires a very complex database design, in addition to a robust infrastructure. Facebook uses a variety of tools to create and manage their data, including Apache Cassandra, which manages data across hundreds of servers; Apache Hive, which facilitates summarizing and retrieving data in very large databases; and Scribe, which reliably delivers billions of Facebook messages each day.

While you may never have to deal with databases this large, you will probably have to use databases throughout your work life. Much of the information you will need to access in order to do your job will be stored in relational databases. Relational databases underlie many of the applications we discuss throughout this book, including enterprise resource planning, customer relationship management, and supply chain management systems you will learn about in Chapter 12. (Note that Facebook uses other types of database technologies in addition to relational databases.)

FOCUSING QUESTIONS:

1. Identify the information elements that are part of a Facebook profile.

2. What information do you think Facebook uses to determine what friend suggestions to make?

Source: http://www.facebook.com/press/info.php?statistics

LEARNING ACTIVITY 5.1   **DATA FOR AN AMAZON ORDER**

Suppose you are ordering something from Amazon. What pieces of data (for example, your name) does Amazon need to fulfill your order?

STATS BOX

How much digital data exists? This is a big, complicated question, but research firm IDC has developed estimates and projections of the amount of data in the "digital universe." According to IDC, in 2009, there were almost 800,000 petabytes of data in the digital universe. (This includes business and personal data, such as digital photos, music, and video.) A petabyte is one million gigabytes. By the end of 2010, IDC estimated that the amount of digital data would grow to 1.2 million petabytes. By 2020, this figure is expected to be 44 times as large as in 2009. With the ever-expanding glut of digital data, you can understand why efficient ways to store, organize, and retrieve the data is increasingly important.

Source: The 2011 Digital Universe Study: Extracting Value from Chaos http://www.emc.com/collateral/demos/microsites/idc-digital-universe/iview.htm

---

Overview of Relational Databases

Databases and Database Management Systems

A **database** is an organized collection of data. In this chapter we focus on a particular type of database called a relational database because this is the dominant type of database for business applications. These databases can store different types of "information" including text, numbers, documents, images and videos. Given the amount and variety of information that businesses deal with, having well-structured databases is a must for any business.

Typically, databases are managed by **database management systems** (DBMS). A database management system provides the means for creating, maintaining, and using databases. For most of you, the "using" part is the most important aspect of a DBMS, although you may create small databases. Professional database designers and administrators handle the creation and maintenance tasks in most organizations.

There are many database management systems used by businesses. Smaller database-oriented tasks can be handled by personal DBMS, such as Microsoft Access and Open Office Base. Larger, more complex databases require enterprise-level DBMS, such as Oracle, MySQL, Microsoft SQL Server, and IBM's DB2. Each of these has its advantages and disadvantages, but all are quite capable. Oracle has been the market leader for many years, but the others are widely used in business.

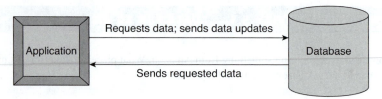

FIGURE 5.1 Interaction between Applications and Databases

Databases are integral elements of information systems. Most information systems today use multitiered architectures that divide processing into different elements. You will learn more about this in Chapter 7. Without going into too much detail, applications handle the processing of data, while the DBMS is responsible for managing the data. As shown in Figure 5.1, the application requests data from the DBMS, which provides the requested data. The application can then manipulate the data (e.g. reducing inventory when a product is ordered) and send updated data to the DBMS. The DBMS updates the actual databases according to the update sent by the application. It is possible to do all of this within the application, but most large systems use the multitier approach.

Databases vs. Spreadsheets (When to Use a DBMS)

Many people get a little confused about whether to use a spreadsheet (such as Microsoft Excel) or a database management system (such as Microsoft Access) for storing and organizing information. One reason for this confusion is that both store information in tables of rows and columns. This similarity is a bit misleading, however. The two applications have very different purposes, strengths and weaknesses.

Spreadsheets are fine for very simple data storage tasks, such as keeping simple lists, like a personal contact list or a home inventory. Unfortunately, spreadsheets have a number of limitations that make them unsuitable for more complex data storage. Some of the problems that you might run into if you use a spreadsheet for data storage include:

Spreadsheet

- Unnecessary data duplication

- Inconsistent data

- Difficulty in data retrieval and search

- Poor data integrity

- Difficulty in relating different data elements (such as customers and orders)

The problems of unnecessary data duplication and poor data integrity are particularly troubling. (Data integrity problems include inaccurate, inconsistent, and out-of-date data.) Some studies indicate that most complex spreadsheets have errors. (See http://panko.shidler.hawaii.edu/SSR/index.htm for a good overview of these studies.) While not all of these errors are due to data issues (for example, formulas could be incorrect), many are. Most database management systems have methods for keeping data up-to-date and consistent. While data stored in databases is not perfect, it typically is of higher quality than data stored in spreadsheets.

Using an out-of-date version can also be a problem with spreadsheets. Businesses sometimes make bad decisions because someone has relied on an old version of a spreadsheet. Often this is due to data not being updated, but there can be other changes that make a spreadsheet out of date. Reports from database management systems draw data directly from databases, which typically contain current information. It is worth noting that spreadsheets can be built to connect to a database to avoid the problem of outdated data.

Because spreadsheets are relatively easy to use and require less planning than database management systems, it is tempting to use a spreadsheet for managing information. For all but the simplest tasks, this is a mistake. In the long run, you are usually much better off to take the time to plan and design a proper database, especially as the amount of information being stored increases.

Databases are good at storing and organizing information. Spreadsheets are good for analyzing and displaying information visually. A complete information solution requires both. Fortunately, it is relatively easy to extract data from a database and import it into a spreadsheet for analysis, so you do not have to make an "either-or" choice. Use a database to store the information; use a spreadsheet to make sense of the information.

Now that you have a general idea of the purposes of databases and their relationship to information systems, we can get into more detail about how relational databases function.

Relational Databases

A **relational database** stores data in the form of connected tables. Tables are made up of records (rows) and fields (columns). A **record** is a set of fields that all pertain to the same thing, while the **fields** represent some characteristic of the thing. An example may make this easier to understand. Consider the Table 5.1.

Each row represents a single instructor. Each column represents a characteristic. The first row of data (not counting the headings) contains data about the

Table 5.1 Instructor Table

InstructorID	Last Name	First Name	Email
1	Smith	Sadie	ssmith@school.edu
2	Jones	Maggie	mjones@school.edu
3	Thurman	Annie	rthurman@school.edu
4	Wilson	Fred	fwilson@school.edu

instructor named Sadie Smith. The table stores four characteristics (fields) about the instructors:

- identification number (InstructorID)

- last name

- first name

- email address

Fortunately, this structure makes intuitive sense for most of us. Things get a little more complicated when we need to store data about multiple things. Take a look at Figure 5.2, which shows a small database about course offerings. This database stores data about three "things" that are related to each other; sections, courses, and instructors. Since we want to store data about three things, we have three tables. This is a key feature of relational databases. Each table stores data about a separate thing. This structure allows for flexibility when retrieving data while minimizing redundancy. When storing data, unnecessary redundancy can be a bad thing because redundancy can lead to inconsistencies. By storing each piece of information only once, we ensure that the data are consistent. We explain more about redundancy and consistency later in this chapter.

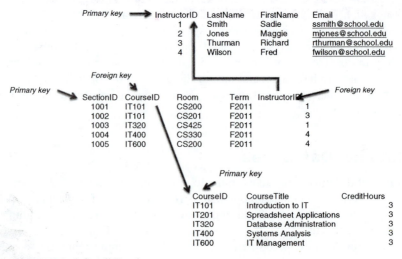

FIGURE 5.2 A Small Database

In order for a database to work, we need some way to uniquely identify each record. You might think that we could use the instructor's name for this purpose, but this will not work because two instructors might have the same name. Sometimes there is a natural choice for this unique identifier called the **primary key**. For example, student ID might be a good choice for a database that tracks members of a student organization. Sometimes, however, you might simply, make up an identifier. Since the identifier typically does not store any meaningful data (other than to identify a row), making up a number is not a problem. Each table in a database has a primary key. Sometimes a primary key is made up of more than one field. We call this a *composite primary key*.

You might have noticed that earlier we said that the tables in our database are related to one another. For example, the Sections table is related to the Instructors table and the Courses table. In a relational database, these connections are implemented by **foreign keys**, which are fields that reference a primary key in a related table. For example, the CourseID field in the Sections table references the CourseID field in the Courses table. This cross-referencing is called a *relationship*. The arrows in Figure 5.2 show how the foreign keys reference the primary keys.

These cross-referencing foreign keys make it easy to combine data contained in multiple tables. See if you can answer this question: What is the title of the course being taught in section 1001? This is a pretty easy question to answer. Section 1001 is Introduction to IT. All you have to do is look at the CourseID in the Sections table, then find the matching CourseID in the Courses table. There is another foreign key in the Sections table. InstructorID references the primary key of the Instructors table. While there are a number of very formal, precise rules that govern relational database design, if you understand this cross-referencing scheme, you understand the basics of relational databases. Even very large, complex databases follow this same basic structure. They just have more tables and fields.

There is an additional characteristic of relational databases that we need to discuss. For reasons that are beyond our scope, in a relational database each row/column intersection can store at most one item of data. For example, if there is more than one section of a course, you must have a separate record for each section.

There are some rules that govern relational database design. These rules, which are called *normal forms*, are in place to ensure data consistency by eliminating unnecessary redundancy. While the particulars of these rules are beyond our scope, we want to use a simple example to show the relationship between redundancy and data consistency. Consider the data shown in Table 5.2.

Table 5.2 Redundancy Example

SectionID	CourseID	CourseTitle	InstructorID	LastName	FirstName
1001	IT101	Introduction to IT	1	Smith	Sadie
1002	IT101	Introduction to Computers	3	Thurman	Maggie
1003	IT320	Database Administration	1	Jackson	Sadie
1004	IT400	Systems Analysis	4	Wilson	Fred
1005	IT600	IT Management	4	Wilson	Fred

Answer the following question about Table 5.2.: What is Instructor #1's last name? You really cannot be sure of the answer to this question. This instructor's last name is Smith in the first row, and Jackson in the third row. We do not really know which one is correct. This inconsistency, which we call an *anomaly*, results from storing the instructor's name in multiple rows. Compare this structure to the one in Figure 5.2. The earlier structure prevents these inconsistencies by storing each item of data only once. (The exception is the foreign key.) This is why each table stores data about one "thing." To summarize simply, if you only store a data element in one place, you cannot have inconsistent values. One of the values could be incorrect (for example an instructor's name could be misspelled), but that is a different problem than inconsistency.

Sometimes a particular row in a table can be related to at most one row in a related table. For example, in most businesses a specific order can only be related to one customer. If we look at this from the other direction, a specific customer can be related to more than one order. This is an example of a *one-to-many* relationship.

Many-to-many relationships also exist. In these relationships a specific row can be related to multiple rows in a related table. But in contrast to the one-to-many relationship, this is true in both directions. Consider the example of students registering for course sections. A specific student can be registered for more than one section (each for a different course), and a specific section can have more than one student registered for it. This is known as a many-to-many relationship.

Because of the structural rules of relational databases, many-to-many relationships require creating a new table that links the two related tables. Not surprisingly, these are called *linking* or *intersection* tables. Figure 5.3 shows a linking table for student registrations. The purpose of the registrations table is to link a student to a section. You can see that student #1 (Pat Johnson) is registered for four sections (1001, 1002, 1004, and 1005). Section 1001 has three students registered (1, 2, and 4).

Students

StudentID	LastName	FirstName	Email
1	Johnson	Pat	pjohnson@school.edu
2	Gonzales	Jorge	jgonzales@school.edu
3	Andrews	Annie	aandrews@school.edu
4	Goldman	Beau	bgoldman@school.edu
5	Simpson	Lois	lsimpson@school.edu

Registrations

Registrations

SectionID	StudentID
1001	1
1001	2
1001	4
1002	5
1002	1
1003	3
1003	2
1004	1
1004	3
1004	5
1004	2
1005	1
1005	5

Sections

SectionID	CourseID	Room	Term
1001	IT101	CS200	F2011
1002	IT101	CS201	F2011
1003	IT320	CS425	F2011
1004	IT400	CS330	F2011
1005	IT600	CS200	F2011

FIGURE 5.3 Many-to-many, Linking Table Example

Although they are more unusual, one-to-one relationships also exist. In these relationships a specific row in a table can be related to at most one row in a related table. This is true in both directions of the relationship. For some businesses, the relationship between customers and accounts could be a one-to-one relationship. (It could be a one-to-many relationship for other businesses.)

As you might imagine, using the actual data to show the structure of a database only works for very small databases. For larger databases, we illustrate structure using database schema diagrams, which we discuss next.

Database Diagrams

Database designers use several different diagrams when coming up with the design of a database. Here we are interested in a view that shows tables, fields, and relationships. (Note that we often call fields *attributes* when discussing database models. We are going to stick to "fields" to make things less confusing.) Some people call these diagrams *entity-relationship diagrams (ERD)* while others call them *database schemas*. There are technical differences between the two, but both essentially show the data elements and relationships among them, which is what we care about here.

Figure 5.4 shows a diagram for a database that stores wish lists for customers. Each rectangle shows the name of the table at the top. Each field is included inside the rectangle. The primary key is indicated by the PK in the left-hand column. Foreign keys have FK beside them to the left. Since tables can have more than one foreign key, the FK notations are numbered. Recall that the foreign keys relate a row in one table to a row in a related table. For example, the field "CategoryID" in the Products table refers to a CategoryID value in the Categories table.

You might find the notation for the WishList table a little confusing. This is an example of a linking table. It links two other tables together. These types of tables are

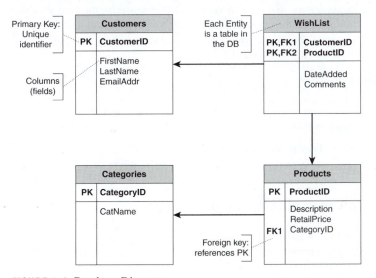

FIGURE 5.4 Database Diagram

necessary to control unnecessary redundancy. Many linking tables have composite primary keys (primary keys comprised of more than one field). In our notation, each field in the primary key is boldfaced, underlined, and has "PK" next to it, as is the case with CustomerID and ProductID in the WishList table. Together, CustomerID and ProductID serve as the primary key of the WishList table. Separately, however, each of these fields acts as foreign keys. You can tell this because of the FK1, and FK2 next to CustomerID and ProductID respectively. The CustomerID value in the WishList table refers to the CustomerID of the specific customer to whom the WishList item is assigned. ProductID in the WishList table serves a similar purpose. An arrow between the tables shows relationships between tables graphically. The direction of the arrow indicates the direction of referencing (from the foreign key to the corresponding primary key).

Note that this is only one way to show a database diagram. Your instructor may prefer another. We use this particular notation simply because it is well implemented in Microsoft Visio and other programs. Once you have the logical design, you have most of the information necessary to create a database, especially for simple applications. More complex applications require additional information, but that is beyond our scope here.

Being able to read a database diagram is important, even if you never design or build a database. The diagram is a key to understanding the structure of the database, which is useful when retrieving data from a database. Learning how to create a database design is beyond the scope of this chapter, but is covered in an In-Depth Guide, which is available through the book's website.

LEARNING ACTIVITY 5.3	FINDING BUSINESS DATABASES ONLINE

Your campus library likely has a variety of business-related online databases. (See http://libraries.slu.edu/databases/databases.php?subject=bus for example.) Visit your library's website and find its list of business databases. Identify and briefly describe one database for each of the related purposes.

- Economic statistics

- Industry information

- Demographic statistics

- Business-related news articles

THE COMPACT DISC DATABASE (CDDB)

Have you ever wondered how your media manager (such as iTunes or Windows Media Player) gets information about your music? When you rip a CD or download music, your media player is usually able to display cover art and track information. Your media player probably downloads this information from CDDB (also known as GraceNote), which is a vast database of music information. This same database is also the brains behind music recognition, such as when you use your mobile phone to identify music at a club. If you are a musician, you can actually send information about your music to CDDB so that anyone who downloads your music will have track titles and other information.

The databases behind CDDB store information about over 7 million CDs and 90 million tracks and support over 250 million users across the world. Literally tens of billions of database queries have been made since CDDB's inception in 1998. This number is growing rapidly, with over 2 billion searches per month.

Source: Gracenote Reaches Global Media Database Milestone, http://www.gracenote.com/press/ 09/09/2010/, checked July 7, 2010

Online Databases

So far in this chapter, we have primarily discussed relational databases that store text and numeric data related to business operations. There are other types of databases that are quite useful for performing research; many of these are accessible through the Internet. You may have used some of these when working on a research paper for class. These databases can also be quite useful in your professional life. For example, if you are a marketing professional you can use these databases to gather information about prospective clients or competitors. Demographic databases are important for understanding markets. For example, retail organizations use demographic databases to gather data to help decide where to locate new stores. These databases serve a different purpose than the databases we discussed earlier. Rather than being containers for raw data, these online databases contain pointers to sources of information.

Knowing what databases exist and how to use them can be very beneficial to you, both personally and professionally. Here are just a few examples of situations you might face and databases that might be helpful. Most of these resources are available through libraries.

- Career research
  - The United States Bureau of Labor Statistics has a searchable database of employment, pay, and benefit statistics and occupation growth projections.
  - Job search sites such as AllianceQ, Monster.com, CareerLink, and "CareerBuilder .com" maintain databases of job openings. You can usually search these databases by a variety of criteria, including occupation and location.

- Preparing for a job interview
  - Article databases such as ABI/Inform and LexisNexis Academic are useful for finding news articles about the company and its executives.
  - The Business and Company Resource Center maintains databases of company and industry-related information.

- Gathering information on customers or competitors
  - The Business and Company Resource Center is also useful for learning more about customers and competitors.
  - Hoovers.com provides extensive information about companies and industries.
- Market research
  - In addition to many of the above, the United States Census Bureau provides access to a variety of demographic and economic data.
- Economic forecasting, investment planning and portfolio management
  - Wharton Research Data Services (WRDS) is essentially a portal that provides a Web-based interface to databases of financial information, including:
    - Compustat: Company financial items such as income statements and balance sheets.
    - CRSP: Historical stock and mutual fund prices, U.S. Treasury interest rates
    - Global Insight: United States and international macroeconomic data
  - Federal Reserve Economic Data (FRED) provides over 21,000 time-series data sets, including interest rates, inflation, and economic growth.

SUMMARY

In this chapter you learned about databases, which are critical to the operation of information systems. The intent of the chapter was to help you gain an appreciation of the importance of databases, with a special emphasis on relational databases. The main points of the chapter are summarized below:

- Database management systems provide the means for creating, maintaining, and using databases.

- Spreadsheets are good for storing simple lists of information. However, they have a number of limitations that render them less effective for more complex data management.

- A relational database stores data in the form of connected tables. Tables are made up of records and fields.

- In a relational database, a record is a set of fields that all pertain to the same thing, while the fields represent some characteristic of the thing.

- In a relational database, foreign keys are fields that reference the primary keys in related tables.

- A database diagram shows the logical structure of a relational database, including its tables, fields, and the relationships among tables. Primary and foreign keys are also indicated.

- There are many online databases that store a vast array of information. These databases include article databases, market and economic databases, and databases of demographic and governmental information, among other topics. Examples include LexisNexis Academic (article database), Federal Reserve Economic Data service (economic data), and Monster.com (employment database).

REVIEW QUESTIONS

1. What are the main functions of a database management system?
2. Name five potential problems that might arise from using a spreadsheet for data storage.
3. Briefly describe how a software application interacts with a database management system in a multitiered architecture.
4. Briefly describe how relational databases store information.
5. What are the main elements of a relational database?
6. In a relational database, what is the function of a primary key?
7. In a relational database, what is the function of a foreign key?
8. What is the purpose of a database diagram?
9. What are the main elements of a database diagram?
10. Name and briefly describe four online databases.

REFLECTION QUESTIONS

1. What is the most important thing you learned in this chapter? Why is it important?
2. What topics are unclear? What about them is unclear?
3. What relationships do you see between what you learned in this chapter and what you learned in previous chapters?
4. Compare and contrast data storage using electronic spreadsheet software and database management systems.
5. Suppose you need to keep track of some data. How would you decide whether to use a spreadsheet or database management system to store the data?
6. As a user of databases, why is it useful to understand how relational databases are structured?

ADDITIONAL LEARNING ACTIVITIES

1. You have just been elected chair of one of your clubs. Your first task is to design a form to keep track of information about your members. For now you just need to track basic information: member's name, email address, mobile phone number, and join date. You want to be able to see the information about multiple members at one time. To keep things simple, you are going to keep the information on paper (at least for the moment). Sketch out a format for how you would store this information.
2. Suppose that you want to store the club member information from the previous question on a computer. Would you use a database (such as Microsoft Access) or a spreadsheet? Explain your choice.
3. Identify the data elements necessary for you to register for a course. Group these elements into tables. Draw a sketch showing how these tables might relate to one another.

PURCHASE ORDER FORM
PO No.:   12548   **Date:**   11/3/2011
Vendor ID: 87459
Name: Bithlo Books
Address   27E. SR 50
                Bithlo, FL 32158

ISBN	Title	Qty	Cost	Extended
1-55860-294-1	Database Modeling & Design	5	10.00	50.00
3-12368-998-2	Guide to the Outback	7	12.00	84.00
2-78912-437-5	Sports Heroes of the 1700's	2	16.25	32.50
	TOTAL COST			**166.50**

FIGURE 5.5 Purchase Order Form

4. Identify the tables and fields that would be a database that stores information for the purchase order form shown in Figure 5.5 above. (Note: "Extended" is the extended cost, or quantity multiplied by cost.) Draw a sketch showing how these tables might relate to one another.

5. Using the database shown in Figure 5.6 below:
   a. Name the tables in this database.
   b. For each table, list its fields and primary key.
   c. List the foreign keys.
   d. For each foreign key list the table to which it refers.

6. Using the database shown in Figure 5.7 on next page:
   a. Name the tables in this database.
   b. For each table, list its fields and primary key.

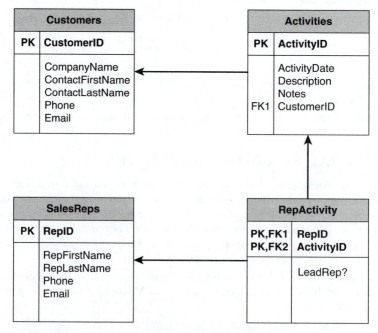

FIGURE 5.6 Customer Activity Database Design

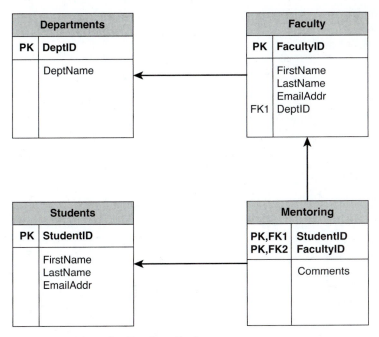

FIGURE 5.7 Mentoring Database Design

   c. List the foreign keys.
   d. For each foreign key list the table to which it refers.
7. You are probably thinking about your future career. One element of your career choice is finding out what industry (or industries) interest you. Visit your library's website and identify three online databases that provide information that can help you evaluate an industry. Briefly describe each database and explain why you think it would be useful in this task.

BIBLIOGRAPHY AND FURTHER READINGS

Spreadsheet vs DB: http://www.databasic.com.au/databases_vs_spreadsheets.htm

GLOSSARY

Database: an organized collection of data.

Database management system (DBMS): set of programs that control the creation, maintenance, and use of databases.

Field: in a relational database, a field stores data about a single characteristic of a record.

Foreign key: in a relational database, a field (or fields) that reference the primary key of a related table.

Primary key: the unique identifier of a record in a relational database.

Record: in a relational database, a set of related fields in a database.

Relational database: a data store that organizes data in connected two-dimensional tables.

Analyzing Information for Business Decision-Making

CHAPTER 6

LEARNING OBJECTIVES

By reading and completing the activities in this chapter, you will be able to:

- Discuss the importance of having good decision-making skills
- Explain how decision-making changes depending on organizational level
- Discuss the role of information in decision-making
- Contrast structured, semi-structured, and unstructured decisions
- Apply a decision-making methodology
- Choose the appropriate technology tool for a given decision-making task

CHAPTER OUTLINE

- Chapter summary

- Review questions

- Reflection questions

- Additional learning activities

- References

- Glossary

Making good decisions requires information, but that is not enough. You must also be able to analyze information. In this chapter we want to help you understand the basics of business-oriented decisions and the process by which they are made. In Chapter 14 you will learn about systems specifically designed to support decision-making. Here the focus is on understanding more about the decision-making process and tools that can help you retrieve and analyze information as part of that process.

A **decision** is simply a choice among alternatives. We make many decisions each day. Sometimes these decisions are trivial, such as deciding what to eat for lunch, while others have enormous consequences, such as deciding whether to accept a job offer. Regardless of the importance of the decision, making the decision requires retrieving and analyzing information.

FOCUSING STORY: HOW A SPREADSHEET SAVED ME (A LOT OF) MONEY

Around 2005, I was fortunate to have some excess money I wanted to invest. This was the boom years of real estate, so that was a natural possibility to explore. "Flipping" houses (buying a house, making improvements and then selling at a profit) was quite popular and I was a big fan of some of the house-flipping shows on television. While on a run, I noticed a small house that looked like a good candidate for flipping. The house seemed to be ideal: It was well within my budget; it was in a good, stable family-oriented neighborhood; and was close to my home. So, I called the real estate agent and arranged for a showing. Despite a number of cosmetic issues, the house was well built and I could easily envision how to improve it. After viewing the house and researching the potential value, I created a simple spreadsheet that analyzed the investment poten-tial of the house. I did a "what if" analysis that examined a range of possible scenarios: worst case, best case, and expected. For example, in the best-case scenario, I estimated that I would have to own the house for six months before I could sell it. In the worst case, I estimated it would take eighteen months. After "running the numbers" it became pretty clear that the investment was not worth the risk (at least to me). The best-case outcome was that I would make around $10,000, but if the worst-case scenario came true, I would lose well over $10,000. The expected scenario would only result in a profit of about $5,000. Some people would have made this investment, but I decided that under this range of possibilities I did not want to invest the time, effort, and money required to improve the house. This turned out to be a good decision; the housing bubble burst at about the time I would have been trying to sell the house. In fact, the house remained for sale for a very long time after I looked at it.

FOCUSING QUESTIONS:

1. What role did information play in this decision?

2. An electronic spreadsheet was very helpful in making this decision. What would have been different if spreadsheet software was not available?

LEARNING ACTIVITY 6.1	INFORMATION AND DECISION-MAKING

Suppose that you are in the market for a new apartment. (Your instructor may give you a different decision-making problem.) How would you go about making the decision of which new apartment to choose? What information would you gather? What would be the consequences of making a bad decision? Be prepared to share your answers in class.

Importance of Good Decision-Making Skills

Good decision-making requires good information along with good decision-making skills, processes, and tools, which is the primary focus of this chapter. The ability to make good decisions is one of the skills that sets apart successful business professionals. There is no escaping decision-making. Being able to make sound decisions that result in positive outcomes is a critical skill for a successful business career. According to a 2010 report by Hart Research Associates, analytical reasoning skills and the ability to solve complex problems are among the most highly sought after qualities for potential employees. These skills are directly related to being able to make good decisions.

Interestingly, while decision-making skills are important at all levels of business, they are increasingly important as one moves up the "organizational ladder." Why is this? First, decisions made by higher-level managers tend to be more complicated. The more complex a decision, the more skilled one must be in order to make effective decisions. Second, higher-level decisions typically have greater impacts. Consider this example. The store manager for a fast-food restaurant makes decisions such as hiring and scheduling hourly workers, and ordering products. A district manager may decide about local marketing campaigns and choosing suppliers. A corporate executive might make decisions about national marketing campaigns and whether to introduce new products. Deciding whom to schedule for the morning shift is much easier than deciding whether to roll out a new product. In addition, a bad decision on scheduling has relatively minor consequences while make a bad product decision can cost millions of dollars.

Let us be quite clear about the importance of decision-making. Virtually everything in this book is related, to some degree, to making better decisions. All of the systems we discuss, all of the tools you will learn about, and all of the information skills you will gain are directed toward helping you better understand and use information so that you can make better decisions. To paraphrase Herbert Simon, Nobel Prize–winning economist and technologist, nothing is more important for the well-being of society than that decision-making and problem-solving be well done.

LEARNING ACTIVITY 6.2	WHAT KIND OF INFORMATION DO I NEED?

You will face many different types of decisions throughout your business career. Some decisions are well defined, and have clear alternatives and information requirements. Others are much less clear. For each decision, answer the following questions:

- What information would you need in order to make the decisions?

- How confident are you that you have accurately identified the needs? Why do you feel this way?

DECISIONS

1. You are the manager of a fast-food restaurant. How many hamburger buns should you order for tomorrow?

2. You are the manager of a retail store and you need a new shift manager. Which employee should you promote?

3. You are an executive for a computer manufacturer. Should your company develop a tablet computer?

Using Information for Decision-Making

Information and decision-making are inextricably linked; much of our information needs are related to decision-making and making good decisions requires information. Insufficient, inaccurate, or untimely information have detrimental impacts on decision-making. You need good information to understand the objectives of a decision, the constraints that limit the number of alternatives, and the alternatives themselves. You also need information to forecast the potential outcomes from each alternative. Finally, information provides the means for comparing and selecting among the alternatives. If you have inadequate information related to any of these, your ability to make the proper decision is limited.

BUSINESS BOX	WHY DO MANAGERS MAKE BAD DECISIONS?

If decision-making skills are so important to business professionals, why are so many bad decisions made? There are a variety of reasons including:

- Poor decision-making skills

- Time pressures (perception that there is not enough time for systematic decision-making)

- Relying too much on intuition rather than engaging in systematic decision-making

- Being overconfident in decision-making skills, intelligence, or knowledge of the decision context

- Going with the group (groupthink)

- Addressing the wrong objective

Decision-making biases also play a role in making poor decisions. A decision-making bias is a cognitive tendency that causes the decision maker to make an incorrect decision. Here are a few of the more common decision-making biases.

- *Negativity bias*: giving more weight to negative than to positive experiences or information

- *Confirmation*: searching for information that supports preconceptions

- *Loss aversion*: making losses more important than equal gains

- *Bandwagon*: tendency to do or believe something because many others do or believe the same thing

- *Gambler's fallacy*: believing that random events are influenced by previous random events

Being aware of these biases is the first step in overcoming them.

Types of Decisions

As a business professional you will face many different types of decisions. Information systems can help you with these decisions. Before getting into how information systems can help you, it may be helpful to understand how information needs vary for different types of decisions. Herbert Simon (1960) developed a widely used view of decisions as falling along a continuum from highly structured to unstructured. (Simon called these *programmed* and *non-programmed*, but others have used *structured/unstructured*, which we prefer.) **Structured decisions** are routine and repetitive and often have well-defined procedures for dealing with them. **Unstructured decisions**, in contrast, are novel and do not have agreed-up procedures for making the decisions. **Semi-structured decisions** are somewhere in between the two extremes; they have elements that are structured and elements that are unstructured. For structured decisions, we know what information we need and how to use that information. For unstructured decisions, we are not sure exactly what information we need nor do we know exactly how to use the information. This is important to grasp as it helps us understand how different types of information systems can help with decision-making.

A complementary view comes from Anthony (1965), who developed a framework of managerial activity that is made up of three categories: strategic planning, managerial control, and operational control. *Strategic planning* entails choosing the organization's objectives and deciding how to achieve them; predicting the future of the organization and its environment; and using creative, nonroutine thinking. *Managerial control* involves ensuring the efficient, effective use of resources in achieving the objectives laid out in strategic planning. *Operational control* makes sure that the tasks of the organization are being conducted efficiently and effectively. These tasks typically are routine and well defined.

Gorry and Scott-Morton (1971) combined Simon's framework with Anthony's framework. This resulted in the framework shown in Table 6.1. Examples of relevant information systems are shown in each row/column intersection. As you can see, information systems are useful at all levels of managerial activity and for all types of organizational decisions.

Let's look at this from the perspective of information needs. Operational control has narrow, well-defined information needs that can be anticipated. Further, the information often comes from internal sources or from external sources that are easily accessed. In contrast, strategic planning's information needs are often broad, poorly defined, and come from both internal and external sources.

Operational, structured decisions often do not require any human intervention. Transaction processing systems (TPS) can deal with these decisions using predetermined rules and processes. There is little or no judgment involved. For example, an order-processing program can "decide" to allow a customer to place an order if the customer's credit card company accepts the charges but will block the transaction if the charge is denied.

Table 6.1 Gorry and Scott-Morton's Information Systems Framework

	Operational control	Managerial control	Strategic planning
Structured	Accounting systems (accounts payable/receivable), order processing, inventory control, order processing	Human resources reporting, short-term forecasting	Investment analysis, distribution system analysis
Semi-structured	Production planning	Budget variance analysis	Compensation planning
Unstructured	Cash management, project management	Budget preparation, sales planning	New product planning, social responsibility planning

Source: Adapted from Gorry & Scott-Morton (1971), Rainer & Turban (2008)

While some managerial decisions are structured, many are semi-structured. Semi-structured decisions can be supported through systems that allow flexible information retrieval. We can anticipate some information needs, but cannot create a program capable of making the decision without relying on human judgment. Since we can anticipate some information needs, information systems often have predefined reports that managers can run to retrieve necessary information. However, it is also important to allow for more flexibility through ad-hoc querying, which lets managers retrieve information on the fly. These decisions also require tools that allow for flexibility in analyzing the information once it is retrieved.

Strategic planning often involves unstructured decisions. It is very difficult to anticipate the information needs of managers involved in strategic planning. They may need information ranging from simple, prebuilt reports from internal sources to economists' projections on the future of the economy. In addition, it is hard to determine what the managers will do with the information once they have it.

It is important understand that as the amount of structure in a decision decreases, the need for flexibility increases. Very structured decisions require little flexibility in terms of information systems. In contrast, the highly unstructured decisions typical of strategic planning require information systems that offer great flexibility.

A Decision-Making Process

Many different decision-making processes exist, each with its own set of proponents. There are many similarities across the various processes. Most seem to fit well with Simon's classic, intelligence/design/choice model, so we start this section with a brief discussion of that model, then provide a more detailed process that you can use to make better decisions.

The intelligence phase of Simon's model includes those activities that alert decision makers that there is need to change the current state. Intelligence, in this context, involves sensing conditions and predicting what conditions will require action. The design phase involves developing alternative approaches to bringing about the required change or achieving the required goals. The most effective and efficient alternative is selected in the choice phase. Some believe that it is worthwhile to add a fourth phase, implementation, in which the activities in the chosen alternative are carried out. Table 6.2 provides some examples of information systems that can be used at each stage of Simon's model.

While we like Simon's model very much, it may be worthwhile to expand his model to provide more actionable details.

❋ Identify and Clearly Define the Problem

In many ways this is the most critical phase in the decision-making process. If you do not clearly define the problem to be solved, you may spend considerable time and energy in solving the wrong problem. A good problem definition should produce a clear, concise problem statement that describes both the initial state (where you are now) and desired state (where you want to be).

Table 6.2   Information Systems and Decisions Stages

Phase	Information System
Intelligence	Data analysis (spreadsheets, statistical software, visualization)
	Communication systems
	Data retrieval and document management systems
Design	Group support systems
	Communication systems
	Document management systems
	Data analysis systems (spreadsheets, statistical software, visualization)
Choice	Data analysis systems
Implementation	Project management systems
	Data analysis systems
	Communication systems

One common issue with problem definition is confusing the core problem with symptoms of the problem. For example, a sales manager might notice that sales from new representatives are decreasing. This could be a symptom of poor training, poor selection of new representatives, or a number of other underlying problems. There are techniques you can use to get at the core problem. The "5-Whys" is a popular example that is easy to understand and apply. To use the technique, simply start with the apparent problem or issue, such as "our sales are declining." Then ask yourself (or your group) "why?" then keep asking "why?" until you uncover the root cause of the problem. By the way, there is nothing magical about the "5" in 5-Whys. It is fine to ask more than five questions to get at the root cause. One criticism of the 5-Whys is that it is sometimes too simple to uncover causes in some situations. Also, the technique does not allow for identifying multiple root causes. Despite its limitations, the 5-Whys remains an effective and popular technique for uncovering root causes.

Having a well-defined, concise problem statement has other benefits as well. One important benefit is that it allows all parties to agree on the core problem. This is very helpful in later phases. In addition, such a statement enables more effective communication of the problem to various stakeholders.

Determine Requirements and Goals

Once you have your problem well defined, you should define the decision's requirements. **Requirements** are the conditions that any acceptable solution must provide. The key word here is "must." Most decisions have conditions that must be met and conditions that are desirable, but not required. One major benefit of having well-defined requirements is that they often help you eliminate infeasible alternatives early in the decision-making process. For example, if you have an absolute budget for a new automobile, you can quickly eliminate many possibilities on the basis of cost.

In contrast to requirements, **decision goals** go beyond the minimum, essential requirements. One way to distinguish between requirements and goals is to think of requirements as "must haves," and goals as "like to haves." Interestingly, goals often conflict with one another. Consider the example of deciding on a new car. Goals might include low cost, excellent fuel efficiency, and high performance. While these are all reasonable goals, fuel efficiency and performance may be in conflict. Another interesting aspect of goals is that they sometimes suggest new requirements. Also keep in mind that as you analyze your decision, you may realize that an original requirement is actually not required, and is therefore a goal. For example, when searching for an apartment you may originally consider having two bathrooms a requirement. However, if you would choose a one-bath apartment that was fantastic in every other aspect, the "two-baths" requirement is really a goal.

Identify Alternatives

Once you understand your problem's requirements and goals, it is time to identify **alternatives**. An alternative is a method for transforming the current condition into the desired state. An alternative often goes through two stages: generation and refinement. Brainstorming is often used to generate alternatives, but there are other methods that can be effective. For example, the *nominal group technique* is a structured method for reaching consensus within a group while encouraging input from all group members. While the technique was developed to help groups reach consensus, it can also be used to generate alternative solutions to a problem. Regardless of the method used to identify alternatives, it is important to provide clear descriptions of each alternative. These descriptions should plainly show how the alternative solves the problem, and how it is different from other alternatives.

Define the Criteria

Decision criteria are objective measures of the requirements and goals that help you discriminate among the alternatives. Criteria are used to determine how well each alternative meets a particular goal or requirement. It is important that each criterion be independent of other criteria (it should stand alone). Also, each goal and requirement should be represented by at least one criterion. You should also avoid redundant criteria. Finally, you should try to use relatively few criteria (keeping in mind that each requirement and goal must be represented by at least one criterion) to keep things manageable.

LEARNING ACTIVITY 6.3	REQUIREMENTS, GOALS, AND CRITERIA

Suppose that you are in the market for a new vehicle. Establish at least five requirements and goals (five combined). For each requirement and goal, determine one or more criteria. Be prepared to share your answers.

Select a Decision-making Technique/tool

There are many decision-making tools that can be applied to various decision-making situations. While it is beyond our scope here to give a comprehensive list, we offer several that are easy to understand and apply while also being quite useful. The book's website gives some resources for learning more about decision-making tools.

The techniques vary in their complexity and level of subjectivity. Generally, you want to use the simplest appropriate decision-making technique. Be sure to also consider the importance of the decision. More important decisions usually benefit from more complex, sophisticated techniques.

Pros/cons analysis

Pros/cons analysis is conceptually simple and requires no mathematical skills. You simply list the advantages and disadvantages of each alternative and then choose the alternative with the strongest advantages and weakest disadvantages. This technique is good for simple decisions that have a small number of alternatives and few discriminating criteria. Where this method gets tricky is in figuring out what "strongest" and "weakest" mean operationally. Also, this method is highly subjective. Despite its weaknesses, a pros/cons analysis is often quite helpful in choosing among alternative courses of action.

Paired comparisons

The paired comparisons technique, as the name implies, requires you to evaluate each alternative against all other alternatives. There are various ways you can carry out this analysis. In its simplest form, it is kind of like a single-elimination sports tournament. Start by picking one pair of alternatives. Compare the two using the criteria you established earlier. The losing alternative is out of the "tournament." Pair the winner against the next alternative. Keep doing this until only one winning alternative remains.

This method, while simple, is inferior to the more sophisticated variation of paired comparisons. In the more complex variant, you build a matrix, such as the one shown in Figure 6.1. The top row of the matrix is partially grayed out because it represents duplicate comparisons. The diagonal is grayed out because there is no need to compare an alternative to itself. Each remaining cell indicates which of the two alternatives is better. (This is easier if you assign a letter to each alternative.) Once all of the comparisons are done, choose the alternative with the most "wins." In our example, you would choose alternative D.

	A	B	C	D
A				
B	A			
C	A	C		
D	D	D	D	

FIGURE 6.1 Paired Comparisons Matrix

Table 6.3 Unweighted Decision Matrix

	Cost	Quality	Experience	Flexibility	Complete	Score
Proposal 1	6	8	4	7	8	33
Proposal 2	8	6	5	8	8	35
Proposal 3	4	4	6	6	9	29
Proposal 4	1	8	7	6	9	31

You can also indicate the strength of the "win" by entering a number following the better alternative. Use a scale such as 0 (no difference) to 5 (major difference). Add up all of the numbers for each alternative and convert them to a percentage. Choose the alternative with the highest percentage.

Decision matrix

The decision matrix technique is widely used in business, especially for choosing among projects or products. The decision matrix uses a grid that lists all of the alternatives in the first column, and all of the criteria in the first row, as shown in Table 6.3. Fill in the grid by rating each alternative on the criteria using a scale to indicate how well the alternative scores on the criterion. In our example we use a 10-point scale, with 10 indicating that the alternative satisfies the criterion very well. Add up the scores for each alternative; choose the one with the highest total score.

The above example considers all criteria to be of equal importance. If this is not the case, you can use a weighted version of the decision matrix. To do this, assign each criterion a weight relative to its importance. One way to do this is to distribute 100% across the criteria, as shown in Table 6.4. Once you have the weights and the ratings for each alternative, multiply each score by that criterion's weight. The sum of these is the overall score for the alternative. Complete this operation for each alternative and choose the one with the highest sum.

Evaluate the Alternatives Using the Criteria

Once you have chosen a decision-making tool, apply it to evaluate each of the alternatives. It is very important that you use your criteria when assessing the alternatives.

Table 6.4 Weighted Decision Matrix

	Cost	Quality	Experience	Flexibility	Complete	Score
Proposal 1	6	7	5	7	8	6.80
Proposal 2	8	6	4	8	8	7.00
Proposal 3	4	4	6	6	9	5.65
Proposal 4	1	8	7	6	9	6.20
Weight	*0.25*	*0.30*	*0.10*	*0.10*	*0.25*	

This may seem obvious, but sometimes the criteria get lost along the way and are not used effectively.

Check That the Solution Solves the Problem

It is worthwhile to validate the chosen alternative to make sure that it actually solves the original problem. Be sure that the alternative will bring about the desired state, meets all requirements, and best achieves the goals.

It is important to understand that the entire process is dependent on the problem definition. If the problem is poorly defined, you are likely to develop inappropriate requirements and goals, which leads to incorrect criteria. If you have the wrong criteria, your alternative evaluation will be faulty, and you are likely to make the wrong choice. So, each step in the process is dependent on the steps that precede it. Because of this, it is important to ensure that each step is carried out correctly.

Information Retrieval and Analysis Tools

Now that you understand more about the relationship between decision structure and information needs, we can discuss how information systems help with decision-making. In this section, we discuss two categories of tools: information retrieval and information analysis tools. (There are other information and communication tools that are helpful for decision-making, such as email and knowledge management systems, but we discuss these elsewhere in the book.) It is worth noting that the tools we discuss here can be considered components of a decision support system, which we cover in Chapter 14.

When you analyze information, the information has to come from somewhere. Often this information comes from an organization's databases. So, you need tools to help you retrieve the information you need. Information may also be stored in organizational documents. Information retrieval tools include database management systems, reporting tools, and document management tools. As we discussed in Chapter 5, one element of database management systems is data retrieval, which is called *querying*. Creating complex database queries requires specialized knowledge, so many managers use reporting tools such as Business Objects or Crystal Reports to generate reports to support their decision-making. These **reporting tools** typically allow users to create reports visually rather than requiring special commands. This allows managers to quickly generate reports as they refine their information needs. Figure 6.2 shows a Business Objects screen. The user simply drags data objects from the left-hand pane to the Results Objects area to create a query, which serves as the basis of the desired report.

Managers sometimes need information that is stored in documents, such as memos and policy documents. **Document management systems** include functions that help users locate and retrieve such documents. There are multiple aspects to a document management system. Some help with the creation of the document, either directly or through integration with other systems. There also must be some means to capture the document (place the document into the document management system). Not all

FIGURE 6.2 SAP Business Objects Screen

documents originate through a computerized system. Non-digital documents must be scanned so that they can be managed by the document management system. Once the document is in the system, it needs to be indexed to facilitate faster and easier retrieval.

In addition, document management systems help with versioning (keeping track of various versions of a document). Some document management systems help workers share documents. The system may also help with distributing documents properly.

LEARNING ACTIVITY 6.4	"WHAT IF" I GET A 75% ON THE FINAL?

"What grade will I get if I score a 75% on the final?" You have probably asked yourself a similar question. While you can certainly figure this out without a computer, a properly designed spreadsheet can make this much easier. Use the spreadsheet available on the book's website to calculate your overall course grade under three different final exam scores. (You can adjust the weights or grades to more closely match the grading scheme for a particular course.)

Spreadsheets are a type of decision support system. (We will discuss decision support systems more in Chapter 14.) The electronic spreadsheet played an important role in introducing the use of personal computers to businesses. For an interesting history of the electronic spreadsheet see: http://dssresources.com/history/sshistory.html.

In terms of decision support, spreadsheets provide two very important functions, "what-if" analysis and goal-seeking analysis. **"What-if" analysis,** which is a form of sensitivity analysis, involves seeing how changes in one or more input variables impact the value of one or more outcome variables. For example, if you are purchasing a car, you can see the impact of changing the interest rate of your loan on the monthly payment, as shown in Figure 6.3. You can change any of the input variables to see a range of possible outcomes.

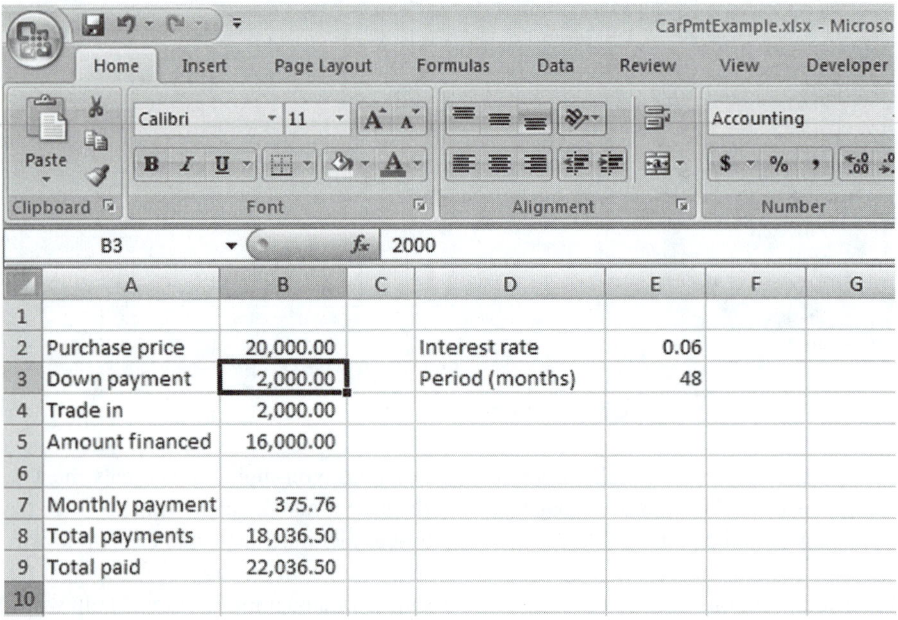

	A	B	C	D	E	F	G
1							
2	Purchase price	20,000.00		Interest rate	0.06		
3	Down payment	2,000.00		Period (months)	48		
4	Trade in	2,000.00					
5	Amount financed	16,000.00					
6							
7	Monthly payment	375.76					
8	Total payments	18,036.50					
9	Total paid	22,036.50					
10							

FIGURE 6.3 Spreadsheet Example

Some electronic spreadsheet software (such as Microsoft Excel) offers ways to quickly generate a number of scenarios so that you can see the impact of various changes on outcome variables. Excel's Scenario Manager is an example. Figure 6.4 shows a Scenario Manager summary for our car payment calculator. There are three scenarios showing the monthly payment, total payments and total paid for three payment periods, 36 months, 48 months and 60 months.

Goal seeking is the opposite of what-if analysis. In a what-if analysis, you specify changes to the input values to see the impact on the outcome variables. In **goal-seeking**

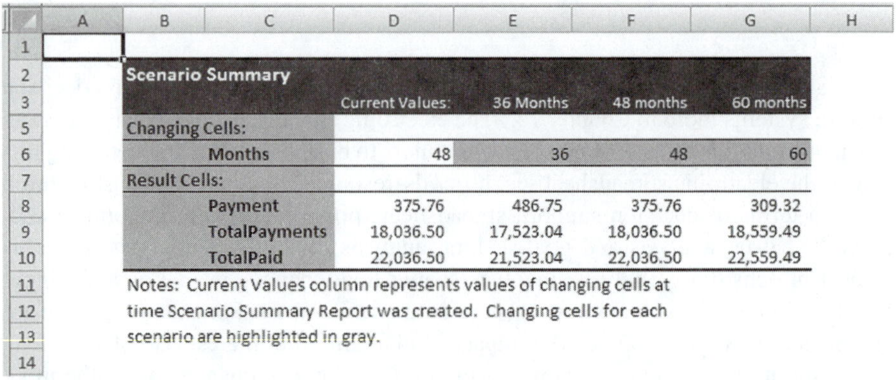

Scenario Summary		Current Values:	36 Months	48 months	60 months
Changing Cells:					
	Months	48	36	48	60
Result Cells:					
	Payment	375.76	486.75	375.76	309.32
	TotalPayments	18,036.50	17,523.04	18,036.50	18,559.49
	TotalPaid	22,036.50	21,523.04	22,036.50	22,559.49

Notes: Current Values column represents values of changing cells at time Scenario Summary Report was created. Changing cells for each scenario are highlighted in gray.

FIGURE 6.4 Scenario Manager Summary

Original

After Goal-Seek Analysis

	A	B	C
1			
2	Purchase price	25,000.00	
3	Down payment	2,000.00	
4	Trade in	2,000.00	
5	Amount financed	21,000.00	
6			
7	Monthly payment	493.19	
8	Total payments	23,672.91	
9	Total paid	27,672.91	
10			

	A	B	C
1			
2	Purchase price	25,000.00	
3	Down payment	5,967.87	
4	Trade in	2,000.00	
5	Amount financed	17,032.13	
6			
7	Monthly payment	400.00	
8	Total payments	19,200.00	
9	Total paid	27,167.87	
10			

FIGURE 6.5 Results of Goal Seek

analysis you specify the value of the outcome variable you seek (the goal) and the spreadsheet software determines the value of a particular input that will produce the desired output. Suppose that you have set a budget of $400 per month for your new car and that you have received a price quote of $25,000 for the model you want to buy and that your current car is worth $2,000 as a trade-in. You could use goal-seeking analysis to determine the down payment you would have to provide in order to meet your monthly payment goal. The "before (original) and after" for this example is shown in Figure 6.5. (Note that we are only showing part of the spreadsheet.) As you can see, you would need almost $6,000 for a down payment to achieve your payment goal.

The reason that spreadsheets can provide such useful tools is that in building the spreadsheet, instead of putting in numbers for some of the cells, you put in relationships in the form of formulas and functions. Figure 6.6 shows the formulas and functions for our car-buying spreadsheet. Because the spreadsheet is built around the formulas and functions, changing one of the input variables quickly shows us the impacts on all related values. If you want to learn more about using spreadsheets, please see the spreadsheet In-Depth Guide (available on the course website).

Payment		=PMT(E2/12,E3,B5)*-1			
	A	B	C	D	E
1					
2	Purchase price	25000		Interest rate	0.06
3	Down payment	2000		Period (months)	48
4	Trade in	2000			
5	Amount financed	=B2-SUM(B3:B4)			
6					
7	Monthly payment	=PMT(E2/12,E3,B5)*-1			
8	Total payments	=B7*E3			
9	Total paid	=B8+SUM(B3:B4)			
10					
11					
12					
13					
14					
15					

FIGURE 6.6 Spreadsheet Showing Formulas

STATS BOX: THE COST OF SPREADSHEET ERRORS

Spreadsheets are widely used analytical tools. Unfortunately, electronic spreadsheets often contain errors that can prove costly. PricewaterhouseCoopers and KPMG estimate that over 90% of corporate spreadsheets contain meaningful errors. These errors could cost as much as $10 billion annually. Here are a few examples of the costs of spreadsheet errors.

- Eastman Kodak Co. had to restate its income statement in 2005 due to several errors. One of the most severe was an $11 million error in an employee's severance pay package. The error was caused when too many zeros were added to the employee's severance accrual.

- Incorrect saving of a spreadsheet file misstated natural gas storage amounts, which resulted in inflated prices. Estimates of the cost to consumers ranged from $200 million to $1 billion.

- Entering numeric data as text, rather than numbers, caused a $50,000 budget shortfall for a UK school.

- The University of Toledo over-projected tuition revenue by over $2 million due to an error in a spreadsheet that projected enrollments.

You can more about these and other costly spreadsheet errors at:
http://www.eusprig.org/stories.htm

While spreadsheets can perform many types of statistical analysis, they typically are unable to perform more sophisticated statistical methods. When more advanced techniques are needed, you must turn to dedicated statistical software, such as SPSS, Stata R, and SAS (among others). These applications have the capability to analyze large numbers of data points quickly and accurately. Some applications specialize in particular families of statistical techniques. For example, Smart PLS (http://www. smartpls.de/forum/) specializes in a technique called *partial least squares*. Others have broad capabilities ranging from simple descriptive statistics to very complex, sophisticated statistical methods such as time-series analysis for economic forecasting. Many include programming languages that can be used to develop custom algorithms. These applications vary widely in their complexity. Some are intended only for expert users with in-depth knowledge of statistics and the program itself. Others are specifically intended for more casual users.

There are also software tools that help you visualize data. While most statistical software applications have some **data visualization** capabilities, there are also programs that are intended specifically for data visualization. Visualizing data can help you uncover trends and relationships in data that might be less apparent when viewing the data in tables. Figure 6.7 shows a variety of graphs on hiring and termination trends. These charts were produced using the spreadsheet application

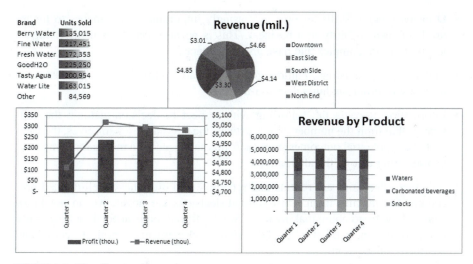

FIGURE 6.7 Visualization Example

Microsoft Excel. It is worth noting that spreadsheet software can produce charts, but typically are not as powerful or flexible as dedicated visualization software.

CHAPTER SUMMARY

The focus of this chapter is using information for decision-making. We discussed a variety of tools that can be used to help retrieve, analyze, and understand information when making decisions. We also presented a systematic process for making decisions. Finally, we provided you with several techniques that are helpful in decision-making.

Here are the chapter's main points:

- Good decision-making requires good information and good decision-making skills, processes, and tools.

- Decision-making skills are critical to a successful business career. These skills are highly sought after by business employers.

- Decision-making skills become increasingly important as one moves to higher levels of responsibility in a business. This is because decisions made at higher levels are more complex and have greater impacts.

- Making good decisions requires good information. Insufficient, inaccurate, or untimely information hurts decision-making.

- Information impacts the following with respect to decision-making: the constraints that limit the number of alternatives, the alternatives themselves, the forecast of the potential outcomes from each alternative, and the means for comparing and selecting among the alternatives.

- Structured decisions are routine and repetitive and often have well-defined procedures for making them. Unstructured decisions are novel; we do not know exactly how to go about making them, what information is needed, or how to use that information. Semi-structured decisions have elements of both structured and unstructured decisions.

- Decision-making can be done by completing the following steps: 1) identify and clearly define the problem, 2) define the requirements and goals of the decision, 3) identify alternatives, 4) define the decision criteria, 5) select the appropriate decision-making tools, 6) evaluate the alternatives using the criteria, and 7) check that the solution solves the problem.

- Many information analysis tools exist, including tools for information retrieval, information analysis, knowledge management, and communication.

- Information retrieval tools include database management systems, reporting tools, and document management tools.

- Information analysis tools include electronic spreadsheets, statistical software, and data visualization tools.

REVIEW QUESTIONS

1. Explain why decision-making skills are more important at higher levels of an organization.
2. Compare and contrast structured, semi-structured, and unstructured decisions.
3. Explain the relationship between decision type (structured, semi-structured, unstructured) and managerial activity (strategic planning, managerial control, and operational control).
4. Name and briefly describe the phases of Simon's model of decision-making.
5. For each phase of Simon's model of decision-making, give an example of an information system that supports the phase.
6. Name the phases in the detailed decision-making process described in the chapter.
7. Contrast requirements and goals in the context of decision-making.
8. Name and briefly describe the decision-making tools discussed in the chapter.

9. Name and briefly describe the information retrieval tools discussed in the chapter.

10. Compare and contrast "what-if" and "goal-seeking" analysis.

REFLECTION QUESTIONS

1. What is the most important thing you learned in this chapter? Why is it important?

2. What topics are unclear? What about them is unclear?

3. What relationships do you see between what you learned in this chapter and what you have learned in earlier chapters?

4. Think about a difficult or important decision you have had to make. What made the decision difficult? How could the material in this chapter have helped you make that decision?

5. Think about a time when you made a poor decision. What could you have done that would have led to a better decision?

6. Briefly discuss how a reporting tool can be used to help you make semi-structured and unstructured decisions.

7. Why are document management systems useful when making unstructured decisions?

8. How can following a disciplined decision-making process (such as the one described in this chapter) help you justify a decision?

9. How do decide how much time and effort to put into making a decision?

10. Suppose that you have several job offers from which to choose. Describe how you would go about deciding which one to accept.

ADDITIONAL LEARNING ACTIVITIES

1. Suppose you have three decisions to make:
   a. What elective class to take in your final semester.
   b. Which of several post-graduation job offers to accept.
   c. Where to go for your graduation trip.

   For each decision, rank the three decisions according to how much time and effort you would put into making the decision. Explain your rating. Be prepared to share your answers in class.

2. Suppose that have three job offers from which to choose.
   a. Determine the requirements and goals for deciding which offer to accept. (Have at least five total requirements and goals.)
   b. Determine the criterion you would use to measure each requirement/goal.
   c. Which decision-making tool would you use to make this decision? Why?

3. Suppose that you are a marketing manager who needs to decide among several different advertising outlets.
   a. Determine the requirements and goals for deciding which outlet to use. (Have at least five total requirements and goals.)
   b. Determine the criterion you would use to measure each requirement/goal.
   c. Which decision-making tool would you use to make this decision? Why?

4. Go to the course website and locate the Car Buying spreadsheet. Use the spreadsheet to determine the monthly payment for two different interest rates for two different periods. For example, 6% and 8% for 36 and 60 months. For each combination, report the monthly payment, total payments, and interest paid. Briefly describe how you could use this spreadsheet when car shopping.

5. Go to the course website and locate the Monthly Commission spreadsheet. Determine how many units you would have to sell to earn $3,000 in commission payments. How did you go about solving this problem? How long did it take you? Be prepared to share your experience in class.

6. Go to the course website and locate the link for the Data Visualization activity (http://www-958.ibm.com/software/data/cognos/manyeyes/datasets/fashion-sales-2003-2006/versions/1). This is a dataset of sales data for a small chain of clothing stores. Click on the "visualize" button. Prepare a visualization that shows the sales revenue for each store by quarter. Which visualization did you choose? Why? How effective was the visualization in helping you understand the data? Be prepared to discuss your experience.

7. Pick four competing elective classes that you might take next semester. (You can only take one of the four.) List the classes, then
   a. prepare a paired comparison matrix to show which class you would take.
   b. prepare an unweighted decision matrix with at least three criteria (such as time of day, or your interest in the class).
   c. prepare a weighted decision matrix using the criteria from (b).

   Which of the three methods was the most effective? Why?

REFERENCES

Anthony, R. N. *Planning and Control Systems: Framework for Analysis*. Cambridge, MA: Graduate School of Business Administration Harvard University, 1965.

Gorry, A. and M. Scott-Morton. "A Framework for Information Systems," *Sloan Management Review*, 13(1)(1971): 56–79.

Rainer, R.K. and E. Turban. *Introduction to Information Systems: Supporting and Transforming Business*, 2nd ed. New York: John Wiley & Sons, 2008.

Simon, H.A. *The New Science of Management Decision*. New York: Harper & Row, 1960.

GLOSSARY

Data visualization: visual representation of data with the goal of clearly communicating or better understanding the meaning of the data.

Decision: a choice among alternatives.

Decision alternative: a method for transforming the current condition into the desired state.

Decision criteria: objective measures of decision requirements and goals that discriminate among the alternatives.

Decision goal: desired decision solution requirements that go beyond the minimum, essential requirements.

Document management system: a system that assists with managing, locating, retrieving, and tracking documents.

Goal-seek analysis: an analysis that determines the value of a particular input variable that will produce the desired output (the goal).

Reporting tools: information systems tools that allow users to create reports without knowing special commands.

Requirement (decision): condition that any acceptable solution must provide.

Semi-structured decision: decision for which some elements are structured and others are unstructured.

Structured decision: decision that is routine and repetitive and often has well-defined procedures for making the decision.

Unstructured decision: decision that is novel and therefore has no agreed-upon, well-understood procedure for making the decision.

"What-if" analysis: analysis that involves seeing how changes in one or more input variables impact the value of one or more outcome variables. (This is also known as *sensitivity analysis*.)

Transmitting Information

LEARNING OBJECTIVES

By reading and completing the activities in this chapter, students should be able to:

- Discuss key components and characteristics of networks

- Explain the different types of networks

- Explain what the Internet is and what it is used for

- Identify the main networking architectures and infrastructures

- Describe various Web 2.0 technologies

CHAPTER OUTLINE

- Focusing story: I want my own WiFi!: The emergence of the MiFi

- Learning Activity 7.1: Online document sharing

- Introduction and definitions

  Network components and characteristics

- Types of networks

  Wired vs. wireless networks

  Broadband networks

  Network coverage

- The Internet

  Internet applications

  Internet vs. intranet

  Virtual Private Network (VPN)

- Learning Activity 7.2: A future Internet? Internet2 and business

- Networking architectures

  Architectural principles

  Client/server architecture

  Peer-to-peer architecture

  Wireless architecture

  Service Oriented Architecture (SOA)

  Software as a Service (SaaS)

  Cloud computing

  Virtualization

- Learning Activity 7.3: architectures and principles

- Communicating information in modern organizations

  Web 2.0

- Learning Activity 7.4: Web 2.0 for business

  Unified Communications (UC)

  Web 3.0

- Chapter summary

- Review questions

- Reflection questions

- Additional learning activities

- References

- Bibliography and further readings

- Glossary

FOCUSING STORY: I WANT MY OWN WIFI!: THE EMERGENCE OF THE MIFI

The interconnected world as most students know it, with easy and often free access to the Internet from home, school, the coffee shop, the airport, and even on the train, is actually fairly recent. We used to need cables (wires) to connect to other systems and the Internet. Really.

But now that we have tasted the freedom of the wireless world, people want more and more. That's where Mi-Fi comes in. Think of the ability to create your own Wi-Fi network wherever you are with a device the size of a credit card (but thicker). Mi-Fi routers became available in 2009 when Novatel introduced the NG-Fi, which uses a 3G connection (third generation cellular network) to obtain a signal that is converted into a password-protected wireless Wi-Fi signal (your own "hot spot"). The Mi-Fi network can support typically up to five users or devices (like an iPhone, a laptop, an iPad, a gaming device, or a Web camera) within 30 feet of the router. The routers are fairly inexpensive ($70 to $300 per router plus the 3G data plan) and run on batteries that can be recharged. Soon after it was announced, Sprint, Verizon, and AT&T started selling the devices to work on their networks in the United States. In December 2009, Bell and Bell Mobility launched their version of the Novatel device, called the MiFiTM 2372 Intelligent Mobile Hotspot, for customers in Canada.

By the end of 2010, creative uses of the Mi-Fi started to appear, with DoCoMo in Japan offering free Wi-Fi in 820 taxis of the Tokyo Musen Cooperative taxi company using Mi-Fi routers. They even offered the service free to customers until April 2011. Passengers can access the taxi's Wi-Fi network using the password indicated in the taxi. Another significant event for the Mi-Fi routers occurred when Virgin Mobile released its Mi-Fi router in 2010 but with a different twist: an unlimited plan (the other plans charge after 5Gb of traffic) with no contract and low monthly costs.

Think about it: by simply pressing a button on a device that you can leave in your pocket, purse, or book bag, you could be a walking hotspot at the beach, in the park, or anywhere else you wish to.

DISCUSSION:

1. Identify potential challenges of using the Mi-Fi for business.

2. What other creative business uses can you think of for the Mi-Fi?

3. Why do you think Virgin Mobile is able to offer a better packaging for its Mi-Fi?

4. What do you think could be the next evolution in wireless networks?

Sources: "Bell Introduces the Award Winning Novatel Wireless MiFi 2372 Intelligent Mobile Hotspot." *Marketing Weekly News* (Dec 19, 2009): 110; Palmer, Jay. "Oh, My! Here Comes Portable Wi-Fi." *Barron's* 89 (43) (Oct 26, 2009): 33; Pogue, David. "Your Own Hot Spot, and Cheap." *New York Times* (September 1, 2010); Shaw, Keith. "Wi-Fi gets personal with Mi-Fi." *Network World* 26 (21) (Jun 8–15, 2009): 38; Wakabayashi, Daisuke. "The Mobile Web in Motion—First Planes and Trains Get Internet Connections, Now Japan Tests Wi-Fi Cabs." *Wall Street Journal* Eastern ed. (Dec 22, 2010): B.6.

Introduction and Definitions

The Focusing Story discussed an interesting new wireless network. But before we explore the various types of networks that exist, we should define what a computer **network** is. Basically, it is a collection of interconnected devices that allow users and systems to communicate and share resources. The devices can be computers, servers, routers, and a wide variety of other telecommunication devices.

LEARNING ACTIVITY 7.1   ONLINE DOCUMENT SHARING

For the purposes of this learning activity your instructor will assign you to a group for answering the discussion questions for the Focusing Story at the beginning of this chapter (or another assignment given to you by your instructor). You will write the group's answers to the questions using an online document-sharing site. You also need to prepare a short (5-minute) presentation on the advantages and disadvantages of using online document sharing based on your experience with this activity. Make sure to discuss those advantages/disadvantages both from a student viewpoint and from a business viewpoint.

Select one of the following online document-sharing sites and start sharing drafts of your documents. You need to make sure you invite your instructor to the site.

• Google Docs: http://Docs.google.com

• Prezentit: http://prezentit.com/

Network Components and Characteristics

Setting up a network requires a variety of devices and, depending on which devices are used, a different type of network is established. For example, the wireless networks discussed in the Focusing Story require a Mi-Fi router to set up the network and devices that have wireless network adapter cards, like the Apple iPad or most laptops, to connect to it.

A **router** is an intelligent device that controls the flow or transmissions in and out of a network (see Figure 7.1). It takes its name from its main purpose, which is routing traffic to appropriate devices on the network (it uses a routing table that

FIGURE 7.1 Router (© Norman Chan/iStockphoto)

FIGURE 7.2 Hub (© Kamil Krawczyk/iStockphoto), (© Krzysztof Kwiatkowski/iStockphoto)

contains address information for the devices on the network) or to other networks. Some networks use bridges or switches instead of routers. **Bridges** are less sophisticated than routers (operating at a lower layer of the network protocol) in that they use broadcasting to all connected ports to find where the traffic should go until they have "learned" on which port each device's address is located. A **switch** is also a less-sophisticated device, but it does forward transmissions only to the ports involved in the communication, based on the devices' addresses rather than all ports connected.

We have been talking about devices having specific addresses. How is that done? It is the result of each device having a **network interface card (NIC or network adapter)** that provides a physical access to a device because it has a unique ID written on a chip that is mounted on the card. Wireless NICs, just like wired NICs, also have their own unique addresses. The network adapter for wired networks is where you plug in an Ethernet cable on your computer.

Finally, basic networks can also make use of hubs and repeaters. The **repeater** retransmits a data signal that it receives after eliminating noise in the signal and regenerating it for strength. A **hub** (see Figure 7.2) is a form of repeater that has multiple ports to connect many devices together.

Types of Networks

Wired vs. Wireless Networks

There are many ways to categorize networks. First, networks can be wired or wireless. **Wired networks** make use of physical cables, which can be copper wires (like the lines to your phones at home or the Ethernet cable we talked about in the previous section), coaxial cables (like the ones used for cable television), of fiber optic cables (which are made of glass fiber and transmit using light signals). Figure 7.3 shows different types of cables. The possible speed of transmission increases from wires to coaxial cables to fiber optic cables, with fiber optic cables allowing speeds hundreds of times faster than coaxial cables and thousands of times faster than basic wires.

FIGURE 7.3 Types of Cables: (from left to right: twisted pair, fiber optic, coaxial)
(© Chris Fertnig/iStockphoto), (© Henrik Jonsson/iStockphoto), (© Mark Coffey/iStockphoto)

There are also quite a few **wireless networks** besides the Wi-Fi you are used to. All of them make use of frequencies to transmit data (and voice). For example, some transmissions are done using microwaves that must be placed no more than 30 miles apart since they must "see" each other to transmit. The satellites used for data transmissions are typically 22,000 miles in space above the equator (they are called *geosynchronous satellites* because they keep a relative position to the earth). Those are the same systems that send you satellite radio signals, GPS coordinates, and TV signals from remote locations. Infrared communication can also be used to create a wireless network for devices in close proximity. For example, wireless mice, keyboards, and other such devices often use infrared to connect to one another. Radio signals are also used for connecting devices. Think of your cordless phone or garage opener. **Cellular networks** also use radio communication technologies to offer another wireless alternative. As you know, cell phones connect to a local antenna that relays calls from one area to the next. Finally, **Bluetooth** is another standard that uses short wavelength radio transmissions to connect devices (like we discussed for infrared technology) such as wireless mice, keyboards, or headphones.

With all of the wireless technology options, what is a wireless, or Wi-Fi, network? First of all, **Wi-Fi** is a name owned by the Wi-Fi Alliance. Today, it has become a standard terminology to refer to a wireless network that you can access with one of your wireless devices such as laptop or personal digital assistant. The Wi-Fi networks also make use of radio technology but in a different way than some of the technologies discussed above. A Wi-Fi network consists of wireless access points (WAP) (or hotspot) that is itself connected to a wired network (see Figure 7.4). The WAP transmits the transmissions it receives from wireless devices to a wired device connected to the Internet.

Broadband Networks

Another way to classify networks, which refers to the speed, frequency, and bandwidth of the network, is whether they are baseband or broadband. Today, the networks you use to connect to the Internet are likely to be broadband networks. They are faster, with download speeds (transfers from the servers to your computer) at more than 256 Kbits per second, although most broadband networks today transfer at rates in the megabytes and even gigabytes per second. The types

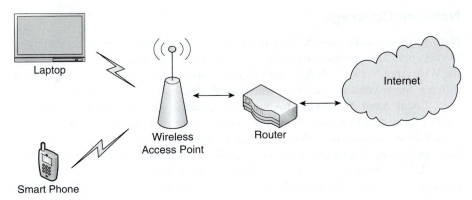

FIGURE 7.4 Wireless Network

of networks that are classified as broadband include the familiar DSL (digital subscriber lines) types of networks and cable connections, as well as some you may not have heard of, like Integrated Service Digital Network (ISDN) and T-lines. We discuss these networks more in depth in the online extension guides on the book website.

STATISTICS BOX 1: BROADBAND PENETRATION IN THE G7 COUNTRIES

The percentage of the population in a country that has access to broadband networks can have a significant impact on the use of applications such as electronic business, electronic government, and other network-dependent applications. The chart below shows the penetration of broadband networks in the G7 (a group of seven industrialized countries).

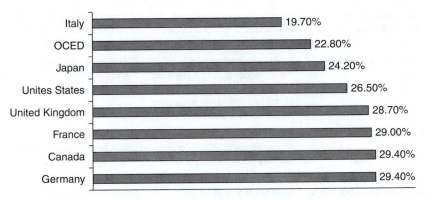

Organization for Economic Co-operation and Development

Source: InformationWeek (July 12, 2010): 23.

Network Coverage

Networks can also be classified as a function of the area of coverage or geography of the network. The two most significant ones are the Local Area Network (LAN) and the Wide Area Network (WAN), but other variations exist. See Table 7.1 for a list of different terms you can hear about when people discuss types of networks.

Local Area Networks (LANs) connect devices in a limited geographical area (a local area of usually less than five kilometers). Examples include homes, departments, school, or a floor of a large office building. Because of the limited geography, LANs can offer very good transmission speeds, especially for wired LANs. To be part of the LAN, a cable must connect the NIC of the computer or device with the router/bridge/switch of the LAN (for wired LANs). The most popular LAN technology today is Ethernet (see Figure 7.5), although some alternatives do exist.

Wide area networks (WANs) connect devices over a large geographic area, which can span any distances you can imagine, from citywide to continent-wide to worldwide. Contrary to LANs, WANs often make use of various communication

Table 7.1 Network Types (Geographical Classification)

Type of Network	Description	
Most Commonly Known Types of Networks		
Local Area Network (LAN)	A network that connects devices in a limited geographical area (a local area of usually less than five kilometers)	
Wide Area Network (WAN)	Network that connects devices over a large geographic area, which can span any distances you can imagine, from city wide to continent wide to worldwide	
Other Types of Networks		**Notes**
Metropolitan Area Network (MAN)	A large computer network that spans a city or a large campus.	It is sometimes difficult to distinguish this from a large LAN or a small WAN.
Personal Area Network (PAN)	A network connecting personal devices to a personal computer (i.e. mouse, microphone, printer, etc.) over a very short distance.	Often uses USB connections (wired) or Bluetooth or infrared technologies (wireless).
Home Area Network (HAN)	A LAN is used within a home office, allowing PCs to share devices such as printers, routers, or scanners.	Sometimes referred to as an office area network (OAN).
Backbone Network (BBN)	Network that serves to interconnect other networks (like LANs) or network segments (sub networks).	Often used in large buildings or areas that have multiple LANs that need to communicate together.

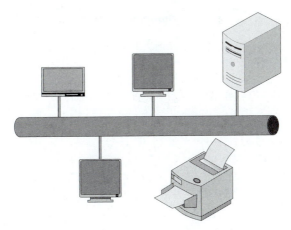

FIGURE 7.5 An Ethernet Local Area Network

media (like phone lines, coaxial cables, and satellite) as well as several different providers (phone company and cable company) even for one given network.

The Internet

One network we have yet to discuss is the Internet. The **Internet** is a publicly accessible worldwide network of networks. One way to explain how the Internet works is to think of a road system (Van Slyke and Belanger, 2003). In many countries, there are interstate highway systems that link major cities together. These interstate highways intersect one another to form a complex road system. However, not every place in the country is accessible directly from an interstate highway. Smaller roads branch off from the highways to allow travelers to reach virtually any area of a country. The Internet works in a similar way. Main connections, called the *Internet backbones*, carry the bulk of the data traffic on the Internet. Networks from major Internet service providers (ISP) make up the backbone. These networks extend across the globe in a similar way that interstate highway systems extend across many countries.

For the Internet to allow global traffic, routers are used to interconnect the various networks together. Every host or computer that is a full participant (permanently connected) on the Internet has a unique address called an *IP (Internet Protocol)* address. The book's website includes more details on the Internet's protocols and addressing, but it is important to note that the IP addressing scheme most students have seen (such as 128.192.68.1) is outdated because it has run out of addresses to allocate to businesses, organizations, and countries. It is called **IPv4** for version 4. The new IP addressing scheme is called IPv6. In simple terms, **IPv6** expands the IP address size from the current 4 bytes (the four sections of the address above) to 16 bytes. In fact, on Thursday, February 3, 2011, the **Internet Assigned Numbers**

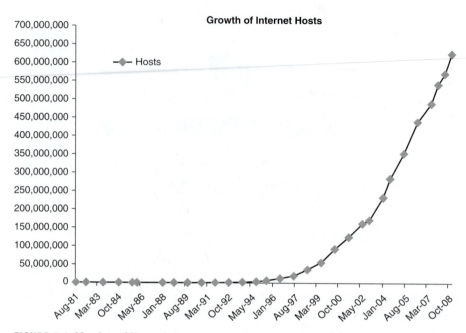

FIGURE 7.6 Number of Hosts Connected to the Internet as of July 2010

(*Source:* Based on data from the Internet Systems Consortium, http://www.isc.org/solutions/survey

Authority (IANA), the organization responsible for assigning IP addresses, assigned the last blocks of IPv4 addresses.

The Internet started as a project by the United States Defense Advanced Research Projects Agency (DARPA) in collaboration with universities. The Internet then grew by absorbing various networks worldwide. Today, the Internet has grown so much that there are more than 750 million host computers connected, based on data collected by the Internet Systems Consortium, which is the developer of BIND DNS, an open source infrastructure software (see Figure 7.6). One of the core characteristics of the Internet that has contributed to this growth is interoperability, which is the ability of heterogeneous systems to communicate with one another. For example, systems based on different hardware platforms and running different software can communicate together on the Internet if they use the Internet's protocols (described on the book's online website).

Internet Applications

The Internet is a network, not an application. When asked what the Internet is students often describe it as a place where there is all this information you can access. But this definition actually refers to the **World Wide Web (the Web)**.

They are not the same. The Web is one application using the Internet as its carrying network. Examples of other applications that make use of the Internet include email, file transfer, instant messaging, Internet telephony, and desktop videoconferencing. Table 7.2 briefly describes some of these other traditional Internet-based applications. Later in the chapter, we will discuss more recent applications, labeled as Web 2.0 applications.

Table 7.2   Traditional Internet-based Applications

Application	Description
World Wide Web (the Web)	Graphical interface to worldwide resources.
Electronic mail (email)	Used to send and receive messages through computer networks.
Instant messaging	Allows multiple users to communicate synchronously by sending and receiving short text messages online.
Voice-over-IP (Internet Telephony)	Allows voice data to be sent over an IP-based network, such as the Internet.
Desktop Video Conferencing	Allows individuals in different locations to communicate via voice and video on personal computers.
Peer-to-Peer file sharing	Allows file sharing between specific individuals or systems across the Internet.
Online application sharing	Allows users to share documents, calendars, or other applications using websites.
File Transfer Protocol (FTP)	Allows users to move files back and forth between nodes on the network. FTP is *Anonymous* when files are loaded on such public sites.
Newsgroups	Allows users to read and post messages to various electronic boards on the Internet.

The Web allows users to access an amazing variety of resources using the infrastructure of the Internet. The Web is the result of work performed by Tim Berners-Lee at CERN (the European Center for Nuclear Research) who proposed the HTTP protocol (hypertext transfer protocol) to interconnect files on the Internet. That is why many web addresses start with http:// indicating that the page is located on a server that supports the hypertext transfer protocol. You are also certainly familiar with hyperlinks, the (often) underlined blue links that allow you to navigate back and forth between pages or to a specific section of a Web page. When you click on a link, your browser sends a request to the Web server that houses the requested page. The server then sends the document over the Internet to your browser. Figure 7.7 illustrates how the Web application makes use of the Internet.

BUSINESS BOX 1	INTERNET APPLICATION OF THE DAY: GET A DEGREE ONLINE!

Ever heard of Phoenix University or Kaplan University? You might have seen the ads about the completely online degree programs available at these and many online universities where one can get a bachelor's, master's, or even Ph.D. degree. Online leaning is not new, but it is growing substantially because it offers a cost-efficient way to deliver education and allows institutions to have a broader reach to individuals who would otherwise not be able to attend school. Today, most traditional universities offer online courses and even online programs, and online universities offer completely online degrees. Have you wondered, however, how employers view these universities' degrees?

The Society for Human Resources Management asked the same question to their members in a survey published in December 2010. What they found surprised some. There was a definite improvement over perceptions of online degrees between 2005 and 2010, and 79% of the respondents said they had hired someone with an online degree in the past 12 month. However, there were still only 34% of respondents who indicated that they considered applicants with online degrees as favorably as applicants with traditional degrees. That leaves 66% who say they are not equal. If applicants had equal job experience, however, the percentage of respondents who said they would consider applicants with online degrees the same as those with traditional degrees went up to 55%. This is echoed by another survey of 240 employers in the North Central region of the United States conducted by researchers Astani and Ready who found that when employers have personal experience with online education, nearly 60% of them view online and traditional learning equally.

Sources: Astani, Marzie and Kathryn J Ready. "Employer's Perceptions of Online vs. Traditional Face-To-Face Learning." *The Business Review, Cambridge* 16 (2) (Dec 2010): 91–96; "Online Degrees Gaining Acceptance," *HR Magazine* 55 (12) (Dec. 2010): 65.

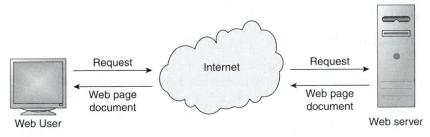

FIGURE 7.7 The Internet and Web

Internet vs. Intranet

Most organizations today, including businesses, schools, and governments, use an **intranet**. It sounds similar to Internet because it is the use of Internet technologies and related applications inside an organization. This means that security controls are in place to ensure that only individuals inside the organization have access to the applications on the intranet.

Virtual Private Network (VPN)

An important use of the Internet is to support **Virtual Private Networks (VPN)**. A VPN is a connection that makes use of an open wired network such as the Internet but that provides a secured channel through encryption and other security features. It is often used for employees to securely connect to their organizations from remote locations. In Chapter 8 (Securing Information), we will discuss the concepts of encryption used to support VPNs.

LEARNING ACTIVITY 7.2	A FUTURE INTERNET? INTERNET2 AND BUSINESS

As we have just discussed, the Internet has been in existence for a very long time. It has grown into a worldwide network that is used extensively for commercial purposes (among other things). Some researchers however, believe that it is important to have an Internet-like network that is not overwhelmed by commercial users, so that they can rapidly exchange research information between researchers, the military, and academics. That is the role of **Internet2™**, which was created by a consortium of research and education institutions, industry leaders, and government agencies. Internet2 is a trademark of the University Corporation for Advanced Internet Development (UCAID). The organization has over 200 members, and operates the **Internet2 network**, a fiber optics-based network used for high-speed transfers between research institutions and is used for testing and researching networking technology. For this activity, research the most up-to-date status of the Internet2 project. Discuss its potential implications for businesses.

Networking Architectures

Architectural Principles

Architecture is the layout or blueprint for how devices are supposed to work together. **Network architectures** can then be implemented as specific **networking infrastructures**. The infrastructure includes the actual hardware, software, and networking components that support the processing and transfer of information. In this section, we focus on the higher-level picture, the networking architectures, which each have specific advantages and disadvantages.

When deciding on an architecture, managers must ensure first and foremost that the architecture will support the business objectives of the organization (ensuring IT and business alignment as discussed in Chapter 4). Then managers must also consider certain architectural principles, such as:

- *Ease of implementation:* Some architectures are easier to implement than others. For example, the SaaS (Software as a Service) architecture we describe below requires limited effort by the organization wishing to use it.

- *Flexibility/interoperability:* In some situations it is important to be able to make changes to how devices are interconnected, or which devices are connected to which ones. Some architectures allow for more flexibility concerning which devices are connectable.

- *Control:* Organizations often want to maintain a certain degree of control over which devices can connect and how they are connected to the network. In the days of the mainframe, where everything was connected to one central large computer, organizations had complete control. Today, they must evaluate how much control they need as they make decisions on which architecture to use.

- *Scalability:* when the number of users or devices increases or decreases substantially, it is important for organizations to be able to grow or reduce the size of the network accordingly. This is the concept of scalability, and is a core consideration in selecting an architecture. In fact, the client/server architecture described below overtook the old mainframe architecture partly because it offered substantial scalability. .

- *Security and reliability:* all technology decisions should take into consideration security, including reliability of the systems, and architectures are no exception. For example, most experts consider a peer-to-peer architecture, where files are shared between computers, as one of the least-secured options for networking. We will discuss security in depth in Chapter 8 (Securing Information).

Client/Server Architecture

In the **client/server architecture**, processing and storage tasks are shared and distributed between two types of network systems: clients and servers (see Figure 7.8).

Clients are processes that request services from servers. **Servers** provide services to clients by responding to their requests. Most computers can perform client or server services, even if we mostly think of clients as the personal computers we use to access larger machines called servers.

An example can help clarify the concept of sharing the workload among clients and servers. When you search the Web for information, you are using a browser on your personal computer. The browser is acting as a client that makes requests to a Web server when you click on a hyperlink, asking for that page to be sent to you. The Web server receives the request, sends the documents back to your browser. Now assume that you need information about prices in that document. The Web server may send a request to a database server for the information, and then sends it along with the other documents to your browser. The browser then displays the requested document. In this case, the client (browser) requests services but also performs the task of displaying the results (presentation task). The Web server receives the requests, makes its own request to the database server (data task), and then packages it to send it back to you (processing or logic task). For servers and clients to communicate, even when they are on different technology platforms, they require some software that can understand each technology's specific formats and communication protocols, and translate them into the other platforms' formats and protocols, enabling interoperability. This is the role of middleware.

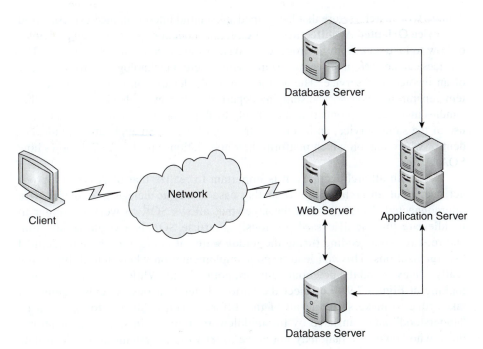

FIGURE 7.8 Client/Service Computing Architecture

Peer-to-Peer Architecture

The **peer-to-peer architecture** is used substantially on the Internet, but not as much in organizations. In a peer-to-peer network, all systems are equal (acting as both clients and servers), sharing their resources with one another. The sharing of resources can include processing power, disk storage, and network bandwidth. Most students are familiar with Napster, the music file sharing system, a prime example of peer-to-peer networking.

Wireless Architecture

We discussed previously how wireless networks are setup. Organizations must evaluate several decisions regarding what to support and whom to allow on the network when they choose to implement a wireless architecture. Think of your university's wireless network. Who should have access to it? If everyone, is it your tuition fees that pay for the network? Which devices should be allowed on it? What level of security should be provided? All of these issues have to be discussed and decided upon by the network architects of your university before they make the wireless network available.

Service Oriented Architecture (SOA)

A more recent architecture that has gained substantial interest in the business world is **Service Oriented Architecture (SOA)**. It is a model or a set of design principles of how to take data from heterogeneous systems and create reusable services. The services can be used in different systems with different technology platforms. Think of an invoice as a service. The accounts payable department probably has a system generating invoices. The shipping department, however, also has a system that handles invoices for products that are ready to ship. The two departments can make use of the same service, an invoice, with each of their own applications, independent of where and on which platform their applications are. Figure 7.9 shows how SOA works.

As with all architectures, it is important to realize that SOA is not a product itself, but an architecture or in this case a way to design how devices are interconnected. Note also that the layer that allows SOA to work is similar to middleware that we discussed previously. Because SOA is a vague architecture and requires some coding (using the middleware), it is often too broadly defined by organizations. This can lead to poor implementation where reusability is not really achieved and the potential gains are not realized. While it seems easy when looking at Figure 7.9 to connect the various heterogeneous systems together, it takes time to make sure that all of the different data fields and formats can be "understood" and translated by the middleware. Further, in some organizations, those who "own" the data may not agree to let various systems access their data and services.

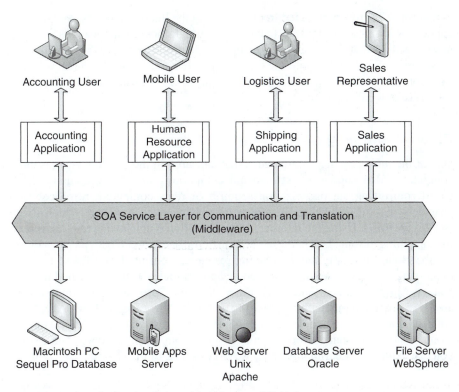

FIGURE 7.9 Sample Service Oriented Architecture (SOA) Layout

Software as a Service (SaaS)

Another recent architecture or model of computing is **Software as a Service (SaaS)** (see Figure 7.10), which is basically the acquisition (or rental) of software via a subscription model. SaaS, often called "software on demand," allows organizations

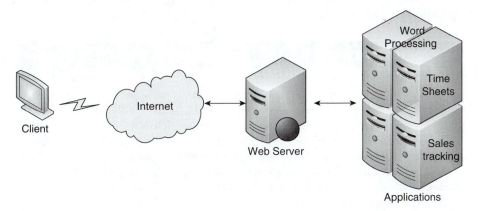

FIGURE 7.10 Software as a Service

to rent software from a provider, frequently using the Internet to access this software application. SaaS software tends to be mostly straightforward applications that businesses need but that do not provide specific competitive advantages. For example, the most popular SaaS applications include customer relationship management software, sales force automation, human resources management software, and desktop applications (like word processing).

Cloud Computing

One of the most popular architectures that appeared in the last few years is cloud computing, also known as "on-demand computing" or "utility computing." In **cloud computing**, an organization acquires or rents computing resources from providers instead of having their own locally managed hardware and software (see Figure 7.11). Using the Internet, the organization is able to increase or decrease its computing resources when the needs arise or decrease. What can be acquired via the cloud? Virtually any computing resource, from hardware for storage and processing, to backup services, to specific applications. Clearly, the cloud includes SaaS we just discussed, and much more. The main providers of cloud services are large organizations with resources to spare, such as Google, IBM, AT&T, and Amazon.com, although specialized providers also exist. An example of using the cloud to store and share information is dropbox.com (http://dropbox.com), which you can explore in Learning Activity 7-A7 at the end of the chapter.

Virtualization

Another recent trend in computing architectures is virtualization (see Figure 7.12 on page 132). **Virtualization** allows one physical device such as a server or computer to operate as if it is several machines. Virtualization software creates virtual environments called *virtual machines* on the hardware platform. Each virtual machine can then run its own operating system and applications. If you own a recent Apple Mac computer, its operating system allows you to perform virtualization so you can run a Windows operating system on your Mac.

LEARNING ACTIVITY 7.3   ARCHITECTURE AND PRINCIPLES

The purpose of this activity is to further explore one of the networking architectures discussed in this chapter. More specifically, the goal is to map each architectural principle to one of the networking architectures, which your instructor will assign to you. Perform necessary research as a group, and clearly highlight how the given architecture ranks on each of architectural principle (high, medium, low), and make sure to describe why. For example, you could state that the client/server architecture ranks high on scalability because clients and servers can be added to the network easily and as needed. Prepare a presentation for the class.

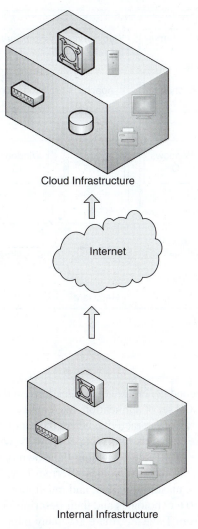

Cloud Infrastructure

Internet

Internal Infrastructure

FIGURE 7.11 Cloud Computing

Communicating Information in Modern Organizations

The previous section briefly reviewed some of the most used or most recent network-ing architectures. How do we make use of these architectures? Well, they serve as the communication backbone for all of the applications that organizations employ to perform tasks. These tasks are called *business processes,* and we will dedicate Chapter 11 to discussing them more in detail. In this section, however, we want to continue our discussion about the communication applications running on networks with a review of the more recent Web 2.0 applications.

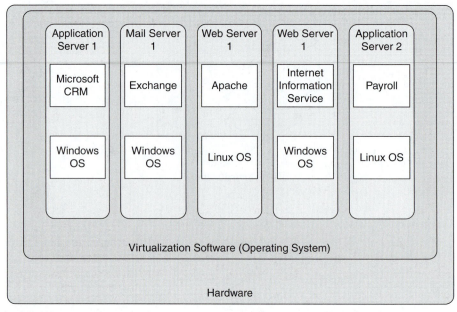

FIGURE 7.12 Virtualization

Web 2.0

Web 2.0 refers to the second generation of applications on the Internet. The main differences between the initial set of application, like email or Web surfing, and Web 2.0 applications is the addition of interactivity, where the user becomes participant in the interaction. For example, in **wikis** like Wikipedia (www.wikipedia.com), users can participate in the design of the site by adding their own definitions and corrections to the information. The set of technologies referred to as Web 2.0 includes wikis, social networking, blogs, mashups, twitter, and much more. Table 7.3 presents a list of some popular Web 2.0 technologies and their description.

As you can see from Table 7.3, there are many interesting Web 2.0 technologies that are changing the way we interact with organizations and with one another. Individuals are increasingly connected via technologies, with many advantages and disadvantages.

Unified Communications (UC)

One technology that cannot be really labeled Web 2.0 but that represents a significant trend for communication is **unified communications (UC)**. As the name suggests, it is the unification or integration of various communication tools such as instant messaging, email, voice mail, video conferencing, and even speech recognition. For example, in a UC environment, an employee may decide that her preference is to receive everything via email. When someone leaves a voice mail for this employee,

Table 7.3   Popular Web 2.0 Technologies

Web 2.0 Technology	Description	Examples
Wiki	Website that allows individuals to jointly create and edit Web pages about a chosen topic.	• The well known Wikipedia: www.wikipedia.com • Setup your own wiki at: http://www.wikispaces.com/
Instant messaging and presence awareness	Allows several individuals to communicate via real-time text-based messages. **Presence awareness** indicates when colleagues are currently online and connected.	• AOL Instant Messaging: www.aim.com • Google instant messaging: talk.google.com
Collaborative content	Allows several individuals to contribute to and share stored data and documents such as text documents, movies, pictures, calendars, and more. The collaborative content systems control for user access and versioning, avoiding two users from changing a document simultaneously.	• Calendaring via Doodle: http://www.doodle.com/ • Document via Google Docs: http://Docs.google.com/ • Presentations via Prezentit: http://prezentit.com/
Web conferencing (voice, video and data)	Allows individuals to conduct live meetings via the Internet, including training sessions or sales presentations. All participants use their own computers to connect to the meeting, and can use voice (voice over IP) and/or video as well as send files, use instant messaging, or even share their personal desktop with others.	• Skype: www.skype.com • Adobe connect: www.adobe.com/ConnectWebConference
Social networking	Allows individuals to participate in a community of users (individuals or organizations) where they are connected with one another via links (for example, friendship or business relationships).	• Friendship social networks: Facebook (www.facebook.com), MySpace (www.myspace.com) • Business social network: LinkedIn (www.linkedin.com).
Blogs	Allow individuals to write commentaries or opinions on anything they want on websites that others can read. Usually, blogs are updated regularly, and allow others to leave comments. The name comes from Web log.	• Create your own blog: www.blogger.com/; http://wordpress.com/.
Mashups	Allow users or developers to combine data or applications from several sources to create new ways to view data or new aggregated results.	• Examples of mashups: http://www.programmableweb.com/mashups

(continued)

Table 7.3 Popular Web 2.0 Technologies (*continued*)

Web 2.0 Technology	Description	Examples
Twitter	Allows individuals to write tweets, which are short text messages of up to 140 characters, on their user page for others to "follow." This has become very popular among celebrities to share their day-to-day activities with fans.	• Create your own twitter: http://twitter.com
RSS	Known as **Really Simple Syndication**, it allows individuals to receive frequently updated information like blogs or news headlines directly to their personal computers.	• Search your university's news pages for where you can sign up to receive news as a RSS feed. • Examples of RSS feeds from Yahoo! Sports: http://sports.yahoo.com/top/rss

the system sends her an email message that can have an audio file of the voice mail as an attachment, a text conversion of the voicemail, or both! While not every organization will likely install the set of products needed to implement UC, a 2010 survey of 249 business professionals by *InformationWeek Analytics* revealed that the top business goals for unified communications are improved collaboration, improved efficiency, the need to replace older telephony technology, creation of a more mobile workforce, and improved communications with customers (Littlejohn, 2010).

THE POWER OF WIKINOMICS

You have heard of wikis and Wikipedia, but what if you could take advantage of everyone's voluntary contributions to knowledge for business purposes. This is referred to by some as **crowdsourcing** or **mass collaboration**, where individuals voluntarily come together to solve a problem. Others have given it the name of **Wikinomics**. More specifically, in a book called *Wikinomics: How Mass Collaboration Changes Everything* (2007), Don Tapscott and Anthony Williams give the example of GoldCorp.

GoldCorp, a Canadian mining company with a 50-year-old mine considered to be tapped out, needed to clearly identify new deposits but in-house geological experts did not seem to be able to find them. The company's CEO, Rob McEwen then took a very unusual step by publishing all proprietary geological data on the Web (mining is usually a very secretive industry). He challenged "Web prospectors" in a contest to find new mining deposits and offered $575,000 in prize money. Approximately 1000 individuals from 50 different countries examined the available information and 110 target locations were submitted to GoldCorp; 50% of them previously unknown to the company. The amazing result is that 80% of the newly identified deposits yielded substantial quantities of gold.

Netflix, the online movie rental company, offers another example of creative use of wikinomics. One of the company's core strengths is to provide users recommendations on movies they may like based on what they have watched or placed in their rental "queue" (list of movies they want shipped to them in order of preference). Up to 60% of their rentals were driven by these recommendations. Netflix had their own developers working this recommendation system, which they called Cinematch. The company, however, wondered if others could develop an even better algorithm, so they turned to the Web and launched a contest where teams could register on the company's website, download the data from a large number of customers' rental preferences, and propose their own recommendation algorithm. If the teams could improve Cinematch's prediction accuracy by 10% or more, they would receive $1,000,000. Netflix also offered a yearly progress prize of $50,000 for teams with the greatest improvements that year. The competition was announced in October 2006 and was set to end on October 2, 2011. On September 2009, one team received the US$1,000,000 grand prize for improving the Cinematch algorithm by approximately 10.10%.

STATISTICS BOX 2

Social networking is everywhere and there is no doubt about its popularity. What is quite interesting is that it achieved this status very rapidly compared to other major innovations. The table below compares how long it took various technologies to achieve one million users. Of course, in the days of the telephone there were fewer people, so this is not a scientific analysis. Yet, it does tell something about today's interconnected world.

Innovation	Year Introduced	Year Reached 150 Million Units	Years It Took
Telephone	1876	1965	89
Television	1928	1966	38
Cellular phone	1983	1977	14
iPod	2001	2008	7
Facebook	2004	2009	5

As of February 2011, Facebook has more than 500 million active users and half of them log on to their accounts every day! The average user has 130 "friends" and overall, users spend over 700 billion minutes per month on Facebook.

Sources: Hempel, Jessi, *"How Facebook is Taking over our Lives,"* Fortune Magazine, Volume 159, No. 4, (March 2, 2009): 51–56; *Facebook Press Releases,* http://www.facebook.com/press/info.php?statistics.

LEARNING ACTIVITY 7.4	WEB 2.0 FOR BUSINESS

The purpose of this activity is to identify creative uses of Web 2.0 technologies for business. Most of you are familiar with several uses of Web 2.0 in society, such as social networking for keeping up with friends or Twitter for knowing up-to-the-minute activities of your favorite celebrities. But Web 2.0 technologies can also be useful for businesses. In this activity, groups of students need to identify creative uses of Web 2.0 specifically for business purposes. Your instructor will assign you one or several Web 2.0 technologies and you must prepare a list of potential uses, highlighting the advantages and disadvantages of using this or these Web 2.0 technology(ies) for the purposes you identified.

Web 3.0

Web 2.0 technologies are all around us today, but researchers and innovators are already working on **Web 3.0**. If Web 2.0 introduced interactivity and user participation, what is Web 3.0 likely to bring to us? The semantic Web. This is when computer systems start to understand the meaning (semantics) of information and data. In other words, the systems will consider the context of the information to give meaning to other information or data connected to it. For example, when you search the Web today you have to identify which keywords are likely to give you the information you need. In the semantic web, the systems will understand what you need and give you exactly that information. Searches will become much more intelligent and results much more personalized.

CHAPTER SUMMARY

In this chapter, we discussed networking concepts and how information is transmitted. We first defined networks and discussed various types, including the Internet and the Web. We then discussed networking architectures and Web 2.0 technologies and concluded with unified communications and Web 3.0.

Here are the main points discussed in the chapter.

• A network is a collection of interconnected devices that allow users and systems to communicate and share resources. The network requires connecting devices such as routers, bridges, or switches. Each device on the network requires a network interface card (NIC or network adapter). Repeaters and hubs can be used to regenerate signals on networks.

• Networks can be classified as wired (using physical connections) or wireless (using airwaves for connections). Wireless networks include Wi-Fi, microwave signals, satellite signals, infrared signals, and radio signals, including cellular networks and Bluetooth. Networks can also be classified as Local Area Networks (LAN), which connect devices in a limited geographical area; or Wide Area Networks (WAN), which connect devices over a large geographic area like a city, a country, or the world. Other networks include Metropolitan Area Network (MAN), Personal Area Network (PAN), Home Area Network (HAN), Virtual Private Network (VPN), and Backbone Network (BBN).

- The Internet is a publicly accessible worldwide network of networks. It uses routers to interconnect the various networks together and every host or computer that is a full participant (permanently connected) on the Internet has a unique address called an IP (Internet Protocol) address. The Internet is a network, not an application. The many applications that can make use of the Internet include the Web, which is a graphical interface to worldwide resources, as well as electronic mail, instant messaging, Voice-over-IP (Internet Telephony), desktop video conferencing, peer-to-peer file sharing, online application sharing, file transfers (FTP), Newsgroups, and many more.

- Network architectures describe how devices are supposed to work together. Every architecture has its advantages and disadvantages in terms of ease of implementation, flexibility and interoperability, control, scalability, and security and reliability. The main networking architectures we discussed include client/server architecture, where processing and storage tasks are shared and distributed between clients and servers; peer-to-peer architecture where systems are equal in sharing their resources with one another; wireless architecture, which defines how devices are to be connected to the wireless network; Service Oriented Architecture (SOA), which allows data from heterogeneous systems to be used to create reusable services; Software as a Service (SaaS) model where software is acquired via a subscription model; cloud computing architecture, which allows an organization to acquire computing resources from providers instead of having their own locally managed hardware and software; and virtualization model where one physical device can operate as if it is several machines.

- Web 2.0 refers to the second generation of applications on the Internet where the user becomes a participant in the interaction. Web 2.0 technologies include wikis, which allow individuals to jointly create and edit Web pages about a chosen topic; instant messaging and presence awareness, which allow several individuals to communicate via real-time text-based messages with presence awareness indicating when colleagues are currently online and connected; collaborative content, which allows several individuals to contribute to and share stored data and documents; web conferencing, which allows individuals to conduct live meetings via the Internet; social networking, which allows individuals to participate in a community of users connected with each other; blogs, which allow individuals to write commentaries or opinions on anything they want on websites others can read; mashups, which allow users or developers to combine data or applications from several sources to create new ways to view data or new aggregated results; Twitter, which allows individuals to write short text messages of up to 140 characters on their user page for others to "follow"; and RSS, which allows individuals to receive frequently updated information like blogs or news headlines directly to their personal computers.

REVIEW QUESTIONS

1. What is a network?
2. What are the key components and characteristics of a network?
3. What is a wireless network and what are some examples of it?
4. What are the differences between Local Area Networks (LANs) and Wide Area Networks (WANs)?
5. What is the Internet and what is the difference between the Internet and the World Wide Web?
6. What is the role of network architectures and what principles should managers take into consideration when evaluating network architectures?
7. Briefly explain each of the networking architecture presented in the chapter.
8. Explain what Web 2.0 means and provide three examples of Web 2.0 technologies.
9. What are unified communications? Give an example.
10. What is Web 3.0?

REFLECTION QUESTIONS

1. What is the most important thing you learned in this chapter? Why is it important?
2. What topics are unclear? What about them is unclear?
3. How can architectures discussed in this chapter be used to create competitive advantages for the organization like we discussed in Chapter 4?
4. Why do many individuals confuse the Internet with the World Wide Web?
5. Why does it make sense for companies to use architectures like SaaS or cloud computing?
6. What issues could exist when companies use architectures like SaaS or cloud computing?
7. Do you think we will eventually live in a completely wireless world or will there always be wired networks? Why?
8. In your opinion, which architectural principle is most important in deciding on a network architecture?
9. Is the Internet likely to continue growing in terms of users, hosts, and connected networks?
10. How can a business use Web 2.0 technologies for competitive advantages?

ADDITIONAL LEARNING ACTIVITIES

1. This activity requires you to complete a case analysis regarding social networking. The case may be accessed through your university website, the Ivey School business case website (http://cases.ivey.uwo.ca), the Harvard Business school cases website (http://cb.hbsp.harvard.edu/cb/web), or may be provided to you by your instructor.

   D. B. Yoffi, M. L. Slind, and N. Achsaf. CASE: LinkedIn Corp., *Harvard Business Case*, Product Number: #9-709-426, 2008.

2. For this activity, read the article "Reputations at Risk," which you can find on the course website. Prepare a report that answers the following questions:

a. What are the various risks companies face with Web 2.0 applications? Support your statements with statistics you find on the Web.

b. What can companies do?

Is it worth it?

Are there other alternatives besides what the article recommends?

c. Which "sites to watch" do you believe offer the greatest risks?

3. This activity requires you to complete a case analysis regarding Web 2.0. The case may be accessed through your university website, the Ivey School business case website (http://cases.ivey.uwo.ca), the Harvard Business school cases website (http://cb.hbsp.harvard.edu/cb/web), or may be provided to you by your instructor.

Steenburgh, Thomas and Jill Avery. CASE: UnME Jeans: Branding in Web 2.0, *Harvard Business Case*, Product Number: #9-509-035, 2008.

4. As a group, research Web 3.0 and develop a presentation for fellow students that can clearly explain what it is and how it is going to function.

5. Locate two undergraduate or master's degree programs that use the Internet and Web to completely replace face-to-face meeting time. Describe each of the programs including the network-enabled applications they use and identify how they could make even better use of Web 2.0 technologies to increase the interactivity of their programs.

6. Research Voice over IP (VoIP) products. Select and download two of them that are either freeware (available for free) or that offer a test version. Use the two products several times and identify their main advantages and weaknesses. Prepare a recommendation report for which one would be most useful for a) students, and b) a small business. Make sure to discuss why.

7. Use the cloud by downloading the dropbox application at http://dropbox.com and share documents with your classmates. Prepare a document discussing the advantages and disadvantages of using the cloud for your schoolwork and for business.

8. This activity requires you to complete a case analysis regarding SaaS. The case may be accessed through your university website, the Ivey School business case website (http://cases.ivey.uwo.ca), the Harvard Business school cases website (http://cb.hbsp.harvard.edu/cb/web), or may be provided to you by your instructor.

Applegate, Lynda M., Robert D. Austin, Kalle Lyytinen, Esko Penttinen, and Timo Saarinen. CASE: F-Secure Corporation: Software as a Service (SaaS) in the Security Solutions Market. *Harvard Business Case*, Feb 26, 2009, product number: 809099-PDF-ENG

REFERENCES

Littlejohn, Jeremy. "UC: Big Promise, Modest Movement," *InformationWeek* (June 19, 2010). http://www.informationweek.com/news/telecom/unified_communications/225700490?queryText=unified communications business driver.

Tapscott, Don and Anthony D. Williams. *Wikinomics: How Mass Collaboration Changes Everything*. New York: Penguin, 2007.

Van Slyke, C. and F. Bélanger. *Electronic Business Technologies*. New York: John Wiley & Sons, 2003.

BIBLIOGRAPHY AND FURTHER READINGS

Greenstein, Shane, Rebecca Frazzano, Evan Meagher. "Triumph of the Commons. Wikia and the Commercialization of Open-Source Communities in 2009," *Kellogg School of Management* (Dec 01, 2009) product number: KEL464-PDF-ENG

GLOSSARY

Anonymous FTP: FTP files loaded on public sites.

Backbone Network (BBN): network that serves to interconnect other networks (like LANs) or network segments (sub networks).

Blog (Web log): website that allows an individual to write commentaries or opinions on anything, for anyone to read.

Bluetooth: wireless network that uses short wavelength radio transmissions to connect devices such as wireless mice, keyboards, or headphones.

Bridge: device used to create a network by broadcasting transmissions to all connected ports to locate device's address.

Cellular networks: network that uses radio communication over local antennas to relays calls from one area to the next.

Client/server architecture: computing model where the processing and storage tasks are shared and distributed between clients and servers.

Clients: processes that request services from servers.

Cloud computing: computing model where an organization acquires or rents computing resources from providers instead of having their own locally managed hardware and software. Also known as *on-demand* or *utility computing*.

Collaborative content: several individuals contribute to and share stored data and documents.

Crowdsourcing: mass collaboration of information to solve a problem; also known as *wikinomics*.

Desktop video conferencing: individuals in different locations communicate via voice and video on personal computers.

Electronic mail (email): applications used to send and receive messages through computer networks.

File Transfer Protocol (FTP): users move files back and forth between nodes on the network.

Home Area Network (HAN): LAN used within a home office, allowing PCs to share devices such as printers, routers, or scanners.

Hub: a form of repeater that has multiple ports to connect many devices together.

Instant messaging and presence awareness: several individuals communicate via real-time text-based messages with presence awareness indicating when colleagues are currently online and connected.

Instant messaging: multiple users communicate synchronously by sending and receiving short text messages online.

Internet Assigned Numbers Authority (IANA): organization responsible for assigning IP addresses.

Internet: publicly accessible worldwide network of networks.

Internet2 network: a fiber optics-based network used for high-speed transfers between research institutions and used for testing and researching networking technology.

Internet2: a consortium of research and education institutions, industry leaders, and government agencies that operates the Internet2 network.

Intranet: the use of Internet technologies and related applications inside an organization.

IPv4: older IP addressing scheme that uses 4 bytes for addresses (such as 128.192.68.1) that ran out of addresses to allocate.

IPv6: new IP addressing scheme that uses 16 bytes for IP addresses.

Local Area Networks (LANs): connects devices in a limited geographical area (usually less than five kilometers).

Mashups: users or developers combine data or applications from several sources to create new ways to view data or create new aggregated results.

Mass collaboration: more than one individual gather information; also known as *wikinomics* or *crowdsourcing*.

Metropolitan Area Network (MAN): network that spans a city or a large campus.

Network: collection of interconnected devices that allow users and systems to communicate and share resources.

Network architecture: layout or blueprint for how devices are supposed to work together.

Network infrastructure: the actual hardware, software, and networking components that support the processing and transfer of information.

Network interface card (NIC or network adapter): provides a physical access to a device because it has a unique ID written on a chip that is mounted on the card.

Newsgroups: users read and post messages to various electronic boards on the Internet.

Online application sharing: users share documents, calendars, or other applications using websites.

Peer-to-peer architecture: computing model where all systems are equal (acting as both clients and servers), sharing their resources with one another.

Peer-to-peer file sharing: file sharing between specific individuals or systems across the Internet.

Personal Area Network (PAN): network connecting personal devices to a personal computer (i.e. mouse, microphone, printer, etc.) over a very short distance.

Real Simple Syndication (RSS): individuals receive frequently updated information like blogs or news headlines directly to their personal computers.

Repeater: retransmits a data signal that it receives after eliminating noise in the signal and regenerating it for strength.

Router: intelligent device that controls the flow or transmissions in and out of a network.

Scalability: ability to grow or reduce the size of the network as required.

Servers: processes that provide services to clients by responding to their requests.

Service Oriented Architecture (SOA): computing model or set of design principles of how to take data from heterogeneous systems and create reusable services.

Social networking: individuals participate in a community of users connected with one another.

Software as a Service (SaaS): architecture or model of computing where the acquisition (or rental) of software is done via a subscription model.

Switch: device used to create a network by forwarding transmissions to the ports where the received devices are located.

Twitter: individuals write short text messages of up to 140 characters on their user page for others to "follow."

Unified communications (UC): the unification or integration of various communication tools such as instant messaging, email, voice mail, video conferencing, and even speech recognition.

Virtual Private Network (VPN): connection that makes use of an open wired network such as the Internet but that provides a secured channel through encryption and other security features.

Virtualization: computing model that allows one physical device such as a server or computer to operate as if it is several machines.

Voice-over-IP (Internet Telephony): voice data that is sent over an IP-based network, such as the Internet.

Web 2.0: second generation of applications on the Internet where the user becomes a participant in the interaction.

Web 3.0: known as the *semantic Web*, computer systems that understand the meaning (semantics) of information and data, resulting in more intelligent searches and more personalized results.

Web conferencing: individuals conduct live meetings via the Internet.

Wide Area Networks (WANs): connect devices over a large geographic area such as a city, a country, or the world.

Wi-Fi: network name owned by the Wi-Fi Alliance; wireless network that uses radio technology.

Wikinomics: individuals who voluntarily come together to solve a problem online.

Wikis: individuals jointly create and edit web pages about a chosen topic.

Wired network: network that makes use of physical cables (copper wires, coaxial, or fiber-optic cables) for connections.

Wireless network: network that makes use of frequencies to transmit signals.

World Wide Web (the Web): graphical interface to worldwide resources available on the Internet.

Securing Information

CHAPTER 8

LEARNING OBJECTIVES

By reading and completing the activities in this chapter, students should be able to:

- Explain the various types of threats to the security of information
- Identify the main goals of information security
- Discuss the different categorizations of security technologies and solutions
- Explain the basic functioning of security technologies and solutions, such as passwords, firewalls, biometrics, encryption, virus protection, and wireless security
- Discuss the main purposes and content of security policies
- Identify risk management options

CHAPTER OUTLINE

- Focusing story: My Mac is more secured than your windows-based PC!
- Introduction and definitions

  Information security concepts

  Security levels
- Learning Activity 8.1: How protected is your computer?
- Information security threats

  Denial of service

  Unauthorized access
- Learning Activity 8.2: Detecting phishing

  Theft and fraud

  Summary of security threats

- Security technologies and solutions

  Security goals

  Preventive, corrective, and detective controls

  Physical security vs. logical security

  User profiles

- Learning Activity 8.3: How strong is your password?

  Biometrics

  Firewalls

  Rendering data unreadable: Encryption

- Learning Activity 8.4: Breaking the encryption

  Types of cryptography

  Virus protection

  Wireless security

- Security policies

- Learning Activity 8.5: Where's the security?

- Risk management

- Chapter summary

- Review questions

- Reflection questions

- Additional learning activities

- References

- Bibliography and further readings

- Glossary

FOCUSING STORY: MY MAC IS MORE SECURED THAN YOUR WINDOWS-BASED PC!

I am sure some of you have heard it, even probably shared the rumors with others. If you get a Mac (an Apple computer with a Macintosh operating system), you are much less likely to have security breaches than if you get a regular PC, plus they're really cool. We might agree with the cool part, but what is the status of Apple computer security?

For quite a while, there were few viruses and other such programs (called malware) that targeted Mac systems. That resulted in a reputation that Mac systems were substantially safer than Windows-based PCs. Experts do recognize that this is still true; Apple computers are less likely to be victims of viruses, but they also warn that this does not mean there are no security issues! One Mac lover, and security researcher, named Charlie Miller revealed in the spring of 2010 that he had identified 20 security vulnerabilities in Apple's software, each of which could result in a computer being compromised (taken over). Miller first hacked an iPhone in 2007, and then a Macbook Air in two minutes at a competition in Vancouver a few months later.

When Apple released the iPhone in 2007, it generated new interest in Apple's platforms and might have attracted the attention of many more hackers who had targeted Microsoft's platforms before. As a result, many hackers started to identify security flaws in the iPhone, such as the ability to bypass the phone's PIN number by placing it in recovery mode, or the ability to extract encrypted data using basic forensic software. The software is available for free online and a YouTube video even explains how to do this. Of course, Apple released fixes for these security issues as soon as they could. Nevertheless, as a result of these, many firms that deal with sensitive data, such as law firms, decided it was too risky for use. More recently, in the summer of 2010, new security issues surfaced with the release of the iPad. One group of computer experts discovered a flaw that allowed them to uncover 114,000 email addresses, including those of prominent officials in companies, politics, and the military. What they did is guess numbers that identified iPads connected to AT&T's mobile network.

In the end, it is still true that Macs face fewer attacks, although they are being hacked. One reason is that Macs only account for 8% of the U.S. market for computers, making this a much smaller pool of potential victims. Some say, however, that with the growth of the iPhone and iPad markets, Macs are becoming much more interesting to hack, and that their software vulnerabilities (bugs) are steadily increasing. As one expert says, Mac users "do have less to worry about than their PC cousins, but still have enough potential vulnerability to justify a solid interest in security safeguards." (Furnell, 2010, p. 10)

DISCUSSION:

1. Why is forensic software available online to everyone?

2. Will increased use of Apple platforms lead to more security issues?

3. Why are security issues in iPhones and iPads of concern for Mac users?

Sources: Ante, Spencer E. "AT&T Says Ipad Owners' Email Data Was Breached." *Wall Street Journal* (Jun 10, 2010): B.1; Ante, Spencer E. and Ben Worthen. "FBI to Probe iPad Breach— Group That Exposed AT&T Flaw to See Addresses Says It Did a 'Public Service.'" *Wall Street Journal* (Jun 11, 2010): B.1; Furnell, Steven. "Mac security: An Apple That Can't Be Bitten?" *Network Security* 2010 (1) (Jan 2010): 7–11; Greenberg, Andy. "The Mac Hacker Strikes Again." *Forbes* 85 (6)(Apr 12, 2010): 40; Monroe, Ian. "Worms in the Apple?" *ABA Journal* 96 (3) (Mar 2010): 33; Hooper, Larry. "iPhone: Apple's Worm?" *CRN* 1256 (Dec 10, 2007): 16.

Introduction and Definitions

Information security is an important topic for everyone in today's interconnected world. What is **information security**? It is defined as the set of protections put in place to safeguard information systems and/or data from security threats such as unauthorized access, use, disclosure, disruption, modification, or destruction.

Information Security Concepts

Whether you need to secure your own computer to prevent a virus from destroying your files or an organization needs to secure access to their data and servers to ensure that hackers cannot get information about their clients, the core concepts of security remain the same.

First, security is not about technology only, but also about management and people. It is possible to acquire the best-ever security tools, but if the employees do not use them or even worse decide to bypass the security protections that are mandated by the organization, the systems and data are vulnerable to attacks or security failures. Top to bottom commitment to security in the organization is needed to ensure that security tools are properly used and security policies are followed adequately.

Second, the world of information security is somewhat unfair. How many security weaknesses does the hacker need to break into a system? One. How many security weaknesses does the organization or individual need to fix or protect against? All of them. This is referred to as **asymmetrical security warfare**. One party must do everything to protect oneself, while the other party (the attacker) only needs to find the one weakness.

Third, as a result of having to protect the computer systems and data from all possible weaknesses, security for individuals, and even more so for organizations, requires what is called defense in depth. **Defense in depth** means that there must be multiple layers of security protections in place. For example, if you have very important data on your computer, such as personal financial information, defense in depth would mean having a lock on the computer, a password to access it, a firewall to protect it against breaches from the Internet, and even encryption of the data so it is unreadable without the encryption passcode or password. We will discuss all of these technologies in this chapter. Below we explore more in depth various levels of security protection possible.

Security Levels

The concept of defense in depth refers to multiple layers of protection, which can include multiple devices performing similar functions. Similarly, there must exist protection technologies and policies to secure stored information. Some like to refer to three main levels: protection of the information itself, of the computer on which the information is stored, and of the network to which the computer is connected. A more fine-grained set of security levels is shown in Figure 8.1. In this case, data can only be accessed with proper authorization for this data, the application that uses the data, the host computer on which the data is stored, and the network to which the host is connected.

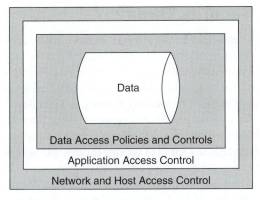

FIGURE 8.1 Access Levels for Information Security

An example of securing access to data could be your university grade entry application that professors use. In order to give you a grade for the semester, the professor needs to have access to the university's network, with a user ID and password. To change grades, the professor is required to connect to a specific application on a specific system. This requires the use of a user ID and password. In addition, only authorized users (the professor) are able to access the grade change application. The student data is protected through an additional level of security since only certain professors are allowed to change certain grades for certain students. At many universities, an employee ID is required in addition to the user ID and password when accessing specific information about students. Finally, data can be encrypted at the data level, providing yet another level of security. In this case, the professor (or her computer) will need to have software to handle the encrypted information and make it legible.

LEARNING ACTIVITY 8.1   **HOW PROTECTED IS YOUR COMPUTER?**

For many individuals, students, and nonstudents, security is the job of IT specialists and something they do not feel comfortable handling themselves. However, many studies show that the weakest link in security is these same individuals who fail to perform basic steps in securing their computers, data, and networks. Maybe it is your case? Let's see how secure your computer is with this learning activity.

1. Run one of the following applications and print (to file) a copy of the vulnerability report.
   a. Shields Up application on the following website: www.grc.com/
   b. Firewall test at Audit My PC: http://www.auditmypc.com/

3. Try to fix the issues identified, if applicable.

4. Bring your online report to class for discussion.

Information Security Threats

Most people think of information security as unauthorized access to individual or organizational data or systems. But it is much broader; it also includes dealing with natural disasters, such as earthquakes and fires, as well as dealing with any threats to computerized systems, such as viruses, hackers, and accidental loss of data or systems.

There are a large number of **security threats** to individuals and organizations alike, particularly today as most people are connected to the Internet on a regular if not permanent basis. Threats are often broadly categorized as denial of service, unauthorized access, and theft and fraud. **Denial of service threats** are those that render a system inoperative or limit its capability to operate, or make data unavailable. **Unauthorized access threats** refer to someone accessing systems and/or data illegally. **Theft and fraud threats** are related to the loss of systems or data due to theft or fraudulent activities.

Denial of Service

Security threats that can cause denial of service can result from intentional acts, careless behavior, or even natural disasters. While natural disasters such as earthquakes, tornadoes, hurricanes, or fires cannot be prevented and can completely destroy systems or data, a careful security **disaster recovery** plan will include steps to recover from such disasters (backups, duplicate systems, etc.). Careless behaviors are numerous, such as forgetting to perform proper backups of one's computer, not installing security updates to an operating system, or failing to update one's antivirus software. Often, individuals even turn off security features because they find them annoying. Was it your case in Learning Activity 8.1? Did you remove password protection from your PC? Forgot to update your operating system software? No one should undermine the potential security issues that careless behaviors can generate. What solutions exist to protect against these? Education is the first one, and second is automation of security tools and updates so that the user does not have to perform security tasks or is prevented from reducing the effectiveness of the current security on the systems and data.

The last category of denial of service security threats includes those that are intentional. Some threats could be fairly simple, like vandalism from a disgruntled employee who reformats a server's main drive or starts a fire in the computer room. Others can involve sophisticated tools meant to disrupt or destroy use of systems or data. They include viruses and other malware, email bombing and other attacks, and break-ins (also unauthorized access, as discussed in that section).

Viruses and Other Malware

Viruses have been around for several decades, and have become a major issue for all organizations, as well as individuals. It is likely that at least one person in your class has been a victim of a virus. Both authors have at some point in time had computer virus issues. Viruses are often referred to as target-of-opportunity, which means they are sent out there to find any victim they can.

What are viruses? What do they look like? **Viruses** are computer programs designed to perform unwanted events. Some cause minor harm, such as sending undesirable messages. Others are very destructive, deleting all files on a computer or creating so much traffic on a network that it crashes and cannot be used by its customary users. The lines of code that make up a virus can be embedded into other files or they can be attached to the boot sectors of disks or USB drives (so they automatically infect anyone using that device).

What a virus looks like is called the **virus signature**; it is the particular bit patterns that can be recognized, which is how virus detection software knows your computer has contracted a virus. If viruses are embedded into a legitimate file, they are often called **Trojan horses**. If they can propagate themselves throughout the Internet with no user intervention, they are referred to as **worms**. A **stealth virus** is a more advanced virus that changes its own bit pattern to become undetectable by virus scanners. Some viruses are downloaded when users access certain websites. Browsers today often protect you from downloading what is called **active content** (for example, ActiveX programs). However, when asked, many users simply say yes to downloading any content from the website. Once viruses are installed on a computer, it may be difficult to remove them (we discuss later how to do this). Viruses can also modify themselves as they move to other computers, changing their signature to become less easy to detect. Finally, **spyware** (which we discuss in Chapter 9) is a form of virus since the software can log everything a user is doing on their computer, unbeknownst to them.

There are also **virus hoaxes** on the Internet. These are not viruses, but false virus alerts being sent and resent by individuals. Their consequences include either substantial unnecessary network traffic, or unwanted actions by users (for example, telling users that certain files must be deleted to avoid the virus). Usually, unsophisticated users who panic at the idea that they might have caught a virus propagate these hoaxes. In case of doubt, the best action is to go to the website of the company that built the targeted application and search for virus hoaxes.

E-mail Bombing and Other Computer Attacks

Computer attacks, including **e-mail bombing**, involve targeting a specific computer or network, with the intent of disrupting its normal functioning. These attacks send a large number of requests, emails, or synchronization (SYN) messages to fill the target's mailboxes, system, communication ports, or memory buffers, with the intent of blocking legitimate messages from entering the systems or overloading the systems to make them crash. When a hacker uses an innocent third party to multiply the messages being sent to the intended target, such as a university server, this is called **smurfing**. To do this, hackers place software agents on the innocent third party's computer. These programs will then help them launch their attacks when they decide to strike. If many computers are being used for such attacks, we call them **distributed denial of service attacks (DDOS)**.

Why would anyone perform such malicious acts? Some may be disgruntled employees. Others may attack a given target for political reasons, for example, protesting a company's stand on some issue. The groups who perform such actions often use the term **hactivism**, which involves finding information that, if revealed, will advance human causes. However, these and other denial of service attacks by hackers continue to be very damaging to organizations. Any downtime in the computer systems or networks can mean lost sales and lost revenues for companies, or major losses in productivity if employees cannot perform their normal duties.

Unauthorized Access

Unauthorized access involves illegal access to systems, applications, or data. One of the biggest worries for organizations is theft of data, including customer information, trade secrets, or other important information regarding the organization, its business partners, or employees. Unauthorized access through break-ins can also be used to damage information or applications on a system, leading to a type of denial of service.

When thinking of unauthorized access, we often imagine a hacker who lives on the margins of society and who tries to access an organization's data files to do something good for the world, or to prove he can. However, the reality is that organizational insiders often perpetrate unauthorized access; they have the knowledge needed to hack into the systems to obtain information, such as credit card numbers. Some incidences of unauthorized access are difficult to identify because they are passive, such as recording transmissions (see Figure 8.2). By doing so, a hacker can obtain passwords, which can then be used to access information on an organization's systems through a valid account. As can be seen from Figure 8.2, breaks-ins can also

Active Unauthorized Access

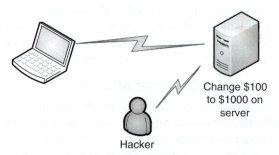

Change $100 to $1000 on server

Hacker

Passive Unauthorized Access

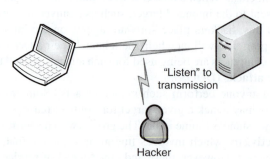

"Listen" to transmission

Hacker

FIGURE 8.2 Passive vs. Active Unauthorized Access

be used to actively modify the system or data being hacked, for example creating false account information for fraud purposes, downloading customer data, or changing the content of messages to falsely implicate the company in certain events or to delay negotiations on an important contract.

How is hacking actually performed? It requires a combination of skills and patience. Most of the tools available for hacking are unfortunately easy to find on the Internet, but not everyone has the skills, patience, or intent (!) to perform break-ins. Software, such as **sniffers**, can be used to map information on someone's network and identify weaknesses in computers and networks. When you performed Learning Activity 8.1, the scanning software identified **open ports** on your computer. This meant that some specific applications are installed and running on your computer. Once this is known, a hacker can test the targeted system for vulnerabilities (like unpatched software), and if a vulnerability is found, s/he can exploit it. Hackers often do these using **spoofing**, which means pretending to be someone else (or another computer). In an email message, you can easily spoof an address by simply changing the information in the "From" line to reflect the name of the person you want to impersonate. This is not very sophisticated and many individuals are able to detect such simple spoofing. More advanced spoofing can be done at the IP address level by changing the source (sender's) IP address to look like it comes from a different address. This is done by changing the information in the address field of the IP packet. A packet is a small unit of data that flows through networks, allowing for the transmission of messages. Hackers usually do spoof IP addresses when they launch spamming denial of service attacks so that the attacks cannot be traced back to them. Spamming involves sending e-mails to many individuals at once, sending unsolicited commercial e-mails to individuals, or targeting one individual computer or network and sending thousands of messages to it.

What are vulnerabilities? They are often called *software security holes*. All operating systems and applications have them. The Internet is again a source of information since vulnerabilities are documented. Software patches (updates) are meant to address these vulnerabilities once they are found. When new software is made publicly available, it usually takes very little time for hackers to identify the security holes. The software developers then have to quickly react by developing fixes for the software, which are made available to users via download on the software developers' website. Unfortunately, many users do not update their operating systems fast enough or even turn off automatic updates.

STATISTICS BOX 1

What systems do the hackers tend to break into the most? Not surprisingly, the database server where most business data is stored is likely to be a main target in terms of percentage of records taken. However, point-of-sales systems, such as cash registers, often have more breaches, because database servers also tend to be the most secured systems in organizations. The figure below shows you other systems that are subject to targeted break-ins.

(*continued*)

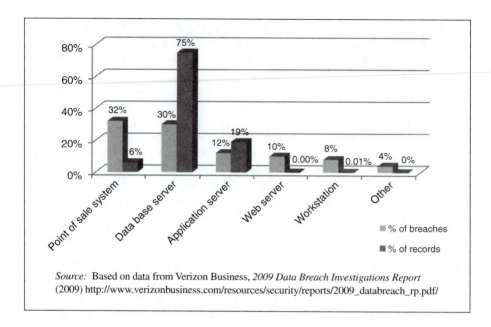

Source: Based on data from Verizon Business, *2009 Data Breach Investigations Report* (2009) http://www.verizonbusiness.com/resources/security/reports/2009_databreach_rp.pdf/

Finally, it is important to reiterate that many unauthorized access situations arise because users have access to someone else's legitimate password and accounts. In many cases, individuals are negligent about protecting their passwords. In other cases, individuals can be tricked into giving out this (and other) information. This is referred to as **social engineering** (and sometimes called *phishing*). Examples of social engineering actions include tricking someone into

From: customer.center@BankOfAmerica.com
To: belanger@vt.edu
Date: Oct-22-10 2:36 PM
Subject: Online Banking Alert

Your Online Banking is Blocked! Please Take Immediate Action.

Dear Belanger,

We recently reviewed your account and we suspect that your Bank of America account may have been compromised by an unauthorized person. Protecting the security of your account is our primary concern. Therefore, as a preventive measure, we have temporarily limited access to important account features.

To restore your online account access, we need you to confirm your information at the following website within 48 hours of receiving this email. It is very important that you update your information within this timeframe if you do not wish your online access to be placed on hold.

https://www.bankofamerica.com/update/

We thank you for your rapid attention to this matter.

FIGURE 8.3 Example of a Phishing Email

telling you their password by claiming to be someone with rights to know it, or tricking them into sending you an important file or opening a link to a dangerous website (See Figure 8.3 for an example). Sophisticated social engineering can even involve listening to lunch conversations among unsuspecting professionals with privileged information. Today, most Internet users are familiar with phishing through email messages sent pretending to be banks or large companies such as eBay.com, PayPal, or Amazon.com. The problem is that for most individuals, it is hard to identify whether such emails are phishing emails when they actually have an account with those companies.

BUSINESS EXAMPLE BOX 1	EVEN BIG TECHNOLOGY COMPANIES CAN BE HACKED

One would think that large technology companies should have the resources and expertise not to be victims of hackers, right? Well, in early 2010, mighty Google was the victim of hackers in China.

In January 2010, Google employees realized that the company's Gmail system (email accounts) had been hacked by individuals in China using systems at two educational institutions. Google has many well-designed and monitored firewalls, but the attackers were able to release malicious code inside those firewalls. The code was meant to attract users to innocent-looking websites that released viruses or other malware onto their computers. The attacks are referred to as *spear phishing*. In this case, there are many hypotheses for what the malware was trying to do. It may have tried to access Gmail records, or it may have tried to access Google's intellectual property. The problem for Google is that many companies are considering migrating part of their own infrastructures to Google (i.e. cloud computing). Security, of course, will be a key concern of managers as they consider whether to migrate to the Google cloud architecture or not.

(*Source:* Anderson, Mark. "Too Big to Hack: To Keep Cyberspace Secure, Must Governments Regulate Mighty Google?" *IEEE Spectrum* (April 2010): 13–14.)

Even when a system has been hacked, organizations do not necessarily know that this has happened, unless a problem occurs immediately. Some organizations have tools to detect hacking attacks, which we will discuss in the next section of this chapter. The hacker, however, will often start the attack by erasing audit logs that would show what has happened and installing **rookits**, software that will allow him to have unfettered access to everything on the system, including adding, deleting, and copying files. The hackers often install **backdoors**, allowing them to re-access the system at their will. Finally, they can install a number of victimization software such as **keystroke capture programs** that will log all information entered into the computer, spyware, attack software for denial of service attacks, or other remote tools for them to control the systems that have been hacked.

LEARNING ACTIVITY 8.2   DETECTING PHISHING

There are many ways to detect phishing emails. The most common things to look for include the following problems in phishing emails:

1. The email is not addressed to you directly.

2. The email is addressed to you using your email account info (without the @provider; e.g. Dear belanger).

3. The email does not have a personalized salutation (i.e. Dear Dr. Belanger).

4. When you hover the mouse over the hyperlink, the site does not seem to be from the proper company (look at the domain name).

5. When you hover the mouse over the hyperlink, the site seems to be located in another country.

6. The email contains poor grammar and spelling mistakes real companies would not make (we hope).

7. The email makes you feel your response is urgent or something bad is going to happen.

Read more about phishing at the following sites:
- http://www.anti-phishing.info/
- http://www.spamlaws.com/detecting-phishing.html

Then, test your skills detecting phishing email on the book's website. You can also identify the problems mentioned above in the sample phishing email in Figure 8.3.

Theft and Fraud

Theft and fraud concerning information has become an important concern of companies. We discussed some fraud and theft of data in the unauthorized access security threat discussion. Two additional issues need to be explored regarding theft and fraud: theft of software or hardware devices that increasingly contain huge amounts of information, and theft of data using small hardware devices.

Theft of software usually occurs when employees copy legitimate software installed on their company's servers to bring home or to give to someone else. These copies do not carry licenses and are therefore illegal copies. This is a major concern for organizations, and many have started to perform audits of installed software. The best control for this problem, though, is user education. Many employees do not see a problem with copying software this way, although it is illegal. Other organizations provide only personal computers that do not allow saving to any external media devices, preventing software from being copied.

FIGURE 8.4 A USB Thumb Drive (© Michael Bodmann/iStockphoto)

As hardware has become more portable and powerful, theft of hardware has become an increasing concern for organizations. Think of how much data can be stored on a laptop, tablet, or even a personal digital device like a BlackBerry or iPhone. Besides the cost of the hardware itself, organizations have to worry about the information contained in these devices, as well as the access that the devices often have to the organization's internal systems.

Finally, theft of data is also possible thanks to storage devices with ever increasing capacities. Today, a small USB thumb drive like the one shown in Figure 8.4, can contain gigabytes of data. Think of a complete list of all of an organization's customers, with addresses and historical purchases; this can fit easily on a thumb drive. An individual can install software that automatically copies everything on a device when the USB thumb drive is inserted. There have been reports of such tools being inserted in computers in hotel business centers, in kiosk devices in shopping mall, and others. A nonemployee roaming an office could easily copy tons of files if allowed in with the device and not supervised while in the organization's offices.

Summary of Security Threats

Before a manager can evaluate security measures and come up with a proper security plan, she must identify all of the threats to security that her organization faces. We have presented some of the most common security threats in this section.

There are, however, other threats to security that can occur. Each year since the late 1990s, the Computer Security Institute and the FBI have conducted a survey of the most prevalent threats (most security incidents). Their data show that viruses, insider abuse of information systems, and laptop theft remain the most important issues. It is necessary to distinguish here between prevalence (how often the threats occur) and impact (cost of the threat). For example, financial fraud is considered a low-prevalence, but high-impact security threat. In 2010, 45.6% of the individuals who reported security problems indicated that they actually had been victim of at least one targeted attack (CSI/FBI Survey, 2011). Of course, not all intrusions are reported because companies do not want to spend the energy on reporting incidents, are afraid of negative publicity or competitors taking advantage of the incidents, or do not believe law enforcement can help or would be interested. Below is a list of the security incidents reported over the years in order of prevalence (those most often reported listed first).

- Viruses

- Insider abuse

- Laptop theft

- Unauthorized access

- Denial of service

- Instant messaging or messaging abuse: people spending more time on chat than work

- Bots: computers that have been compromised (hacked) and used to relay attacks

- Theft/loss of customer data from mobile devices

- Theft/loss of customer data from all other sources

- Abuse of wireless network: unauthorized users accessing the company's wireless network

- System penetration

- Financial fraud

- Misuse of Web applications

- Theft/loss of proprietary info from mobile devices

- Theft/loss of proprietary info from all other sources

- Password sniffing

- DNS attacks: denial of service or other attack meant to bring down the Domain Name Server (used for translating URL to access Web pages)

- Website defacement: hackers accessing the company's Web page and changing it

- Telecom fraud: people using the telecom infrastructures of the company with authorization

- Sabotage

Security Technologies and Solutions

Security Goals

Before we discuss each of the security tools, we need to briefly mention that all tools and policies are meant to address one or more core security goals, which are known as CIA – Confidentiality, Integrity, and Availability.

Confidentiality involves making sure that only authorized individuals can access information or data. **Integrity** involves making sure that data are consistent and complete. For example, as a message is transmitted, its content is not modified unwillingly during the transmission. Finally, **availability** involves ensuring that system and/or data are available when they are needed. For systems to be considered highly available, the organization must protect them from disruptions not only due to security threats such as denial of service attacks, but also due to power outages, hardware failures, and system upgrades.

There are two additional goals of security to consider: authentication (or authenticity) and nonrepudiation. **Authentication** is basically making sure that the parties involved are who they say they are, and that transactions, data, or communications are genuine. **Nonrepudiation** is particularly important in e-commerce, and refers to making sure one cannot renege on their obligations, for example by denying that they entered into a transaction with a Web merchant. In e-commerce, digital signatures and encryption are used to ensure that the goal of nonrepudiation is met.

Preventive, Corrective, and Detective Controls

A large number of security technologies and solutions exist to address the threats we have discussed so far. One way to classify the security solutions and tools (often called security controls) is to consider whether they are preventive, detective, or corrective controls. The goal of **preventive controls** is to stop or limit the security threat from happening in the first place. For example, **antivirus software** scans computers and programs and alerts users if potential viruses exist before they can infect files or computers. The goal of **detective controls** is to find or discover where and when security threats occur. For example, **audit logs** can be used to track all accesses to a system to see if multiple false attempts are made from a particular user ID. Finally, the goal of **corrective controls** is to repair damages after a security problem has occurred. An example is the antivirus software previously discussed, which can remove a virus, quarantine the file with the virus, or simply delete the problematic file.

Physical Security vs. Logical Security

Security solutions can also be classified as physical or logical. **Physical access controls** are those security solutions that involve protecting the physical access to systems, applications, or data, whereas **logical access controls** include security solutions that protect access to systems, applications, or data by ensuring users or systems are authenticated and allowed to have such access.

Physical access controls can include locks for laptops, locked computer rooms, and secured rooms for backup storage. Once devices are no longer needed, software programs called drive shredders should be used to make sure that all discarded disk drives cannot be read again. Physical security also involves ensuring that wiring closets, where all of the routers and connections are located, are properly locked and secured. Another important aspect of physical security is selection of personnel. Remember that insider abuse is one of the most significant security threats. Organizations must ensure that only proper personnel have access to key information systems and data. Organizations should run background checks on such personnel and provide appropriate training. Several surveys have identified onsite contractors as a major threat to security for organizations.

Logical access controls use many technologies to require authentication of users and systems trying to access specific applications, networks, data, or computers. These include user profiles, biometrics, firewalls, and encryption.

User Profiles

User profiles are one of the main solutions used to prevent unauthorized access to systems, data, and applications. Users are assigned profiles that consist of a user identification (self-selected or assigned by the organization) and a set of privileges. Once the user confirms his identification, he can access the system, application, or data with the level of privileges given to him. For example, faculty can view student data but cannot modify some of that data (such as personal address). This is considered the principle of least privilege. Give users only access to what they need and no more!

User profiles require that individuals be differentiated from one another using one or several levels of identification: possession, knowledge, or trait.

- **Possession** is when an individual owns a form of identification. For example, your driver's license, your student ID, and your passport are possession forms of identification.

- **Knowledge** is when an individual needs to know something to gain access. Passwords are a good example of knowledge required to access systems. Combining possession and knowledge, such as requiring a personal identification number (PIN) with a banking card, provides more security.

- **Traits** require recognition of physical or behavioral human characteristics, such as a fingerprint or a signature style, to gain access to systems, data, or applications. This is part of biometrics, which will be described in the next section.

LEARNING ACTIVITY 8.3   **HOW STRONG IS YOUR PASSWORD?**

Passwords are one of the most used security solutions to control access to systems, applications, and data. We have no doubt that you have several passwords you use on a regular basis. But how strong are these passwords? Let's see what a strong password is.

1. Select two passwords you use frequently, and test their level of security using one of the following password checkers:
   - http://www.microsoft.com/protect/fraud/passwords/checker.aspx/
   - http://www.passwordmeter.com/

2. Read the information on how to create a strong password at:
   - http://www.microsoft.com/protect/fraud/passwords/create.aspx/

3. Create a strong password. Test it. Do not use it for your accounts!

4. Bring the following to class:
   - The level of security of your two passwords (be honest; but do not tell the passwords!)
   - The strong password you created and what it stands for.

User profiles remain one of the most used security solutions for access to systems and data. Yet, there are many issues with using user profiles for authentication. First, users often use words or numbers that are easy to remember. Many systems today will not accept such passwords, which can be easily "broken" with a **dictionary attack**, where all words of several dictionaries in multiple languages are tested as passwords with numbers before and after the words. This often takes only a few seconds for a password to be discovered. The second problem is that users also write their password down on a sticky note taped to their computer or taped to the inside of their desk drawers because they have too many passwords to remember. Alternatively, they use the same password for everything. If someone finds out about it, all systems the user accesses are compromised. Password recovery can be a problem too, since it is often easy to know the name of a person's pet, family members, school attended, or city of birth, as well as birthday or important numbers. Just think how much of that information can be found on social networking sites like Facebook!

To increase the effectiveness of user profiles, security systems now often require users to change their passwords regularly, like every one, three, or six months. Many systems will not allow more than a few attempts at entering a password before they block access to the user account. Most systems also require the use of strong passwords. As discussed in Learning Activity 8.3, strong passwords require a mix of uppercase letters, lowercase letters, alphanumeric characters, and numbers. Tools exist to help manage passwords. For example, **password crackers** are available online for various systems to recover passwords that are forgotten. Of course, they can also be used to crack someone else's password, for example with a

Table 8.1 Top Twenty Passwords Used in Hotmail Accounts Hacked in October 2009

Rank	Password	Count	Rank	Password	Count
1	123456	64	11	iloveyou	7
2	123456789	18	12	daniel	7
3	alejandra	11	13	000000	7
4	111111	10	14	roberto	7
5	alberto	9	15	654321	6
6	tequiero	9	16	bonita	6
7	alejandro	9	17	sebastian	6
8	12345678	9	18	beatriz	6
9	1234567	8	19	mariposa	5
10	estrella	7	20	america	5

Source: Based on data from Acutenix, available at http://www.acunetix.com/blog/news/statistics-from-10000-leaked-hotmail-passwords/.

stolen laptop. There are also password generators that can help you generate strong passwords. Even with all of these tools, however, most individuals still create poor passwords. In October 2009, ten thousand Windows Live Hotmail email accounts were hacked and their passwords were posted online to another site. An analysis of these passwords revealed that most users had really weak passwords, with the top 20 passwords shown in Table 8.1.

Biometrics

Another security method used to authenticate users and control access to systems, data, and applications is **biometrics**, which use human traits and characteristics to recognize individuals. While they go beyond possession and knowledge, biometrics can be used in conjunction with these to provide strong security, for example requiring a card with a password and a fingerprint to have access to certain data. Fingerprinting is a low-cost example of biometric technology. There are several other biometric technologies, which can be classified as **physiological biometrics** (those that use physical traits) or **behavioral biometrics** (those that use behavior). Table 8.2 briefly describes these security solutions.

Law enforcement agencies have used fingerprinting for a long time to identify criminals. Today, many laptops have fingerprinting scanners to restrict access or replace passwords, such as the one shown in figure 8.5. Iris scanning offers some of the best security because the iris is unique among all individuals. (The iris is the colored portion of the eye.) Immigration services in the United States use fingerprinting for noncitizens and iris scanning for frequent travelers who have special cards identifying them as trusted travelers. The English government in the United Kingdom has a large database of earprints because no two ears are said to be the same.

Table 8.2   Sample Biometric Solutions

Physiological Biometrics		Behavioral Biometrics	
Fingerprint recognition	Analyses ridges and valleys (minutiae) on the surface tips of human fingers.	Signature recognition	Analyses the signature. **Static signature recognition** compares scanned or ink signatures with stored signatures while **dynamic signature recognition** analyses not only the signature but how it is written using pressure points—how much an individual pushes on the pen when she writes her name.
Facial recognition	Analyses facial features or patterns (faceprints).	**Gait recognition**	Analyses the walking style or gait of individuals.
Finger geometry recognition	Analyses 3D geometry of the finger.	**Keystroke recognition**	Analyses rhythm and patterns of keystroke of individuals on keyboards.
Hand geometry recognition	Analyses geometric features of the hand such as length of fingers and width of the hand.		
Iris/retina recognition	Analyses features (eyeprints) in the iris (iris) or the patterns of veins in the back of the eye (retina).		
DNA recognition	Analyses segments from an individual's DNA.		
Odor recognition	Analyses an individual's odor to determine identity.		
Voice recognition (speaker recognition)	Analyses voice to determine the identity of a speaker (who is speaking). Different from speech recognition (what is being said).		
Ear recognition	Analyses the shape of the ear.		

Source: Based on information provided by Biometrics Institute, available at http://www.biometricsinstitute .org/displaycommon.cfm?an=1&subarticlenbr=30

Biometrics are used in one of two ways: authentication or identification. In **authentication**, also called *one-to-one matching*, the goal is to match the individual with their stored biometric data. Fingerprint biometrics on laptops are good example of that. In **identification**, also called *one-to-many matching*, the goal is identify an individual from an entire population of individuals with stored biometric data. An example is facial recognition at airports used to identify potential terrorists entering a country from a database of facial prints stored by law enforcement agencies.

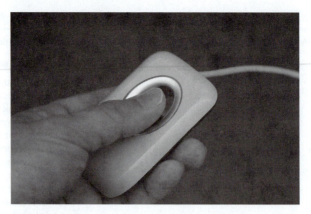

FIGURE 8.5 Fingerprinting Scanner (© Mike Liu/iStockphoto)

The processes of authentication and identification are shown in Figures 8.6 and 8.7.

Firewalls

At the beginning of the chapter you tested your computer security using an online tool. What the software was looking for was whether your computer was letting information out about itself and whether there were open ports or software applications running. The best protection against these potential problems is a firewall, and if your computer's firewall was running and up-to-date, your computer should have resulted in stealth ratings (not visible to outsiders).

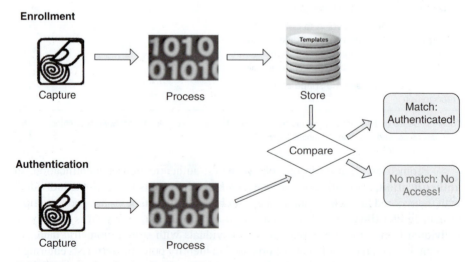

FIGURE 8.6 Authentication in Biometrics

Enrollment

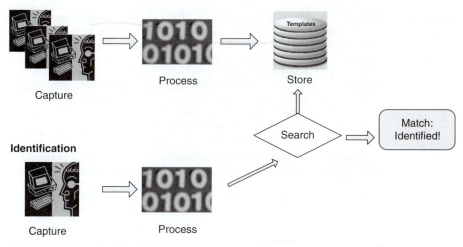

FIGURE 8.7 Identification in Biometrics

A **firewall** is a computer or a router that controls access in and out of the organization's networks, applications, and computers. The term *firewall* comes from the construction industry where it represents a wall built with fire-resistant materials. If a fire starts in one room of a building, it won't spread to other rooms if firewalls are used. In computer security, firewalls control the transmissions that are attempting to enter and/or leave the organization's networks or computers, as shown in Figure 8.8.

There are several types of firewalls, which vary in how they control access into and out of the organization. Table 8.3 lists various terms used to describe firewalls.

Firewalls are great security tools, but they cannot handle all security threats. For example, they cannot protect an organization from a virus that is attached to a message with appropriate destination and source addresses, or that is introduced by an individual on a portable storage device. Firewalls also cannot prevent hackers

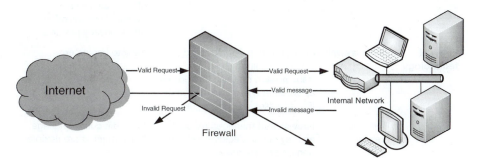

FIGURE 8.8 Firewall

Table 8.3   Firewall Types and Terminology

Firewall type	Packet-level firewall (also called screening router firewall)	Works at the network level, looking at information within the data packets (see online In-depth Guide). If the source address of the packet is from an "acceptable" computer, the firewall will let the message through, assuming that the destination address is also a valid internal address.	Easy to implement and prevents most basic attacks such as email bombing and other denials of service. Sophisticated attacks can often bypass these.
	Application-level firewall (one form is called *proxy server*)	Firewall that verifies access to applications. Users must log into the firewall before they can access applications inside the organization (from outside).	More complex to install and manage. Also slows down communication. But, provides better security than packet-level firewalls.
	Firewall appliance	A firewall that is self-contained. In other words, the hardware and software are built to perform only one function, that of a firewall.	Very useful for small businesses with limited technical knowledge that require more protection than a simple host firewall on their personal computers.
Firewall location	Internal firewall	Firewall used between departments or divisions inside the organization.	Organizations can use these to isolate departmental data and provide greater defense in depth protection.
	External firewall	Firewall used to protect access to the internal network and computers of the organization.	This is the type of firewall that is usually referred to in most definitions.
	Host (personal) firewall	Firewall installed on a computer.	Good option for all computers. In addition to protecting the computer from outsider attacks, and warning of arrival of malicious files, the personal firewall often offers privacy features.
Firewall technology	Static firewall	Firewall with predetermined ways of dealing with transmission requests based on application types and ranges of IP addresses.	Easy to implement.
	Dynamic firewall	Firewall that manages requests as they occur, deciding on both denials and permissions as they arrive.	More difficult to manage but is much more flexible.

from exploiting an unsecured computer, keep disgruntled employees from copying sensitive information, or stop employees from losing sensitive data loaded on an unsecured laptop, PDA, or cellular phone, for example. Nevertheless, firewalls are part of the main line of defense for organizations. Consistent with the principle of defense in depth, different firewalls should be implemented at different locations in the organization, as shown in Figure 8.9.

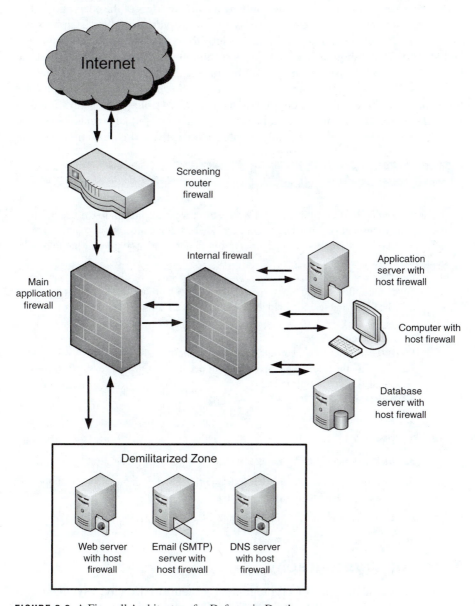

FIGURE 8.9 A Firewall Architecture for Defense in Depth

Rendering Data Unreadable: Encryption

Encryption, also known as *cryptography*, is the use of mathematical algorithms to convert a message or information into scrambled text that makes it unreadable. The original message is called **plaintext**. The converted or unreadable text is called **ciphertext**. When the ciphertext is converted back to plaintext, this is referred to as **decryption**. The algorithm used to convert the message is called the **cipher**. The **encryption or decryption key** is information known only by the proper users of the encryption tool.

The ciphers used in Learning Activity 8.4 are very simplistic. Ciphers are much more complicated and use complex algorithms (not simply adding numbers and letters). The strength of an encryption technique is related to the length of the key. This is usually expressed in the number of bits the key has. The larger the size of the key, the more secure the encryption. This is because larger keys are harder to break since there are more combinations of bits possible. Today, keys in commercial use are 256-bit or longer. It is estimated that a 64-bit key can be broken in 33 to 34 days or less. Understandably, a 256-bit key is therefore much more secure.

LEARNING ACTIVITY 8.4	BREAKING THE ENCRYPTION

Security technologies are unlikely to be able to prevent all unauthorized access to data, applications and systems. One way to provide additional protection for important data is encryption. Before we discuss encryption in depth, let us explore what makes data unreadable.

Part 1.

Given the following plaintext: a b c d e f g h i j k l m n o p q r s t u v w x y z
and the following resulting ciphertext: b c d e f g h i j k l m n o p q r s t u v w x y z a

What is the cipher?

Part 2. Using the cipher, convert the words: computer lab closed

Part 3. Using the following cipher and your personally selected keys below, convert the text: Fun for Spring Break.

dpnqvufs mbc dmptfe

Key selection:

1. Pick a number from 1 to 5

2. Pick a sign + or −

3. Pick a symbol (!,@,#,$,%,^,&,*)

4. Use this cipher to encode: new letter = original letter (sign selected) number, spaces replaced with symbol selected.

5. Compare your results with classmates.

Types of Cryptography

There are two main types of cryptographic system used today: asymmetric or symmetric, as shown in Figure 8.10. This is based on whether the same key is issued to encrypt and decrypt the data or not. In **asymmetric encryption**, two

Asymmetric Encryption

It is a beautiful day!
(Plaintext)

Public Key   Cipher

1010 0101(
Cyperthext

Private Key   Cipher

It is a beautiful day!
(Plaintext)

Symmetric Encryption

It is a beautiful day!
(Plaintext)

Private Key   Cipher

1010 0101(
Cyperthext

Private Key   Cipher

It is a beautiful day!
(Plaintext)

FIGURE 8.10 Symmetric vs. Asymmetric Encryption

keys are used. The public key is used to encrypt messages. It is sent to any person or system with whom one wishes to exchange encrypted messages. Using the public key, anyone can encrypt messages for the intended recipient, who will then use their private key to decrypt those messages. The public key and the private key are linked (forming a **key pair**), but only the recipient has the private key. This is also *called public key cryptography* since one of the keys can be shared with anyone (public).

In **symmetric encryption**, the same key is used to encrypt and decrypt data. In this case, individuals have to be very careful with whom they share their encryption keys because these individuals or companies will also be able to decrypt their messages. It is very efficient, but requires that both parties know the key and no one else. The problem is therefore how to distribute the key without having it intercepted by others. This is why both types of encryption are often used together, with public key encryption used to distribute a secret key to a party you wish to interact with. Once the secret key is received, it can be used for symmetric encryption since both parties know it. Finally, it is important to realize that encryption can be used for more than transmission of data. It can be used to protect data on servers and computers.

For example, you could encrypt your data on your personal computer so that no one could access it without the proper key.

Encryption has many applications for securing data and transmissions. One of them is the Virtual Private Network we discussed in Chapter 7. Recall that VPNs are used to create a secured tunnel of communication over the Internet between two parties (often an employee and her company). The way VPNs function is through the use of encryption. When the employee wishes to connect to the company's internal network, she requests a VPN connection. After inputting secret information, the employee's computer establishes an encrypted session with the company's server (this is called a *handshake*). Once both computers share the secret key (which is only for that session), all transmissions are encrypted until the VPN connection is dropped.

Encryption is also used for protecting information in business transactions online. When you shop online and have to enter your credit card information, you typically look for the lock icon or the https:// in the URL to indicate that the site is secure. If you double click on the icon, you will see the security certificate that was issued to the website by a certificate-issuing organization such as VeriSign. Figure 8.11 shows a sample certificate located in the Internet options of a browser application. This certificate includes a public key, which is sent to your browser when you connect to this secure Web page. The browser can then generate a secret key and send it to the server using the public key encryption since only the server can decrypt this information (via the private key). Once the server receives the secret key, your browser and the server can communicate

FIGURE 8.11 Sample Security Certificate

securely using this secret key (called a *session key*). The transmissions will be encrypted until the current session is dropped.

Virus Protection

Viruses are one of the most prevalent security threats in organizations. You should not underestimate the amount of money involved in terms of support personnel time involved in fixing virus problems. Fortunately, today antivirus software has become very easy to use and to keep up-to-date. Recall that a virus has a signature, the bit pattern that represents the virus. Antivirus software looks for these signatures or variations of them in files and systems. If they are found, the software can remove the virus, quarantine the file, or delete the file. The software can even detect viruses in emails and files as they are loaded but before they are opened. Once a new virus is identified, it usually takes less than 24 hours for specialists to decode it and write a protection for it. But viruses are easy to write, with several tools for writing viruses available online. Symantec, one of the leading providers of antivirus software, states that there are now over one million computer viruses in existence.

Unfortunately, most antivirus programs are primarily reactive. They only detect existing viruses or ones that look similar to an old virus archived in the software's database. Newer virus protection tools, called **behavioral-based anti-virus protection tools**, look for suspicious behaviors in programs instead of just a virus' signature. One of the most important protections, however, remains user education about updating software and not downloading unknown executable files to their computers.

Wireless Security

As more and more individuals connect their devices to the Internet and their organizations via wireless networks, we need to briefly discuss the additional issues related to wireless security. In reality, all of the security solutions discussed so far can be used in the wireless environment. However, because the wireless networks typically broadcast their communications over the "airwaves" they are more susceptible to security breaches since they can be intercepted without physical connections to the devices.

The best protection for wireless networks remains encryption. The standards for wireless encryption are numerous, with the most popular ones in America called WEP and WPA. **WEP, the Wired Equivalent Privacy** is an older encryption algorithm, which today can be easily cracked within minutes (with proper knowledge and software tools). **WPA, the Wi-Fi Protected Access**, is a more recent and powerful encryption algorithm widely available in most routers. So when setting up a home wireless network, users should select WPA encryption if their devices support it. A further protection for home wireless networks is to disable the broadcasting of the network's ID (SSID). Only with knowledge of the network's name can someone find it and connect to it (with the WPA or WEP encryption key information).

STATISTICS BOX 2

Even when security is a top priority for organizations, employees can often find ways to bypass the security controls that are used, such as firewalls, restricted access, or automatic logoff systems. In a survey of over 400 senior IT professionals conducted in 2008, Cyber-Ark Software found that close to three quarters (74%) of the respondents said they could get around the security controls their organization had implemented.

Security Policies

Most medium to large organizations today have security policies, which describe what the general security guidelines are for an organization. **Security policies** tend to be for internal use. The policies include a number of **security procedures**, which are specific statements describing how to implement the security policies. For example, a security policy could be "All users must change their passwords every two months." One of its related security procedures could then describe steps to be taken to change one's password. Another procedure could involve an automated system to force users to change their password every two months, while an additional one could include actions that should happen if a user attempts to enter an unacceptable (not strong) password. A security policy should have clear goals and objectives, a detailed list of security policies and procedures, and also a list of actions for the enforcement of procedures.

Even with the best policies and procedures in place, and with the best security technologies available, an organization may not be well protected if its users and employees fail to follow the policies and procedures, or fail to use the technologies properly. This is where security education and training becomes very important. Users must be made aware of the risks involved, the tools available, and the consequences of not performing the proper security behaviors that are asked of them. Refer to the book's website for several tips on how to secure your computer, network, and data properly.

BUSINESS EXAMPLE BOX 2	HOW TO RESPOND TO A SECURITY CRISIS

While certain individuals in an organization are more concerned about being hacked (usually a chief officer or a security person), many believe that it is unlikely to happen to them. But what if it does? How should a company react? Organizations can learn from what happened to Heartland Payment Systems in 2008–2009, and from how they reacted.

Heartland Payment Systems, a financial transaction company, discovered in late 2008 that their system containing more than 600 million credit card holders' information had been hacked. Unfortunately, the company did not have a security crisis plan in place. Fortunately, they were quick to act and hired a crisis response corporation. The first order of business? To develop a plan to deal with employees, Wall Street, the media, and the customers, and to do it quickly as opposed to waiting weeks or months after the breach happened. The company decided that it was better to provide full disclosure about what happened and be transparent about what was being done to address the situation. The company and their consultant agreed on two key objectives: 1.) Show that they were going above and beyond expectations in terms of responsibility and accountability to deal with the huge data loss, and 2.) Develop a leadership position on dealing with identity theft after the crisis was over.

To achieve their objectives, the officers of the company quickly announced what type of data was hacked and what was not, conducted a great number of media interviews, and contacted a large number of their customers directly. They also discussed the situation with influential financial bloggers and industry analysts, created a dedicated website, and communicated all of this to their employees fully and clearly.

In the end, the company was mainly successful in handling the crisis. They then explored new security programs and formed a security group. They shared some of their key lessons learned: "Be prepared," "Have a war room," and "Figure out how you can make a difference in a bad situation."

(*Source:* "Case Study: Credit Card Payments Company 'Runs to the Light' as Security Breach Puts Reputation and Profits in Jeopardy." *PR News* 66 (35) (Sep 13, 2010).

STATISTICS BOX 3: SECURITY POLICIES COMPLIANCE

Security policies are very important in ensuring overall information security in organizations. However, policies are only useful if they are followed. The Ponemon Institute asked survey respondents: How well does your organization make sure policies for the following tasks are performed? Below is the percentage of respondents who said they were excellent (5 of 5) or good (4 of 5) in their 2010 surveys.

Percentage of Respondents Stating Their Organization Does an Excellent or Good Job Making Sure Policies Are Followed for These Tasks

Source: Based on data from the Ponemon Institute© Research Report. *2010 Access Governance Trends Survey* (April 19, 2010).

LEARNING ACTIVITY 8.5	WHERE'S THE SECURITY?

Now that we have explored all of the security threats and solutions, we need to see how they all fit together. For this learning activity, you need to map the threats to security and the goals of information security to the security solutions available. Prepare a table that contains the following information:

1. Column 1: List all of the main security threats that we discussed.

2. Column 2: List all of the security solutions that can address each of the security threats you have identified (there might be many solutions for each threat).

3. Column 3: For each security solution in column 2, indicate which security goal is met by the security solution.

Risk Management

No matter what efforts an organization may make to provide the best security possible, and all of the technologies and tools they might invest in, there are always security risks involved. **Risk management** is the process of identifying, assessing, and prioritizing the security risks an organization may face. As a result of this process, organizations may decide to accept the risks, try to mitigate or prevent those risks by investing in security protections, or share the security risks with another organization, for example by buying insurance. Organizations can refer to different standards for risk management that are available from organizations like the Project Management Institute, the National Institute of Science and Technology, and the International Standards Organization.

While security and risk management do go hand in hand, they have a few differences as well. **Security** is focused on protecting the assets a company has from both external and internal threats. External threats such as hackers and viruses threaten the valuable information a company collects while in business. Security must be able to secure this data from these attacks to ensure the company can run smoothly without interruption. Internal threats are important to guard against as well. For example, security involves monitoring the network to make sure policies are not being breached in a harmful way, and that employees are only able to access systems they are authorized to do so. Risk management has a broader focus, analyzing and balancing risks with the resources available to mitigate them. Risk management determines where the company is most vulnerable and how likely it is a risk would affect it. While weighing these risks, they look at the cost of addressing these issues and make decisions based on both the financial aspect as well as the acceptable level of security needed to protect different areas in the company.

CHAPTER SUMMARY

In this chapter, we discussed the security of information. We first defined information security and described the threats to information security. We then discussed the technologies and solutions related to information security and concluded the chapter with a discussion of information security policies.

Here are the main points discussed in the chapter.

- There are three main categories of information security threats: denial of service, unauthorized access, and theft and fraud. Denial of service threats are those that render a system inoperative, limit its capability to operate, or make data unavailable. They include intentional acts such as viruses, malware, and email bombings; careless behavior such as lack of backups; and natural disasters. Unauthorized access threats refer to someone accessing systems and/or data illegally. Theft and fraud threats are related to the loss of systems or data due to theft or fraudulent activities, including illegal downloading or copying of software and theft of data using small hardware devices.

- There are three main goals that security tools and policies are meant to address: Confidentiality, Integrity, and Availability (CIA). Confidentiality involves making sure that only authorized individuals can access information or data. Integrity involves making sure that the data are consistent and complete. Availability involves ensuring that system and/or data are available when they are needed. Two additional goals are authentication (or authenticity) and nonrepudiation. Authentication involves making sure that the parties involved are who they say they are, and that transactions, data, or communications are genuine. Nonrepudiation refers to making sure one cannot renege on his/her obligations, for example by denying that he/she entered into a transaction with a Web merchant.

- Security solutions and tools (also called security controls) can be classified as preventive, detective, or corrective controls. The goal of preventive controls is to stop or limit the security threat from happening in the first place. The goal of detective controls is to find or discover where and when security threats occurred. The goal of corrective controls is to repair damages after a security problem has occurred. Security controls can also be classified as physical or logical. Physical access controls are those security solutions that involve protecting the physical access to systems, applications, or data; whereas logical access controls include security solutions that protect access to systems, applications, or data by ensuring users or systems are authenticated and allowed to have such access. Physical access controls can include locks for laptops, locked computer rooms, and secured rooms for backup storage. Logical access controls include user profiles, biometrics, firewalls, encryption, virus protection, and wireless security.

- There are many security solutions. The security solution of user profiles requires users to be assigned profiles that consist of a user identification (self-selected or assigned by the organization) and a set of privileges. Biometrics use human traits and characteristics to recognize individuals to grant them access or to identify them among other individuals. Firewalls are computers or routers that control access in and out of the organization's networks, applications, and computers. Encryption, also known as cryptography, is the use of mathematical algorithms to convert a message or information into a scrambled message or information that makes it unreadable. Antivirus software looks for virus signatures (patterns) in files and systems to prevent them from being executed. Wireless security is mostly done through encryption such as WEP and WPA.

- Security policies describe what the general security guidelines are for an organization, including procedures, enforcement mechanisms, objectives, and also list actions for the enforcement of procedures.

- Risk management is the process of identifying, assessing, and prioritizing the security risks an organization may face, and deciding whether to accept the risks, mitigate the risks, or share the security risks by buying insurance.

REVIEW QUESTIONS

1. Briefly explain the three main goals of security and the additional two discussed in the text.
2. What is a denial of service attack and what kind of events can lead to such an attack?
3. Explain how unauthorized access threats can occur.
4. Define preventive security controls, detective security controls, and corrective security controls. Provide two examples of each.
5. What are the various purposes of biometrics and how do they work?
6. What is a firewall and how does it work?
7. What are the two types of encryption discussed in the chapter and how do they differ?
8. How does antivirus software work?
9. What are the key steps required for wireless security?
10. What are security policies and procedures, and how are they related?

REFLECTION QUESTIONS

1. What is the most important thing you learned in this chapter? Why is it important?
2. What topics are unclear? What about them is unclear?
3. For each of the following security threats, suggest one preventive, one detective, and one corrective security control.
   a. A virus is affecting the organization's intranet.
   b. A hacker accesses consumer data on the company's database server to commit fraud.
   c. A disgruntled employee steals trade secrets from the company's computers.
   d. A construction worker breaks the data communication and electrical cables coming into the company's building.
4. Which biometric technologies are better used for identification and which for verification? Explain why.
5. Explain what happens when you request your antivirus software to scan your hard drive.
6. A friend wants to send you encrypted messages. She asks you to send her both your public and private keys. What should your response be? Why? What should you send her? How will you send it? Does it matter?

7. List at least three security threats that a firewall will not protect a company against. Explain why.

8. Is a Virtual Private Network a network or a security tool? Explain.

9. What do you believe are the most serious security concerns for the different types of networking architectures discussed in Chapter 7?

10. If an organization decides to accept a security risk instead of trying to mitigate it, would this still be considered risk management? Why or why not?

ADDITIONAL LEARNING ACTIVITIES

1. Identify all of the security threats individuals can face when using social networking sites such as Facebook, MySpace, LinkedIn, and others. Create a table that lists the threats, your estimate of how serious the threat is (low, medium, high), and a suggestion of how such sites should go about addressing these security threats.

2. Perform research on various encryption software that individuals can use for emails, their hard drives, or even mobile devices. Create a table that lists the various features of each major vendor and the costs for individual users like you. Then select one the products and try it. Be prepared to discuss the advantages and disadvantages of the product you selected both for you as a student, and for businesses that might want to use it.

3. A popular public key encryption tool is PGP (Pretty Good Privacy). Developed by Phillip Zimmermann, it was offered on the Internet for free on the MIT website for a while, but then became a commercial product. Today, one can still get freeware PGP at the PGP International website: http://www.pgpi.org/products/pgp/versions/freeware/. Install the PGP and create your key pair. Then exchange encrypted e-mail messages with your teammates and encrypt files on your hard drive. Discuss how this could or could not be used for business.

4. Read the Constellation Energy Group security case on the course website. Prepare a report answering the following questions. You may need to perform extra research on the topic.

   a. What is the case about?
   b. Explain what converged security operations means.
   c. Explain what is meant by political, logistical, and cultural challenges to implementing converged security operations. Provide some examples.
   d. What are the similarities and differences between security and risk management?
   e. What do you believe are the most important factors that help make converged security possible at Constellation?

5. Read the online In-depth Guide that discusses how to implement a security plan for an organization. Select a local small business that has at least 10 employees and develop a security plan for this business.

6. Find your university's security policy and identify the main components of this policy. Be prepared to discuss the following:

   - What threats are referred to?
   - What security technologies are included in the policy?
   - Select one example each of a specific policy and a specific procedure.
   - Who is responsible for ensuring that you, as a student, follow the policy?
   - What happens if you do not follow the policy?

7. Compare and contrast the security policy you found in learning activity 8-A6 with the templates for security policies provided by the SANS organization: http://www.sans.org/security-resources/policies/.

8. Read the article A. S. Horowitz, "Top 10 Security Mistakes," Computerworld (July 9, 2001): http://www.computerworld.com/securitytopics/security/story/0,10801,61986,00.html. Briefly explain each of the 10 mistakes. Then answer the following questions:

   1. Where do we stand today on these security mistakes?

   2. Why have we not improved more?

REFERENCES

Computer Security Institute/ FBI Security Survey 2011, http://gocsi.com/.

Cyber-Ark Software, Inc. Trust, Security & Passwords Survey Research Brief (June 10, 2009) www.cyber-ark.com.

BIBLIOGRAPHY AND FURTHER READINGS

APWG. *Phishing Activity Trends Report, 4th Quarter 2009.* www.apwg.org.

Berinato, Scott. *Anatomy of a Fraud, CSO Security and Risk.* (October 1, 2004). www.csoonline.com.

Brandel, Mary. "Are you Listening?"*Computerworld* 44 (14) (July 12, 2010): 13.

Scarlet, Sarah D. "Death to Phishing." *CSO Security and Risk* (October 1, 2005). www.csoonline.com/.

Toonkel, Jessica. "SEC Said to 'Sweep' Advisory Firms for Social-Media Info." *Investment News,* (February 14, 2011). http://www.investmentnews.com/article/20110214/FREE/110219962?template=printart.

Weise, Joel and Charles R. Martin. *Developing a Security Policy, Sun Microsystems.* http://www.sun.com/blueprints/1201/secpolicy.pdf.

Phishing Resources

http://www.anti-phishing.info/

http://www.spamlaws.com/detecting-phishing.html/

GLOSSARY

Active content: executable files on websites.

Antivirus software: programs that look for virus signatures or variations of them in files and systems.

Application-level firewall: firewall that verifies access to applications by requiring users to log into the firewall before they can access applications inside the organization (from outside).

Asymmetric encryption: uses two keys: a public key for encrypting and a private key for decrypting.

Asymmetrical security warfare: one party must do everything to protect itself, while the other party (the attacker) only needs to find the one security weakness.

Audit logs: software programs that can scan for unexpected actions to detect potential hackers

Authentication (biometrics): matching the individual with his/her stored biometric data.

Authentication: process by which the identity of a transacting party is verified.

Availability: system and/or data are available when needed.

Backdoors: ways for hackers to re-access the compromised system at will.

Behavioral biometrics: biometrics that use human behaviors.

Behavioral-based antivirus protection tools: programs that look for suspicious behaviors in programs instead of just a virus' signature.

Biometrics: technologies that use human features to recognize individuals and grant them access.

Cipher: algorithm used to encrypt and decrypt plaintext.

Ciphertext: encrypted (unreadable) message.

Confidentiality: making sure that only authorized individuals can access information or data.

Corrective controls: controls meant to repair damages after a security problem has occurred.

Decryption key: key used to convert the unreadable text into its original form.

Decryption: converting ciphertext back to plaintext.

Defense in depth: multiple layers of security protections in place.

Denial of service threats: threats that render a system inoperative or limit its capability to operate, or make data unavailable.

Detective controls: controls meant to find or discover where and when security threats occur.

Dictionary attack: when all words of several dictionaries in multiple languages are tested as passwords with numbers before and after the words.

Disaster recovery: Procedures and tools to recover systems affected by disasters and destruction.

Distributed Denial of Service Attacks (DDOS): when many computers are being used for DOS attacks.

DNA recognition: Analyses segments from an individual DNA.

Dynamic firewall: manages the requests as they occur, deciding on both denials and permissions as they arrive.

Dynamic signature recognition: analyses not only the signature but how it is written using pressure points.

Ear recognition: Analyses the shape of the ear.

Email bombing: sending a large number of requests, emails, or synchronization (SYN) messages to fill a target's mailboxes, systems, communication ports, or memory buffers, with the intent of blocking legitimate messages from entering the systems or overloading the system to make it crash.

Encryption key: key used to convert the text into an unreadable form

Encryption: application of a mathematical algorithm to a message or information that scrambles that message or information to make it unreadable.

External firewall: Firewall used to protect access to the internal network and computers of the organization.

Facial recognition: Analyses facial features or patterns (faceprints).

Finger geometry recognition: Analyses 3D geometry of the finger.

Fingerprint recognition: Analyses ridges and valleys (minutiae) on the surface tips of human fingers.

Firewall appliance: the hardware and software to perform firewall function.

Firewall: computer or a router that controls access in and out of the organization's networks, applications, and computers.

Gait recognition: Analyses the walking style or gait of individuals.

Hactivism: hackers that try to find information that, if revealed, will advance human causes.

Hand geometry recognition: Analyses geometric features of the hand such as length of fingers and width of the hand.

Host firewall: Firewall installed on a computer.

Identification (biometrics): identifing an individual from an entire population of individuals with stored biometric data.

Information security: set of protections put in place to safeguard information systems and/or data from security threats such as unauthorized access, use, disclosure, disruption, modification, or destruction.

Integrity: when data are consistent and complete.

Internal firewall: firewall used inside an organization, between departments or divisions.

Iris/retina recognition: Analyses features (eyeprints) in the iris (iris) or the patterns of veins in the back of the eye (retina).

Key pair: a set of linked public key and private key.

Keystroke capture programs: software that logs all information entered into a computer.

Keystroke recognition: Analyses rhythm and patterns of keystroke of individuals on keyboards.

Knowledge: when an individual needs to know something to gain access.

Logical access controls: security solutions that protect access to systems, applications, or data by ensuring users or systems are authenticated and allowed to have such access.

Nonrepudiation: Making sure a party cannot renege on obligations, for example by denying that they entered into a transaction with a Web merchant.

Odor recognition: Analyses an individual's odor to determine identity.

Packet-level firewall: also called a screening level firewall, controls access by looking at the source and destination addresses in data packets.

Packets: small units of data that flow through networks, allowing for the transmission of messages.

Password crackers: software used to recover passwords that are forgotten.

Personal firewall: firewall installed on a given personal computer.

Physical access controls: controls that involve protecting the physical access to systems, applications, or data.

Physiological biometrics: using physical traits to identify individuals.

Plaintext: original message before it is encrypted.

Possession: when an individual owns a form of identification.

Preventive controls: controls meant to stop or limit the security threat from happening in the first place.

Risk management: the process of identifying, assessing, and prioritizing the security risks an organization may face, and deciding whether to accept, mitigate, or share the security risks..

Rookits: software that allow hackers to have unfettered access to everything on the system, including adding, deleting, and copying files.

Security: protection against security threats.

Security levels: the layers of protection technologies and policies used to secure stored information.

Security policies: descriptions of the general security guidelines for an organization.

Security procedures: specific statements describing how to implement the security policies.

Security threat: broadly categorized as denial of service, unauthorized access, and theft and fraud.

Smurfing: a hacker uses an innocent third party to multiply the messages being sent to the intended target.

Sniffer: software that monitors transmissions, capturing unauthorized data of interest.

Social engineering: (sometimes called phishing) tricking individuals into giving out security information.

Software ports: applications installed and running on a computer.

Spamming: sending e-mails to many individuals at once, sending unsolicited commercial e-mail to individuals, or targeting one individual computer or network and sending thousands of messages to it.

Spoofing: pretending to be someone else (or another computer) to enter a system or gain attention.

Spyware: a form of virus that logs everything a user is doing on their computer, unbeknownst to them.

Static firewall: a firewall that has predetermined ways of dealing with transmission requests.

Static signature recognition: compares scanned or ink signatures with stored signatures.

Stealth virus: more advanced virus that changes its own bit pattern to become undetectable by virus scanners.

Symmetric encryption: encryption where the same key is used to encrypting and decrypting data.

Target-of-opportunity threats: threats (such as viruses) sent out to find any victim possible.

Theft and fraud threats: threats related to the loss of systems or data due to theft or fraudulent activities.

Traits: physical or behavioral human characteristics are needed to gain access to systems or data.

Trojan horses: viruses embedded into a legitimate file.

Unauthorized access threats: individuals who access systems and/or data illegally.

User profile: assigned profiles that consist of a user identification, a password, and a set of privileges.

Virus hoaxes: false virus alerts sent and resent by individuals.

Virus signature: bit patterns of the virus that can be recognized.

Virus: computer program designed to perform unwanted events.

Voice recognition (speaker recognition): Analyses voice to determine the identity of a speaker; different from speech recognition (determining *what* is being said).

Wi-Fi Protected Access (WPA): recent and powerful encryption algorithm for wireless security.

Wired Equivalent Privacy (WEP): older encryption algorithm for wireless security.

Worms: viruses that can propagate themselves throughout the Internet with no user intervention.

Protecting the Confidentiality and Privacy of Information

CHAPTER 9

LEARNING OBJECTIVES

By reading and completing the activities in this chapter, students should be able to:

- Understand the various threats to information privacy

- Identify technologies and solutions used to protect the confidentiality and privacy of information

- Explain how information privacy is a component of the PAPA ethical framework

- Discuss the relationship between information privacy and information security

CHAPTER OUTLINE

Privacy statement or policy

Privacy seals

- Learning Activity 9.4: Why your advisor can't talk to your parents

- Government information privacy regulations

- Privacy and ethics

- Learning Activity 9.5: PAPA, privacy policies, and FERPA

- Relationship between security and privacy

- Chapter summary

- Review questions

- Reflection questions

- Additional learning activities

- References

- Bibliography and further readings

- Glossary

FOCUSING STORY: THE RESELLING OF CUSTOMER DATA: THE CHOICEPOINT STORY

ChoicePoint was created in 1997 as a spinoff of the insurance services unit of the Equifax corporation. The company's business model involves collecting public data about individuals, organizing the data into databases, and selling the resulting information to Fortune 1000 companies, small businesses, law firms, insurance companies, private investigators, and government entities. These companies, in turn, use the information to assess potential customers or employees. ChoicePoint also provides intelligence information to law enforcement and counterintelligence agencies.

In 2002, ChoicePoint used its huge database of customer information to start offering direct marketing services. By 2005, it was one of the leading data brokerage firms, but in late January 2005, ChoicePoint mistakenly released data on thousands of Americans (approximately 162,000) to fraudsters who created false accounts. By the end of 2006, at least 440 cases of identity theft were linked to this breach. The incident brought widespread attention to the data brokerage industry, and many citizens and governments called for stricter controls on personal information. Many individuals also realized that the data ChoicePoint collected about them and sold to others often had inaccuracies, sometimes affecting their ability to be hired for a job. ChoicePoint, however, maintained that it was not the fault of the data aggregator but instead of the source of the data. ChoicePoint's stated position is that the entities maintain the source data and are therefore responsible for keeping them accurate.

In 2006, the Federal Trade Commission (FTC) fined ChoicePoint $10 million for the breach that resulted in 162,000 cases of compromised data. Additionally, the company paid $5 million to the individuals affected by the breach. The company decided to settle with the FTC, while not admitting fault, instead of fighting the matter for years in court. In early 2008, the parent company of Lexis-Nexis (Reed Elsevier), another data aggregator, announced its plans to purchase ChoicePoint for U.S. $4.1 billion. Again, privacy advocates saw the merger as an increased threat to the public's right to privacy. After the Committee on Foreign Investment in the United States stated that there were no issues with the sale and the U.S. Federal Trade Commission gave the regulatory go-ahead, Reed Elsevier proceeded with the acquisition.

DISCUSSION:

1. How much data do you think ChoicePoint has about you? Give specific examples.

2. Where do you think the data that ChoicePoint has about you come from?

3. Why is ChoicePoint allowed to sell your data to companies and agencies?

4. Should ChoicePoint be held accountable for the accuracy of the data they sell to companies and agencies?

Sources: Bosworth, Martin H. "Lexis-Nexis Parent To Buy ChoicePoint." *Consumeraffairs.com.* (February 23, 2008) and (August 31, 2008) http://www.consumeraffairs.com/news04/2008/02/choicepoint_sale.html; "CFIUS Completes Review of Proposed ChoicePoint(R) Acquisition." *WSJ.com.* (Sep. 2, 2008) *Wall Street Journal* (Sep. 4, 2008) http://online.wsj.com/article/PR-CO-20080902-906169.html?mod=wsjcrmain; Gatzlaff, K. and McCullough, K. "The Effect of Data Breaches on Shareholder Wealth." *Risk Management and Insurance Review* 13(1) (2010): 61; 3. Paine, L. and Phillips, Z., ChoicePoint (A). *Harvard Business School* Case (# 9-306-001).

LEARNING ACTIVITY 9.1   **FINDING MINDY**[1]

Students often wonder if information privacy is really as much of a problem as the media tries to convey. In order to start looking into an answer for this question, let us see how information privacy can affect the lives of individuals. Please read the following story and be prepared to discuss the questions in class.

After a long week of school, Mindy was anxious to get home, grab a snack, and relax in front of the computer. Signing on with her screen name SftBallGrl16, she noticed Jimmyg114 was online, whom she met a month ago in a sports chat room.

(continued)

---

[1]This story circulated on the web at a certain time period in the mid-2000s. We do not know the author of the story.

SftBallGrl16:
Hey you! I think I'm being stalked LOL!

Jimmyg114:
LOL really, why?

SftBallGrl16:
Well I thought this car was following me on my walk home today. But I think it was just my imagination LOL

Jimmyg114:
Haha someone's paranoid! Better stop giving out your info online.

SftBallGrl16:
No way. I don't do that. I've heard the terrible stories.

Jimmyg114:
Anyway didn't you have a game today?

SftBallGrl16:
Yeah and we won again. 3 in a row!

Jimmyg114:
Nice, who did you guys play?

SftBallGrl16:
The Warriors. They were pretty good.

Jimmyg114:
What is your team called?

SftBallGrl16:
We are the Newtown Hawks. We just got new uniforms I love them.

Jimmyg114:
Really what do they look like?

SftBallGrl16:
They are blue and white with an awesome hawk logo on the front.

Jimmyg114:
Nice, what position do you play?

SftBallGrl16:
Third base. We play them again for our homecoming in 2 weeks. My parents and friends are all coming. It is a big game. Well I have to get going. My parents will be home any minute and I was supposed to do the dishes. LOL

Jimmyg114:
LOL ok catch you later.

Later, Jimmyg114 went to the member's menu and to search for her profile. He began to write everything down he knew about SftBallGrl16 so far.

Her name: Mindy

Birthday: July 19, 1996

Age: 13

Location: Maryland

Hobbies: softball, jogging, skiing, and hanging out at the mall.

Besides this information, he knew she lived in Newtown because she had just told him.

He knew she stayed by herself until 6:00 p.m. every evening until her parents came home from work. He knew she played softball on Thursday evenings on the school team, and the team was named the Newtown Hawks. Her favorite number 19 was printed on her jersey. He knew she was in the eight grade at the Newtown High School. This information had been gathered over the past couple weeks.

By Tuesday, Mindy forgot about the car following her.

Her game was well under way when she noticed a man she had never seen before staring at her. This startled her at first. Occasionally she would glance over at him, and he would smile. He seemed harmless. When the game finished, he wandered around, watching Mindy as she talked with her coach. Mindy began to walk home and the man followed quietly behind her. Keeping a safe distance, the man watched Mindy walk into her house. He now knew the exact location.

DISCUSSION QUESTIONS:

1. How much of the information provided by Mindy to Jimmyg114 would you consider *private*?

2. How much of that information would be available online if Mindy did not interact with Jimmyg114?

3. What types of personal information do you as students care about protecting normally? Are you going to be more careful?

4. What potential risks do Mindy and her family now face?

Information Privacy Threats

Privacy of information is the confidentiality of the information collected by organizations about the individuals using their services (Van Slyke and Bélanger, 2003). It can also be defined as one's ability to control information about oneself (Bélanger, Hiller & Smith, 2002). The privacy of information is a very important concept for individuals and organizations alike. Many students may have faced issues with the privacy of their information when friends posted something about them on Facebook or MySpace without their prior approval. This may have been just for fun or may have caused some tensions between friends. However, as students move to the workplace, they will realize that organizations need to be even more keenly aware of information privacy concepts since workers, professionals, and managers have access to and deal with great amounts of information on a daily basis. Therefore, everyone has to be concerned not only about their own information privacy, but also about the privacy of information of others, including customers, employees, business partners, students, parents, children, and more.

There are many possible threats to information privacy, for example dealing with the collection, unauthorized secondary use, improper access, and errors in data (Smith et al., 1996). We discussed the privacy threat related to errors in the Focusing Story on ChoicePoint. Inaccuracies or **errors in data** can have serious impacts on individuals, for example for those applying for jobs or loans. **Improper access to data** deals more with the security of information as discussed in the previous chapter with the security threat of unauthorized access. The information privacy threats of data collection and unauthorized secondary use, however, are worth discussing more in depth.

Data Collection

The collection of data from individuals is not a new concern, and the concept of privacy has been explored and discussed for centuries. One of the major differences today, however, is that as communications and information have been digitized, it has become easier and faster to collect ever increasing amounts of information. Specifically, with the advent of advanced information and communication technologies, the **data collection threat** means that data can be collected, aggregated, and analyzed at a faster pace and in larger volume than ever. Of a greater concern sometimes, is the fact that data can be collected without anyone's awareness, for example through the use of cookies. **Cookies** are small text files that store information on your computer about you or your computer when you browse or enter information into certain websites.

Another hidden data collection approach is **clickstream data**, which tracks online browsing behaviors. The tracking is done by software that looks at the IP address of the computer connecting to a site, identifying what page the computer connected from, what page it goes after the current one, how often it connects to this site, and whether actual purchases are made from this site. Thorough analysis of this data can then give marketers an indication of successful and unsuccessful online ads, referring sites, and other information on the preferences of each user. Customized ads can also be delivered to the consumer's screen. Interestingly, no one would probably agree to be followed in his or her buying decision process in a physical retail store. Imagine someone walking with you and observing you as you stroll through a Wal-Mart and look at various products! Yet, online tracking of consumers is a regular occurrence.

The proliferation of online sites collecting data, of data sources, and of tools to manipulate these data in today's interconnected society, leads to more data being available, and to individuals being increasingly concerned about the privacy of their information. Current technology allows easy loading of information from online forms directly into databases. For companies, this is a major advantage, since the data are loaded immediately (faster) and accurately (no transcribing errors and no problems dealing with unreadable writing) (Van Slyke and Bélanger 2003). However, a Pew Internet Project survey found that 85% of adults believed it was very important for them to control access to their personal information (Madden and Smith, 2010). Information privacy is also an important concern for corporations. Another survey found that 85% of responding companies experienced some sort of reportable privacy breach during the previous year; and 63% reported multiple breaches. The majority of the reporting companies stated that they spent their time reacting to privacy breaches as opposed to being proactive in their attempts to prevent them (Deloitte, 2007).

Secondary Use of Information

Unauthorized secondary use of information refers to the use of data for purposes other than those for which they were originally collected. For example, you enter your information on a website to register for the warranty of your new digital camera, but then the company uses your information to send you marketing ads about their other products. Information privacy refers to having some level of control over these potential secondary uses of one's personal information. Function creep is another terminology used to refer to data being used for other functions beyond those purposes for which they were collected. Often, individuals are given the option to opt-in or opt-out of secondary use on websites. When you **opt-in**, you have to specifically state that you agree that your data can be used for other purposes, often to receive special deals or information from partner companies. When you have to **opt-out**, you have to make sure you tell the company you do not want your data shared with others or used for other purposes. The trick is that sometimes you have to click a box to opt-out, and sometimes you have to unclick one. If you forget, by default you are agreeing to let the companies share or use your information.

In summary, when information collection and use is not regulated, individuals have the responsibility of protecting their own (or others') information. However, it is often the case that individuals are not aware of the risks, or do not know how to protect their own information. Often, people make a choice to give this information because it provides convenience or personalization of one's online experience.

LEARNING ACTIVITY 9.2	PRIVACY PIZZA

Your instructor will present a video entitled Privacy Pizza in class, or may direct you to the course website for you to watch the video individually before class. As you watch the video, make notes on the types of information and technologies that are discussed and/or used in the video. The Privacy Pizza video can also be found at: http://www.aclu.org/pizza/. Be prepared to answer the following questions:

1. Do you think access to the various types of information identified is regulated or not?

2. For the technologies identified, are the technologies widely available today?

3. How likely is it that a pizza shop/company can use such technologies?

4. What can someone do to avoid this situation from happening to him or her?

STATISTICS BOX 1: CONCERN FOR INFORMATION PRIVACY

Different age groups are believed to have different levels of concerns over information privacy. The Pew Internet and American Life Research Center studied this question by surveying 2,253 adults and found that indeed there are some differences, as can be seen from the figure below (Madden and Smith 2010).

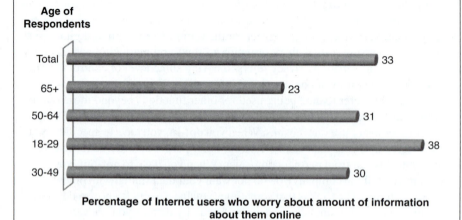

Age of Respondents

Total	33
65+	23
50-64	31
18-29	38
30-49	30

Percentage of Internet users who worry about amount of information about them online

Source: Based on data from Madden, M. and A. Smith (2010). *Reputation Management and Social Media, Pew Internet and American Life Project,* http://www.pewinternet.org./

Consequences of Privacy Violations

Individual Consequences: Identify Theft

The issues faced by Mindy are very serious since her physical well-being could have been at stake in the scenario presented in Learning Activity 9.1. Others, including adults, elderly parents, and small business owners, can also face serious consequences when others take their personal information for fraudulent activities. This is the concept of **identity theft**.

Identity theft cases have been increasing substantially in recent years. The Javelin Strategy & Research Center (https://www.javelinstrategy.com/) reports that there were almost 10 million identity theft victims in 2008 in the United States, representing a 22% increase from 2007. They also report that 71% of fraud happens within a week of stealing a victim's personal data. However, the surprising finding from their study published in 2009 is that low-tech methods for stealing personal information are more popular than technology-driven methods for identity thieves. These include stealing wallets and physical documents, which accounted for 43% of identity theft (online methods accounted for only 11%). Online identity theft is often the result of data access breaches where large numbers of records are copied from a company's database. As seen in the previous chapter, transmitting information online is relatively secure, but what happens after the information is received by the local organizations can sometimes not be as secure. Identity theft can have several negative consequences for individuals, including financial, social, and emotional impacts.

STATISTICS BOX 2: FRAUD TYPE FROM IDENTITY THEFT

Every year, the Federal Trade Commission (FTC) collects information on identity theft complaints and on fraud committed with someone else's identity in the United States. The figure below shows the types of fraud that are committed this way, computed from FTC complaint data. As can be seen, credit card fraud is by far the largest type of fraud being committed. This involves using someone else's credit card to illegally acquire goods or services. Other large categories of fraud include receiving benefits illegally from the government, obtaining utility services under someone else's identity, getting a job under someone else's identity, or accessing someone else's bank accounts. Some of these types of frauds often involve individuals with poor credit (for utility fraud) or with no legal right to work (for employment fraud).

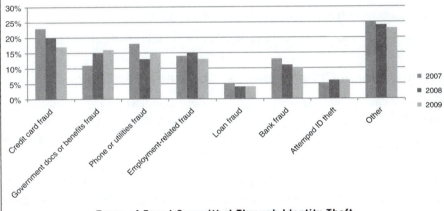

Types of Fraud Committed Through Identity Theft

Source: Based on data published by the Federal Trade Commission, available at http://www.ftc.gov/bcp/edu/microsites/idtheft/reference-desk/national-data.html.

Students are often concerned that their data is being stolen from the Web when they acquire some goods or services online. In reality, as stated in the previous paragraph, the risks are greater that fraudsters or identity thieves access large amounts of information from unsecured databases. Often, individuals who illegally access this data then resell it on the black market. It is difficult to have precise numbers on the size of this market, but various researchers and centers have identified the value of your information on the black market. How much would you be willing to pay for:

- A valid credit card number with a security code?

- Valid bank account details including the PIN (Personal identification Number)?

- A valid social security number?

- A complete new (valid) identity?

The best way for individuals to protect themselves from identity theft is to follow basic security guidelines and common sense. The Identity Theft Center (www.idtheftcenter.org), a not-for-profit organization, has been created to help identity theft victims and offers very useful information about protection against identity theft and what to do if it happens to you.
Typical topics include actions such as:

1. Watching for shoulder-surfers who observe what you are typing.

2. Request photo identification when someone asks for your information.

3. Shred everything that has any data about you.

4. Destroy digital data by going beyond a simple delete.

5. Really check the statements you receive.

6. Limit the information provided on your checks.

7. Request your free annual credit report and check it!

8. Do not use your Social Security Number unless it is absolutely needed.

Organizational Consequences: Company Reputation

For organizations, information privacy violations also have serious consequences. There are, however, two sides to the issue here. Organizations have the responsibility of protecting their customers' data, but they are sometimes the ones infringing on the privacy of their clients.

If organizations fail to protect the privacy of their customers' information, then their reputation can suffer. There are many examples of companies' reputations being at stake. In March 2007, TJX Co., owner company of approximately 2,500 retail stores including TJ Maxx, Marshals, Winners, and Homesense, among others, reported it had experienced a serious (and extended) breach of its databases, exposing information on more than 45.7 million credit and debit cards. The same year, Talves, a subsidiary of the Canadian Imperial Bank of Commerce (CIBC), lost a backup hard drive that contained personal information on approximately 470,000 clients, with information on addresses, signatures, names, dates of birth, social insurance numbers, and financial information (Stewart 2007; Charters 2008). In both cases, many customers stopped doing business with these companies.

The costs of privacy breaches can be enormous for the companies involved. First, they may lose current and future customers. Second, they have to repair the breaches. And third, they have to compensate customers for their potential identity theft issues. Remember the ChoicePoint case that started this chapter? The company had to send notices to all customers, provide credit reports and one year of credit monitoring to all the affected customers (for a cost of about U.S. $ 2 million), open a toll-free line to deal with the issues, re-credential all of its small business "clients," and settle with the Federal Trade Commission for $ 15 million, which included a fine of $ 10 million and $ 5 million for identify theft victims (Paine 2006).

Finally, but not least, privacy breaches in organizations can have impacts directly on the organization if the information that is leaked concerns the organizations' patents, trade secrets, or other intellectual property.

STATISTICS BOX 3: REPUTATION RISKS OF SOCIAL NETWORKING

Social networking, which was discussed in a previous chapter, is one application that can create many privacy threats for individuals if they post too much personal information. However, companies' reputations can also be at risk when employees post information about what they do. See the statistics below about social networking and privacy below.

Percentage of employees who say that it's easy to damage a company's reputation on social media.

Percentage of employees who say they consider what their clients would think before posting comments, photos, or videos online.

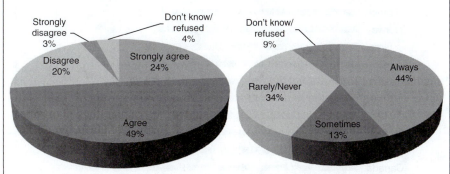

Survey of 2008 Employees in United States Companies

Source: Deloitte LLP. *Ethics & Workplace Survey* (2009). http://www.deloitte.com/assets/Dcom-UnitedStates/Local%20Assets/Documents/us_2009_ethics_workplace_survey_220509.pdf.

Technologies and Solutions for Information Privacy

Now that we understand the broad concepts of information privacy threats, it is important to further discuss the particular roles that technology can play in both infringing on information privacy and protecting one's information privacy. One technology that we will discuss is cookies. Some of the tools that we describe in this section, however, are more approaches to information privacy rather than tools. For example, a privacy policy on a website is more about the content and whether it is applied properly than about technology to create a policy. Similarly, privacy seals and government regulations toward privacy are ways to protect you online, but are more tools and techniques than they are technologies.

STATISTICS BOX 4: SURVEILLANCE SOCIETIES AROUND THE WORLD

We discussed privacy as having consequences for individuals and organizations. Privacy can also have global aspects as well. The organization International Privacy (www.privacyinternational.org/) produced a privacy index for many countries worldwide. Some of the countries' scores from 2007 are presented in the figure below. A score of 1 means highest level of surveillance while a score of 5 means the lowest level of surveillance.

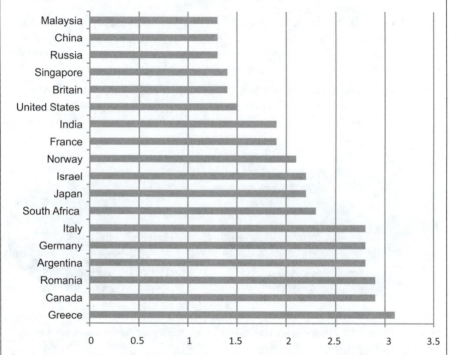

Source: Based on data from Privacy International, available at http://www.privacyinternational .org/article.shtml?cmd[347]=x-347-559597&als[theme]=Data Protection and Privacy Laws

Cookies and Cookie Managers

Websites often use **cookies**, small text files located on your computer, to store temporarily (or sometimes for as long as you have your computer) information about you, your accounts, and your computer. Every time you enter information and you are asked, "Do you want this to be remembered?" information is stored in a cookie. Cookies provide convenience to individuals. Because the information is stored on the computer, you do not have to retype all the account information, or addresses, or even remember your passwords to access a website that has stored information in the cookie file. Information not typed in can also be stored in cookies. For example,

FIGURE 9.1 Cookies identified with IECookiesView (NirSofer; see Table 9.1)

the website can record information such as your IP (Internet Protocol) address, the domain name of your computer, the length of time you stay on a specific Web page, etc. When the user accesses one of the addresses in the address range of the website that stored the cookie, the browser transmits all of the information retained in the cookie to the website's server the user is currently browsing. Any item used to personalize your experience on the Web uses a set of cookies.

In terms of technologies to deal with cookies, there are many options. The most simple is the settings you use on your Internet browser. The privacy settings allow you to state whether or not you allow cookies, and what types of cookies should be automatically accepted. If you set your computer to be super "private," most cookies will not work, but then many websites will not allow you to use their pages. If you set it too low on privacy settings, then most information about you and your computer will be stored and can be used by websites. The right balance depends on your privacy preferences. Different operating systems and browsers have different ways to deal with cookies. One organization, AboutCookies.org (www.aboutcookies.org) shows you different ways to control or delete cookies from your computer.

There are also **cookie managers** that can be downloaded for free or for a fee (an example is provided in Figure 9.1). These give you more details about which cookies are stored, what is stored in them, and gives you the ability to delete them. Table 9.1 shows you sample cookie managers, but many more exist on the Web. Finally, several new antivirus software, antispyware, and other security software automatically scan for and delete unnecessary cookies.

Table 9.1   Sample Cookie Management Tools

Name	Description	Creator and Link
Cookie Cruncher	Freeware cookie manager	Rendering Better Avenues Software http://www.rbaworld.com/Programs/CookieCruncher/
Cookie Crusher	Cookie manager	The Limit Software http://download.cnet.com/Cookie-Crusher/3000-2144_4-10006576.html
Cookie Monster	Cookie manager	AMPsoft, http://www.ampsoft.net/
Maxa Cookie Manager	Freeware cookie manager	Maxa Research http://www.maxa-tools.com/cookie.php
Cookie Pal	Cookie manager	Kookaburra Software, http://www.kburra.com/cpal.html

(continued)

Table 9.1 (Continued)

Name	Description	Creator and Link
Extended Cookie Manager	Cookie Manager for Firefox browser	Sven Jost, https://addons.mozilla.org/en-US/firefox/addon/extended-cookie-manager/
IECookiesView	Cookie Manager for Mozilla and Internet Explorer browsers	NirSofer http://www.nirsoft.net/utils/iecookies.html
Window Washer	General cleaner with cookie manager	Webroot Software http://www.webroot.com/En_US/consumer-products-windowwasher.html

LEARNING ACTIVITY 9.3   PRIVACY POLICY CREATION

This activity will allow you to explore contents of privacy policies. Based on the scenario below, create an appropriate policy.

    Scenario: Two of your best friends from class have asked you to join them in a new venture: They are starting to sell customized high-quality university-branded apparel to fellow students, and mostly wealthy alumni. They want you to be the Chief Technology Officer, and you have enthusiastically joined with them. As you oversee the development of the website for the company, which you are outsourcing, you have been asked to provide a privacy policy regarding your handling of customer data. This policy will be on the website at the bottom of the pages, in small print.

Activity:

1. Go to one of these sites (or other free tool) to create your privacy policies.
   OECD: http://www2.oecd.org/pwv3/
   or
   The Direct Marketing Association (use the visitor sign on)
   http://www.dmaresponsibility.org/PPG/

2. Bring your resulting policy to class (if the activity is performed before class).

3. Be prepared to discuss how you created your policy and which decisions you had to make.

Privacy Statement or Policy

Most serious companies who do business online have privacy policies. A **privacy policy** is a statement that describes what the organization's practices are with respect to the privacy of its customers. In general, most privacy policies include some or all of the following information: what data they are collecting, how the data are collected, what the organization is doing with the data, why it is collecting the data, what other companies it may or may not share the data with, what actions the company is taking to protect the data, how you can access the data the company has about you and how you can fix errors about you, and finally whether or not you can opt out of the company collecting data about you.

The information contained in the privacy policies of companies usually follow the **Fair Information Practices principles** (FIP) set forth by the Federal Trade Commission (FTC) and a number of other organizations. These principles are derived from a number of studies, guidelines, and reports coming from a variety of countries (see http://www.ftc.gov/reports/privacy3/fairinfo.shtm for details). The FIP principles provide guidance for how to deal with personal information, and include: (1) Notice/Awareness; (2) Choice/Consent; (3) Access/Participation; (4) Integrity/Security; and (5) Enforcement/Redress. Table 9.2 shows how the FIP principles can be mapped to what privacy policies include.

It is important to note that privacy policies, like privacy seals we will discuss below, are considered self-regulation mechanisms for information privacy. This means that most companies are not legally required to have a policy. **Self-regulation** is often an attempt by industry leaders to avoid government regulations. In this case, businesses do not want the government to impose privacy rules they would have to follow. Instead, they suggest that privacy policies provide sufficient protection for individuals. Do you think this is true? Well, the first question you should ask is who reads privacy policies? Research clearly shows that most individuals never read privacy policies on websites. Now that you do know what policies contain, do you feel protected? What would you do if a company fails to follow its own policies? The **Federal Trade Commission (FTC)** is in charge of ensuring that privacy policies are respected. However, there is not a "privacy policy police." It is up to consumers to make complaints to the FTC in the United States. With enough complaints about a particular site, the FTC will investigate. So, if you find that a company fails to follow its own policy, you must turn to the FTC with your complaint in the United States, or the privacy & data protection regulators of European countries, the European Commission, or the EU Commissioners Data Protection Working Group in Europe. Companies dealing with customers in Europe have to be aware that the privacy laws are more stringent than in the United States. To allow international business to prosper, however, a Safe Harbor Program was developed so that companies in the United States can certify their practices with the U.S. Department of Commerce if they host or use European customers' data in the United States. More details on this program can be found at: http://www.export.gov/safeharbor/.

Table 9.2   Mapping Fair Information Practices to Privacy Policies

Fair Information Principle	Privacy Policies
Notice/Awareness	what data we are collecting
	how the data are collected
	what we are doing with the data
	why we are collecting the data
	which other companies we may or may not share the data with
Choice/Consent	how you can (or not) opt out of us collecting these data about you
Access/Participation	how you can access the data we have about you
Integrity/Security	what actions we are taking to protect the data
Enforcement/Redress	how you can fix errors in our data about you

BUSINESS EXAMPLE 1   PRIVACY AND FACEBOOK

Which students are not on Facebook? Not many, right? Everyone seems to be on Facebook. Why? It's easy to communicate with so many people, so fast, from anywhere, and at any time. It's a great place to share pictures and keep in touch. It's addictive. By early 2010, Facebook was the most commonly used social networking site by adults, with 73% having a Facebook profile, as opposed to 48% on MySpace and 14% on Linked In as reported by a Pew Internet and American Life Project report.

Facebook likes to collect information on their users because it is their business model. Using profiles, Facebook is able to offer targeted marketing for companies. Facebook clearly says that they do not provide the information directly to its clients, but rather use their access to your information to provide targeted advertising for its clients. Think about the information available: what you like, where you shop, when you date, when you break up, when someone in your family gets a job, gets fired, gets married, etc. So, is information privacy an issue on Facebook? Ahh. Some will say yes, but I don't care. Others will say no, not at all. And few, very few, will say yes, and I quit. Where do you stand?

Let us look at some of the complaints against Facebook. In 2006, Facebook released a newsfeed application that displayed changes to a friend's page directly to your computer, without you having to access their page. In 2007, Facebook released an application called Beacon that showed information on your page (available to all your friends) when you performed actions on partner sites such as what movie you rented on Blockbuster or what you bought on eBay. Following class actions and a settlement, Facebook discontinued this application but launched a similar program called Connect, which is intended to have better privacy settings.

In Spring 2010, Facebook changed settings to allow private information from users to be displayed to all users irrespective of the initial choice of keeping this private, including job title, music preferences, school attended, and home city. The information is also shared with selected business partners of Facebook through the "instant personalization" application. After complaints, Facebook offered ways to control this setting (opt-out), but many users never changed them. It is apparently not an easy task to change the settings. As a result, European Union regulators filed complaints against Facebook, alleging the users did not have effective control over their information. The Federal Trade Commission also started to investigate, and later asked the company to simplify privacy controls for users (which the company later did) and to provide more opt-in options rather than opt-out (which the company did not do).

Sources: Cowan, J. "Why We'll Never Escape Facebook." Canadian Business 83(10) (2010): 28–33; Gelles, D., S. Kirchgaessner, et al. "Virtually Insecure." Financial Times (Jul 29, 2010): 7.; Gelles, D. and M. Palmer. "Facebook in Privacy Action." Financial Times (Jul 8, 2010):16; "Getting Personal. But Too Personal? Facebook's Mark Zuckerberg on What Information People Should Share—and Who Gets to Decide." Wall Street Journal (July, 7, 2010); Hamaker, C. "Facebook Fans Pay Price in Privacy." Rural Telecommunications 29(4). (2010): 8.; Lenhart, A., K. Purcell, et al. "Social Media & Mobile Internet Use Among Teens and Young Adults." P. I. a. A. L. Project (2010).; Lyons, D. "Facebook's False Contrition; A Business Built on Your Data." Newsweek 155(23) (2010).; Lyons, D. "The High Price of Facebook; You Pay for It with Your Privacy." Newsweek 155(22) (2010).

Privacy Seals

Privacy seals offer another attempt by companies at self-regulation regarding privacy of consumers, while offering a way for companies to reassure consumers about transacting with them online. The way it works is that some company or organization, such as the Better Business Bureau, develops a seal program with a **seal**—a logo that companies can post on their website if they follow certain rules. There are several **seal programs** that businesses can participate in to show their commitment to trustworthiness (i.e. this website can be trusted). These seal are also called **reputation seals** and are issued by such sites as TRUSTe (www.TRUSTe.com), WebTrust, and BBBOnLine (www.bbbonline.org/online). Security seal programs assure consumers that the website follows a set of security procedures protecting their data; examples include those offered by Verisign (www.verisign.com) and McAfee Secure (secureshopping.mcafee.com). Privacy seals ensure that the website follows certain privacy guidelines, such as ESRB Privacy Online (www.esrb.org/privacy/). Even general trust seals often deal directly with privacy. For example, TRUSTe states to consumers: "When you see the TRUSTe seal, you can be assured that you have full control over the uses of your personal information to protect your privacy." (www.TRUSTe.com). Seals are then supposed to instill consumer confidence in the website, but studies have shown that even experienced Web users are less familiar with privacy and security seals than with security technologies (Cheskin 1999). In general, only 25% of consumers seem to recognize seal features on websites (Harris 2001), and many users will acquire goods or services independent of whether trust seals are present or not (Bélanger et al. 2002). Some popular seal programs include WebTrust, BBB Online, TRUSTe, Verisign, and Trust Guard. There are many other seal programs, some specific to other areas of the world such as TrustUK for the United Kingdom and eTICK for Australia.

LEARNING ACTIVITY 9.4	WHY YOUR ADVISOR CAN'T TALK TO YOUR PARENTS

Legislation exists to protect information privacy of individuals in a number of specific cases, such as financial information, health information, children, and even students. The purpose of this activity is to allow you to explore how your information privacy is protected and to better understand the difference between legitimate and inappropriate uses of information.

1. Go to the **Family Educational Rights and Privacy Act (FERPA)** website for students: http://www.ed.gov/policy/gen/guid/fpco/ferpa/students.html. FERPA protects the privacy of student education records. This link is available on the book website.

2. Read the information on the main page. Pay particular attention to the types of information covered by FERPA and individuals to whom protected information can be released.

(continued)

3. Answer the following questions and be prepared to discuss them in class.
   a. What types of information are protected under FERPA?
   b. Under what conditions may school officials provide protected information to parents? In your opinion, how do these conditions relate to the concept of "owning" your personal data?
   c. Why do you think FERPA was created? What problem did it solve?
   d. Compare the protections afforded by FERPA to the privacy policies you examined in Learning Activity 9.3. What elements do they have in common? How are they different? Which has stronger protections?

Government Information Privacy Regulations

Even though information privacy is largely our responsibility as individuals, there are specific situations where governments have created regulations to protect information privacy. There are actually many such regulations throughout the world. In the European Union, for example, the **Data Protection Directive** regulates how

Table 9.3 Sample Privacy Regulations

Law	Description	Source
Children's Internet Protection Act of 2001 (CIPA)	Regulates access to offensive content over the Internet on school and library computers.	http://www.fcc.gov/cgb/consumerfacts/cipa.html
Children's Online Privacy Protection Act of 1998 (COPPA)	Prevents websites from collecting personally identifiable information from children without parental consent.	http://www.ftc.gov/ogc/coppa1.htm
Electronic Communications Privacy Act of 1986 (ECPA)	Regulates access, use, disclosure, interception, and privacy protections of electronic communications.	http://legal.web.aol.com/resources/legislation/ecpa.html
Family Educational Rights and Privacy Act (FERPA)	Protects the privacy of student education records.	http://www2.ed.gov/policy/gen/guid/fpco/ferpa/index.html
Gramm-Leach-Bliley Financial Services Modernization Act of 1999 (GLBA)	Provides regulations to protect consumers' personal financial information held by financial institutions.	http://www.ftc.gov/privacy/privacyinitiatives/glbact.html
Health Insurance Portability and Accountability Act (HIPPA)	Provides regulations to protect personal health information held by covered entities and gives patients an array of rights with respect to that information.	http://www.hhs.gov/ocr/privacy/hipaa/understanding/index.html

personal data is processed and protected in the European Union. In the United States, there are many specific privacy laws. Some that students might be more familiar with include the **Gramm-Leach-Bliley Financial Services Modernization Act of 1999 (GLBA),** which regulates use of private information by financial institutions, the Family Educational Rights and Privacy Act (FERPA) discussed in Learning Activity 9.4, the **Children's Online Privacy Protection Act of 1998 (COPPA)**, which prevents websites from collecting personally identifiable information from children without parental consent, and **HIPPA, the Health Insurance Portability and Accountability Act**, which protects your medical information (and requires you to sign a form at the doctor saying you are aware of their privacy practices). Table 9.3 describes a few of these specific privacy protection regulations. Note that there are many more privacy regulations around the world that are not included in the table.

BUSINESS EXAMPLE BOX 2	HIPPA AND IDENTITY THEFT

As discussed in this chapter, HIPPA was enacted to protect personal health information that health organizations hold and to give patients an array of rights with respect to that information. While HIPPA was not meant to provide identity theft protection, one case actually led to HIPPA being used to prosecute a healthcare worker who used his access to health information to steal identities and use them for his own personal gain. Richard Gibson was employed by the Seattle Cancer Care Alliance where he took personally identifiable information from patients, including name, social security number, and date of birth, to fraudulently obtain credit cards that he then used to purchase electronics for about $9000. Once this was discovered he was investigated and prosecuted for failing to safeguard the privacy and integrity of patents' health information. He was sentenced in late 2004 to 16 months in federal prison. The company he worked for was not found responsible for the employee's actions, although in many cases employers can be held responsible for criminal activities their employees may perform.

Source: Annulis, B. D. "Identity Theft Case Creates New HIPPA Concerns for Hospitals." *Health Care Strategic Management* 23(1) (2005): 11–12.

Privacy and Ethics

As discussed at the beginning of the chapter, information privacy and confidentiality is not a new issue, but the increased use of technology has created new concerns about the use of data, and not only information privacy concerns. In the mid-1980s, Mason (1986) suggested that the increased use of information technologies, which was labeled the Information Age, would lead to four major concerns about the use of information: privacy, accuracy, property, and accessibility (PAPA). Table 9.4 shows the **PAPA framework**. The framework can be used by managers to consider areas of concerns about information they handle in their organizations.

Table 9.4 PAPA Ethical Framework – For Students (Mason, 1986)

PAPA Component	Description	Questions to Ask Yourself
Privacy	The confidentiality of the data collected about you is maintained.	• What information about you must you reveal to others? • What information should others be able to know about you—with or without your permission? • How is your information protected?
Accuracy	The data about you is what it is supposed to be. It does not include errors.	• Who is responsible for the accuracy of your information? • Who is accountable for errors about your information? • How do you remedy errors about your information?
Property	The ownership of the data about you.	• Who owns your information? • Who has the legal rights to your information? • How is the distribution of your information regulated?
Accessibility	The access to the information systems and the data that they hold about you.	• Who can have access to your information? • Which companies can have access to your information? • What safeguards are in place when someone accesses your information?

LEARNING ACTIVITY 9.5	PAPA, PRIVACY POLICIES, AND FERPA

This activity is meant to bring together various concepts you have learned throughout the chapter.

First, you must review the privacy policies you created earlier in this chapter and the information on FERPA regulation you read earlier. Answer the following questions and be prepared to discuss them in class.

1. How is each element of the PAPA model addressed in the privacy policy? Are any aspects of PAPA not addressed? Which ones (if any)?

2. How is each element of the PAPA model addressed by FERPA? Are any aspects of PAPA not addressed? Which ones (if any)?

3. Explain how the conditions under which a university can disclose information to parents relates to the property element of PAPA.

Relationship between Security and Privacy

In the previous chapter, we discussed information security. After reading this chapter on information privacy, you should realize that these concepts are very much related in practice. Security is the protection of information against threats such as unauthorized access to data, falsification of data, or denial of service. A company can provide every security protection possible for your information against these threats without necessarily having the intent of protecting the confidentiality of your information. Thus, information privacy is different than information security, even if these concepts are often used interchangeably.

CHAPTER SUMMARY

In this chapter, we discussed information confidentiality and privacy. We first described the threats to information privacy and the consequences of privacy violations for individuals and organizations. We then discussed the technologies and solutions related to information privacy. We concluded the chapter with a discussion of the PAPA framework, and of the relationship between security and privacy.
Here are the main points discussed in the chapter.

- There are four main categories of threats to information privacy: data collection, unauthorized secondary use of data, improper access to data, and errors in data.

- We identified several technologies used to infringe on and/or protect information privacy, such as cookies, cookie managers, privacy statements and policies, trust seals, and government regulations.

- Information privacy is one of the four components of the PAPA ethical framework, which include Privacy, Accuracy, Property, and Accessibility. The framework can be used to identify concerns about the use of information.

- Information privacy and information security are related concepts since it is mandatory for the information to be secured before it can be private. The reverse is not necessarily true since information that is protected from a security standpoint can still be shared with others, infringing on the privacy of the information.

REVIEW QUESTIONS

1. Explain briefly the four main threats to information privacy.
2. What is the difference between opt-in and opt-out options in privacy policies?
3. What are some of the possible consequences of privacy violations?
4. What are cookies and what should individuals do about them?
5. What is the purpose of privacy policies or statements? Who regulates them?
6. What are the Fair Information Principles? What is their purpose?

7. What are privacy seals and what is their purpose?

8. Briefly describe some of the key regulations protecting information privacy in the United States.

9. What is the PAPA framework? Explain its components. What is its purpose?

10. What is the difference (if any) between information privacy and security?

REFLECTION QUESTIONS

1. What is the most important thing you learned in this chapter? Why is it important?

2. What topics are unclear? What about them is unclear?

3. Are there any overlaps between the information privacy threats discussed in the chapter and the components of the PAPA framework?

4. How are privacy policies, cookies, and privacy seals related?

5. A well-known online retailer reveals that a hacker successfully accessed the personal information of 500 of their consumers. Is this a threat to privacy or security for the consumers? Explain.

6. Give examples of five types of data that could be stored in a cookie set up by your university when you browse the main student pages.

7. What is the difference between information privacy and information security? Can one exist without the other?

8. Why are data collection and secondary use of information threats to information privacy?

9. Can businesses be victims of identity theft? Why or why not?

10. When should organizations consider trust seals when they design a website?

ADDITIONAL LEARNING ACTIVITIES

1. This activity requires you to complete a case analysis regarding information privacy. It actually takes the Focusing Story at the beginning of the chapter to a full-length case analysis. The case may be accessed through your university website, the Ivey School business case website (http://cases.ivey.uwo.ca), the Harvard Business school case website (http://cb.hbsp.harvard.edu/cb/web), or may be provided to you by your instructor.

   CASE: Paine, L. and Z. Phillips. ChoicePoint (A), *Harvard Business School Case*, Product Number: # 9–306–001.

2. This activity allows you to explore more in-depth two privacy seal programs. First, visit five websites and note which privacy seals are common to the websites. Identify trends: Do better sites use particular seals? Then, select the two most popular privacy seals and find their website. Identify the requirements and costs for organizations to participate in each of the two seal programs and create a comparison table that includes whether a fee is charged (high/low), policies for affixing the seal, disclosures required, consumer redress options, and any other important information.

3. This activity requires you to listen to an interesting series of broadcasts on information privacy presented on the National Public Radio's *All Things Considered* program called

"The End of Privacy." Listen to each segment, and then write a short essay on one of these questions:

a. Is privacy still possible? Why?
b. Is real-time tracking a concern for privacy, or a security advantage? Why or why not?
c. Is social networking worth the privacy risks? Why or why not?
d. Can online information about you come to haunt you? How?

- October 26, 2009 —Online Data Present a Privacy Minefield (7 min 49 seconds)
  - http://www.npr.org/templates/story/story.php?storyId=114163862
- October 27, 2009 — Is Your Facebook Profile as Private as You Think? (5 min 47 seconds)
  - http://www.npr.org/templates/story/story.php?storyId=114187478&ps=rs
- October 28, 2009 — Digital Bread Crumbs: Following Your Cell Phone Trail
  - http://www.npr.org/templates/story/story.php?storyId=114241860 (7 min 50 seconds)
- October 29, 2009 — Digital Data Make for a Really Permanent Record
  - http://www.npr.org/templates/story/story.php?storyId=114276194 (7 min 46 seconds)

4. Select two websites you regularly transact with or send information to. Obtain their privacy policies and map them to the Fair Information Practices and privacy policy contents as done in Table 9.2. Do all privacy policies include the proper content? Explain.

5. Investigate two of the laws discussed in this chapter more in-depth (COPPA, HIPPA, FERPA, etc.). Draw a table that shows how each law addresses the Fair Information Practices principles.

6. Find three examples of websites that ask you to provide personal information and discuss the reasons why you would. Then find three examples of websites that you would not want to provide with personal information and discuss why.

7. Compare and contrast the information privacy threats discussed in the chapter with the components of the PAPA framework. Identify any overlaps and differences.

REFERENCES

Bélanger, F., J. Hiller, and W.J. Smith. "Trustworthiness in E-Commerce: The Role of Privacy, Security, and Site Attributes." *Journal of Strategic Information Systems* 11(3/4) (2002): 245–270.

Bélanger, F. and J. S. Hiller. "A Framework for E-Government: Privacy Implications." *Business Process Management Journal* 12:1(2006): 48–60.

Charters, D. "Addressing Privacy Breaches." *CMA Management* 81(9) (2008): 34.

Cheskin. "eCommerce Trust Study." *Cheskin Research and Studio Archetype/Sapient.* (1999).

Deloitte. (2007). "Enterprise@Risk: 2007 Privacy & Data Protection Survey." Retrieved January 16, 2008, from http://www.deloitte.com/dtt/cda/doc/content/us_risk_s%26P_2007%20 Privacy10Dec2007final.pdf.

Harris "Why Some Companies Are Trusted and Others Are Not: Personal Experience and Knowledge of Company More Important than Glitz." *Harris Interactive.* (2001).

Madden, M. and A. Smith. "Reputation Management and Social Media." *Pew Internet Life and Society Project.* (2010).

Mason, R. O. "Four Ethical Issues of the Information Age." *MIS Quarterly*10(1) (1986): 5.

Paine, L. and Z. Phillips. ChoicePoint (A & B) Teaching Note. *Harvard Business School* 5(2006): 307–08.

Smith, H. J., S. J. Milberg, et al. "Information privacy: Measuring individuals' concerns about organizational practices." *MIS Quarterly* 20(2) (1996): 167.

Stewart, R. "Commentary: Legal Effect of Revealing Private Information in the US and Abroad." *Information Systems Management* 24(4) (2007): 343.

Van Slyke, C. and F. Bélanger. *Electronic Business Technologies*. New York, NY, John Wiley & Sons, 2003.

BIBLIOGRAPHY AND FURTHER READINGS

Anderson, J. "How to Fix Your Facebook Settings," *Kiplinger's Personal Finance* 64 (8) (2010): 61.

Anti-Phishing Game: Used to be at Carnegie Mellon University but is being commercialized by Wombat technologies. Students can still play the demo game at the following website: http://wombatsecurity.com/antiphishing_phil/index.html.

Deloitte, LLP. *Social Networking and Reputational Risk in the Workplace* (2009), http://www.deloitte.com/assets/Dcom-UnitedStates/Local%20Assets/Documents/us_2009_ethics_workplace_survey_220509.pdf.

Deloitte LLP. Ethics & Workplace Survey results (2009). http://www.deloitte.com/assets/Dcom-UnitedStates/Local%20Assets/Documents/us_2008_ethics_workplace_survey_150509.pdf.

Kugler, Logan. "The Smart Paranoid's Guide to using Google: Here are Down-and-Dirty Details on How to Maintain Your Privacy While Using Google's Myriad Services. *Computerworld* (May 25dex.html.

GLOSSARY

Accessibility: refers to who has access to the information systems and the data that they hold.

Accuracy: when data is what it is supposed to be. It does not include errors.

Children's Internet Protection Act of 2001 (CIPA): law that regulates access to offensive content over the Internet on school and library computers.

Children's Online Privacy Protection Act of 1998 (COPPA): law that prevents websites from collecting personally identifiable information from children without parental consent.

Clickstream data: tracking of online browsing behaviors.

Cookie manager: software application that allows you to view which cookies are stored on your computer, what's in them, and gives you the ability to delete them.

Cookies: small text files located on your computer, to store information about you, your accounts, and your computer.

Data collection threat: privacy threat resulting from the fact that data can be collected, aggregated, and analyzed at a faster pace and in larger volume than ever, and without the individuals' awareness.

Data Protection Directive: law that regulates how personal data is processed and protected in the European Union.

Electronic Communications Privacy Act of 1986 (ECPA): law that regulates access, use, disclosure, interception, and privacy protections of electronic communications.

Errors in data: privacy threat where there are inaccuracies in data.

Fair Information Practices principles (FIP): guidelines for how to deal with personal information, which include notice/awareness; choice/consent; access/participation; integrity/security; and enforcement/redress.

Family Educational Rights and Privacy Act (FERPA): law that protects the privacy of student education records.

Federal Trade Commission (FTC): government agency responsible for (among other things) ensuring that privacy policies are respected.

Gramm-Leach-Bliley Financial Services Modernization Act of 1999 (GLBA): law that provides regulations to protect consumers' personal financial information held by financial institutions.

Health Insurance Portability and Accountability Act (HIPPA): law that provides regulations to protect personal health information held by covered entities and gives patients an array of rights with respect to that information.

Identity theft: using another person's personal information for fraudulent activities.

Improper access to data: privacy threat where unauthorized individuals have access to one's private information.

Opt-in: privacy option where individuals state they agree that their data can be shared with others or used for other purposes, often to receive special deals or information from partner companies.

Opt-out: privacy option where individuals must state to companies they do not want their data shared with others or used for other purposes.

PAPA framework: framework that identifies four major categories of concerns about the use of information: privacy, accuracy, property, and accessibility.

Privacy policy: statement that describes what the organization's practices are with respect to the privacy of its customers.

Privacy seal: seal that businesses can post on their website to show their commitment to privacy.

Privacy: one's ability to control information about oneself.

Property: refers to who has ownership of the data.

Reputation seal: seal that businesses can post on their website to show their commitment to trustworthiness.

Seal program: program offered by an organization, which post a set of rules that companies must follow to be a part of the seal program.

Security seal: seal that businesses can post on their website to show their commitment to security.

Self-regulation: attempt by industry leaders to avoid government regulations by suggesting (rather than requiring) that companies have privacy policies, for example with privacy seals and privacy policies.

Unauthorized secondary use of information: privacy threat resulting from the use of data for purposes other than those for which they were originally collected.

Developing Information Systems

LEARNING OBJECTIVES

By reading and completing the activities in this chapter, you will be able to:

- Explain the benefits of a software development methodology
- List and describe the phases in the traditional systems development life cycle
- Compare and contrast the traditional systems development life cycle with alternative methodologies
- Explain factors that influence the decision to build custom software or purchase commercial, off-the-shelf software
- Define open source software
- Describe major outsourcing models
- List the benefits and risks of outsourcing

CHAPTER OUTLINE

- Focusing story: The $6 billion software bug
- Time, cost, and quality
- Learning Activity 10.1: Determining requirements
- Software development methodologies
- Traditional systems development life cycle

    Planning phase

    Requirements phase

    Design phase

    Development phase

    Implementation phase

Maintenance phase

- Learning Activity 10.2: Advantages and disadvantages of the SDLC
- Alternative methodologies

Prototyping

Rapid application development (RAD)

Spiral model

- Learning Activity 10.3: Comparing the methods
- Build or buy decision
- Learning Activity 10.4: How open source software impacts build vs. buy
- Using open source in business
- Learning Activity 10.5: What to outsource
- Outsourcing information systems

Outsourcing models

Benefits and risks of outsourcing

Making the outsourcing decision

Geographic considerations

- Chapter summary
- Review questions
- Reflection questions
- Additional learning activities
- References
- Glossary

In this chapter you will gain a basic understanding of the software development process. In addition, the chapter will help you learn about alternatives to building software from scratch. Outsourcing information systems are also discussed.

FOCUSING STORY: THE $6 BILLION SOFTWARE BUG

In August 2003, the largest power blackout in North American history hit the northeastern United States and southeastern Canada. Fifty million people lost power, some for up to two days. At least 11 people died as a result of the blackout. Total cost: $6 billion. Investigators concluded that the initial problem started when a power line in Ohio sagged and hit an overgrown tree. Normally this is an isolated incident. When such an incident occurs, alarm systems alert power systems operators of the problem so they can take appropriate steps to make sure that the problem remains isolated. Unfortunately, in this case a software bug caused the alarm system to malfunction. This started a cascade of errors that led to over 50 million people losing electrical power. The lack of power also led to water supply problems, and the shutdown of major transportation systems, including railroads and airlines. Gas stations could not dispense fuel. Cell phone service was interrupted (although wired phones continued working).

While lack of proper maintenance was the root cause of the blackout, without the software bug, the impact would have been small and limited to relatively few people. With the software error, tens of millions of people were affected and there were billions in economic costs.

There are many other examples of the high consequences of faulty software:

- In 2005, Toyota recalled over 150,000 Prius hybrids to fix software that caused the gasoline engine to shut down unexpectedly.

- In 2004, a software error disrupted communication at LAX airport's air traffic control system; 800 flights were disrupted. Fortunately, there were no midair collisions, although there were several near misses.

- In 1985 to 1987, software errors in the Therac-25 radiation therapy device allowed the device to deliver lethal doses of radiation to patients. At least five patients died.

- In 1990, an error in the control systems of AT&T's long distance switches left 60,000 people without long distance service.

FOCUSING QUESTIONS:

1. Have you ever experienced software that did not operate correctly? What consequences did you experience?

2. What can be done to limit software errors?

3. Why is it important to catch software errors early in the development process?

Time, Cost, and Quality

Every software development project faces a tension among time, cost, and quality. This reality, which applies to all sorts of projects, is known by several names, including the *project triangle,* the *engineering triangle,* and the *design triangle.* The basic idea is that there are tradeoffs among the three dimensions. The three constraints are described below.

- Time: How long will the project take to complete?
- Cost: What resources are required to complete the project?
- Quality: How well does the completed project meet user requirements?

Some versions of the triangle substitute scope (what is done as part of the project) for quality. Scope and quality are closely related, especially when considering an overall project. Quality is related to user requirements, and increasing the scope of a software development project adds new requirements that need to be met. So, increasing the scope of a project also makes it harder (more costly and/or longer in duration) to meet quality goals.

There is an old saying, "You want it fast, good, and cheap? Pick any two." Increasing the speed with which a project is delivered, and you will have to compromise on either quality or costs. Decreasing the cost requires longer completion time or accepting lower quality. It is important to understand these tradeoffs when making software development decisions. Typically, one of the three constraints is fixed (for example, you may have a strict budget or delivery date). As a result, the other two constraints must be managed against each other. For example, if you have a fixed budget, moving to an earlier delivery date requires changes in quality or scope. You can learn more about this in relation to project management in the In-Depth Guide on Funding and Managing Projects, which is available from the book's website.

LEARNING ACTIVITY 10.1   **DETERMINING REQUIREMENTS**

Determining system requirements is a major step in the software development process. One method for uncovering requirements is to interview the intended users of the software. Suppose that a club you belong to wants to create a system for keeping track of members. Get in pairs. One of you acts as the interviewer who is trying to discover requirements. The other acts as the user. Document at least 10 requirements for the system.

Software Development Methodologies

Developing software is a complex, time-consuming, and costly endeavor. Because of this, it is often useful to have a framework for planning, structuring, and controlling software development projects. Such frameworks are commonly called **software development methodologies**. These methodologies provide discipline to the software development process by defining processes, roles, and deliverables related to software development. Typically the methodologies break down software development into phases, each of which has its own set of processes, roles, and deliverables. In some methodologies, the deliverables of one phase provide the inputs for the next phase.

Most large organizations have a standard software development methodology that is used across the organization, although many organizations may allow different methodologies for particular projects. For example, Web-based system development projects may follow a different methodology than a transaction processing system development project.

The main reason to use a formal software development methodology is that it provides discipline by clearly defining how the project should proceed, what work should be done, how that work should be done, and what outputs should be produced. Having a standard methodology in an organization also allows individuals to more easily join a project in progress. The standardized roles, processes, documentation, and deliverables make it easier for a new team member to become familiar with what has been done on the project. It also makes it easier for the new member to find relevant information.

Traditional Systems Development Life Cycle

Traditionally, many systems development projects have followed a semi-sequential, phased approach, which is typically called the **systems development life cycle** (SDLC). The SDLC provides a disciplined approach to systems development. Projects follow a well-defined set of phases that have related objectives, processes, and deliverables. The traditional SDLC is sometimes called the *waterfall method* since the results of one phase flow as inputs into the next phase. It is important to realize that there are many different versions of the "traditional" SDLC. The differences boil down to how the phases are divided; some versions have more phases than others. The versions with fewer phases collapse multiple phases from the more complex versions into a single phase. In this chapter we present a relatively typical version with six phases, as shown in Figure 10.1. Note the dashed feedback lines on the left-hand side of the diagram. Sometimes you need to go back and refine an earlier phase based on new information that emerges.

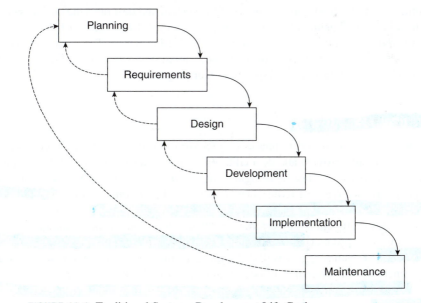

FIGURE 10.1 Traditional Systems Development Life Cycle

Planning Phase

The goal of the planning stage is to define the overall goal and scope of the system and determine the feasibility of the project. Essentially, you want to answer the question, "Why build the system?" In addition, you need to establish whether the project is feasible. There are several different aspects to feasibility:

- *Technical feasibility* concerns whether the proposed system can be completed from a technical standpoint. It is important to consider whether the system fits with the existing technical infrastructure.

- *Economic feasibility* relates to whether the proposed system is affordable and worth the investment.

- *Organizational feasibility* concerns whether the project fits with the organization's existing strategies and practices. If the system does not fit with current ways of operating, the organization needs to determine what needs to be changed and whether these changes are feasible. Organizational feasibility should also consider whether the organization has access to the human resources necessary to complete the project.

- *Legal feasibility* concerns whether the proposed project violates any laws or regulations.

- *Ethical feasibility* considers whether the system fits within the ethical guidelines and practices of the organization and its industry.

The major deliverables of the planning phase are the feasibility analysis, project initiation document, and the project management plan. The project initiation document specifies the high-level goals of the system and describes the business case for the system. (A business case describes the system and why it is needed.) The feasibility analysis results are often included in the business case. The project management plan documents the scope of the project, identifies major tasks and resources, and describes any interrelationships with other projects.

Requirements Phase

The goal of the requirements phase is to uncover and document the functions that the system should provide and desired levels of performance. In other words, in the requirements phase the task is to figure out and document what the system should do. There are two types of requirements: functional and nonfunctional. **Functional requirements** describe how the system should interact with users and other systems. An example of a functional requirement is "the system shall allow customers to look up the price of a product. **Nonfunctional requirements** are related to constraints on the system, for example, how well it should perform. An example of a nonfunctional requirement is, "the system shall be available at least 23 hours per day."

Requirements elicitation involves gathering requirements from various stakeholders and is a primary task in the requirements phase. Gathering the requirements

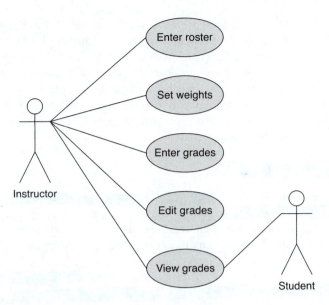

FIGURE 10.2 Use Case Diagram Example

for a system is often a difficult, time consuming, and error-prone process. To make things worse, requirements may change during the process. Despite the difficulties, it is very important to fully understand the system's requirements; they form the foundation for the rest of the development project.

The output of the requirements phase is a specification of the system's functional and nonfunctional requirements. Typically, this takes the form of a set of requirements statements (sometimes called *system shall* statements) or a set of use cases, either in text or diagram form. A *system shall* statement simply defines a requirement, such as "The system shall allow teachers to enter student grades." A **use case** describes a sequence of actions that results in an outcome for some actor. An actor can be a user or another external system. Figure 10.2 shows a use case diagram. (Use case diagrams are part of the Unified Modeling Language, which was developed as a standard way to specify models related to software systems.)

It is important to understand that requirements should specify *what* the system must do, but not *how* the system should meet the requirements. This allows the systems designers flexibility in the design of the system, which is covered in the next phase.

Design Phase

The main goal of the design phase is to describe in detail how the system will meet the requirements specified earlier. The requirements specified earlier form the foundation of the system design. The focus here is on *how* the system will satisfy the requirements, although there are elements of the design phase that still deal with what the system is intended to do. These elements are known as the *logical system design,* which includes abstract models of what the system is intended to do. An example of such a model is the database diagram we saw in Chapter 5. In addition to the database model, the user interface and business rules enforced by the system need to be designed. The design phase also specifies the plans for implementing and testing the system. The system design document is a major deliverable of the design phase. This document describes, in detail, the system requirements, operating environment, database design, user interface, and processing logic. Other deliverables include an implementation plan and a training plan.

Development Phase

During the development phase, the outputs of the design phase are converted into the actual information system. This is the phase in which the system is actually constructed. The software is written, databases are created, and any necessary hardware is installed. It is often necessary to integrate the new system with existing information systems; if needed, the integration occurs during the development phase. System testing is a critical part of the development phase. Testing occurs both during the development of the software and when the entire system is complete and integrated. Software testing is a complex, time-consuming, but critical aspect of systems development. It is necessary to thoroughly test the system prior to actual implementation. Errors are very expensive to correct when they are not discovered until after the system is implemented. The errors may also lead to business disruptions. The development phase's deliverables include the application software, data and files for testing, and documentation on how the software components interact with one another and external systems.

Implementation Phase

The goal of the implementation phase is to make the system operational in a production environment. One important implementation phase activity is to notify users of the rollout of the new system. This notification should include the implementation schedule, differences in work processes and responsibilities brought about by the new system, and the process for obtaining technical support for the new system. User training is also an important activity in this phase. Often, it is also necessary to convert data from the existing system into the new system. For example, a new product cataloging system might need to have data from the old system migrated into the new system. Finally, it is a good practice to have a post-implementation review that documents the project to date and make recommendations for improvements for future projects. The main deliverable of the implementation phase is the system itself, installed and running correctly. The post-implementation review report is another deliverable from this phase.

There are several approaches to changing from an existing system to the newly developed system. There are four common approaches to system migration.

- *Direct changeover* (also called *immediate changeover*): At a specific point in time, the old system is no longer used and is replaced with the new system. While this has the advantage of being rapid, it is very risky. If the new system has problems, the functions available in the old system are also unavailable.

- *Parallel operation*: Both the old and new systems operate for some period of time. The parallel approach is lower risk than direct changeover, but also takes longer and is more expensive. The parallel approach is necessary for systems that cannot be taken out of service while changing from the old to the new system.

- *Phased implementation*: The new system is implemented in stages. This approach is an attractive compromise between direct and parallel approaches. However, it is best suited for systems that have clear modules that can be implemented in a phased manner. Systems with significant interdependencies between modules are not suitable for phased implementation.

- *Pilot operation*: The new system is implemented in a business unit (such as a store or department) or location (such as a state or country). The initial pilot is followed by other pilot changeovers or a full changeover to the new system. Each pilot changeover must use one of the other approaches.

Maintenance Phase

The final phase in the SDLC is the maintenance phase. This is usually the longest, most costly phase of the life cycle. It is not unusual for more than half of the total system cost to occur in the maintenance phase. The goal of this phase is ensuring that the system operates properly to meet current needs. This involves fixing any problems that are uncovered and may also involve modifying or adding to the programs to meet new needs. In addition, the system may be modified to improve performance or take advantage of new technologies. For example, an online ordering system may be modified to allow customers to order from their smart phones.

Although we presented the SDLC as a very linear process, where one phase follows the next in an orderly fashion, reality is rarely so neat. During the systems development process, it is often necessary to revisit an earlier phase when new needs arise or problems are discovered.

LEARNING ACTIVITY 10.2	ADVANTAGES AND DISADVANTAGES OF THE SDLC

The traditional SDLC has been around for a long time (that is why it is called "traditional") and has been used successfully for many systems development projects. However, it is not without its drawbacks. With a partner, research the SDLC approach and develop a list of three advantages and three disadvantages to the traditional SDLC. Be prepared to share your list.

As you discovered in Learning Activity 10.2, there are advantages and disadvantages to the traditional SDLC. These drawbacks led to the development of alternative methodologies. In the next section we describe several of these alternative approaches.

STATS BOX: STANDISH CHAOS REPORT

Cancelled IT projects and incorrect software cost the global economy billions of dollars each year. The Standish Group's CHAOS Report provides data on the failure rates of IT-related projects. Project outcomes are divided into three categories. Successful projects are delivered on time, on budget, and meet requirements. Challenged projects are late, over budget, and/or do not meet some requirements. Failed projects are cancelled before they are completed or are delivered, but not used. For 2009, 32% of the IT projects studied were successful, while 44% were challenged, and 24% failed. This is a significant improvement over the first CHAOS report, which found that only 16% of IT projects were successful, while 53% failed. There are many causes for software failure. In some cases, the initial estimates of the costs, resources, and delivery date are unrealistic. Other causes include misunderstanding requirements, "feature-creep" (expanding requirements), and inadequate testing. The costs of these failures are staggering. One controversial estimate puts the global price tag of IT failure at over $6 trillion (http://www.zdnet.com/blog/projectfailures/worldwide-cost-of-it-failure-62-trillion/7627).

Alternative Methodologies

Prototyping

Prototyping is an approach to deal with aspects of a full methodology; it is not a complete, stand-alone methodology. In a prototyping approach to systems development, you begin with an initial investigation of the main requirements of the system. It is not necessary to have a full understanding of all requirements. After the initial investigation, a small-scale mock-up of the system (called the **prototype**) is built and reviewed by stakeholders. The stakeholders point out flaws, which reveals new or misunderstood requirements. The prototype is refined and reviewed. This cycle repeats until the stakeholders are satisfied that all requirements are met. Then the full system is implemented. Some prototypes are "throw-away" prototypes, which means that they are not intended to be part of the final system; their purpose is to uncover requirements and problems. Sometimes, however, prototypes become part of the final system. This is known as evolutionary prototyping.

Increased stakeholder involvement is a major benefit of the prototyping approach. The stakeholders know the particular business area addressed by a system much better than the systems developers and having them involved throughout the development process can lead to systems that better meet their needs. In addition, stakeholder involvement may increase satisfaction with the final system.

Prototyping is also potentially more effective for uncovering system requirements. This is especially important when requirements are unclear, ambiguous, or difficult to define. In some cases, a prototyping approach may be less expensive than a traditional SDLC approach.

There are also drawbacks to the prototyping approach. Prototyping can lead to poorly designed systems that do not perform well when scaled up for actual use. It is also difficult to estimate how many iterations are required, which makes it difficult to estimate costs and schedules. Usually, prototyping results in less-well-documented systems, which may cause problems later (for example, when the system needs to be revised or integrated with new systems). Finally, nonfunctional requirements (such as performance requirements) are difficult to establish using prototypes.

Prototyping is best for systems that require extensive user interaction and for which the analysts have some understanding of the business issues to be addressed, especially when functional requirements are not well understood. Prototyping is less well suited for systems that have well-defined requirements, when nonfunctional requirements are especially important or when future scalability is important.

Rapid Application Development (RAD)

As the name implies, rapid application development (RAD) is intended to develop systems more quickly than traditional methods. It is an iterative method that uses rapid development of prototypes rather than engaging in extensive up-front planning. RAD typically breaks software development projects into smaller chunks in order to reduce overall project risk. This also facilitates making changes as the project's requirements emerge. The focus is usually on filling organizational needs rather than creating technically perfect systems.

Active user involvement is a key aspect of RAD. The idea is to work with users to determine high-level requirements and then build a prototype based on those requirements. Developers review the prototype with the users, who provide feedback. The prototype is refined based on the feedback. This process continues until the full system is developed. Interestingly, some of the same methods used in the traditional SDLC approach can also be applied in RAD. The RAD process is illustrated in Figure 10.3.

Development tools are integral parts of a RAD system. Computer aided software engineering (CASE) tools, for example, automate many software design and development tasks. Tools for quickly developing graphical user interfaces are often included in a RAD environment. These tools allow developers to build user interfaces by dragging and dropping interface elements onto a screen instead of having to write the software code.

In addition to delivering systems more quickly than the traditional SDLC, RAD often results in lower costs as well. Because user involvement is such an important aspect of RAD, systems developed using RAD often have greater buy-in from users. RAD also facilitates evolving requirements well. However, the speed of RAD may result in lower-quality software. Because users often want more and more features,

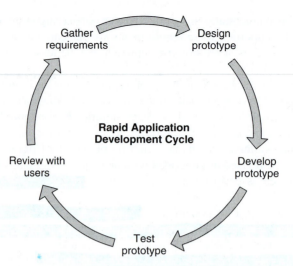

FIGURE 10.3 Rapid Application Development Cycle

"feature-creep" may be more likely with RAD. Since there is less focus on nonfunctional requirements, systems may not perform well when scaled to more users or greater volumes of processing.

RAD is best suited for smaller-scale projects with well-focused organizational objectives and committed users. RAD does not work as well for very large projects or systems where performance and quality is critical. For example, you might not want to use RAD for a safety-critical system such as an air traffic control system.

Spiral Model

The Spiral Model, which is shown in Figure 10.4, is basically an iterative version of the standard "waterfall" SDLC. It is a risk-driven model, which focuses reducing project risk by identifying risks and ways to reduce those risks throughout the development process (Boem, 1988). Think of the development process as trips around the spiral. For each trip, you would perform the same steps:

- *Identify objectives, alternative approaches, and constraints*
  Objectives correspond to the requirements we discussed earlier. They may include both functional and nonfunctional requirements. In addition, alternative means of achieving the objectives are identified. These might include different designs, purchasing the system, etc. Constraints would include time, resources, costs, and the systems with which the new system must interact.

- *Evaluate the alternatives and identify and resolve risks*
  Identifying potential risks is important. These risks are associated with project uncertainties. Developing effective methods for reducing these uncertainties is

critical. For example, prototyping may help reduce risks related to misunderstanding functional requirements.

- *Develop and verify the deliverables from this iteration*
  The prototype (or other deliverable) from the current iteration is developed and evaluated. Evaluation includes making sure that the prototype meets the current requirements. In early iterations, this may simply be a proof-of-concept. In later iterations verification may include detailed testing.

- *Plan the next iteration*
  Determine what should be accomplished in the next iteration. Also determine the resources needed.

  The Spiral Model's focus on risk and risk reduction is a major advantage over other methods when developing critical systems. The approach also involves users throughout the process, which can build user commitment to the project. The Spiral Model allows developers to incorporate other approaches, such as the traditional SDLC and prototyping when appropriate for individual iterations. Like RAD, the

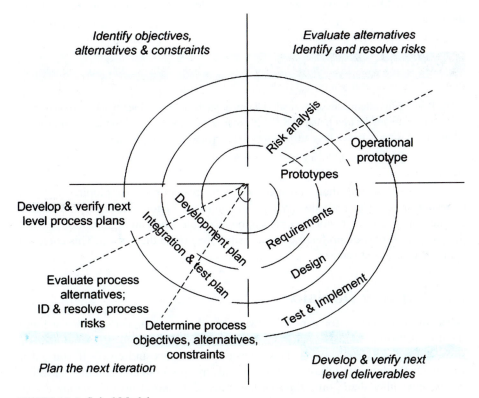

FIGURE 10.4 Spiral Model

Source: http://www.maxwideman.com/papers/linearity/spiral.htm

Spiral Model considers evolving requirements. Effectively using the Spiral Model requires highly skilled project managers. In addition, it is often difficult to known when to stop. Although originally intended to run for four cycles, there is a temptation to keep going to add more features.

The Spiral Model is most appropriate for critical systems where there is a high priority on minimizing risk. It is less appropriate for projects where risk avoidance is not critical and when costs are especially important.

This is just a sampling of some of the more common systems development methodologies. There are many others. Several of these fall into the category of agile development methodologies. *Agile development* occurs in self-managed, cross-functional teams whose members include information systems professionals and user representatives. Rather than being process-oriented, agile methods are people-oriented. Agile methods emphasize multiple iterations and continuous feedback from user representatives. There are many specific methodologies that fall into the family of agile methods. These include Extreme Programming (XP), which uses frequent releases with short development cycles, and Scrum, which features work "sprints" of one to several weeks at the end of which the development team meets with stakeholders to assess progress and plan what needs to be done next. As software and its uses continue to evolve, we expect that software development methodologies will do the same.

LEARNING ACTIVITY 10.3	COMPARING THE METHODS

Pick one of the alternative software development methodologies described in the chapter. Compare it with the traditional SDLC. Find at least three ways in which they are similar, and three ways in which they are different. Be prepared to share your answers.

As you can see, there are many different methods for developing systems; choosing the correct methodology depends on many factors. However, developing a system from scratch is not the only option available when an organization needs a new system. It may be preferable to buy rather than build the system. This choice is the topic of the next section.

Build or Buy Decision

When the need arises for a new software-based system, managers face a long-standing decision, whether to create the software or purchase existing commercial, off-the-shelf (COTS) software. This decision is complex and costly if you get it wrong. On the surface, it may seem like it is always preferable to purchase an existing system rather than going through the time, cost, and effort of creating a new system. However, the decision is not that easy. Often the COTS software will need significant customization in order to meet business needs. In these cases, it may be more effective to build a new system. In between the extremes of custom and COTS software lie hybrid approaches. These hybrid approaches involve modifying COTS software to better fit organizational needs or combining COTS components to create the desired solution.

Custom-built software is software that is built from scratch using few commercially obtained components. The main benefit of the custom approach is that the resulting system will likely be a better fit with business requirements. As a result, the custom system may be used to create a competitive advantage. In addition, the organization will have greater control over adding or modifying functions after the initial system is implemented. However, custom solutions usually take much longer and are more costly to develop than COTS or hybrid solutions. In addition, custom solutions are more prone to errors, which can further increase costs and time to delivery.

COTS software is a complete (or nearly complete) solution obtained from a third party. Examples range from office productivity systems to ERP systems. Often, COTS is less expensive than custom or hybrid approaches. COTS may also be higher quality, especially if it is a widely used system. Usually (although not always) COTS-based solutions can be provided in a much shorter timeframe than custom or hybrid solutions. There are downsides to COTS, however. First, COTS often requires changing existing business practices to fit the COTS. Second, you are largely at the mercy of the vendor or consultants for support, including enhancements and fixes. In addition, a financially weak vendor may be unable to provide proper support or maintenance. In extreme cases, the vendor may go out of business.

Hybrid solutions may use components from different vendors to create the complete solution or may involve customizing COTS by modifying programming code or adding small programs called scripts. In ideal cases, the hybrid solutions offer the best of custom and COTS approaches. The hybrid solutions usually better fit business requirements and existing processes, but can be delivered less expensively and more quickly than custom solutions. However, hybrid solutions also suffer from some of the same drawbacks as custom-built systems and COTS. In addition, it may be difficult to find the expertise necessary to modify or combine the COTS components. Figure 10.5 provides an overview of some of the characteristics of the three approaches.

When making the build vs. buy decision, there are a number of questions that must be addressed:

- *Is there COTS software that will meet the business needs?*
  If the answer to this question is "no," your choices are narrowed to custom development or a hybrid approach. If no COTS software can meet your organization's needs, you have to create the software or customize COTS. In these cases, you may have the option of outsourcing the development or customization. (We discuss outsourcing later in this chapter.)

- *Will the software give your company a competitive advantage?*
  If COTS is an option, the next question is to consider whether the system will give your company a competitive advantage. If so the scale is tipped towards building custom software. If not, COTS may be a better choice. To understand why, think about the example of a hotel chain. To such a company, a payroll system would

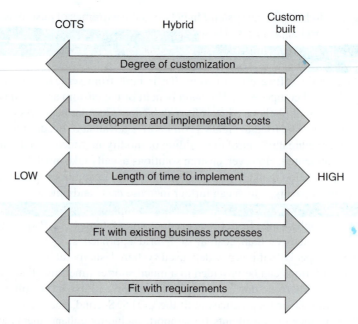

COTS   Hybrid   Custom
                                            built

Degree of customization

Development and implementation costs

LOW   Length of time to implement   HIGH

Fit with existing business processes

Fit with requirements

FIGURE 10.5 Comparing COTS and Custom Development

Source: Adapted from: http://www.baselinemag.com/index2.php?option=content&task=view&id=5113&pop=1&hide_ads=1&page=0&hide_js=1

not be likely to provide any competitive advantage. Payroll is a routine function so it is a good candidate for COTS. In contrast, having a custom system for analyzing the behaviors and preferences of frequent guests may give them an advantage over the company's competitors and is therefore a better candidate for building a custom system.

- *Does the COTS fit with business processes?*
  COTS will rarely match exactly with existing business processes. As a result, you will usually have to modify at least some business processes in order to use COTS. Often this is not a problem, but sometimes the changes necessary are so extensive that it may be better to build a custom system. The key issue is whether it is practical to alter existing processes in order to fit the way the COTS software operates.

- *Does the COTS fit with existing IT architecture and staff?*
  To be successful, COTS must fit with your organization's existing IT. Here is a simplistic example. Suppose that your organization used only Windows-based PCs. Macintosh-only COTS would not be a good fit with your existing IT. It is also important that your IT staff be able to support any COTS you use. If the existing staff cannot provide support you will either need to contract with an outside company for support, train your existing staff, or hire new staff. All of these add to the cost and complexity of implementing the COTS.

- *Do you have the capability to create the required system?*
  There are times when an organization simply does not have the capability to create a system that meets requirements. In these cases, COTS is often an attractive option. Outsourcing the development of the system is another option.

- *When is the system needed?*
  A COTS solution can almost always be implemented faster than a custom-built system. As a result, you should consider the "go-live" goal for the new system when making the build-buy decision.

- *What is the total cost of ownership for each approach?*
  Finally, you should compare the total cost of ownership (TCO) for both approaches. The cost of purchasing or building the system is not the only cost you should consider. There are also support and maintenance costs, costs to integrate the system into the existing architecture, and costs related to enhancing the system in the future. One important point to keep in mind is that COTS usually are changed much more often than custom-built systems. When the vendor releases a new version of the software, you may incur additional costs related to deploying the new version. Of course, you could stay with the old version, but vendors often drop support for older versions, which may lead to problems.

LEARNING ACTIVITY 10.4   **HOW OPEN SOURCE SOFTWARE IMPACTS BUILD VS. BUY**

Open source software is software that provides access to the program's code, which means that it can be freely modified. Often organizations must decide whether to build custom software or purchase a commercial software package. In pairs, discuss how open source software might impact the build vs. buy decision. Prepare a bullet list of your findings.

Using Open Source in Business

Open source software is software that allows users to access the underlying source code for an application. Having the **source code** for a program allows users to modify the program's functions. The source code is the human-readable form of a software program. Typically, this source code is translated into computer instructions through a process called *compiling*. The compiled code is not in a form that is easily understood by a human. The licensing for open source software also allows users to modify the program, subject to some conditions. The Open Source Initiative provides a detailed definition for "open source" at http://www.opensource.org/docs/osd.

Open source software is usually available free of charge, although it is common for companies to distribute (for a fee) open source software along with support contracts or other enhancements. Open source software has been in existence for many years, but has been largely unknown to the general population until recently. The rise of popular open source applications such as Mozilla Firefox (a Web browser), Open Office (a productivity suite), and operating and systems software such as the Linux operating system and Apache Web server have increased the awareness of open source software.

More recently Google's open source Android operating system has been credited with a rapid rise in the number of smart phones running Android. According to the Nielsen Company, in the second quarter of 2009, Android-based phones accounted for only 1% of the new smart phone purchases in the United States. By November 2010 they accounted for over 40%. Some believe that Android's openness is one reason for its rapid rise. The fact that Android was open allowed many smart phone manufacturers to implement Android on their handsets. The manufacturers were also able to modify Android to take advantage of their phone's specific features.

Businesses are adopting open source software for a variety of uses. For many years the Apache Web server has held over 50% of the U.S. Web server market. Most large organizations use Linux servers to some extent. According to the Linux Foundation, over three-quarters of large organizations plan to add more Linux servers in the near future. Open source is less popular for personal computer operating systems, with slightly more than 1% of personal computers using Linux. Open source for end users may be on the rise, however. The recent economic downturn has led some organizations to take another look at open source applications. In addition, many governments are actively promoting the use of open source alternatives to proprietary software among both governmental departments and citizens. Time will tell whether this trend continues.

Why would businesses use open source software? There are a variety of reasons. The most obvious is the potential cost savings. Most open source software can be acquired without charge. It is important to note that this does not mean that the software can be implemented without cost. There are ongoing costs associated with installation, support, and continuous training; these costs should not be ignored. Another reason businesses use open source software is to avoid being dependent on proprietary software vendors for ongoing development and support. For example, users of Microsoft Office are completely reliant upon Microsoft for current developments (such as fixing errors or enhancing the software). With open source software, the larger community can carry out these functions. This means that continuous development and support is possible even if the creator of the software goes out of business. There is also some evidence that mature open source software is often more reliable than proprietary software. In addition, open source software is more likely to use open standards for things such as file formats. This reduces the reliance on any particular software vendor. Additional flexibility comes from the fact that users have the ability to modify the software as needed. This is not possible with proprietary software. (It should be noted that most users lack the technical skills necessary to modify software, which reduces the value of this benefit.)

One interesting aspect of open source software is that a community of volunteer programmers often does ongoing development. You can think of the structure of an open source development community like an onion. Core developers are at the center and passive users are at the outermost layer. The core developers do most of the programming for both the original creation and ongoing development. Developers at outer layers report errors and request features and may also contribute fixes for the errors. Active users also report problems, but do not contribute any programming code, and often help less experienced users in community forums. Thus the community not only supports current users, but also provides a platform for ongoing enhancements.

BUSINESS BOX	BAD ECONOMY LEADS TO MORE OPEN SOURCE SOFTWARE

According to Forrester Research, 87% of companies in a survey claimed that they saved money by using open source software. Almost all of these organizations found that open source software met or exceeded quality expectations. Over a third of the companies solve business problems by combining open source and proprietary software.

   The recent economic downturn may be a driver for open source adoption. The savings in software development costs can be significant. One estimate puts the savings at almost $400 billion. According to the Gartner Group, cost savings are the main reason companies adopt open source, but flexibility is also an important driver.

Sources: http://webdevnews.net/2009/05/forrester-87-companies-save-money-open-source-solutions/

http://www.businessweek.com/print/technology/content/nov2008/tc20081130_319283.htm

http://www.gartner.com/it/page.jsp?id=801412

LEARNING ACTIVITY 10.5	WHAT TO OUTSOURCE

Outsourcing occurs when a company turns to an outside vendor to provide some service. While the definition of outsourcing is easy to understand, deciding what to outsource is much harder. For each of the business scenarios below, decide whether the system or operation should be outsourced. Explain your answer.

Organization	System/function
1. Engineering company	Payroll and benefits management system
2. Regional beer brewery	Customer relationship management
3. University	Learning management system (e.g. Blackboard, Moodle)
4. Financial portfolio management company	Investment analysis software
5. Public radio station	Donor management system

Outsourcing Information Systems

Information technology **outsourcing** occurs when an organization goes to an outside company to provide IT services that were previously provided internally. (Outsourcing is not unique to IT. For example, some companies outsource the manufacturing of products that they sell.)

Outsourcing Models

There are many different outsourcing models. These differ in the degree of outsourcing and in what is outsourced. Some organizations contract with a service provider to provide all IT-related services. This is known as **full or complete outsourcing**. Full outsourcing allows an organization to focus on its core activities and may also reduce IT costs. Service providers may be able to provide services less expensively due to economies of scale.

In contrast, in **selective or partial outsourcing** only certain aspects of IT are outsourced to a service provider. For example, AT&T recently outsourced the maintenance of its ERP system to Accenture. There are different approaches to deciding what to outsource. Under **process-based outsourcing** an organization outsources a particular function or business process. Functions that are often outsourced include help desk support, payroll and benefits processing, and telecommunication services. Outsourcing specific functions is not new. For example, ADP has been providing payroll services to organizations for over 50 years.

Personnel outsourcing is another form of outsourcing that has a long history. This form of outsourcing allows organizations to meet staffing needs without the long-term costs associated with hiring permanent workers. Bringing in temporary, contract-based workers may be effective when an organization needs specific expertise on a short-term basis or when the current workload is more than the internal IT staff can handle. In these cases, outsourcing can speed time to deployment for a system and avoid costs related to training the current staff.

Another approach is **project-based outsourcing**. As the name implies, this involves contracting with a vendor for a specific project. Since projects have specific start and end points, when the project is finished, the outsourcing engagement ends. Organizations outsource projects when they lack the internal resources necessary to complete the project. Earlier we mentioned outsourcing as an alternative for developing a custom system. This is an example of project-based outsourcing. Then the system is developed and deployed, and the outsourcing engagement ends. Interestingly, upgrades to the system may lead to future outsourcing engagements.

Application outsourcing involves a service provider handling activities related to a specific software application for a fee. There are different forms of application outsourcing. With application hosting, the client organization is responsible for operating the IT infrastructure associated with the application, but the client must purchase the software and pay any annual license or maintenance payments to the software publisher. Amazon's Web Services is an example of application hosting. Organizations can deploy applications on Amazon's systems. Amazon handles keeping the servers up and running, but is not responsible for maintaining the application.

This arrangement is often very cost effective, especially when there are demand spikes that may require additional server capacity. Software as a service (SaaS) provides on-demand Web-based access to an application on a per-use or per-user basis. Salesforce.com is a well-known provider of SaaS. Salesforce.com provides organizations with customer relationship management software for a monthly per-user fee. Different features lead to different fees. For example a simple contact management currently costs $5 per user per month while a full CRM system costs $125 per user per month. The SaaS model provides a large degree of flexibility and can be cost effective. The client organization does not have to worry about maintaining the software or the servers. SaaS also provides very good scalability. However, there are security and privacy concerns with SaaS.

Benefits and Risks of Outsourcing

Outsourcing, when done well, can result in a variety of benefits. A major benefit of outsourcing is that it can give organizations access to specific expertise not available in-house. There can also be cost savings with outsourcing. These are normally associated with the vendor having lower cost structures, either through economies of scale or lower wage rates. Outsourcing also shifts employee-related fixed costs to variable costs. In addition, outsourcing may allow for more rapid delivery of projects through additional expertise and personnel and can be an effective means of managing capacity. It is generally easier to contract for additional capacity than to add it through other means. Selective outsourcing allows management to focus on core business activities. Finally, when outsourcing sites are spread across time zones, offshore outsourcing can lead to 24-hour productivity.

There are also risks associated with outsourcing. In some cases, outsourcing can lead to a loss of competencies within the organization. This is especially problematic when this loss is related to the core activities of the organization. There are also risks related to the outsourcing relationship. There is a risk of becoming dependent on the service provider, which can lower bargaining power in later negotiations. In addition, there is a danger that the vendor may behave opportunistically and take advantage of the organization's lack of expertise or inadequate monitoring. Risks from opportunism are especially high when the outsourcing contract is not well structured. Outsourcing may also hurt the morale of the remaining workforce. Finally, there are risks related to confidentiality. Outsourcing vendors must ensure that sensitive information is properly protected. This is both a technical and human problem. Even when the proper technical security measures are in place, the employees of the service provider can compromise confidentiality. The benefits and risks of outsourcing are summarized in Table 10.1.

Making the Outsourcing Decision

The decision whether to outsource is very complex and depends greatly on the particular set of circumstances. There are some consistent factors that should be considered (Grover & Teng, 1993):

Table 10.1   Benefits and Risks of Outsourcing

Benefits of Outsourcing:	Risks of Outsourcing
• Access to expertise not available in-house	• Loss of internal competencies
• Potential cost savings	• Becoming dependent on service provider (lowers bargaining power)
• Shifting fixed costs to variable costs	• Opportunistic behavior by service provider
• Effective way to manage capacity	• Lower morale of remaining workers
• Focus on core activities	• Confidentiality may be compromised
• Potential for 24-hour productivity	

• *How mature is the IT system in question?*
  Systems that have been around a long time are better candidates for outsourcing. There are several reasons for this. First, if the system is mature, you are less likely to be able to gain a competitive advantage from the system. Second, it is easier to find competent vendors for mature systems. This also means that you are more likely to have a choice of vendors, which is helpful during negotiations both initially and in the future.

• *How significant is the system to the organization's competitive advantage?*
  One common reason for outsourcing is to allow the organization to concentrate on core activities. Outsourcing is more suitable for systems that do not provide

---

BUSINESS BOX   **REVERSING THE OUTSOURCING DECISION**

In 2005, Houston, Texas–based utility Reliant Energy outsourced some of its IT jobs to Accenture. As a result, Reliant cut approximately one-third of its 340 IT jobs. In 2009, Reliant reversed this decision and began hiring IT workers so it could bring the outsourced work back in-house. Neither Reliant or Accenture would comment on the reason for the reversal.

   While still relatively rare, there are numerous other examples of "backsourcing" (bringing a previously outsourced function back in-house). In 2004, JPMorgan Chase cancelled a multibillion dollar outsourcing contract with IBM. IBM lost another contract when the UK Automobile Association canceled a £50 million outsourcing contract. In both of these cases, mergers were cited as the reason for the backsourcing. Poor performance can also cause backsourcing. In 2005, Sears Roebuck cancelled a $1.6 billion contract with Computer Sciences Corporation due to what Sears claimed was a failure to meet obligations.

Sources: http://www.reuters.com/article/2010/01/30/urnidgns852573c400693880002576ba 006e69d-idUS96268580820100130

http://www.computerweekly.com/Articles/2007/09/24/226946/AA-cancels-16350m-IBM-outsourcing-contract.htm

http://www.smh.com.au/news/Breaking/Sears-cancels-big-outsourcing-contract/2005/05/20/1116533524145.html

a competitive advantage. There is also greater risk of loss of control when you outsource strategic systems; problems with strategic systems usually have serious consequences.

- *How does the organization's IT capability compare with competitors'?*
  In cases where an organization has relatively weak IT capabilities it may be better to outsource. This is particularly true if the organization is weak in IT related to the system in question.

- *Are there cost advantages to outsourcing?*
  Of course, the question of costs is also important. Even if there are no savings through outsourcing, it may still be a good idea if outsourcing allows the organization to focus on critical areas or if the organization lacks the necessary capabilities.

Geographic Considerations

Where to outsource is an important aspect of outsourcing. (Note that choosing a vendor is also important, but here we focus on location.) **Offshore outsourcing** involves using a vendor that provides services from a location outside the client organization's region. A U.S. computer manufacturer outsourcing technical support to India is an example of offshore outsourcing. This is often done to reduce costs. Developing countries have much lower wages than developed countries, so offshore outsourcing can be very cost effective. However, there may be a backlash to offshore outsourcing. This can be a result of customers being upset about jobs being sent overseas. Resistance can also come from poor language skills or cultural differences. Language and cultural differences, along with distance, can make offshore outsourcing arrangements difficult to manage.

    Nearshore outsourcing is similar to offshore outsourcing. The difference is that nearshore outsourcing occurs close to the client's home location. If a U.S. company outsources to a Canadian firm, this would be a nearshore arrangement. The reduced travel times may make management easier. Cultural and language differences may be reduced, but this is not always the case. A U.S. company outsourcing to Mexico may still face considerable language and cultural barriers. A nearshore arrangement often results when a company wants to gain some of the cost savings of offshore outsourcing while reducing some of the management, language, and cultural difficulties.

    Onshore outsourcing is outsourcing to a firm located in the same country. Onshore outsourcing may offer significant cost savings while eliminating the cultural and language barriers of offshore outsourcing. In addition, onshore outsourcing is less likely to bring about a customer backlash since the jobs are staying in the country. Cost savings result from differences in wage rates for different areas of a country. Wages in rural areas are often considerably lower than in urban areas. According to Rural American Outsourcing, Inc. (http://www.ruralamericaonshore. com/) rural onshore outsourcing can save 40% over urban areas and is only 17% more costly than offshore outsourcing.

CHAPTER SUMMARY

- Software development methodologies provide discipline to the development process by defining processes, roles, and deliverables.

- The traditional systems development life cycle is a semi-sequential, phased approach. There are different versions of the traditional SDLC.

- The SDLC described in this chapter consists of six phases: planning, requirements, design, development, implementation, and maintenance.

- Alternatives to the traditional SDLC include prototyping, rapid application development, and the Spiral Model.

- The decision whether to build custom software or purchase commercial, off-the-shelf software is complex.

- Open source software allows users to access the underlying source code for the application, which allows users to modify the program.

- Open source software is usually free, although some companies charge a fee for ongoing support or enhancements.

- Outsourcing occurs when an outside organization provides IT services that were previously provided internally.

- Outsourcing models include full (complete), process-based, personnel, project-based, and application outsourcing.

- There are both benefits and risks associated with outsourcing.

- Factors affecting the outsourcing decision include the maturity of the system, the system's significance to the organization's competitive advantage, the organizations IT capability, and cost.

- Offshore outsourcing occurs when an organization receives services from a company outside the organization's geographic region.

- Nearshore outsourcing occurs when an organization receives services from a company within the organization's geographic region, but outside its home country.

- Onshore outsourcing occurs when an organization receives services from a company in the same country.

REVIEW QUESTIONS

1. What is the major benefit of a software development methodology?
2. What aspects of software development does a methodology specify?
3. Name and briefly describe the phases of the systems development life cycle described in the chapter.

4. Name and briefly describe the aspects of feasibility described in the chapter.

5. Name and describe three alternatives to the traditional SDLC.

6. Name the advantages and disadvantages of each of the software development methodologies described in the chapter.

7. List the advantages and disadvantages of custom, COTS, and hybrid approaches to software.

8. List the main characteristics of custom-built and commercial, off-the-shelf software.

9. What are the main factors to consider when deciding whether to build or purchase software?

10. Define open source software.

11. What advantages does open source software offer to businesses?

12. List and briefly describe the outsourcing models presented in the chapter.

13. List the major benefits and risks of outsourcing.

14. What factors should organizations consider when deciding whether to outsource?

15. How do offshore, nearshore, and onshore outsourcing differ?

REFLECTION QUESTIONS

1. What is the most important thing you learned in this chapter? Why is it important?

2. What topics are unclear? What about them is unclear?

3. What relationships do you see between what you learned in this chapter and what you have learned in earlier chapters?

4. How is the traditional systems development life cycle related to systems theory? (Recall that you learned about systems theory in Chapter 2.)

5. What is the difference between functional and nonfunctional requirements? Why are they both important? Which do you think is harder to determine? Why?

6. Your organization needs to build a system to help users carry out a business process that is very unique to your organization.
   a. Should your organization build this system from scratch or use COTS? Why? What additional information would be helpful in making this decision?
   b. Do you think this should be outsourced? Why? What additional information would be helpful in making this decision?

7. Commercial, off-the-shelf software is often of higher quality than custom-built software. This is especially true if the COTS is widely used.
   a. Why might COTS be higher quality?
   b. Why would this be more likely if the COTS is widely used?

8. What ethical issues are related to the decision to outsource a function? Are these issues different for offshore, nearshore, and onshore outsourcing?

9. There have been several instances of software development companies making formerly proprietary software open source. (See http://en.wikipedia.org/wiki/List_of_formerly_proprietary_software for a partial list of proprietary software that has been shifted to open source.) Why would a software development company do this? What would the company potentially gain? What would it potentially lose?

ADDITIONAL LEARNING ACTIVITIES

1. Form groups of two or three:
   - One of you (the *explainer)* answer the following question: What are possible consequences of incorrect or poorly stated requirements?
   - When the first person finishes, the other person (the *questioner*) seeks clarification and provides her/his own ideas.
   - Record and be prepared to share your answer.

2. You need to recommend a software development methodology for an upcoming project. From the methodologies presented in this chapter, choose a methodology for each of the following projects. Briefly provide the rationale for each choice.

   a. A system for monitoring electrical surges in an electrical power grid. The requirements for the system are well understood. Users will be required to use the system.
   b. A contact management system. The systems potential users are unsure of exactly what they want the system to do. Use of the system will be voluntary.
   c. A relatively small order tracking system. The objectives of the system are well known, and potential users very much want such a system.

3. For each of the following, recommend whether the organization should build or buy the system in question. Explain your recommendation.

   a. A medium-sized company that sells roofing materials to contractors needs a system that will allow customers to check product inventory through a website.
   b. A large (Fortune 500) retailer with a large, well-skilled IT department needs a system that will track the purchasing habits of its frequent customers.
   c. A large (Fortune 500) defense contractor needs a system that will track payments to vendors.

4. For each of the systems described in #3 above, what additional information would be useful in making your recommendation? Explain why the information would help in the build vs. buy decision.

5. Locate open source alternatives for each of the following:

   a. Microsoft Access database management system
   b. Microsoft Outlook (email)
   c. Adobe Photoshop
   d. Salesforce.com customer relationship management system
   e. iTunes media player

6. Find two examples of backsourcing (bringing back in-house previously outsourced functions or personnel) other than the examples described in the chapter. Provide a brief (one-paragraph) description of each. Include the reason for the backsourcing in your description.

7. Find two examples of outsourcing (do not include examples from the chapter). Provide a brief (one-paragraph) description of the outsourcing arrangement. Include the reason for outsourcing in your description. Also, indicate which outsourcing model best describes the example.

REFERENCES

Boehm, B. "A Spiral Model of Software Development and Enhancement," *IEEE Computer*, 21(5), (1988), 61–72.

Grover, V., and J.T.CTeng, "The Decision to Outsource Information Systems Function. *Journal of Systems Management*, (1993), 44(11), 34–38.

GLOSSARY

Application outsourcing: an outsourcing arrangement that involves a service provider handling activities related to a specific software application.

Full Outsourcing: outsourcing arrangement where an organization contracts with a service provider to provide all IT-related services.

Functional requirements: describes how a system should interact with users and other systems.

Nearshore outsourcing: using a vendor that provides services from a location close the client's location.

Nonfunctional requirements: constraints on a system.

Offshore outsourcing: using a vendor that provides services from a location outside the client organization's region.

Onshore outsourcing: outsourcing to a firm located in the same country.

Open source software: software that allows users to access the underlying source code for an application.

Personnel outsourcing: outsourcing arrangement in which a service provider places workers into an organization on a temporary contract basis.

Process-based outsourcing: organization outsources a particular function or business process.

Project-based outsourcing: outsourcing arrangement that involves contracting with a service provider to complete a specific project.

Prototype: a small-scale mock-up of a system or a portion of a system.

Requirements elicitation: gathering system requirements from various stakeholders.

Selective (partial) outsourcing: An outsourcing arrangement in which only certain aspects of IT are outsourced to a service provider.

Software development methodology: framework for planning, structuring, and controlling software development projects.

Source code: text-based computer programming language statements that can be read by humans.

Systems development life cycle (SDLC): semi-sequential, phased approach to systems development.

Use case: describes a series of actions that results in an outcome for an actor.

Information-Based Business Processes

CHAPTER 11

LEARNING OBJECTIVES

By reading and completing the activities in this chapter, students should be able to:

- Explain what a business process is
- Perform business process modeling
- Discuss the impacts of technology on business processes
- Explain how business process improvement can be achieved with Business Process Reengineering (BPR)

CHAPTER OUTLINE

- References

- Bibliography and further readings

- Glossary

FOCUSING STORY: IMPROVING PROCESSES IS FOR EVERYONE!

This book is about information, and many of our examples seem to showcase technology companies. However, when we talk about business processes, or the way things are done in organizations, everyone can benefit from improvements, even companies that are in basic manufacturing industries like the cement industry.

Cemex is a 100-year-old multinational cement corporation based in Monterrey, Mexico. For years it functioned pretty much like every other cement company, with limited communications between its various plants, constantly changing order information (customers cannot pour concrete on bad weather days), and having a difficult time confirming precise deliveries to customers due to weather, traffic, and labor problems. Needless to say, customer satisfaction is not always high in this industry.

When Lorenzo Zambrano, the grandson of Cemex's founder, was appointed CEO, he looked for ways to improve processes. To handle unpredictable demands and changing conditions, the company realized they needed better real-time communications. They therefore implemented a satellite communication system (which they called Cemexnet) to connect all of their cement plants. They also linked all offices via satellite and the Internet, and created a central office for coordination. This allowed plants to be constantly aware of fluctuating supply and demand. The second main aspect of the overhaul was to develop a new tracking, scheduling and routing system (which they called Dynamic Synchronization of Operations). This logistics application uses GPS transmitters in each delivery truck, allowing dispatchers to allocate trucks to the plants closest to where they are at a given time. With detailed information on traffic conditions, inventory, and the customers' location, trucks can be rerouted as needed. Finally, suppliers, distributors, and customers of Cemex can use an online application to check order status.

The results have been impressive for Cemex: decreased delivery time span from 3 hours to 20 minutes (98% of the time), increased customer satisfaction, substantial increases in net sales, decreased number of delivery trucks (35% decrease in the first year), and substantial cost savings overall (think fuel, maintenance, and payroll).

DISCUSSION QUESTIONS:

Identify specific ways in which the new technologies at Cemex changed how

- customers do business with Cemex

- delivery truck drivers do their work

- office staff work at Cemex

- plant managers handle business at Cemex

Source: Kaplan, Simone. "Business Process Improvement at Concrete Co. Cemex." *CIO Magazine* (August 15, 2001). http://www.cio.com/article/print/30445 3/17/2011/.

LEARNING ACTIVITY 11.1	HOW MANY STEPS IN THIS PROCESS?

The organization you work for sells university-trademarked items to various consumers. It has traditionally sold goods through the bookstore, but is now going to sell items (clothing, memorabilia, etc.) online. In this activity, your group represents a team of managers assembled to identify all of the steps involved in managing the inventory for supporting the sale of goods online. Identify all of the steps and substeps necessary for this to occur. Make a list of all of the steps you think of.

What Is a Process?

A **process** is a series of steps or tasks required to achieve a specific goal. The definition of the word "process" in the dictionary is a "series of actions, changes, or functions bringing about a result." In organizations, everything that happens is based on a series of processes or key activities. They are often called *business processes*, but they could more precisely be labeled *organizational processes*, since processes exist not only in businesses, but also in government agencies, charities, schools, and other noncommercial organizations. Figure 11.1 shows an example of a process, the process of acquiring materials needed for the production of an enterprise's main goods. It should be noted that while the process looks to be linear, it is not necessarily the case, since several activities can take place at the same time (concurrently).

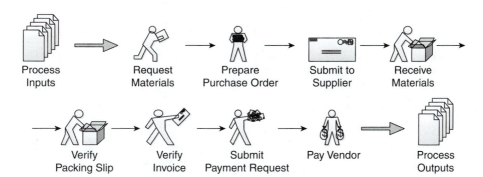

| Process Inputs | Request Materials | Prepare Purchase Order | Submit to Supplier | Receive Materials |

| Verify Packing Slip | Verify Invoice | Submit Payment Request | Pay Vendor | Process Outputs |

FIGURE 11.1 Example of a Process to Acquire Materials

Processes are not limited to one functional area of the organization. For example, in Figure 11.1, it is likely that a production department will request materials, while an accounting department will pay vendors. This is an important point: Processes extend across many organizational boundaries and tend to involve several individuals. Another key characteristic of processes is the **all-or-nothing concept.** This implies that a process needs to be completed or not done at all. Looking again at Figure 11.1, requesting materials requires purchase orders, receiving materials, and so on. The process is not complete if there is no payment request or no payment made.

Every business process can usually be decomposed into several tasks, also called **sub-processes**. This is because processes usually require several decisions and actions to be made along the way. In general, there can be several levels of sub-processes, all the way down to specific activities or tasks. For example, in the process shown in Figure 11.1, the sub-process of verifying the invoice involves viewing the invoice, viewing the ordering information, and comparing what was ordered with the charges. It can involve making sure that the proper discounts are given, which can require several steps (searching for discounts, comparing quantities, etc.) (See Figure 11.2 for some possible sub-processes).

Mapping the processes and subprocesses is called process modeling, which we describe in more detail below. There are many examples of processes you are familiar with even if you do not realize they are considered processes. Think of course registration. What are the various steps involved? You need to identify the courses required for your program and the requirements for each course. You must then login to the registration system, enter your information, and make the requests. Next you need to react to those requests that were denied. You can appeal them, try to force-add the course, or decide to take a different course. There are also processes for requesting transcripts, updating your personal information, or for professors to enter grades, just to name a few.

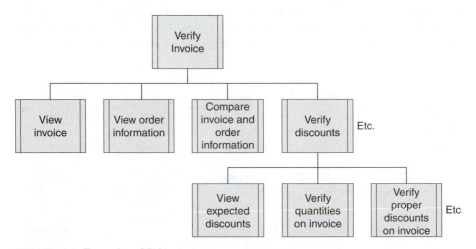

FIGURE 11.2 Examples of Subprocesses

Process Modeling

Process modeling is the mapping of processes and subprocesses used in an organization or division. Examine the process of acquiring materials needed for the production of an enterprise's main goods in Figure 11.1. Only the steps involved are identified. In process modeling, we need to expand the steps to identify when they are occurring, and which decisions are involved. We must also recognize if there are any relationships between processes. The bottom line is that understanding the various processes that occur at different levels in the organization and how they interrelate is necessary to really understand how an organization works. Figure 11.3 shows a process model for customers acquiring goods from a firm.

A process model should clearly describe what happens as a process is performed. As analysts are modeling the processes, they should not analyze the process for improvements (yet); the goal is to describe the process as is. Process modeling can also be explanatory, in that the process modeling effort can identify the rationale

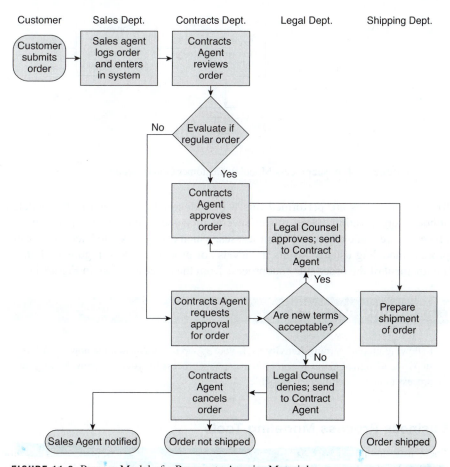

FIGURE 11.3 Process Model of a Process to Acquire Materials

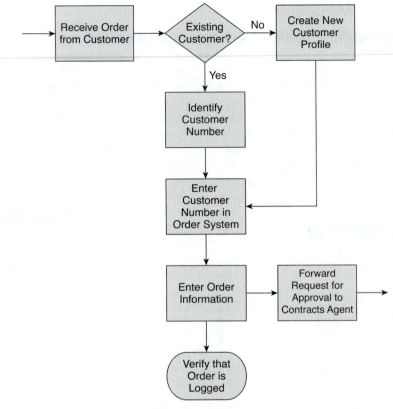

FIGURE 11.4 A Subprocess Model of Customer Goods Acquisition

for why processes are performed this way. Individual processes can be modeled, although organizations often model several processes simultaneously. Recall that processes are made of several subprocesses, which can also be modeled. As a result, process modeling usually results in "levels" of process models. Figure 11.4 shows a refinement of the order entry subprocess from the process shown in Figure 11.3.

LEARNING ACTIVITY 11.2   MODEL THIS!

Following up on Learning Activity 11.1, your group of managers must now model the steps you identified in the inventory management process for your company. Make your process model as complete as possible.

Business Process Modeling Tools

There are many **process modeling tools** and software available to help analysts describe business processes and create business process models or diagrams. Mili et al. (2010)

Table 11.1   Examples of Business Process Modeling Tools (Mili et al. 2010)

Category of Modeling Tool	Description	Sample Languages
Traditional process modeling languages	Software engineering and information systems modeling languages mostly used in business process engineering.	• Event Process Chains (EPC) • Role Activity Diagrams (RAD) • Resource-Event-Agent (REA) • Architectural Modeling Box for Enterprise Redesign (AMBER)
Object-oriented modeling languages	Process modeling languages supporting the object-oriented approach to software development.	• Object-Oriented Role Analysis Methodology (OORAM) • Enterprise Distributed Object Computing (EDOC) • Unified Modeling Language (UML) 1 and 2
Dynamic process modeling languages	Process modeling language standards proposed by various—mostly industrial—organizations.	• Workflow Process Description Language (WPDL) • Business Process Modeling Language (BPML) • Web Services Business Process Execution Language (WS-BPEL) • Business Process Modeling Notation (BPMN) • Business Process Definition Metamodel (BPDM)
Process integration languages	Process modeling languages for the purposes of integrating the processes of two or more business partners in electronic business.	• RosettaNet • Electronic Business Extensible Markup Language (ebXML) • Web Services Choreography Description Language (WS-CDL)

Source: **Mili et al. 2010.**

identify four types of such tools: traditional process modeling languages, object-oriented modeling languages, dynamic process modeling languages, and process integration languages. Table 11.1 describes these various categories and shows some examples of these languages.

Analysts can become well versed in some of the languages presented in Table 11.1, but to facilitate business process modeling, several companies have developed software specifically targeted at creating business process models. Table 11.2 shows a few of the popular process modeling companies and software. There are many more companies and software tools available. You can get an updated list at the Workflow and Reengineering International Association's website (http://www .waria.com/).

Table 11.2 Sample Business Process Modeling Companies and Software Products

Company	Product	Address
Corel Corporation	DESIGNER® Technical Suite X5.	http://www.corel.com/
CSG International	Business Support Systems	http://www.csgsystems.com/
Global 360	AnalystView	http://www.global360.com/ products/process-discovery-analysis/
Interfacing Technology	Enterprise Process Center	http://www.interfacing.com/
KBSI, Knowledge Based Systems Inc.	Business Process Solutions (several)	http://www.kbsi.com/COTS/ BusinessProcesses.htm/
Microsoft Corporation	Visio Modeling Software	http://www.microsoft.com/en-us/ visio/
OpenText	Business Process Management	http://www.opentext.com/2/global/ products/products-business-process-management.htm/
Oracle Corporation	Oracle Business Process Management	http://www.oracle.com/us/ technologies/bpm/index.html
Silverrun BPM	Silverrun Modeling Tools	http://www.silverrun.com/
Software AG	Business Process Excellence	http://www.softwareag.com/

Technology and Processes

Business processes have existed since organizations started to organize work activities into tasks. Today, however, information technologies play an ever-increasing role in how business processes are performed, since technology is embedded in most work environments, but also in how business processes are modified or improved. We discuss business process improvement in the next section. Before we discuss how things can be done better, however, it is important to realize that technology is not only enabling new business processes but can also be a barrier or constraint to business process improvement.

Think about how much the tasks individuals do in organizations are dependent on how the technology they use functions. It might be more efficient to input data a certain way, but the system will not let you do it. It could be useful to create a new report, but the system does not allow collating the data appropriately. This is even more visible when we talk about legacy systems. Recall from the previous chapters that **legacy systems** are often older, large applications that may be mission critical. They are hard to replace and can be somewhat inflexible. In addition, they are often still used to support key business processes. Even if an organization creates a new graphical friendlier interface to access information, what can be done with the information can be highly dependent on the type of data warehouse or application performing the back-office processing.

Process Improvement

Once business processes are properly modeled, they can be analyzed for improvement. Business process improvement is an important goal for managers, and it is often labeled **Business Process Reengineering (BPR)**. BPR involves the redesign of business processes to improve how work is done, which of course means that BPR requires that business process modeling be done well first. It is important to realize that BPR often involves changing the way tasks are performed instead of just automating the tasks. It requires rethinking about what is done and how it is done (and even whether it should be done!). In one of their books on BPR, Michael Hammer and James Champy (2003) suggest that BPR involves the fundamental rethinking (really asking why an organization performs tasks in a certain way) and radical redesign of business processes (meaning that there is re-invention or re-creation, not just simple minor changes done) in order to obtain dramatic improvements in performance (meaning that the goal is to achieve significant improvements for the organization whether in terms of cost, efficiency, satisfaction, or other important measures).

There are usually four key areas for business process improvement: effectiveness, efficiency, internal control, and compliance. These goals are summarized in Table 11.3.

Summarizing our discussion so far, it is clear that BPR involves several phases, and just like our strategic planning process did in Chapter 4, it starts with a clear vision of what the goal of the redesign is. It follows with an understanding of what the current processes are, how they work, who performs them, and who uses their outcomes. At the same time, redesign involves rethinking business processes, so analysts should not end up limiting themselves by focusing too much on how things are done as opposed how they should be done. Finally, a very important part of the redesign process is ensuring that there are measurements to make

Table 11.3 Typical Goals for Business Process Reengineering

Effectiveness	The extent to which the expected outputs of the process are obtained as expected.
Efficiency	The average time it takes for the process to be completed.
Internal Control	The extent to which the information and data used in the performance of the process cannot be changed by error or illegally.
Compliance	The extent to which the process follows the regulatory or statutory obligations of the organization.

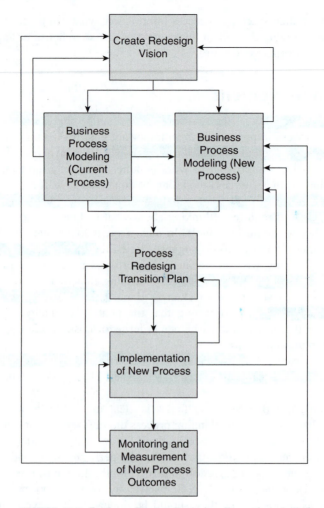

FIGURE 11.5 Business Process Redesign (Reengineering) Stages

certain that improvements are indeed being made. As you can expect, the Business Process Redesign effort is an iterative process where what is done or found in later stages may result in the need to revisit earlier stages. Figure 11.5 shows a sample BPR process.

Remember that in the end, managers performing BPR need to ask themselves key questions like: What are our key business processes? Do we have to execute each process? How can we use information technologies to perform these processes in better ways? And, what are the likely impacts of the business process redesign? The result of a business process improvement effort should be a document that defines how the new business processes should or could be performed, indicating clear rules and guidelines that the processes must or should follow. For organizations, the results of a redesign of

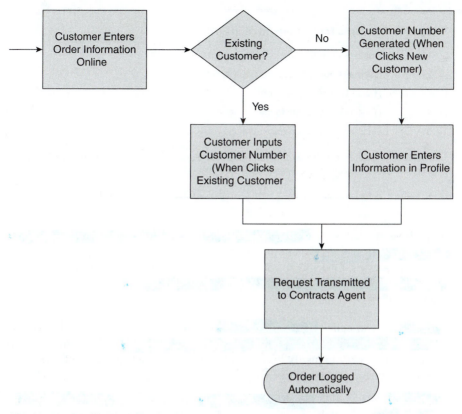

FIGURE 11.6 Online Ordering Redesign

business processes often means streamlined ways of doing business. Figure 11.6 shows an example of the redesign of the business process from Figure 11.4 once the organization offers online ordering.

Levels of Change

In Chapter 4, we introduced the idea that information technology can be implemented in organizations for strategic purposes, or in other words to create

---

STATISTICS BOX 1: IMPORTANCE OF PROCESS REDESIGN

Improving business processes is a very important concern for chief information officers. Almost every year, the Society for Information Management (SIM) asks its members (top management IT executives) what their top concerns are. As can be seen from the table below, business process reengineering is one of the top concerns of IT leaders surveyed in June 2010.

(*continued*)

Top Five Concerns for IT Executives in 2010

1	Business productivity and cost reduction
2	Business agility and speed to market
3	IT and business alignment
4	IT reliability and efficiency
5	Business process reengineering

Source: Luftman, Jerry and Tal Ben-Zvi. "Key Issues for IT Executives 2010: Judicious IT Investments Continue Post-Recession." *MIS Quarterly Executive* 9 (4) (Dec 2010): 263–273.

---

competitive advantages. When new IT is implemented, it can have differing effects on organizations depending on the role it plays in changing or supporting business processes. One way to categorize these impacts is whether they represent changes that automate, informate, or transform organizations (Dehning et al, 2003; Schein, 1992).

- *Automate,* also called *first order change,* involves using technology to perform a process more efficiently, often by replacing human labor with technology. It is usually fairly easy to justify because managers can quantify the benefits (such as reduced wages, reduced errors, etc.).

- *Informate,* also called *second order change,* involves using technology to better inform people, which as a result can change how they perform business processes. Whenever people have to change how they perform business processes, it is more difficult to implement systems. Recall from our earlier discussions that people often resist technology implementations when they have to change their work habits.

- *Transform,* also called *third order change,* requires a fundamental redefinition of the business processes, or how work is done. Obviously, since Business Process Reengineering (BPR) involves the redesign of business processes, it is a third order change. This is the most difficult level of change to deal with when implementing information systems.

LEARNING ACTIVITY 11.3   REDESIGN THIS!

This activity builds on what you have accomplished in Learning Activity 11.2. Now that your team of managers has become more familiar with the inventory management system, and has gained knowledge on business process improvement, your team should perform a redesign of the business process model you previously completed.

BUSINESS EXAMPLE BOX 1	CHOICECARE PHYSICIANS: CHANGING ACCESS TO PATIENT RECORDS

Most students have gone to small doctors' offices where the receptionists and nurses have folders marked with different colors that contain tons of details about you, including a variety of paper charts. ChoiceCare Physicians, an eight-doctor private practice, is one of those offices that had a very large room specifically dedicated to storing all of the charts and reports needed by doctors, nurses, and staff. When staff needed to access documents, they had to look for the charts that, depending on the situation, could be in a variety of locations. This was quite inefficient when patients called for results, with documents sometimes logged in the existing system, and sometimes not because they were not yet completed. Similarly, insurance companies would request documents that were in different formats and locations. Staff had to spend a significant amount of time finding these different documents, if they could be found. In the end, it was easy to misplace a document and it was very hard to find other documents.

To solve this situation, ChoiceCare implemented a document management system that allowed them to digitize all documents and store them together in one place. Staff personnel register every document in a digital format as the document is created, filled, or signed. When anyone (with proper access) needs a document, it can be easily accessed as needed. Since the documents are digitized, it is harder to lose them (with proper backup facilities) and easier to find them (since they can be indexed and/or searched). The system also avoids duplication of files for a same patient since the document management system can flagged a file that has a similar name.

Source: "Change Unmanageable Work-Flow Procedures." *Health Management Technology* 31(4) (April 2010): 18–19.

CHAPTER SUMMARY

In this chapter, we explained more in depth what business processes are, how they can be modeled, and how organizations seek to improve business processes through Business Process Reengineering (BPR). More specifically, we discussed the following:

- A business process is a series of steps or tasks required to achieve a specific business goal of organizations.

- Business process modeling is the mapping of processes and subprocesses used in an organization or division. We demonstrated business process modeling with graphic models of a materials acquisition process and its subprocesses. Business process modeling helps us understand the various processes that occur at different levels in the organization and how they interrelate.

- Technology impacts business processes because it is embedded in how work is done in most work environments. Technology could be a constraint to business processes, especially when legacy systems are involved.

- Business process improvement can be achieved with Business Process Reengineering (BPR), which involves the redesign of business processes to improve how work is done. BPR often involves changing the way tasks are performed instead of just automating the tasks. There are usually four key areas for business process improvement: effectiveness, efficiency, internal control, and compliance.

REVIEW QUESTIONS

1. Explain what a business process is and give an example from your school environment.
2. Identify some of the important characteristics of processes.
3. What is business process modeling and what is the purpose of business process modeling?
4. Identify some of the important characteristics of a process model.
5. What kinds of tools are available for business process modeling?
6. How does technology impact business processes?
7. What is Business Process Reengineering (BPR) and what does it involve?
8. What are the four key areas for business process improvement?
9. Briefly explain the main steps involved in performing business process redesign.
10. What are some of the results expected from a business redesign effort?

REFLECTION QUESTIONS

1. What is the most important thing you learned in this chapter? Why is it important?
2. What topics are unclear? What about them is unclear?
3. Identify all of the processes a student encounters during the first week of class as a freshman.
4. How does the material in this chapter (business processes) relate to security topics in Chapter 8?
5. How does the material in this chapter (business processes) relate to privacy topics in Chapter 9?
6. Can all business processes be redesigned? Why or why not?
7. What are the similarities and differences between process modeling as discussed in this chapter, and data modeling as discussed in Chapter 5?
8. Should informal business processes (representing how things are really done, even if they do not follow recognized or documented procedures) be modeled or just formalized (documented by the organization)?
9. What would be an example of technology being a barrier to redesign in a school setting?
10. Why do you think business process reengineering is an important concern for CIOs?

ADDITIONAL LEARNING ACTIVITIES

1. This activity allows students to get some additional practice at business process redesign. First, you need to download the template of one of the business processes (your instructor will tell you which one) from Global 360: http://www.global360.com/process-templates/. In small groups, examine the template, and then with business process redesign in mind, modify the business process you downloaded to improve it.

2. This activity requires you to complete a case analysis regarding business processes. The case may be accessed through your university website, the Ivey School business case website (http://cases.ivey.uwo.ca), the Harvard Business school cases website (http://cb.hbsp.harvard.edu/cb/web), or may be provided to you by your instructor.

   Raghu, T.S. CASE: "Creating a Process-Oriented Enterprise at Pinnacle West." *Ivey School of Business* Product number: 910E02-PDF-ENG, Feb 05, 2010.

3. Examine Figure 11.2, identify one of the subprocesses of the order entry process and model it, as was done in Figure 11.4 for the order entry part in the sales department.

4. Select one of the key processes needed at your school and model it. You can select from one from the following list: class registration, final grade assignment, student enrollment, tuition payment, requesting transcripts; or you can identify another important process and model it.

5. Use the process modeling tools in the Visio software to create your models in Learning Activities 11.A3 or 11.A4.

REFERENCES

Dehning, Bruce, Vernon J. Richardson, and Robert W. Zmud, "The Value Relevance Of Announcements Of Transformational Information Technology Investments, *MIS Quarterly* 27 (4). (December 2003): 637–656.

Hammer, Michael and James Champy. *Reengineering the Corporation: A Manifesto for Business Revolution*. New York, NY: HarperCollins, 2003.

Mili, Hafedh, Guy Tremblay, Guitta Bou Jaoude, Éric Lefebvre, Lamia Elabed, and Ghizlane El Boussaidi. "Business Process Modeling Languages: Sorting Through the Alphabet Soup." *ACM Computing Surveys* 43(1). (Nov 2010): 7–62.

Schein, E. H. "The Role of the CEO in the Management of Change: The Case of Information Technology," in *Transforming Organizations*, T. A. Kochan and M. Useem (eds.), Oxford University Press, Oxford, (1992): 325–345.

BIBLIOGRAPHY AND FURTHER READINGS

Global 3060. *Business Process Modeling Demos*. http://www.global360.com/resource-center/tours/.

Business Processes: http://publib.boulder.ibm.com/infocenter/dmndhelp/v6rxmx/index.jsp?topic=/com.ibm.wbit.help.bpel.ui.doc/concepts/cunder.html/.

GLOSSARY

All-or-nothing concept: idea that a process needs to be completed or not done at all.

Business Process Reengineering (BPR): redesign of business processes to improve how work is done.

Compliance: BPR goal that involves the extent to which the process follows the regulatory or statutory obligations of the organization.

Dynamic process modeling languages: process modeling language standards proposed by various (mostly industrial) organizations.

Effectiveness: BPR goal that involves the extent to which the expected outputs of the process are obtained as expected.

Efficiency: BPR goal that looks at the average time it takes for the process to be completed.

Internal Control: BPR goal that involves the extent to which the information and data used in the performance of the process cannot be changed by error or illegally.

Legacy systems: older, large applications that may be mission-critical.

Object-oriented languages: process modeling languages supporting the object-oriented approach to software development.

Process: series of steps or tasks required to achieve a specific goal.

Process integration languages: process modeling languages for the purposes of integrating the processes of two or more business partners in electronic business.

Process modeling tool: tools and software available to help analysts describe business processes and create business process models or diagrams.

Process modeling: mapping of processes and subprocesses used in an organization or division.

Subprocesses: decomposition of business processes into several tasks.

Traditional process modeling languages: software engineering and information systems modeling languages mostly used in business process engineering.

CHAPTER 12

Enterprise Information Systems

LEARNING OBJECTIVES

By reading and completing the activities in this chapter, students should be able to:

- Identify the main characteristics and types of enterprise systems

- Discuss the purposes of Enterprise Resource Planning (ERP) systems

- Explain the purposes and functioning of supply chain management systems (SCM)

- Identify the components of customer relationship management (CRM) systems

- Apply the customer life cycle concepts to customer relationship management (CRM)

CHAPTER OUTLINE

- Customer relationship management systems

  Customer service life cycle

  Components of CRM

- Learning Activity 12.4: Self-servicing

  CRM implementation options

  Benefits and limitations of CRM

- Customer managed interactions (CMI)

- Chapter summary

- Review questions

- Reflection questions

- Additional learning activities

- References

- Bibliography and further readings

- Glossary

FOCUSING STORY: SUPPLY CHAIN INNOVATIONS AT WAL-MART

You need a new pair of inexpensive jeans or maybe just a new set of travel speakers for your iPod. Where would you go to buy these? Many students would turn to a local Wal-Mart store since the company is well known throughout the world as a low-cost retailer of goods. What makes it possible for the company to offer prices that often seem to be well below what competitors can afford to offer? Of course, there are many answers to this, but one of the most important factors is how Wal-Mart manages the way it gets the products sold in its stores. This is the supply chain. Wal-Mart calls this the *productivity loop*: lower cost products lead to lower prices for consumers, which lead to more sales, which increase profits; and then they repeat the loop as quickly as possible. However, there are many other benefits for Wal-Mart and its partners in the supply chain, as explained below.

Wal-Mart is well known for its innovative strategies regarding its supply chain and its tight management of its distribution channels. By 2010, Wal-Mart had established four very large global merchandising centers that are responsible for ordering goods and clothing (also called *sourcing*) products for the company's stores in 15 countries. It also uses direct purchasing of fresh fruits and vegetables from producers on a global basis, bypassing traditional suppliers.

Wal-Mart's supply chain strategies cover many aspects, but in a speech given at the Council of Supply Chain Management Professionals (CSCMP) annual conference in 2009, Gary Maxwell, then senior vice president of International Supply at Wal-Mart, explained that effective inventory management may be the most critical element to master for an efficient supply chain.

To improve the effectiveness of its supply chain, Wal-Mart mandated in 2003 that its largest suppliers use **RFID (Radio Frequency Identification Tags)**. This required suppliers to insert electronic tags on pallets of goods to be shipped to Wal-Mart. Using readers, both Wal-Mart and the supplier can then track the pallets as they move through the various distribution centers all the way to the store. Wal-Mart has been a leader in the development of the RFID technology. However, while it has successfully reduced out-of-stock items (8% worldwide) and improved its overall inventory data (they can resupply three times faster), the adoption of the technology was slower than expected. For many companies, the cost was quite high (from US$100,000 to US$300,000 for small companies to US$20 million for larger ones). In 2003, first-generation chips sold for US$1.25 each. In 2009, second-generation chips cost 7¢ to 10¢. By late 2008, 600 of Wal-Mart's 60,000 suppliers plus 750 Sam's Club (owned by Wal-Mart) suppliers deployed RFID to some degree. On Wal-Mart's end, RFID is deployed at about 1,000 of the roughly 4,000 Wal-Mart and Sam's Club stores in the United States.

Today, suppliers and Wal-Mart reap many other benefits from RFID, such as knowing in real-time how long it takes for items in the promotional areas of stores to sell. They can even evaluate where in the store items sell better. This is a win-win situation for Wal-Mart and suppliers. Some suppliers have even built the use of RFID tags into their whole IT infrastructure, from acquisition to sales to replenishment.

Wal-Mart continuously strives to innovate in its supply chain. Its most recent effort is convincing its suppliers that reducing gas emissions and becoming more "green" in their delivery of products to Wal-Mart can result in profitability and sustainability. Wal-Mart is asking some suppliers to report how much energy they use in manufacturing the products Wal-Mart buys from them, and requires them to meet stricter quality and environmental standards.

DISCUSSION QUESTIONS:

1. What do you believe are the key success factors for the supply chain implementation at Wal-Mart? What would be those factors for other companies trying to imitate Wal-Mart's supply chain efforts?

2. What is your assessment of Wal-Mart's move into RFID technology as a leader? Could there be an issue being at the leading edge of technology?

3. How can technology be used to help Wal-Mart in its next endeavor—its green supply chain?

Sources: Compiled from Berman, Jeff. "Wal-mart's Maxwell Cites Keys to Developing Best-in-Market Global Supply Chains." *Logistics Management* 48 (10) (Oct 2009): 18.; Birchall, Jonathan. "Wal-mart Takes Aim at Supply Chain Cost." *Financial Times* (Jan 4, 2010): 1.; Cassidy, William B. "Wal-Mart Squeezes Costs from Supply Chain." *Journal of Commerce* (Jan 5, 2010).; McCrea, Bridget. "This Is Why "Green" Equals Good Business." *Supply Chain Management Review* 14 (2) (Mar 2010): 56.; Webster, John S. "Wal-Mart's RFID Revolution a Tough Sell." *Network World* 25 (36) (Sep 15, 2008): 34–36.

LEARNING ACTIVITY 12.1	FINDING THE COMPONENTS OF AN ENTERPRISE SYSTEM

The Supply Chain Management System at Wal-Mart represents only one type of enterprise system companies can use for running their businesses efficiently. One of the most popular enterprise systems in organizations is Enterprise Resource Planning (ERP). We will discuss enterprise systems and ERP later, but for now, we want you to identify the components of an ERP system offered by the one of the larger companies such as SAP, Oracle PeopleSoft, or Microsoft Dynamics.

Please prepare a short report for class that identifies the company that sells the ERP, a brief background on the company, the components of the ERP system, and a brief description of each component. The report should be less than two pages long.

Enterprise Systems

Personal vs. Enterprise Systems

There are many information system applications used by individuals and companies to perform tasks. For example, if you think of applications you use that are for individuals only, you might find that Quickens is used to manage your finances, or that Microsoft Word is used to write your term papers. Those are considered **personal information systems**. Conversely, **enterprise systems** are information systems that serve the needs of the organization or parts of the organization. For example, the organization may use SAP's Enterprise Resource Planning (ERP) applications to manage the finances of the company, including paying bills, receiving invoices, and paying employees. In Learning Activity 12.1, you identified many other components of an ERP. As you recall, many modules are available to perform functions needed across several departments in the organization.

Three perspectives on developing enterprise systems have emerged: the hierarchical perspective, the functional perspective, and the process perspective (Piccoli, 2008).

In the **hierarchical perspective**, software developers build information systems to mirror the organization, so that applications are built to meet the needs of individuals at a given level in the organization. The idea is that executives need strategic types of information they can use for decision-making, whereas middle managers and front line managers need tactical and operational information respectively. Table 12.1 shows the type of information needed at each level and the characteristics of that information, which is also reproduced in Figure 12.1.

As a result, systems are built for operations, tactical, or strategic management, with sometimes limited interaction and consistency across these systems. Redundancy is also a problem, with different systems sometimes performing fairly similar functions.

Table 12.1   Types of Information Required by Hierarchical Level

Activity	Time Horizon	Hierarchical Level	Characteristics
Strategic	Long term	General management, Functional management	• Externally focused • Highly unstructured
Tactical	Mid term	Middle management	• Semi-structured • Recurrent
Operational	Short term	Operation management, Employees	• Highly structured • Transaction focused

Source: adapted from Piccoli, 2008.

In the **functional perspective**, information system applications are developed to meet the needs of individuals in a functional area, such as human resources or marketing. With this perspective, information system developers build a "financial" system, a "marketing" system, a "production" system, or a "human resources" system. The systems tend to serve the functional area well as they are customized to the needs of the department. Again, when thinking about the various functional areas in an organization (often called *departments*), you can see that information system applications built this way could result in redundancy and inaccuracy of data (think of having to update customer information in five different departments). This perspective also limits communication across functional areas.

Finally, in the **process perspective**, information systems applications are developed to support the task being done (or process) irrespective of the organizational level or functional area of the individual using the system. A process is a series of steps required to perform a task.

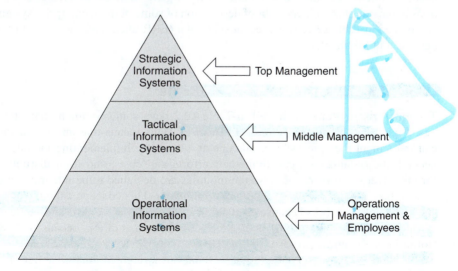

FIGURE 12.1 Hierarchical Information Systems

Integration and Enterprise Systems

The discussion of the three perspectives for the development of enterprise systems highlights some of the issues that arise when systems are not developed with the organization as a whole in mind. In particular, we discussed the issues of redundancy (identical data stored in multiple locations), and lack of communication across departments. To solve these problems, the process perspective focuses on integration. Integration is the unifying, or joining together, of resources and assets. This is clearly one of the primary advantages of enterprise systems, which are designed to integrate either across business processes or across information systems.

Business integration is the unification of business processes previously performed as separate activities, in order to create cohesive and streamlined business processes. In other words, business integration refers to ensuring that processes are performed the best way they can be, without having barriers along the functional areas (departments) or hierarchical levels. This is accomplished by making sure the processes are performed at the best location, and by allowing access to the necessary information to everyone who needs it. This is also called **data integration**. Examples of enterprise systems that provide business integration include customer relationship management (CRM) and enterprise knowledge management. **Systems integration** is the unification of information systems and databases that were previously operating as separate systems. Systems integration focuses on the technological components of information systems. Examples of enterprise systems that are used for systems integration include Enterprise Resource Planning (ERP), Content Management Systems (CMS), Supply Chain Management (SCM), Unified Communications, and Enterprise Application Integration. As you can see, most enterprise systems are designed to facilitate the flow of information between all business functions inside the boundaries of the organization and to manage connections to outside stakeholders. A brief description of some of these enterprise systems is provided in Table 12.2. The three most popular (ERP, SCM, and CRM) are further described in the chapter.

Characteristics of Enterprise Systems

The enterprise systems presented in Table 12.2 have some common characteristics. First, many of these systems are modular. This means that an organization can implement the "pieces" it needs one at a time. By implementing modules as needed, the organization can limit their efforts and costs, and limit disruptions for employees. However, because the modules are designed to be integrated with one another, they function more efficiently together. This concept, called **application integration**, works because an event that occurs in one module automatically triggers events in one or more of the other modules. In addition, because data are stored in one central database, by offering data integration, companies avoid the data redundancy and inaccuracy issues found in hierarchical or functional information systems.

Table 12.2   Examples of Enterprise Information Systems

Tool	Description
Customer Relationship Management (CRM)	An organization-wide strategy for managing an organization's multiple interactions with customers. It allows organizations to attract, retain, and manage customer relationships, for example by offering personalized services and self-servicing tools. It also allows companies to analyze customer data to find its most profitable products, services, and customers. It involves both technology and a philosophy of customer service.
Enterprise Knowledge Management (also called Business Intelligence; BI)	A set of tools used to analyze business data to find trends, issues, and opportunities. Companies have accumulated large amounts of data such as sales, revenues, or expenses, to name a few, and BI tools show various views of this data to help decision makers. BI tools include a wide variety of analysis approaches such as online analytical processing, business analytics, or data and text mining.
Enterprise Resource Planning (ERP)	ERP software allows organizations to manage resources throughout the organization, independently of which business function controls the resource. Typical modules in ERP include financial management, order processing, or human resources management.
Content Management Systems (CMS)	CMS applications allow companies to manage the vast amounts of information of various types (content) they have stored. This includes the capture, storing, preservation, and delivery of content. CMS refers to technologies, strategies, and approaches to managing content.
Unified Communication (UC)	UC is a framework for the integration of the various modes of communication used by an organization, including email, voicemail, videoconferencing, instant messaging, texting, and Voice-over-IP. For example, a customer may leave a voicemail that is automatically sent as an email to the account representative (based on preferences). Similarly, instead of sending an email, the voicemail can be transferred immediately to an instant message if the representative is currently online.
Enterprise Application Integration (EAI)	EAI is a set of tools and services (a framework instead of a single technology) to allow various enterprise systems (such as ERP or CRM) to share the data. It makes use of middleware (see Chapter 7) to perform this communication.
Supply Chain Management Systems (SCM)	SCM software helps organizations manage the movement of materials or products from provision to production to consumption. SCM involves collaboration between partners both upstream and downstream from the focal organization (upstream and downstream flows are shown in Figure 12.3).

Source: adapted from Pearlson and Saunders, 2010; Piccoli, 2008; Wikipedia.com.

Enterprise Resource Planning (ERP)

As previously discussed, an **Enterprise Resource Planning (ERP)** system is a set of information systems tools that are used to manage an organization's resources and enable information flow within and between processes (and departments). Before ERP, organizations developed different applications to manage information processing and management needs of the different functional areas of the organization. With ERP, various modules offer integrated management of these resources. Typical modules in ERP systems include financials (accounts receivable, general ledger, accounts payable, etc.), distribution services, human resources, and product life cycle management (marketing). Some ERP systems also include other enterprise systems applications such as Customer Relationship Management (CRM), Supply Chain Management (SCM), and Warehouse Management Systems (WMS).

Like other enterprise systems, ERP applications are built on a centralized database, as shown in Figure 12.2, and offer system and business integration. The ERP system itself can reside on a centralized server or it can be distributed across modular hardware and software units that are interconnected. Many vendors offer commercial ERP packages (such as SAP, Oracle PeopleSoft, Microsoft Dynamics, etc.) that tend

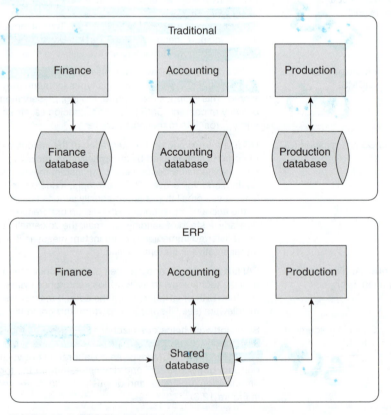

FIGURE 12.2 ERP Shared Database

to include the collective experience of its consultants. As a result, such packages are said to include best practices from the industry. However, the biggest challenge with ERP systems is to customize them to the needs of the organization and to the computing platforms used within the organization.

Benefits and Disadvantages of ERP Systems

There are many benefits for organizations that successfully implement an ERP system. Efficiency is the most important of these as it is quantifiable. Efficiency is achieved because ERP systems can reduce data redundancy (reduce direct costs of operation), improve communication (reduce indirect costs of operation through the streamlining of business processes), and in general allow complex systems to work together in an integrated fashion (also streamlining business operations and making sure tasks are performed in a standardized way). If properly implemented, ERP systems can also offer responsiveness to various stakeholders, including customers and suppliers, by providing more accurate information and more rapid responses to demands. ERP systems are also adaptable since they can be configured to fit the organization's needs. However, when an ERP system becomes too customized, it can lose some of the advantages of integration and standardization offered by the standard packages. Finally, ERP systems benefit from the expertise of ERP software vendors and consultants who, through experience implementing many of these systems over the years, have embedded into their software packages the state-of-the-art processes used in an industry.

BUSINESS EXAMPLE BOX 1	THE POWER OF ERP DATA: HOW SLUMBERLAND FURNITURE CLEANED UP ITS SUPPLIER LIST

Slumberland Furniture is a private bedding and furniture chain of 120 stores based in Little Canada, Minnesota. The company sells furniture it buys from a number of suppliers. As with many companies, Slumberland management had some perceptions as to which suppliers were better providers than others. This all changed, however, in 2008 when the company started an ERP business intelligence project to understand which furniture suppliers were most profitable. The company wanted to focus on facts instead of perceptions.

Slumberland's ERP system includes point-of-sale and order-management applications, and provides sales information, including which products sell fastest in which stores and at what prices. Collecting information from the ERP application, together with the retail system and the warehouse management system, Slumberland identified data such as how many times a dresser or La-Z-Boy recliner had been moved around a warehouse or from one distribution center to another, and who moved it. In performing their analyses, the company also considered subjective information like ratings by its managers of how well suppliers responded to questions or helped solve problems that occurred.

(continued)

After analyzing its supply chain data found in the ERP system, Slumberland found some surprising revelations. For example, they realized that the more they moved a large, heavy piece of furniture (like the La-Z-Boy), the more they risked damaging it (which means they had to either spend money repairing it or send it back to the manufacturer). In the words of the company's director of information services, "analyzing this data showed the true cost of doing business with each supplier," including shipping delays, or how often some items are moved between or within warehouses. They were surprised to find that some vendors, previously thought to be their most profitable partnerships, were in reality not working out well for them. For example, some offered discounts, but repeatedly delivered orders late. Others had packaging that was complicated and costly in labor to remove. As a result of analyzing their ERP data, Slumberland "cleaned up" its list of suppliers and started working more closely with better-performing vendors. In the end, the company believes it was able to reduce its inventory (and therefore costs) by 10%.

Source: Nash, Kim S. "Furnishing Higher Profits; A BI Project Using ERP Data Allowed Furniture Retailer Slumberland to Find Its Most Profitable Suppliers." *CIO* 23(3) (Nov 1, 2009).

ERP systems also suffer from a number of significant disadvantages. First, they represent an enormous amount of work and very high costs. Because most organizations do not use directly "off-the-shelf" applications but instead customize them substantially, ERP implementations can take anywhere from six months (for a few modules) to six years (for a full implementation). There are even stories of implementations lasting up to 12 years. One study reveals that in recent implementations of ERP, 57% of organizations said the implementation took longer than expected (Panorama Consulting Group, 2010). Costs of ERP implementations vary depending on the size of the implementation, from a few hundred thousand (US) dollars to many millions. One reason why implementing an ERP system is not as simple as simply loading the software is that it involves changing the way business is done. Business processes that have been in place for a long time may need to be redesigned. Users accustomed to the old way of doing business may offer significant resistance to an ERP implementation. Departments that have to relinquish control of some data or applications may also be resistant to the implementation. The bottom line is that an ERP implementation is often risky and complex, but that the benefits can be substantial and worth the effort.

A recent study confirms that the typical disadvantages of ERP implementations still exist. The study shows that ERP implementations take longer and cost more than expected, and under-deliver business value. The study also reveals that organizations do not do a good job managing the organizational changes that result from an ERP implementation (Panorama Consulting Group, 2010). Why is it that many ERP implementations are so difficult? Because, as we said, they often involve changes in processes and people's jobs; they therefore represent a third order change (Chapter 11). In addition, they are often very large in scope, and may require more customization than initially expected. Finally, ERP implementations require a strong champion, a person who believes enough in the implementation to see it through the many obstacles and years of efforts.

BUSINESS EXAMPLE BOX 2	ERP IS NOT ALWAYS A HORROR STORY: CISCO IMPLEMENTATION ON TIME AND BUDGET

Enterprise Resource Planning (ERP) implementations make good horror stories for IT and business managers to talk about. As discussed in this chapter, they are often way over budget and delayed by months and sometimes years. However, there are also some good stories. For Cisco Systems, Inc., an ERP implementation went well, and achieved its planned budget and time objectives.

Cisco, founded in 1984, produces telecommunications equipment. They quickly became a Fortune 500 company as a result of the growth of the Internet. To support its core business operations in the mid-1990s, Cisco used a UNIX-based software package that handled its finance, manufacturing, and order entry core functions. At the time, each functional area (business unit) used the system but made its own decisions regarding the future of their IT systems. As a result, the systems were often "upgraded" by each department for their own needs. When the CIO of Cisco at the time, Pete Solvik, decided to analyze the software applications, he found that the software package in use lacked reliability, maintainability, and redundancy (backup) needed. A failure in the legacy system in 1994 that led to a two-day shutdown of operations, resulted in a need for a new system.

As with many CIOs, Cisco's CIO was trying to avoid ERP because he was concerned that an ERP solution would involve implementation headaches and cost overruns. In particular, the independent department structure would not work well with an integrated ERP. However, the ERP did seem the best solution for the company's needs and so a consulting company was hired to help Cisco select a vendor and implement the ERP system. KPMG Consulting helped prepare the ERP Request for Proposal and then helped Cisco select Oracle as their ERP vendor. The agreement also involved Cisco helping Oracle to market new releases to potential customers, in exchange for a successful implementation within budget and time.

The implementation team then prepared a budget and schedule, committing to top management that everything would be done within nine months for $15 million. Using a rapid iterative prototyping to implement the ERP, 30 developers spent three months modifying the Oracle ERP system to support Cisco's business processes. After several phases of analysis, development, implementation, corrections, and training, the final implementation was done on time and below the $15 million budget. Meeting its goals, Cisco management offered the implementation team a bonus pool of over $200,000.

Source: Datta, Avimanyu. "Cisco Systems: Implementing 'Customized' ERP in Nine Months and within Budget." *Journal of Cases on Information Technology* 11(2) (Apr–Jun 2009): 56ff.

STATISTICS BOX 1: TOP SEVEN SELECTED ERP VENDORS

In a 2010 survey of companies that have implemented an ERP system, Panorama Consulting identified the top seven vendors that are most often selected (percentage of time the company's software is selected from a short list of vendors), as per the table below.

Selected ERP Vendor	Selection Rate *
Oracle PeopleSoft	66.7%
Oracle eBusiness Suite	54.2%
SAP	54.1%
Infor Global Solutions	38.5%
Oracle JD Edwards	37.5%
Epicor Software Corporation	33.3%
Microsoft Dynamics	22.9%

*Percentage of time the company's software is selected from short list of vendors.
Source: Panorama Consulting, *From Magic Quadrant to Top 10 ERP Vendors, 2010 Report* (August 25, 2010).

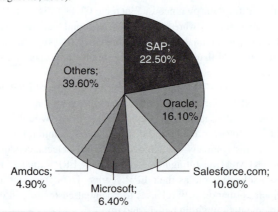

LEARNING ACTIVITY 12.2   THE ONLINE BEER GAME

As seen in the Focusing Story, supply chain systems are very important enterprise systems for organizations who must receive raw materials or products needed for their manufacturing or resale operations. Before we discuss the concepts more in depth, students should experience the issues surrounding proper management of supply chains. To do so, please connect to the Beer Game developed by MIT (Massachusetts Institute of Technology) professors, which can be found at http://beergame.mit.edu/. Use the web-based version of the Beer Game for this exercise. Login to the course website for a direct link to the Beer Game, the guide to the game, and hints from prior students. Your instructor should let you know whether a specific game has been created for you (and give you the password) or if you are expected to create a new game.

After you have completed the game for the time allotted by your instructor, be prepared to discuss the following questions:

1. How does information impact your supply chain decisions?

2. How could information systems help with the information needs of managing a supply chain?

Supply Chain Management Systems

The Focusing Story at the beginning of the chapter introduced the concept of Supply Chain Management (SCM) at Wal-Mart. We discussed how managing the flow of goods in its supplier and distribution channels helps the company tightly control its inventory and reduce its costs. Supply chain management, however, can also apply to services, financial products, knowledge, and relationships, as well as goods.

The typical **supply chain** involves the flow of goods from the manufacturer to the wholesaler to the retailer and to the consumer. A typical supply chain is shown in Figure 12.3. Firms that provide or supply an organization's products or services are considered upstream, while firms that distribute an organization's products or services are considered downstream.

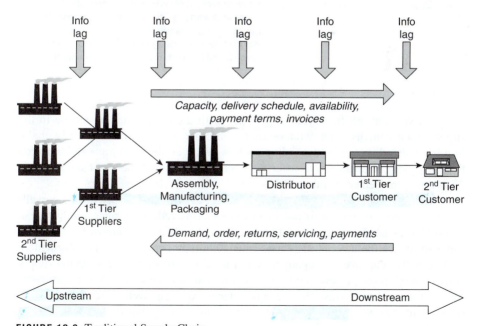

FIGURE 12.3 Traditional Supply Chain

Table 12.3 Supply Chain (and Other) Disaster Examples

Year	Company	What Happened?
1999 – Christmas	Toys R Us.com	On-line retail division cannot make Christmas delivery commitments to thousands; infamous "We're sorry" emails sent on Dec. 23; eventually, Amazon takes over fulfillment.
1999 – Halloween	Hershey	New order management and shipping systems (implementing both ERP and SCM simultaneously); Hershey could not fulfill critical Halloween orders; $150 million in revenues lost as stock drops 30%.
2001	Cisco	Lack of demand and inventory visibility as market slows leads to $2.2 billion inventory write-off and stock price cut in half.
2001	Nike	New planning system causes inventory and order woes; blamed for $100 million in lost sales and depressed stock price by 20%; triggered a flurry of class-action lawsuits.
2005	Loblaws	Plans for a significant logistics network makeover ran into poor execution problems; company blames two quarters of poor results on high costs and lost sales from the effort; CEO apologizes to shareholders; even though the logistics issues largely stabilized by early 2006, the stock price never recovered from the hit.
2007–2009	Boeing	Plans to radically overhaul the supply chain for the new *Dreamliner* 787 aircraft sound good, but massive problems with component deliveries leads to two-year delay in aircraft launch and some $2 billion in charges to fix supplier problems.

Source: Gilmore, 2009.

As you can tell from your experience with the Beer Game, everyone in the supply chain benefits from collaborating with other members of the supply chain. You have also discovered (depending on how well you did) that a poorly managed flow of goods can result in a disaster for a company. Some of the worst supply chain disasters are presented in Table 12.3.

Enterprise systems are key to the management of the supply chain. A well-managed supply chain can result in inventory costs reduction since products can be ordered as needed as opposed to have them stored for long amounts of time. It can also reduce the amount of returned items through better inventory information. SCM can also improve a company's overall relationships with partners in the supply chain through more accurate and timely communication about the flow of products, information, and payments. These can be referred to respectively as the product flow (movement of goods), information flow (orders and delivery status), and financial flow (credit terms, payment schedules, and consignment and title ownership arrangements).

A good SCM system also allows companies to offer just-in-time (JIT) inventory. This is when firms are able to maintain the lowest level of inventory while still being able to fulfill demand. Because SCM systems provide notices of inventory stock depletion in real time, personnel (or systems) are able to order new stock immediately.

The key to SCM's success rests in the sharing of information both upstream and downstream. Today, most companies use Web-based interfaces to access inventory, delivery, and other information from the SCM system. The SCM systems also tend to be increasingly integrated with other enterprise systems such as ERP and Customer Relationship Management (CRM) systems.

STATISTICS BOX 2: SUPPLY CHAIN'S IMPACT ON COMPANY VALUATION

Statistical evidence suggests that companies with well-run supply chains continue to outperform other companies. Here are some of these statistics:

- According to Boston-based AMR Research, the average total return on investment of companies in AMR's "Supply Chain Top 25" in 2007 was 17.89%, compared with returns of 6.43% for the Dow Jones Industrial Average and 3.53% for companies in Standard & Poor's 500 Index.

- According to a Georgia Tech study, a company's stock price can drop as much as 8% on the day a supply chain glitch is announced.

- A study by Dr. Thomas Speh of Miami University of Ohio showed that when a company adopts a new distribution or logistics innovation, the company's stock price increases.

- A study by Bain & Company showed that companies employing sophisticated supply chain methods enjoyed 12 times greater profit than companies with unsophisticated methods.

Source: Council of Supply Chain Management Professionals, http://cscmp.org/press/fastfacts.asp/.

LEARNING ACTIVITY 12.3   CUSTOMER RELATIONSHIP MANAGEMENT

An enterprise system that has gained importance in recent years is Customer Relationship Management (CRM). Before we discuss the concept more in depth, learn about CRM by viewing one of the following demonstrations:

- Salesforce (Salesforce.com CRM: Centralize your Accounts); http://www.salesforce.com/video/search.jsp?t=CRM_Overview_Demo&v=_r1H7OK8lzY&s=crm

(continued)

- Microsoft Dynamics' CRM; http://uscrmdynamics.cloudapp.net/demos/Dynamics-CRM-2011-Driving-Sales-Productivity/CRM-2011-Driving-Sales-Productivity.html

Be prepared to discuss the following points in class:

1. What are the purposes of a CRM?
2. What are the various types of tasks that can be accomplished with a CRM?
3. Who benefits from a CRM system?
4. What are the benefits for each stakeholder?
5. What types of companies should have a CRM? Why?

Customer Relationship Management Systems

Customer Relationship Management (CRM) refers to an organization-wide strategy for managing an organization's multiple interactions with customers. For example, when dealing with a company to buy a product, you might talk to a person via a toll-free phone number, send an email, chat in an instant messaging box with a customer representative, or simply perform your transaction online without "talking" with anyone. These are all channels of interaction.

CRM involves a set of activities (including a philosophy of customer service) and technologies (the CRM system) meant to help understand the needs of current and potential customers. The CRM system allows organizations to attract and retain customers, and to manage customer relationships, for example by offering personalized services and self-servicing tools. It also allows companies to analyze customer data to find its most profitable products, services, and customers.

Broadly speaking, there are three main goals for CRM, as shown in Table 12.4 (META Group, 2001). First, CRM systems help organizations manage multiple channels of interaction with customers in ways that the customers prefer. The second goal of CRM systems is to provide an integrated picture of the customer across the various customer-facing parts of the organization. The third major goal of CRM systems is to enable the analysis of customer-related information. This information is gathered through interactions with customers, although external data (such as census data) may also be involved.

Customer Service Life Cycle

The **Customer Service Life Cycle (CSLC)** is a framework to help us understand the various tasks a CRM can be useful for. The CSLC is a series of phases that customers

Table 12.4 Goals of CRM (META Group, 2001)

Manage multiple channels of interaction with customer
Provide a unified view of the customer across the enterprise
Analyze information collected to improve campaigns, services, products

Table 12.5   Phases in Customer Service Life Cycle

Phase	Description	Example of CRM Use
Engage	Creating customer awareness of the product or service. The goal of the engage stage is to generate leads and then convert those leads into buying customers.	**Campaign management** Email marketing **Lead processing** **Sales force automation** Web-based catalogs
Transact	All activities associated with the purchase process. The goal of this phase is to efficiently and effectively complete the purchase process so that customers do not abandon the purchase process in the middle.	Order management Payment process and options Product configuration Product pricing
Fulfill	Delivery of the product or service to the customer.	**Order tracking** Supply-chain integration
Service	Supporting the customer during the ownership of a product or service.	**Call center automation** Customer issues management Self Service

Source: adapted from Van Slyke and Belanger, 2003.

pass through when interacting with an organization. There are a number of variations on the phases, but they are all similar. Our simplified CRM includes four phases; engage, transact, fulfill, and service. Table 12.5 summarizes the phases and shows some specific CRM-related applications that can be useful for each CSLC phase. The combined phases are referred to as a cycle, as shown in Figure 12.4, because completion of one

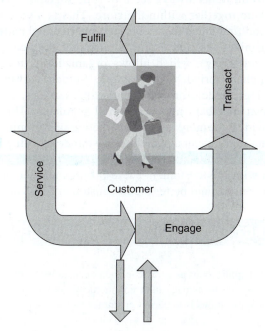

FIGURE 12.4 Customer Service Life Cycle

round of the cycle often leads to another round. Note that in the following discussion, we refer to products, but similar statements could be made about services.

Components of CRM

CRM systems have three main components: operational, collaborative, and analytical CRM (Van Slyke and Bélanger, 2003). Figure 12.5 shows how the components work together.

The **operational** components of a CRM system help an organization improve day-to-day interactions with customers. They are involved with the operations of the company such as sales or repairs.

The **collaborative** components of a CRM system help the organization interact and collaborate with their customers. They include older applications such as email and automated response systems, but also newer ones such as interactive chat facilities for customer service, **Interactive Voice Response (IVR)** systems, and Voice over IP (VoIP), which allows a customer to talk to a "live" customer service representative while online.

The **analytical** components of CRM consist of technologies and processes organizations can use to analyze customer data. A critical analytical component in most CRM systems is the data warehouse, which we discussed earlier. **Data mining** technologies and methods are often used to discover patterns and groups in the data stored in a data warehouse. Data mining involves using software that performs analyses of large data sets to find patterns that repeat themselves. For example, a grocery store might find that on college football weekends certain items always seem to sell "together." The grocery store can then locate them together within the store. This is a very simple example, and data mining can find much more complex and detailed patterns. One analysis that many organizations find useful is customer segmentation (sometimes called customer clustering), which allows organizations to group customers that share certain characteristics. For example, Student Advantage, a company that provides college student-oriented marketing services, uses segmentation to place its student members into very small segments. This allows Student Advantage to provide extremely targeted marketing opportunities to a wide variety of clients. Data mining can also help in customer profiling. **Customer profiling** lets companies build a picture of a customer through data collected from their interactions with this customer. These profiles allow companies to better anticipate customer needs and better predict customer behavior.

| LEARNING ACTIVITY 12.4 | SELF-SERVICING |

We discussed CRM applications as a way companies can gather information about their customers and as a way to manage their communications with them. An additional function of CRM applications is to permit **customer self-service**, allowing customers to take care of their service problems themselves. Before we discuss the pros and cons of doing this, you should try self-servicing.

- Scenario: you ordered a new noise-free headphone for taking on your multiple trips. You bought it on Amazon.com for $65. You opened the shipping package two months ago but never opened the actual package completely (it has the original packaging). You were busy with the start of classes so you did not think about it again, but now your parents gave you the exact same item as a gift, so you want to return the package to Amazon.com.

- Go to the Amazon website (www.amazon.com).

- Figure out how much you are going to receive as a refund (not counting taxes, if any).

- Estimate how long it is going to take for you to get your money once the headphones are shipped back to Amazon. Identify why this time is needed.

- Figure out what you have to do to return the headphones.

DISCUSSION QUESTIONS:

1. How difficult was it to find the information needed?

2. How difficult do you think it would be to actually complete the return?

3. How likely are you to use this self-servicing application (Return Center) instead of calling someone at Amazon? Why?

4. What are the benefits to customers of self-servicing CRM applications?

5. What are the benefits to companies of self-servicing CRM applications?

KEY STATISTICS BOX 3: CRM VENDORS

The CRM market has been growing, with revenues of $8.13 billion in 2007 and $9.15 billion in 2008 (DestinationCRM.com, 2009). Research from Gartner, Inc. suggests that for 2008, the top vendors were SAP with 22.5% of the CRM market, Oracle with a 16.1% share, and Saleforce.com with 10.6% of the market (Beal, 2009).

CRM Implementation Options

Like most other enterprise systems, there are two main ways that CRM can be implemented: on-premise or on-demand. **On-premise CRM** implementation means that the CRM is acquired, leased, or developed by the organization and

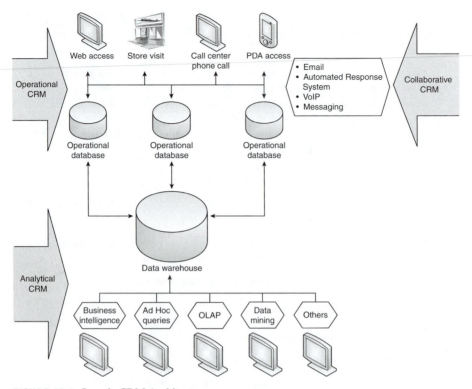

FIGURE 12.5 Sample CRM Architecture

BUSINESS EXAMPLE BOX 3	NOT JUST TECHNOLOGY: TRAINING PEOPLE FOR CRM AT BRITISH TELECOM

British Telecom (BT) is the largest telecommunication provider in the United Kingdom, holding approximately 45% of the UK broadband market. One of the most important business functions at BT is Business Sales, which is a division in charge of responding to customer inquiries and making sure customers use BT services. Every week, BT Business Sales handles 60,000 customer contacts. This typically generates US$4.05 million (£2.75 million) in revenues per year.

To handle customer calls, BT has a CRM system that is available to its 540 call-handling advisors and 92 managers across the 9 sites used by BT Business Sales throughout the United Kingdom. However, over the years BT management realized that there was a lack of consistency on how advisors serviced customers. For example, various advisors did not ask their customers some relevant questions (even though the CRM system requested this information) while others did not properly acknowledge or record replies from their customers. Not surprisingly, even when customers called to obtain information or service, advisors were trying to sell them something instead of helping the customers.

To improve the customer relationships and the use of CRM, BT decided to develop a customer-oriented culture and a coaching philosophy through training of all call-center managers, first-line managers, and call-handling advisors. Part of the training was focused on improving the team culture in the call centers. The training effort did include new technology (to capture screens advisors used for training purposes), but was also heavily focused on offering practical, skill-based behavioral training. The company recognized that new technology was not enough to create the change of culture that was required. The program included measurement of performance, both in terms of perceptions and actual performance.

BT achieved the expected results from the training program and the use of CRM. First, they created a culture of coaching employees among managers. Second, they now measure performance by receiving inputs from customers and others, not just measuring performance based on sales (this is called 360-degree feedback). Third, they created an emphasis on ongoing relationships, which has led to stronger relations between advisors and customers, and between advisors and managers.

Source: Pollitt, David. "BT Business Sales Dials Up a Customer-focused Coaching Culture." *Human Resource Management International Digest* 18 (Nov.4, 2010): 9.

installed on its local servers. This often has the advantage of providing a customized solution. However, the costs of development and maintenance could be substantial. **On-demand CRM,** also known as **Software-as-a-Service (SaaS) CRM,** refers to the remote use of a CRM provider's applications through the Internet. This offers advantages like up-to-date applications and no maintenance or implementation costs. Of course, the company has to use the standard functions, also known as *plain vanilla* software.

Benefits and Limitations of CRM

There are many expected benefits from the use of CRM systems for organizations. First, CRM systems are expected to provide greater customer satisfaction because customers can receive personalized services and products, faster response time to their questions, and more streamlined interactions with the company. For companies, this results in improved customer relations, which should lead to repeat business (called *customer retention*). In addition, CRM systems can help an organization maximize its profits by reducing the costs for acquiring a customer and servicing customers, and increasing overall revenues. Revenues can increase because of customer loyalty, but also because of what is called cross-selling, or the selling of products to customers based on other products they acquired. For example, Amazon.

com often sends its customers book recommendations based on books they have previously bought.

There are also some potential disadvantages to the use of CRM. First, the implementation of a CRM system requires more than simply installing the software application. In order to be successful in implementing a CRM system, organizations must look beyond purely technical issues and ensure that all customer-facing employees are customer-minded. The company must also make sure that it identifies all channels of interactions with customers. The ability to achieve buy-in from various areas of the organization is key to a successful implementation. Of course, there are complicated technological issues that also must be addressed. First, the organization must ensure that its CRM architecture is scalable so that growth in customer demands is met without problems. Just like ERP systems, CRM systems can be customized to meet the specific needs of the organization. Overall, the ability to deal with both nontechnical and technical issues is a requirement for successfully implementing almost any enterprise system.

Customer Managed Interactions (CMI)

One issue with CRM systems is that they are very firm centric in the sense that they focus on the existing transactional and behavioral data collected by the organization based on the prior and current interactions of the customer with the organization. While trends can be used to predict what customers might buy in the future, there are some acquisitions and customer activities that are unforeseeable unless the customer tells the company about it. For example, a customer might be interested in some products for a friend's upcoming wedding but the company would not know of this "need." To address this lack of information, some companies have turned their focus to Customer Managed Interactions (CMI).

Customer Managed Interactions (CMI) involve letting customers store and manage data about themselves. Why would customers willingly tell companies of their buying intentions? For convenience, money, or to obtain personalized service. Think of all of your friends who create wish lists at some of the major online retailers like Amazon.com or Target.com. There is even a site dedicated to helping anyone create wish lists (WishList.com). Customers tell the company what they intend to buy; therefore, this information tends to be accurate. Once the company knows about intended purchases, it can perform targeted marketing, for example giving a specific discount, which may push the customer over into the buying phase of the Customer Service Life Cycle.

CHAPTER SUMMARY

In this chapter, we discussed enterprise systems. We first presented the main components, characteristics and types of enterprise systems. We then explored more in depth three enterprise systems: Enterprise Resource Planning (ERP) systems, supply chain management systems (SCM), and customer relationship management (CRM) systems. Here are the main points discussed in the chapter.

- Enterprise systems are information systems that serve the needs of the organization or parts of the organization.

- Enterprise systems are modular; they are integrated with one another (offering application integration), and use a central database (offering data integration).

- The purpose of Enterprise Resource Planning (ERP) systems is to manage an organization's resources and enable information flow within and between processes (and departments) via a set of integrated information systems tools.

- Supply Chain Management (SCM) systems help organizations manage the flow of goods in its supplier and distribution channels to better control inventory, reduce costs, and improve communication with its business partners.

- Customer relationship management (CRM) systems have three main components: the operational component that helps an organization improve day-to-day interactions with customers; the collaborative component that helps the organization interact and collaborate with its customers; and the analytical component, which consists of technologies and processes organizations can use to analyze customer data.

- The customer life cycle is a series of phases that customers pass through when interacting with an organization, and it can be used to identify important CRM applications.

REVIEW QUESTIONS

1. What is the difference between a personal and an enterprise information system?
2. How are applications developed using the functional perspective? The hierarchical perspective?
3. Define business integration and systems integration.
4. What is an Enterprise Resource Planning system, and how does it support systems integration?
5. What is the purpose of a Supply Chain Management (SCM) system?
6. What is Customer Relationship Management?
7. What are the main components of a CRM? Briefly describe each.
8. What are the main goals of a CRM?
9. What is the difference between on-premise CRM and on-demand CRM?
10. What are Customer Managed Interactions? How do they differ from CRM?

REFLECTION QUESTIONS

1. What is the most important thing you learned in this chapter? Why is it important?
2. What topics are unclear? What about them is unclear?

3. How does the process perspective provide integration, and what types of integration are provided?

4. How does cloud computing relate to ERP and CRM applications?

5. How does the material in this chapter relate to the content of Chapter 4 on strategic information systems?

6. Explain how data integration is essential to the success of ERP, SCM, and CRM systems.

7. Which issues are similar for both the process and the hierarchical perspectives of developing enterprise systems? Why?

8. How can process modeling (Chapter 11) enable firms to successfully implement enterprise systems?

9. We discussed different types of integration in this chapter (system, business, and data). How do they relate to one another?

10. Can a very small business implement a CRM? What would be the advantages and disadvantages of doing so?

ADDITIONAL LEARNING ACTIVITIES

1. This activity requires you to complete a case analysis regarding an ERP acquisition. The case may be accessed through your university website, the Ivey School business case website (http://cases.ivey.uwo.ca), the Harvard Business school cases website (http://cb.hbsp.harvard.edu/cb/web), or may be provided to you by your instructor.

   Source: Canniff, Mike. Case: Enterprise Resource Planning Software—Ongoing Maintenance Cost Benefit Analysis, *Ivey School of Business*, Product Number: 906E12-PDF-ENG.

2. View the video by Salesforce.com entitled *Bigger* and *Better Data*. You may watch only the first 30 minutes at http://www.salesforce.com/video/search.jsp?t=Bigger_and_Better_Data_for_Healthy_CRM_in_2010__For_Professional_and_Group_Edit&v=eZ3EOS_gKGk&s=crm

   The video discusses CRM but is focused more extensively on the use of the data available from CRM and the marketing that can be done with these data. Prepare a short report describing the main points of the video. Make sure to address the following questions:
   - Who benefits from bigger and better data?
   - How does one obtain better quality CRM data?
   - How should strategy, process, and technology integrate to provide a better CRM?
   - What is data migration and how does it improve data quality?

3. Select a small organization you are familiar with. This could be your employer, a company where you parents or friends work, or just a company you know well. First, evaluate the company's need for a CRM based on your knowledge from the readings, discussions, and activities you have done in this chapter. Prepare a short report including your recommended features, applications, and strategies for this small business.

4. After completing Learning Activity 12-A3, watch the *Small Business CRM demo* from Salesforce.com. Include any changes to your report based on the information in the demo.
   http://www.salesforce.com/video/search.jsp?s=small+business

5. Compare and contrast in a table the advantages and disadvantages of each enterprise system perspective (hierarchical, functional, and process).

6. Imagine that you are a new student at a university that requires each student to have a computer, but does not provide guidelines beyond the fact that they have to be laptops, use wireless networks, and have capability to use basic office applications and statistical analyses. The laptops have to be useful for three years. Develop a list of activities from the Customer Service Life Cycle that apply to this situation. Identify the CRM applications that can be used for each activity.

REFERENCES

Barney Beal, "Gartner releases CRM market share report and SAP leads, but how much does it matter?", *IT Knowledge Exchange*, (July 22, 2009), http://itknowledgeexchange.techtarget.com/voices-of-crm/gartner-releases-crm-market-share-report-and-sap-leads-but-how-much-does-it-matter/

DestinationCRM.com *CRM Market Grows for Fifth Straight Year* (2009).

Gartner, Inc. "Gartner Says Worldwide Customer Relationship Management Market Grew 23 Percent in 2007." (Sept. 12, 2008) Press release. http://www.gartner.com/it/page.jsp?id=715308. Retrieved 2008-08-15.

Gartner, Inc. "Gartner Says Worldwide CRM Market Grew 12.5 Percent in 2008." (June 16, 2009). Press release. http://www.gartner.com/it/page.jsp?id=1074615. Retrieved Oct 27, 2009.

Gilmore, Dan. "The Top Supply Chain Disasters of All Time." *Supply Chain Digest* (May 7, 2009). http://www.scdigest.com/assets/FirstThoughts/09-05-07.php?cid=2451&ctype=content.

META Group. *Integration: Critical Issues for Implementation of CRM Solutions*. Paper commissioned by Oracle Corporation, 15 February 2001. Available at http://www.oracle.com/applications/crm/metacrmwp.pdf.

Panorama Consulting Group. *2010 ERP REPORT*. http://panorama-consulting.com/resource-center/2010-erp-report/.

Pearlson, Keri and Carol Saunders. *Managing and Using Information Systems* 4th ed., Hoboken, NJ: Wiley, 2010.

Piccoli, Gabriele. *Information Systems for Managers* 1st ed. Hoboken, NJ: Wiley, 2008.

Van Slyke, C. and F. Bélanger. *Electronic Business Technologies*. Hoboken, NJ: Wiley, 2003.

BIBLIOGRAPHY AND FURTHER READINGS

Gulati, R. and J.N. Oldroyd. "The Quest for Customer Focus." *Harvard Business Review*, Product number: 9645 (2005).

Piccoli, G and R. Watson. "Profit from Customer Data by Identifying Strategic Opportunities and Adopting the 'Born Digital' Approach." *MIS Quarterly Executive* 7(3) (Sep 2008): 113–122.

Reinhartz, W. and Kumar. "The Mismanagement of Customer Loyalty." *Harvard Business Review*, Product number: #R0207F (2002).

SAP Information

• http://www.sap.com/solutions/business-suite/erp/index.epx

- http://www.sdn.sap.com/irj/scn/go/portal/prtroot/docs/business_maps/99B4D4E97A624B
  E5987BC14633908B9B/78590453EC454B8986A933EBB7E84848/82087E7A8EB94E1
  F885C5A1F62C789FB.xml
- http://web.mit.edu/sapr3/docs/webdocs/getstarted/gsOVERVIEW.html

Supply Chain Management videos

- http://www.sap.com/solutions/business-suite/scm/demos/index.epx
- http://www.youtube.com/watch?v=dDmGtPQAI24 (MS Dynamics)

CRM videos

- http://www.youtube.com/watch?v=-_6c018ZI2g

Social CRM article

- http://www.pcworld.com/businesscenter/article/200897-3/how_savvy_firms_monitor_
  customers_online_chatter.html

GLOSSARY

Analytical components of CRM: technologies and processes organizations can use to analyze customer data.

Application integration: applications where modules are designed to be integrated with one another.

Business integration: the unification of business processes previously performed as separate activities, in order to create cohesive and streamlined business processes.

Business Intelligence (BI): a set of tools used to analyze business data to find trends, issues, and opportunities.

Business process reengineering (BPR): the redesign of business processes to improve how work is done.

Call center automation: applications that support call centers, which are often the main contact point between an organization and its customers.

Campaign management: applications that help organizations plan, carry out, and analyze the results of marketing campaigns.

Collaborative components of CRM: applications that help the organization interact and collaborate with their customers.

Customer issues management: applications that help organizations with tasks such as scheduling, dispatching and communicating with field service personnel.

Content Management Systems (CMS): applications that allow companies to manage the vast amounts of information of various types (content) they have stored. This includes the capture, storing, preservation, and delivery of content.

Customer Managed Interactions (CMI): applications that let customers store and manage data about themselves.

Customer profiling: applications that help organizations group customers according to demographic characteristics or behaviors.

Customer Relationship Management (CRM): an organization-wide strategy for managing an organization's multiple interactions with customers.

Customer self-service: software that allows customers to find solutions to problems without interacting with a customer service representative.

Customer Service Life Cycle (CSLC): a series of phases that customers pass through when interacting with an organization.

Data integration: applications where data is stored in one central database.

Data mining: applications used to analyze data to discover patterns and groups in the data gathered through other components of a CRM system.

Enterprise Application Integration (EAI): a set of tools and services (a framework instead of a single technology) to allow various enterprise systems (such as ERP or CRM) to share the data.

Enterprise Resource Planning (ERP): software that allows organizations to manage resources throughout the organization, independently of which business function controls the resource.

Enterprise systems: information systems that serve the needs of the organization or parts of the organization.

Functional perspective: software development approach where information systems applications are developed to meet the needs of individuals in a functional area, such as human resources or marketing.

Hierarchical perspective: software development approach where software developers build information systems to mirror the organization, so that applications are built to meet the needs of individuals at a given level in the organization.

Interactive voice response (IVR): applications that allow customers to use a telephone to navigate through various types of systems, such as product request systems or customer service systems.

Lead processing: applications used to qualify, assign, and track sales leads to maximize the probability that the leads eventually turn into sales.

On-demand CRM: remote use of a CRM provider's applications through the Internet.

On-premise CRM: CRM specifically developed for the organization and installed on its local servers.

Operational components of CRM: applications that help improve day-to-day interactions with customers such as sales, repairs, etc.

Order tracking: applications that allow customers to determine the status of their order.

Personal information systems: information systems applications for individual use.

Process perspective: software development approach where information systems applications are developed to support the task being done (or process) irrespective of the organizational level or functional area the individual using the system.

Product configuration: applications used to properly configure or choose complex products.

Radio Frequency Identification Tags (RFID): electronic tags that can be tracked remotely using wireless networks.

Sales force automation: applications that provide functions directed at making sales representatives more efficient and effective.

Software-as-a-Service (SaaS) CRM: remote use of a CRM provider's applications through the Internet.

Supply Chain Management Systems (SCM): software that helps organizations manage the movement of materials or products from provision to production to consumption.

Supply chain: entities involved in the flow of goods from the manufacturer to the wholesaler to the retailer and to the consumer.

Systems integration: the unification of information systems and databases that were previously operating as separate systems.

Unified Communication (UC): a framework for the integration of the various modes of communication used by an organization, including email, voicemail, videoconferencing, instant messaging, texting, and Voice-over-IP.

CHAPTER 13

Information for Electronic Business

LEARNING OBJECTIVES

By reading and completing the activities in this chapter, students should be able to:

- Describe the concept of e-business and various e-business models
- Identify the business-to-consumers (B2C) business models, enablers, and impacts
- Explain search engine optimization
- Discuss the main business-to-business (B2B) e-business models
- Identify the major trends related to e-business

CHAPTER OUTLINE

E-channel expansion

- Learning Activity 13.2: Why would I trust them or buy from them?
- Design for B2C e-business
- Business-to-Business (B2B)

B2B e-business models

- Learning Activity 13.3: Where is my Web page?
- Search engine optimization
- Trends in e-business

Mobile business

Global e-business

- Learning Activity 13.4: USA.gov

E-government

- Chapter summary
- Review questions
- Reflection questions
- Additional learning activities
- References
- Bibliography and further readings
- Glossary

FOCUSING STORY: THE IPOD AND THE MUSIC INDUSTRY

Who would have thought that a small device like an iPod could literally change a well-established major industry? Yet, that is what happened when Apple Inc. launched the iPod and electronic music downloads. Because of this new way of selling songs and albums, the music industry has been one of the most affected by e-business.

In the "old" music industry, artists recorded songs and albums through record companies, which were the major players in the industry. Companies could sell CDs (and before the 1980s, LPs) and make significant profits on each album customers bought, with some fees (rights) going to the artists, and some commissions going to distributors and retailers. Eventually, the record companies decided not to release singles, only albums. That was not to the liking of music listeners. Then came the iPod, announced on October 23, 2001. It allowed users to download only the songs they wanted to a very portable device. The industry was never the same. Two significant problems occurred with the growing use of the Internet for access to digital music. The first one is that digital music is easy to steal, and users started to download music illegally and share it with one another. In this scenario, everyone in the industry lost money. Even though illegal downloads had started years before, with Napster allowing illegal downloads for free between 1999 and 2001, the iPod made it easy to copy songs. At the same time, however, many users are happy to spend small amounts of money for legal downloads of the songs they really want. That is why Apple is said to have sold over six billion songs by the end of 2009 on iTunes.

A second phenomenon that occurred with the ability of downloading songs through the Internet was that some artists decided to sell their own music online. They were able to charge less to consumers because they only had to pay the e-business website for selling their music; they also made more profits this way. It is suggested that on a 99¢ song, 29¢ goes to Apple and 70¢ goes to the label and artist. When artists produce their own music, they get the full 70¢ that normally goes to the artist and label. Record companies changed their licensing approaches to embrace new online services in response to this major threat to the industry. However, they did not envision online streaming: the new online threat to the music industry. Online music streaming services allow listeners to play music on their computers or Internet-enabled devices instead of buying CDs or downloading music to their MP3 players (one of which is the iPod). These services, like Pandora (www.pandora.com), Last.fm (www.last.fm), or Imeem (music.inboxtoolbar.com), are free or relatively inexpensive. As users listen online instead of purchasing music, sales of music keep going down every year. The total music industry sales in 2000 were approximately US$14 billion, but were down to US$10 billion by 2008. It is predicted that the downward slide of paid music sales will continue.

DISCUSSION QUESTIONS:

1. Will the streaming audio approach change the music industry once more? How?

2. How can the streaming audio business model be successful?

3. What other ways could companies use to leverage digital music?

Sources: Cranford, Buffy. "How Apple and the iPod Have Changed the Music Industry." *Helium* (December 14, 2009). http://www.helium.com; Harrison, Joyce V. "How Apple and the iPod Have Changed the Music Industry." *Helium* (December 12, 2009). http://www.helium.com/; Hawkins, Dawn. "How Apple and the iPod Have Changed the Music Industry." *Helium* (February 17, 2010). http://www.helium.com/; MacMillan, Douglas. "The Music Industry's New Internet Problem." *Bloomberg BusinessWeek* (March 6, 2009). http://www.businessweek.com/print/technology/content/mar2009/tc2009035_000194.htm;

LEARNING ACTIVITY 13.1	WHY IS E-BUSINESS IMPORTANT?

Most of you have already experienced electronic business, the topic of this chapter, when you acquired products electronically. E-business, however, is much broader than just buying something online. In this learning activity, we want you to think broadly about what e-business is and find two interesting up-to-date statistics online about the size of electronic business. These can be for a subset (such as B2C or B2B), an industry, or a market segment. Make sure your statistics are current, say within the last two years. Be careful about some of the older information available online. For example, you may find predictions from five years ago about expected e-business sales. It is much better to find out what current e-business sales are. Prepare a short report of your two statistics (make sure to include your citations!) and a brief discussion of why you think e-business is important today.

Introduction to E-business

In Learning Activity 13.1, you found several statistics about e-business. What you found should have already convinced you of the importance of e-business in today's economy. However, the importance of e-business goes beyond any number you could find online. The reality is that e-business changed how most organizations interact with their customers, suppliers, and even how they interact with the government. More importantly, complete industries have been transformed with the emergence of e-business applications. This is the case in the opening story that shows how e-business completely changed the music industry. What other industries have been changed by e-business? You may think of travel, publishing, and even education, just to name a few. We discuss later in this chapter specific impacts e-business has had on these industries.

What is e-business exactly? There are many definitions. Table 13.1 provides some terminology used when discussing e-business. Note that Electronic Funds Transfers (EFT) and Electronic Data Interchange (EDI) provide tools for transferring documents or financial data between organizations, and we discuss them in Chapter 7 on transmitting information. The other terms include variations on whether only the Web, other Internet tools, or any other electronic means are used for business transactions, such as collaboration software, kiosk technologies, and so on. For our purposes, we will use the term e-business, which is often recognized as the broader term that includes various electronic means of conducting business, as shown in Figure 13.1.

Types of E-businesses

In Table 13.1 and Figure 13.1, we differentiate between commerce and government. There are other ways to categorize the various types of e-business. Some of the most common categorization are as follows:

Table 13.1 E-business Terms and Terminology

Electronic Funds Transfer	Electronic means to conduct financial transactions such as payments and remittances.
Electronic Data Interchange	Electronic means to transfer documents between organizations.
Web commerce	Electronic means to conduct business transactions using the Web as an interface.
Internet commerce	Electronic means to conduct business using the Internet (for example email, the Web, or file transfers).
Electronic commerce	Electronic means to conduct business transactions, including the Internet, Electronic Data Interchange, or private networks.
Electronic government	Electronic means to interact or conduct transactions with government agencies.
Electronic business	Electronic means to interact or conduct business with individuals, companies, or government agencies.

- **Business-to-Consumer (B2C):** This is when interactions are taking place between a consumer and a business. For example, when you buy books on Amazon.com, you are conducting a B2C e-commerce transaction.

- **Business-to-Business (B2B):** This is when interactions are taking place between two businesses. For example, when Wal-Mart sends electronic requests for inventory to their suppliers, they are conducting a B2B e-commerce transaction.

- **Consumer-to-Consumer (C2C):** This is when interactions are taking place between two consumers. For example, when you buy goods from another individual on eBay.com, you are conducting a C2C e-commerce transaction.

- **Government-to-Constituent (G2C):** This is when interactions are taking place between a government agency and a constituent. Constituents could be citizens, businesses, or even other agencies. For example, when you pay your taxes online,

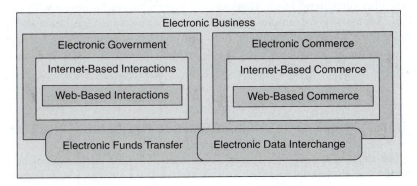

FIGURE 13.1 E-Business Terminology

Table 13.2   Types of E-businesses

E-business Type	Acronym	Definitions	Parties Involved
Business-to-Consumer	B2C	When interactions are taking place between a consumer and a business.	• Consumers • Businesses
Business-to-Business	B2B	When interactions are taking place between two businesses.	• Businesses
Consumer-to-Consumer	C2C	When interactions are taking place between two consumers.	• Consumers
Government-to-Constituent (e-government)	G2C	When interactions are taking place between a government agency and a constituent.	• Citizens • Businesses • Government agencies

you are having a G2C interaction with the government. This is most often referred to today as *electronic government,* or *e-government.*

There are many more types of e-business, although they tend to be variations of the definitions in Table 13.2; for example, consumer-to-business (C2B), business-to-employee (B2E), government-to-government (G2G). The main ones outlined above, however, seem to be the most popular categories.

There is another way to categorize commercial electronic business, and it refers to the online versus offline structure of the organization. There are three main categories used:

- **Bricks and Mortar:** This category represents traditional organizations with physical locations. For example, large automobile manufacturers tend to have physical offices and operations.

- **Bricks and Clicks:** This category represents traditional organizations with physical locations but that also operate an online business. There are many such companies today that have physical stores and online stores; for example, Wal-Mart has Walmart.com, BestBuy has BestBuy.com, and so on.

- **Pure Play (or Click Only):** This category represents organizations with only an online business. For example, Amazon.com and eBay.com started as online companies only, where you could not go to a physical store to conduct a transaction. Many pure play companies, like Google, exist in the online world only, although they still have offices for people to work at.

STATISTICS BOX 1: RETAIL E-COMMERCE IN THE UNITED STATES

As you might have found in Learning Activity 13.1, there are many statistics on e-business that are often not consistent with one another. One good source of statistics for the United States is the U.S. Census Bureau, which provides quarterly statistics on retail e-commerce. The table below shows the statistics available when this book was written. You can obtain the most recent statistics at the following site: http://www.census .gov/retail/#ecommerce/. Note that while the numbers are impressive, e-commerce still represents less than 5% of all retail sales in the country, as can be seen from the figure.

Estimated Quarterly Total and E-commerce U.S. Retail Sales, 2010–2011

Quarter	Retail Sales Total (millions)	Retail Sales E-commerce (millions)	E-commerce as Percent of Total
1st quarter 2011	1,030,038	46,023	4.5
4th quarter 2010	1,003,648	44,517	4.4
3rd quarter 2010	972,440	42,381	4.4
2nd quarter 2010	971,434	39,707	4.1
1st quarter 2010	960,469	38,719	4.0

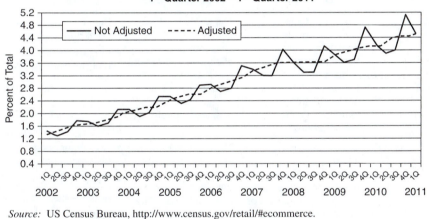

Estimated Quarterly U.S. Retail E-commerce Sales as a Percent of Total Quarterly Retail Sales:
1st Quarter 2002 – 1st Quarter 2011

Source: US Census Bureau, http://www.census.gov/retail/#ecommerce.

E-business Models

The various types of e-business previously discussed refer to who participates in the e-business interaction, and whether this organization uses offline, online, or both business environments. Another important way to classify e-businesses is with respect to their business model.

What Is a Business Model?

A **business model** represents the way the organization functions and creates value. In other words, it is how an organization makes money. The business model often identifies the market that a business is in, the products or services that it offers, and the strategies and major activities it uses to seek competitive advantages in that market. Importantly, the business model should identify the organization's key business processes and organizational capabilities that allow the business to generate revenues and profits.

B2C E-business Models

There are many different business models in the world of e-business, some more popular than others, and many that did not really exist before the increased use of the Internet for business. Table 13.3 shows a variety of B2C e-business models.

The e-business models presented in Table 13.3 continue to evolve as individuals find new ways to use the Internet, and increasingly mobile technologies, to create new approaches to generate revenue. In fact, with the use of location-based services on mobile devices (knowing where you are based on your cell phone's location)

Table 13.3 B2C E-business Models

E-business Model	Description	Important Facts	Examples
Online Retailing	Offers products or services for sale to consumers online. Some businesses acquire the products for resale while others act as electronic intermediaries for selling products.	The ability to distribute products efficiently and effectively (fulfillment and logistics functions) are critical to success in this business model.	• Pure play: Amazon.com, Buy.com, etc. • Bricks and clicks: BestBuy.com, Staples.com, etc.
Infomediary	Offers specialized information to consumers via the Internet that aggregates or analyzes products or services from several providers. The term comes from **Info**rmation inter**mediaries**.	These companies do not sell products or services directly, and they do not have any inventory. The ability to maintain up-to-date information is crucial in this business model.	• Consumer goods: MySimon.com • Travel: Kayak.com • Automobiles: Edmunds.com
Content Providers	Offers consumers content or relevant information, and receives money from vendors for ads or downloads, or from consumers for subscriptions.	Content can be generated and published by the organization or it can be user-generated content that the business published.	• News: Bloomberg Solutions (www.bloomberg.com/solutions/) • Entertainment: Eonline.com • Historical and reference: Britannica.com • Travel: Tripadvisor.com

Exchanges	Offers a location (marketplace) for buyers and sellers to transact online. Revenues come from fees for sellers or buyers, or commission on sales.	Generating a large number of buyers and sellers (a critical mass) is crucial for success in this business model.	• eBay.com • uBid.com
Online Community or Social Media	Offers individuals with similar interest and /or goal an online meeting place to interact with one another. Many start as not-for-profit, but end up charging for select services or information, or allow ads to be posted on the community.	Online communities are virtual, in the sense that the meeting place is online only.	• Facebook.com • MySpace.com • Talkcity.com
E-business Infrastructure Provider	Offers infrastructure hardware, software, or services to other organizations for e-business. Revenues come from fees paid for the services.	Online businesses can use these infrastructures through cloud computing (Chapter 7) or directly through the provider. This has reduced the cost of starting online businesses substantially.	• PayPal.com: online payment service. • MerchantExpress.com: credit card processing service. • Rackspace.com: Web and database hosting services • GoDaddy.com: domain name registration and Web and database hosting

allows marketing firms to offer targeted advertising and services that you may need at a specific moment, based on where you are. Some of the business models would not exist without the Internet, like the infrastructure companies such as PayPal. com or MerchantExpress.com, or the social media websites like Facebook.com or Talkcity.com. There are even some fairly unique business models in existence today like the name your own price model of priceline.com (http://www.priceline.com).

It is necessary for business models to evolve with today's rapid changes in technology and the changes in the way individuals interact with one another. For example, as many students know, changes in your online profile on a social networking site result in changes in the types of ads you see when accessing the site. This change in the social media business model has occurred in the last few years. However, while keeping up with the technological and social changes is important, the most important factor for success is to start with a proper business model. Back in the early days of e-business, many entrepreneurs jumped on the bandwagon of e-business without proper business models. Not surprisingly, many of them failed.

This is one reason behind what is today called the *dot-com bust:* when many individuals and companies lost money in attempts to take advantage of e-business. Today, there are too many e-business successes to even attempt to summarize them. Some are very innovative, while others simply follow solid business models.

BUSINESS EXAMPLE 1	CHANGING THE BUSINESS MODEL: FURNITURE.COM

When the dot-com bust happened in the early 2000s, many e-businesses simply went out of business, not able to generate sufficient revenues to cover their costs. Others, however, were able to survive by changing their business model. Such was the case of Furniture.com Inc.

Founded in 1998, Furniture.com was already in trouble by 2000 because even though the company was selling US$80 million worth of merchandise per year, it was losing an average of $900 per order. This was due to high costs of warehousing and delivery associated with the furniture they were selling to consumers. Executives at the company decided, however, that there was value in the company's IT infrastructure, website, and name, and decided to acquire these. They reopened the company in 2002 under a different business model. This time, they offered furniture for sale, but not their own. In other words, they operate a shopping portal and intermediary for furniture retailers. It now has far fewer employees and has integrated its website ordering system with its suppliers' selling systems, allowing orders placed online to be automatically logged into their partners' systems, and allowing customers to track inventory at local stores. With a name like Furniture.com, it is relatively easy to find for customers searching for furniture!

(Source: Weiss, Todd R. "Failed Online Retail Site Revived as Web Portal: Furniture.com Acts as Middleman via Links to Brick-and-Mortar IT Systems." *ComputerWorld* (November 28, 2005). http://www.computerworld.com/s/article/print/106514/Failed_Online_Retail_Site_Revived_as_Web_Portal/.)

B2C E-business Enablers

The statistics previously presented and those that you found in Learning Activity 13.1 clearly show that B2C e-business continues to increase in value worldwide. What has made this growth possible? A combination of technological and social factors can help explain why B2C e-business has grown so much over the years.

Technological Enablers

There are several technological requirements that must be met for consumers to successfully acquire goods or services online. First, there must be an easy-to-navigate website. The graphical user interfaces of today's browsers and the search tools available on websites are examples of technological improvements that have enabled e-business to grow. In addition, e-business requires that consumers have sufficient network bandwidth to access e-businesses' websites. Think of how much time it takes sometimes to download images for goods you want to purchase. If it takes too long, you might end up going to a different site. The bandwidth required depends on the images and other features of the site, and the overall bandwidth is a function of the vendor's network bandwidth (and server processing capability) and the consumer's Internet access bandwidth. In recent years, the use of broadband networks for Internet access (see Chapter 7) has significantly improved the overall bandwidth availability and therefore, the online shopping experience for consumers.

A less visible but just as critical technological requirement is interoperability. We discussed **interoperability** in Chapter 7, where we defined it as the ability of heterogeneous systems to communicate with one another. Interoperability is key to e-business success since by definition e-business allows individuals using a wide variety of platforms (PCs, Macs, laptops, tablets, smart phones, etc.) to access businesses that also use a wide variety of platforms (with different operating systems, databases, web servers, etc.).

Critical Mass

Beyond technological factors, one key social factor that has had a huge impact on the growth of e-business is the attainment of a critical mass of users. The impact of critical mass is best understood under the concept of network effects, which we define further below. For e-business, attaining **critical mass** means that there are sufficient buyers to sustain the business of vendors, and sufficient vendors to attract buyers to the Internet.

Network effects or network economics can be used to discuss how value is created in a network. Recall from Chapter 4 that a firm can get competitive advantages when they own a resource that is rare or unique. This is considered *value in scarcity*. In networks, however, there is also something completely opposite, which is *value in plentitude*. In a network (think of a group of people), the value of the network increases every time a new member is added to the network. Let us take the example of email. If only two of you use email, it makes one possible link. You might find it limiting eventually to only be able to send email to this one other person. Now if you add a third person to your group, you each have two potential people to email to (or the existence of three links in the network). The addition of the third person adds value to your network. Now consider the networks in Figure 13.2. How many links are possible now?

Extend this concept to e-business, and you realize that the more vendors there are on the Internet, the more interesting it is for you to shop online. For vendors, the same is true; the more consumers there are shopping online, the more interesting it is to use the Internet to sell their goods or services. Today, as we saw in previous chapters, there are close to 1 billion hosts (servers) on the Internet and over 30% of the world population with Internet access. We could say that the Internet and the Web have reached critical mass.

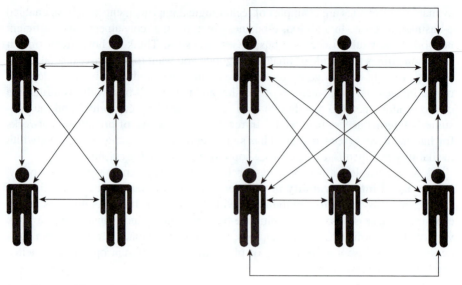

FIGURE 13.2 Networks of People

B2C E-business Impacts

We discussed early in the chapter how e-business has changed industries. For some, these changes have been extremely positive (lower costs) while for others the changes may be perceived as very negative (loss of profits or even disappearance of some businesses). There are two specific terms used to refer to two impacts of e-business: channel compression and channel expansion.

E-channel Compression (Disintermediation)

Channel compression is an impact on the downstream portion of the supply chain. Recall from Chapter 12 that the supply chain consists of several distributors and retailers upstream and downstream of the focal firm. In the distribution channel, the distributors and retailers are called intermediaries. **E-channel compression** refers to situations when the distribution chain is shortened by eliminating some or all of these intermediaries between the focal firm (product producer) and the end consumer. For this reason, channel compression is also called *disintermediation*. As previously discussed, this change in the distribution structure has led to some major restructuring in several industries, including the music, publishing, and travel industries. When organizations have to decide whether or not to eliminate members of their distribution channel, they are often faced with channel conflict, or when to eliminate distributors and when to work with them. For example, if the Dell company decides to offer products through Dell retailers but also to sell directly online, how can they price products so that their resellers can make a profit but their consumers still feel they are getting the best prices when they buy directly online?

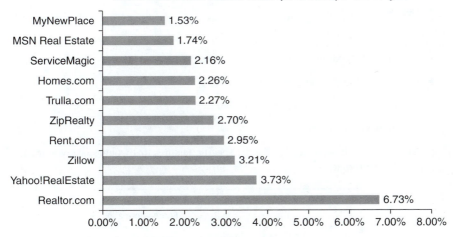

Online Real Estate Market Share (% of visits) in January 2010

FIGURE 13.3 Top Real Estate Websites in January 2010

Source: Based on data from Experian Hitwise, available at http://www.hitwise.com/.

E-channel Expansion

While e-channel compression has resulted in fewer organizations involved in the supply chain for some industries, e-channel expansion offers the reverse impact. **E-channel expansion** is the addition of intermediaries in an industry whose purpose is to aggregate and provide information or brokering functionalities. In other words, they facilitate bringing buyers and sellers together or bringing relevant information to buyers and sellers. Think of the role of kayak.com. They do not offer their own flights, but pull information from different vendors (airlines), as well as other search engines (like expedia.com or priceline.com). These intermediaries can make money by receiving fees from vendors, or by allowing ads on their site. The larger the volume of users, the better they can sell ad placement (selling ads on their website based on number of viewers). An overall important effect of these intermediaries is to reduce search costs and the information asymmetries that existed before the Internet and e-business. A good example is provided by real estate e-brokers. Figure 13.3 shows the most visited real estate websites in January 2010. How many of these companies existed before e-business?

LEARNING ACTIVITY 13.2   **WHY WOULD I TRUST THEM OR BUY FROM THEM?**

In this activity, we want you to visit two retail websites and identify the factors that would make you more willing to trust the web merchant, and to buy and/or share information with the website. Select two of the following Web merchants:

(continued)

- Dell: www.dell.com

- Amazon: www.amazon.com

- BestBuy: www.bestbuy.com

- Sierra: www.sierratradingpost.com

- Road Runner: www.roadrunnersports.com

- Murad: www.murad.com

Create a table as shown below, to list the specific features that would make you trust, buy, or share information:

	Trust	Intentions to Buy	Willingness to Share Information
Site A	Feature 1	Feature 1	Feature 1
	Feature 2	Feature 2	Feature 2
	Etc.	Etc.	Etc.
Site B	Feature 1	Feature 1	Feature 1
	Feature 1	Feature 2	Feature 2
	Feature 2	Etc.	Etc.
	Etc.		

Design for B2C E-Business

There are many important design features that can make e-business websites more or less successful. In Learning Activity 13.2, you identified several of them. For example, most of you will have identified the security of the website as a requirement for trusting the Web merchant and the privacy practices as a requirement for being willing to share information with the website. In Chapters 8 and 9, we discussed various features that increase (or reassure customers about) the security and privacy of information systems. In fact, many researchers have identified trust as one key determinant of individuals' intentions to buy from online merchants. Ease of use of the system in terms of navigation, checking out, and accessing information, are usually important design features as well. The overall look of the website is also a factor in online buying decisions. Sites that are overloaded with information can be distracting for some users, while sites that have too simplistic features and graphics may look unprofessional. There are also nontechnological features for website success, such as return policies, shipping policies, and communication tools. Research also suggests that websites that offer customer reviews see increased site traffic and overall conversion rate (www.emarketer.com). The conversion rate is the rate at which consumers who are browsing the website end up buying from the website. Other features that are found to annoy customers on websites include pop-up ads, the need for extra software to view a site, dead links, confusing navigation, requiring users to login to view content, slow loading pages, and out-of-date content, to name a few (eMarketer.com, 2009).

Business-to-Business (B2B)

Most of this chapter so far has discussed B2C e-business, mainly because you are more familiar with this type of e-business, but also because many of the basic principles also apply to B2B e-business. However, there is a significant difference between B2C and B2B e-business beyond the type of players involved, and that is the size of the market that is involved. B2B e-business represents a significantly larger market than B2C. In fact, the e-commerce data from the United States Census Bureau for 2009 shows that B2C e-commerce was US$298 billion, whereas the sale for B2B was US$ 3,073 billion (http://www.census.gov/econ/estats/2008/all2008tables.html).

STATISTICS BOX 2: B2B VS. B2C E-BUSINESS

Every year the U.S. Census Bureau collects data on e-commerce. At the beginning of the chapter, you saw the most recent e-commerce retail data. For B2B, there is usually a greater time lag necessary to report actual e-commerce sales each year, which is why 2009 data are reported below (the report was published May 27, 2011). The figure below highlights the significant differences in the market sizes of B2C and B2B e-business sales during the 2002–2009 time period. For the most up-to-date data, refer to http://www.census.gov/econ/estats/index.html.

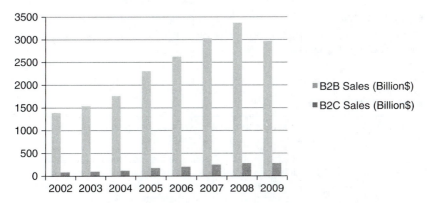

Source: Based on data from the US Census Bureau, available at http://www.census.gov/econ/estats/index.html/.

There are several other differences between B2B and B2C. Of course, B2B involves two or more organizations as opposed to individual consumers. In B2B, these organizations typically know their trading partners fairly well, and as a result, B2B is often relationship-based, except for marketplaces that we will describe later.

B2B E-business Models

B2B involves the sharing of electronic documents, funds, and/or information between organizations. There are many ways to implement this (see Table 13.4). First, B2B e-business includes Supply Chain Management, which we discussed in Chapter 12. In fact, when organizations share knowledge electronically across the supply chain to facilitate inventory control, reduce time delays in billing, and improve customer handling, they are conducting B2B e-business. Two other models of B2B e-business need further explanation: Electronic Data Interchange and e-marketplaces.

Electronic Data Interchange (EDI) is the electronic exchange of information between two or more organizations using a standard format. The types of information exchanged are defined within the standards that are used, and usually include business documents like bills, purchase orders, payment slips, invoices, and so on. EDI has been in existence for a very long time, allowing trading partners to lower transaction costs and improve profits through faster billing cycles, reduced errors, and improved customer responsiveness. Figure 13.4 shows a simplified sample set of EDI transactions.

An important characteristic of EDI is that organizations must use standardized formats for the documents they are exchanging. In fact, every organization has its own internal systems to handle purchase orders, invoices, and other business documents; therefore, each organization stores and handles data in different formats. An EDI transaction starts with the conversion of the documents and data from the format used by the internal system of the organization to an EDI format. This is called the **outbound transformation**. The EDI documents are then sent to the partner organization where the company's systems must perform an **inbound transformation**, which involves the system converting the EDI documents into the format used by the internal systems of that organization. The most used standardized formats for EDI are **ANSI X.12** and **EDIFACT**.

Table 13.4 B2B E-business Models

Electronic Data Interchange (EDI)	Electronic exchange of information between two or more organizations using a standard format.
Supply Chain Management (SCM)	Allows organizations to manage the movement of materials or products from provision to production to consumption. SCM involves collaboration between partners both upstream and downstream from the focal organization.
E-marketplaces	Also known as an *exchange*, it allows vending companies and buying companies to "meet" electronically to conduct transactions.

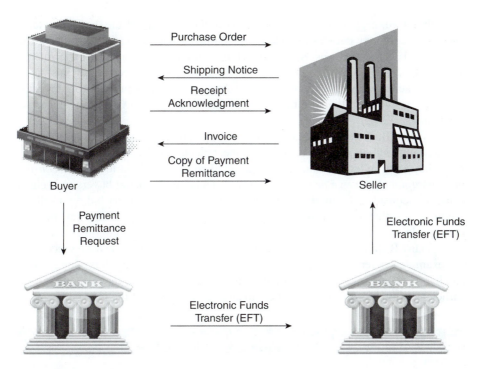

FIGURE 13.4 Electronic Data Interchange Example

EDI used to be limited to one-to-one communications between two trading partners. Today, it has evolved to a multipartner environment, allowing transmission of documents across a variety of information systems, even if they are incompatible in terms of hardware and software since EDI documents themselves have to be in a very strict format. The use of a strict format is both an advantage and a disadvantage of EDI systems; on the one hand, it allows for fast processing and support for the various platforms, but on the other hand, it limits the flexibility of transmission that organizations want. Today, organizations want to conduct more complex activities than simply trading documents with one another to support their business processes, and they want to use the Internet as opposed to proprietary networks for the transmissions. This is where **Extensible Markup Language (XML)** becomes a popular way of conducting B2B transactions. XML is a markup language that allows organizations to give meaning to their data by inserting tags that describe the data within documents. A markup language (such as HTML or XML) is used to give "meaning" to information by placing a beginning and end tag around the information. For example, to bold text in HTML, if we use the tag this is bolded, this will show as **this is bolded** on the Web page.

XML is very flexible since organizations can define their own tags. Once documents are tagged with XML, a variety of systems can read and understand the documents, as long at the systems know the definitions of the tags. In conducting

B2B, therefore, organizations have to agree on the meaning of the tags. For example, if one company decides to code its standardized documents in XML using the term (<CLIENT>Mr. Jones</CLIENT>) but its trading partner uses the term *customer* (<CUSTOMER>Mr. Jones</CUSTOMER>), their respective systems could not read each other's data. Some industries are tackling this problem by developing industry-wide XML definitions or standards, such as **ebXML** for e-business **(E-business XML)**.

Finally, B2B can also be conducted in marketplaces, also known as exchanges. An **exchange** allows vendors or sellers to meet electronically. When a limited number of buyers or sellers are allowed to use a marketplace, we refer to this as a *consortia marketplace* or even a *private market*. When a large number of buyers and sellers exist, it is considered a **neutral auction**. Sometimes many buyers bid on a seller's products (a **seller-oriented or forward auction**), or sometimes many sellers offer their products to a single buyer (a **buyer-oriented or reverse auction**). Over the years, many B2B marketplaces have come and gone, although some have succeeded. For example, Buyerzone.com allows small businesses to buy and sell products to one another. However, marketplaces are difficult to sustain because they need to have a sufficient number of buyers and sellers to ensure the growth of the marketplace.

LEARNING ACTIVITY 13.3　　**WHERE IS MY WEB PAGE?**

In this activity, you will select two different Internet search engines to find some specific items. Record your results in a word processing file.

   a. First, search for "intellectual property rights." Identify the top three sponsored (if any) and the top three nonsponsored links found.
   b. Use the same two search engines to find the following products: a Trek mountain bike and an iPod Touch 4G.

Indicate in your document the search engine used, the links you found, and your preferred search engine. Explain why you prefer a specific search engine.

Search Engine Optimization

Anyone involved in B2C e-business today would probably tell you that one of the most important factors for success online is being visible, which means showing up in searches. In fact, research has shown that if an organization's link is not in the top 30, it does not exist. Other research says that it is the first page of results that count. In a study of which links individuals click on the search results page, 42% of individuals clicked on the first nonsponsored link (explained below), 12% on the second, 8% on the third, then 6%, 5%, and 4% on the following ones, with 3% for the remainder of the links on the first page of search results (http://www.redcardinal. ie/search-engine-optimisation/). Clearly, being at the top of the search results page is important for e-businesses. But how does an organization make sure they show up toward the top of the search results? This is the role of **search engine optimization**

(SEO), which is the series of practices an organization can use to improve their visibility, or optimize how their Web pages or website show up on the search engine results pages. SEO uses a combination of how the Web page is designed, which keywords and languages are used on the Web page, and which search engines are most used by specific audiences.

SEO is not a one-time effort since search engines change their requirements often, people change their searching patterns, and competitors also try to optimize their own websites. In terms of design, one of the most important first steps for an organization is to clearly identify which keywords best represent what the organization's *intended audience* would use to find them. The key is to identify what the targeted audience thinks when they search online. It is also important to note that a keyword could actually be a keyword phrase, such as "mortgage lender" or "best place to eat." With this information, the Web designers can do several things to help the ranking of the Web page. They can include the main keywords more often on the page, and in more prominent places (headings, for example). They can include keywords in meta tags, which is information included with the page but not seen on the Web. There are many other factors that impact the ranking, such as including in-links, or inbound links, where other sites link to the organization's website, the age of the website domain (the longer the better), and the overall size of the website. The exact details of how a website is better ranked vary over time, and across search engines. This is why many consultants have started to offer SEO services to small, medium, and even large e-businesses.

Another way to have an organization's website show up higher in the rankings is to pay for placement. These are considered **sponsored links**, as opposed to **organic links** (ranked by design and SEO only). Some research suggests that most individuals prefer organic links, with 80 to 90% of the clicks being on organic links (http://www.redcardinal.ie/search-engine-optimisation/). Sponsored links show separate from the search results, and are based on the keywords entered in the search engines, as seen in Figure 13.5. The figure shows search results from a search of the keyword iPad on the Google search engine.

Keyword bidding is another form of paying for better ranking. It is also known as Pay-Per-Click (PPC). The concept is that organizations pay the search engine owners only when someone clicks their link on the search results page. In most cases, companies bid for keywords, and the company that bids the highest will show up higher in the results when someone uses the keywords in a search. There is another type of PPC called *flat-rate*, where the price of keywords is fixed. Nevertheless, you can easily see why PPC is an important source of revenues for companies like Google AdWords, Yahoo!, Search Marketing, or Microsoft AdCenter. Every time a user clicks on a link, the organization pays the search engine. In fact, many companies increased their paid search engine use for the holiday season 2010, and saw up to 69% increases in online sales directly attributable to paid searches (Enright, 2011). What does it cost to "buy" a keyword from a search engine? The cost varies substantially depending on the month of the year and what is going on at that time. An updated list can be found at http://www.spyfu.com/TopList.aspx?listId=3. In June 2011, the most expensive keywords were "Exchange server email hosting"

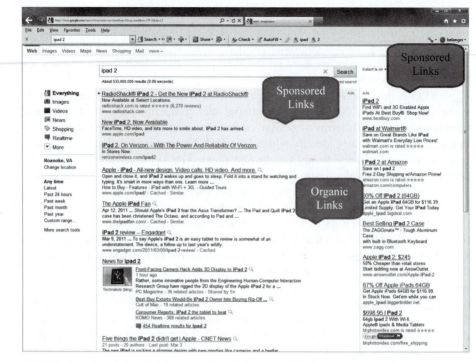

FIGURE 13.5 Search Results for Organic and Sponsored Links

at $110.26 per click and "for mesothelioma" at $109.93 per click. Table 13.5 shows some of the other popular keywords at that time. As can be seen, keywords can be very expensive. Therefore, organizations are often told to find the best and most representative keywords for their business, and to target to be number two instead of number one in the search results.

Paid search engine is a huge business, and the main players in the United States are Google, Yahoo!, and MSN. As of mid-2009, Google owned about 78% of the market, Yahoo! 17%, and MSN 5%. However, the story is slightly different when we consider other search engines around the world. In China, for example, the search engine Baidu owned about 73% of the search engine paid market at the end of 2010 (http://www.resonancechina.com/2011/01/31/q4-2010-china-search-engine-revenue-market-share/).

Trends in E-business

E-business has become mainstream, with individuals and organizations increasingly comfortable transacting and interacting electronically. We discuss three major trends in e-business in the remainder of the chapter. Students, however, can go to the book website for more interesting trends.

Table 13.5   Most Expensive Keywords – June 2011

1	Exchange server email hosting	$110.26
2	for mesothelioma	$109.93
3	christian residential drug treatment	$108.72
4	creditworthiness	$108.06
5	fire training university	$107.95
6	www blinds com	$107.34
7	charitable automobile donations	$107.23
8	attorney cancer law mesothelioma	$106.72
9	insurance quotes vehicle	$106.47
10	college art courses	$105.97
11	booking railway tickets	$105.23
12	atlanta mesothelioma claims	$104.95
13	donate your car san francisco	$104.69
14	d 108	$104.49
15	wedding the	$104.28
16	technical college illinois	$102.90
17	firm law mesothelioma texas	$102.90
18	asbestos attorney cancer lawyer mesothelioma settlement	$102.76
19	villa di piazzano cortona	$102.37
20	florida small business insurance	$102.22

Source: Based on data by SpyFu : Keywords with Highest Cost per Click, available at http://www.spyfu .com/TopList.aspx?listId=3/.

Mobile Business

Today, many individuals use sophisticated Internet-enabled mobile technologies, such as cellular phones, personal digital assistants, and tablets in their daily work and personal lives. This has enabled another form of e-business known as **mobile business (m-business)**, which is when individuals conduct commercial transactions and interactions using handheld mobile devices and wireless communication networks. With mobile devices, users have access to critical information anywhere and anytime, which allows them to seize business opportunities (such as enjoying the sale of the day on Woot! [www.woot.com]). As discussed in a prior chapter, with the advent of **location-based services** (LBS), it is even possible to provide targeted advertisements to users like discounts based on their current location. Therefore, as the user walks in front of a certain restaurant at mealtime, a coupon appears on the user's handheld device.

STATISTICS BOX 3: MOBILE BEHAVIORS

Mobile phones have gained visibility worldwide. Contrarily to many people's beliefs, usage of mobile phones in North America is not as advanced as in some other countries. In the table below, results from a comScore MobiLens study shows that Japanese users are much more likely to use their cellular phones for Web access.

Mobile Behaviors in Japan, United States, and EU5 (UK, DE, FR, ES and IT), June 2010

	Percent of Total Mobile Audience		
	Japan	United States	Europe
Total Audience: 13+ yrs old	100.0%	100.0%	100.0%
Used connected media (Browsed, Accessed Applications or Downloaded Content)	75.2%	43.7%	38.5%
Used browser	59.3%	34.0%	25.8%
Used application	42.3%	31.1%	24.9%
Messaging Usage			
• Sent text message to another phone	40.1%	66.8%	81.7%
• Used major instant messaging service	3.3%	17.2%	12.6%
• Used email (work or personal)	54.0%	27.9%	18.8%
Social Media/Entertainment			
• Accessed Social Networking Site or Blog	17.0%	21.3%	14.7%
• Listened to music on mobile phone	12.5%	13.9%	24.2%
• Took photos	63.0%	50.6%	56.8%
• Captured video	15.4%	19.2%	25.8%
• Watched TV and/or video on mobile phone	22.0%	4.8%	5.4%
• Played games	16.3%	22.5%	24.1%
Financial Information			
• Accessed bank accounts	8.0%	9.4%	7.1%
• Accessed financial news or stock quotes	16.1%	10.0%	7.2%
Retail/Travel			
• Accessed online retail	7.2%	5.5%	4.1%
• Accessed classifieds	4.2%	6.6%	4.2%
• Accessed travel service	3.3%	4.7%	4.1%

Other			
• Accessed maps	15.7%	16.0%	10.8%
• Accessed traffic reports	12.6%	8.2%	5.9%
• Accessed weather	34.1%	22.3%	13.7%

Source: http://www.comscore.com/.

Global e-Business

Another important trend for e-business is the global nature of the phenomenon. Usage of electronic means for business is growing everywhere in the world. In fact, the Internet is also becoming multilingual, facilitating e-business. As of the end of June 2010, there were 536.6 million users of English websites on the Internet (www .internetworldstats.com/stats7.htm). At the same time, 444.9 million used Chinese, 153.3 million used Spanish, and 99.1 million used Japanese websites. It is not surprising then that the China e-Business Research Center reported that e-commerce sales in China grew to 4.5 trillion yuan (US$684 billion) in 2010 (AFP, 2011). Similar statistics exist for e-business worldwide, as you might have found in Learning Activity 13.1. The business statistics box below, for example, lists some of the e-business facts published by the government of Ontario, Canada.

STATISTICS BOX 4: E-BUSINESS IN ONTARIO

E-business is a global phenomenon. The Ministry of Economic Development and Trade of the Province of Ontario, Canada, offer the following statistics.

- In 2009, 76% of all Ontario users made purchases online, compared to 70% in 2007.

- Online purchasing by businesses has steadily increased in Ontario, from 26% in 2001 to 74% in 2009. The most common online business purchases are office supplies, followed by computer software and hardware.

- In 2009, 90% of Ontario companies used the Internet, compared to 68% six years before.

- In 2009, almost 82% of businesses in Ontario had high-speed access to the Internet, compared to 27% in 2001.

- More than three-quarters of Ontario businesses see high-speed access as very important to their company's success.

- In 2009, almost half of Ontario companies felt that e-business was critical to their bottom line, compared to 30% in 2001.

- In 2009, 80% of Ontario companies felt that the Internet is a safe place to do business when proper security measures are in place, compared to 59% six years ago.

(continued)

- Internet banking by Ontario companies has tripled in the past six years to 57% in 2009.

- In 2009, six in 10 Ontario companies had a website, almost double the number eight years before.

- E-mail is now used by 90% of Ontario businesses, an increase of 22 percentage points since 2001.

Source: E-Business Facts, Ontario Ministry of Economic Development and Trade, http://www .ontariocanada.com/ontcan/1medt/smallbiz/en/sb_ebiz_facts_en.jsp/.

LEARNING ACTIVITY 13.4   USA.GOV

Government websites are sometimes different than e-commerce websites. In this learning activity, you are to interact with the usa.gov website (www.usa.gov) or your local government's website. Identify five similarities and differences between this e-government site and e-commerce sites used in Learning Activity 13.2.

E-government

A final trend we discuss is e-government, which was introduced at the beginning of the chapter. **E-government** involves using information technologies to enable and improve the efficiency with which government services are provided to citizens, employees, businesses, and agencies. It can occur at various levels of governments, such as municipalities, counties, districts, states, provinces, or countries. It has become popular for not only obtaining information from government agencies, but also for conducting transactions such as paying taxes, renewing licenses, or downloading government forms. According to Smith (2010), 82% of Internet users search for government information or complete government transactions online. The most leading edge applications in e-government include creating platforms for citizen feedback via blogs, Twitter, or social networking sites. The future of e-government is also likely to include some form of **Internet voting**, where citizens will be able to cast their votes electronically via the Internet. In fact, some countries and states have already started to allow citizens to vote via the Internet.

CHAPTER SUMMARY

In this chapter, we discussed e-business. We first presented various ways to categorize e-business, and then explored specific business models more in depth. More specifically, we explained how business-to-consumer (B2C) is conducted, and what its enablers and impacts are. We also discussed business-to-business e-business models in depth. The chapter concluded with search engine optimization and a discussion of important trends related to e-business.

Here are the main points discussed in the chapter.

- E-business involves electronic means to interact or conduct business with individuals, companies, or government agencies. E-business can be classified according to type: Business-to-Consumer (B2C: interactions are taking place between a consumer and a business), Business-to-Business (B2B: interactions are taking place between two businesses), Consumer-to-Consumer (C2C: interactions are taking place between two consumers), and Government-to-Constituent (G2C: interactions are taking place between a government agency and a constituent). E-businesses can also be classified according to their online component: bricks and mortar are traditional organizations with physical locations, bricks and clicks are traditional organizations with physical locations but that also operate an online business, and pure plays are organizations with only an online business.

- Business-to-Consumer (B2C) e-business models include online retailing (offering products or services for sale to consumers online), infomediaries (offering specialized information to consumers via the Internet that aggregates or analyzes products or services from several providers), content providers (offering consumers content or relevant information), exchanges (offering a location [marketplace] for buyers and sellers to transact online), online communities or social media (offering individuals with similar interest and /or goal an online meeting place to interact with each other), and e-business infrastructure providers (offering infrastructure hardware, software or services to other organizations for e-business). Enablers of B2C e-business include technological enablers (ease of use, bandwidth, and interoperability), as well as a social enabler (critical mass). Finally, impacts of e-business include channel compression and channel expansion.

- Search Engine Optimization (SEO) is the series of practices an organization can use to improve its visibility, or optimize, how its Web pages or website show up on the search engine results pages. SEO uses a combination of Web page design, keywords and languages used on the Web page, and listing on search engines most used by specific audiences. One way to optimize placement is through sponsored links, where the company pays for placement or uses keyword bidding, which gives companies with the highest bids higher placement in search engine results.

- Business-to-Business (B2B) e-business involves the sharing of electronic documents, funds, and/or information between organizations. B2B e-business models include Supply Chain Management, Electronic Data Interchange, and e-marketplaces. Electronic Data Interchange (EDI) is the electronic exchange of information between two or more organizations using a standard format. The most used standardized formats for EDI are ANSI X.12 and EDIFACT, but organizations are increasingly using XML (Extensible Markup Language) to conduct B2B transactions because it is much more flexible in what types of information it allows organizations to exchange with one another. B2B marketplaces, or exchanges, allow vendors or sellers to "meet" electronically.

- Three major trends in e-business are mobile business, global e-business, and e-government. Mobile business, or m-business, occurs when individuals conduct commercial transactions and interactions using handheld mobile devices and wireless communications networks. Global e-business is occurring because usage of electronic means for business is growing everywhere in the world and the Internet is increasingly becoming multilingual. E-government involves using information technologies to enable and improve the efficiency with which government services are provided to citizens, employees, businesses, and agencies.

REVIEW QUESTIONS

1. Define e-business and compare this to e-commerce, e-government, and Internet commerce. Is Internet-commerce considered e-business?
2. Explain what a business model is and what it should include.
3. Describe the various ways to classify e-business models, including B2C and B2B models.
4. Identify the main technological factors that have enabled e-business growth and compare them to the technological enablers of m-business.
5. Explain the concept of network effects or network economics and its importance to e-business.
6. Explain how e-business has led to disintermediation and provide examples.
7. Explain how e-business has led to e-channel expansion, discuss its impacts, and provide examples.
8. Describe the goals of search engine optimization, the various ways in which it is performed, and other options organizations have for marketing their websites.
9. Compare and contrast B2B e-business to B2C e-business.
10. Describe how Electronic Data Interchange (EDI) functions and how it is evolving today.

REFLECTION QUESTIONS

1. What is the most important thing you learned in this chapter? Why is it important?
2. What topics are unclear? What about them is unclear?
3. Is it important to distinguish between e-business, e-commerce, and Internet commerce? Why or why not?
4. How is the material in this chapter related to the transmitting information material in Chapter 7?
5. What is the relationship between network effects and the material on competitive advantages in Chapter 4?
6. What is the role of security in e-business success?
7. What is the role of privacy in e-business success?
8. If in an industry both channel compression and channel expansion occur because of e-business, does that mean that e-business had limited impacts on that industry? Why or why not?

9. A businessperson the authors know said to us that Search Engine Optimization is as much art as science. What does he mean?

10. Why is mobile commerce more popular in other areas of the world compared to the United States?

ADDITIONAL LEARNING ACTIVITIES

1. For this activity, read the article "Failed E-businesses" on the book website. Identify three common mistakes made by the e-businesses that failed during the dot-com bust era. Pick two of them and identify what could you do to make that business work today.

2. This activity requires you to complete a case analysis regarding e-business. The case may be accessed through your university website, the Ivey School business case website (http://cases.ivey.uwo.ca), the Harvard Business school cases website (http://cb.hbsp.harvard.edu/cb/web), or may be provided to you by your instructor.

    Upton, D. and Fuller, V. **CASE:** The ITC eChoupal Initiative. *Harvard Business Case,* Product number: #9-604-016, 2004 (revised).

3. E-business has become a global phenomenon. However, not all countries are equal when it comes to having infrastructures, laws, and business practices that support e-business. The Economist Intelligence Unit (EIU) (www.eiu.com) ranks every country on their digital economy readiness. In this learning activity, you will be assigned one or several countries and explore their e-business readiness. Your instructor will assign you which country you are going to research. Bring a short report to class that will include:

    • The country you are assigned.
    • The EIU ranking for digital economy readiness.
    • Any e-business statistics you can find about your assigned country.
    • Your research of potential explanations for the ranking of your country (you will have to make assumptions).

4. Conduct research on the Web to give examples of each type of e-business defined in Table 13.1.

5. Extend the existing business models presented in Table 13.2 with the use of Location-Based Services (LBS). Describe how mobile users could make use of these models.

6. Identify the business model of the following websites: www.pandora.com, www.consumerreports.org, www.yahoo.com, and www.weightwatchers.com.

7. Identify additional major trends in e-business beyond the ones presented at the end of the chapter.

REFERENCES

Agence France Press. "China e-commerce sales up 22% in 2010."(January 22, 2011) reported in: http://www.independent.co.uk/life-style/china-ecommerce-sales-up-22-in-2010-report-2191373.html

Enright, Allison. "Paid Search Pays Off over the Holidays: Budgets Were up 52% during November and December, and Related Sales Rose 69%." *Internet Retailer,* (January 13, 2011) http://www.internetretailer.com/2011/01/13/paid-search-paid-over-holidays/.

Smith, A. "Government Online: the Internet Gives Citizens New Paths to Government Sevices and Information." *Pew Internet and American Life Project Report* (2010). Retrieved January 26, 2011, from http://pewinternet.org/Reports/2010/Government-Online.aspx/.

BIBLIOGRAPHY AND FURTHER READINGS

Chaffey, Dave. "Boo.com Case Study – a Classic Example of Failed E-business Strategy." *Digital Marketing Case Studies* (February 15, 2010).

Segal, David. "The Dirty Little Secrets of Search." *New York Times* (February 12, 2011) NYTimes.com/.

GLOSSARY

ANSI X.12: one of the most used standardized formats for EDI.

Bricks and Clicks: traditional organizations with physical locations as well as an online business.

Bricks and Mortar: traditional organizations with physical locations.

Business model: the way the organization functions and creates value.

Business-to-Business (B2B): type of e-business where interactions are taking place between two businesses.

Business-to-Consumer (B2C): type of e-business where interactions are taking place between a consumer and a business.

Buyer-oriented or reverse auction: many sellers offer their products to a single buyer.

Consumer-to-Consumer (C2C): type of e-business where interactions are taking place between two consumers.

Content providers: e-business model where companies offer consumers content or relevant information, and receive money from vendors for ads or downloads, or from consumers for subscriptions.

Critical mass: a point when there are sufficient buyers to sustain the business of vendors, and sufficient vendors to attract buyers to the Internet.

E-business infrastructure provider: company that offers infrastructure hardware, software, or services to other organizations for e-business.

ebXML for e-business (E-business XML): an industry-wide set of XML definitions or standards for e-business.

E-channel compression (disintermediation): situations when the distribution chain is shortened by eliminating some or all of these intermediaries between the focal firm (product producer) and the end consumer.

E-channel expansion: addition of intermediaries in an industry whose purpose is to aggregate and provide information or brokering functionalities.

EDIFACT: one of the most used standardized formats for EDI.

Electronic business (e-business): electronic means to interact or conduct business with individuals, companies, or government agencies.

Electronic commerce (e-commerce): electronic means to conduct business transactions, including the Internet, Electronic Data Interchange, or private networks.

Electronic Data Interchange (EDI): a B2B e-business model focusing on the electronic exchange of information between two or more organizations using a standard format.

Electronic Funds Transfer (EFT): electronic means to conduct financial transactions such as payments and remittances.

Electronic government (e-government): electronic means to interact or conduct transactions with government agencies.

E-marketplaces (exchanges): allows vendors or sellers to "meet" electronically.

Exchange: e-business model where companies offer a location (marketplace) for buyers and sellers to transact online.

Extensible Markup Language (XML): a markup language that allows organizations to give meaning to their data by inserting tags that describe the data within documents; a popular way of conducting B2B transactions.

Government-to-Constituent (G2C): type of e-business where interactions are taking place between a government agency and a constituent.

Inbound transformation: converting the EDI documents into the format used by the internal systems of that organization.

Infomediaries: e-business model where companies offer specialized information to consumers via the Internet that aggregates or analyzes products or services from several providers.

Internet commerce: electronic means to conduct business using the Internet (for example email, the Web, or file transfers).

Internet voting: when citizens are able to cast their votes electronically via the Internet.

Interoperability: the ability of heterogeneous systems to communicate with each other.

Keyword bidding (pay-per-click: PPC): when organizations pay the search engine owners when someone clicks their link on the search engine results page.

Location-based services (LBS): services that make use of knowing where the user is, based on their cell phone location to offer targeted advertising or services at a specific moment.

Markup language (such as HTML or XML): used to give "meaning" to information by placing a beginning and end tag around the information.

Mobile business (m-business): when individuals conduct commercial transactions and interactions using handheld mobile devices and wireless communications networks.

Network effects or network economics: explains how value is attained in a network when critical mass, or plentitude of members, is achieved. The value of the network increases every time a new member is added to the network.

Neutral auction: marketplace with a large number of buyers and sellers exist.

Online community or social media: e-business model where organizations offer individuals with similar interest and /or goal an online meeting place to interact with one another.

Online retailing: e-business model where companies offer products or services for sale to consumers online.

Organic links: links on search engine results achieved by design and search engine optimization.

Outbound transformation: conversion of the documents and data from the format used by the internal system of the organization to an EDI format.

Pure Plays (Click Only): organizations with only an online business.

Search engine optimization (SEO): series of practices an organization can use to improve their visibility or optimize how their Web pages or website show up on the search engine results pages.

Seller-oriented or forward auction: many buyers bid on a seller's products.

Sponsored links: links on search engine results that companies paid for placement.

Supply Chain Management (SCM): a B2B e-business model focusing on electronic exchange of information along the supply chain.

Web commerce: electronic means to conduct business transactions using the Web as an interface.

Information and Knowledge for Business Decision Making

CHAPTER 14

LEARNING OBJECTIVES

By reading and completing the activities in this chapter, you will be able to:

- Explain why knowledge management is important to organizations
- Compare and contrast explicit and tacit knowledge
- Describe the main processes for knowledge management
- Compare and contrast major knowledge management technologies
- Apply a framework for making ethical decisions

CHAPTER OUTLINE

Communication-based tools

Executive information systems and dashboards

Expert systems

- Learning Activity 14.3: Using a decision support system
- Decision support systems and group decision support systems
- Business intelligence

  Data warehousing

  Data mining
- Learning Activity 14.4: Making ethical decisions
- Ethical decision-making
- Chapter summary
- Review questions
- Reflection questions
- Additional learning activities
- References
- Bibliography and further readings
- Glossary

Ultimately a business' ability to compete depends heavily on how its employees apply knowledge to make decisions and solve problems. Information systems and technologies can help organizations better manage knowledge. In addition, information systems and technologies can facilitate better decision-making. In this chapter we help you understand knowledge management and how technologies can help organizations manage knowledge. Knowledge is often applied to decision-making. Because of this, we also discuss decision support systems. As organizations gather an increasing amount of data, being able to leverage this data for decision-making and action is an increasingly important aspect of business. Business intelligence systems, which we also discuss in this chapter, help organizations make sense of this sea of data. Because of the importance of ethical decision-making, we close the chapter with a framework and process that you can use to help you make more ethical decisions.

FOCUSING STORY: MANAGING KNOWLEDGE BY TEXTING

Several years ago, I was teaching an onsite class to IT professionals working at a major logistics company. While waiting for class to start one night, I overheard one of the students asking another if he had received a text message regarding a problem he was having with a computer program. This surprised me. At the time such messaging was generally done more for personal than business reasons. So, I asked the student who sent the text how frequently they exchanged such messages. The student replied, "All the time. Whenever one of us runs into a problem we haven't seen before, we send a message to the group. Usually someone has seen a similar problem so they can help." Essentially the group had informally created a "knowledge network" of shared expertise. By sending a simple text message, an individual worker can tap into the knowledge of the entire group. The result is hours of saved time and frustration.

More recently, people are using social networking sites such as LinkedIn and Facebook as a means of accessing the knowledge of others. For example, when I had to write a job description for an unusual faculty job, I turned to several LinkedIn groups for advice. Some individuals responded with helpful advice. When you are faced with a decision, you often find it necessary to reach out to those who may have knowledge useful for the decision. This may be as simple as calling your car-loving brother when you are buying a new vehicle, or it may mean convening a meeting of experts to help a corporate board decide whether to pursue a merger. Regardless of the decision, the intent is the same. Additional knowledge can have great value to decision-making. Whether you use text messaging to get help solving a computer problem or you fly in experts from around the world, you are still trying to leverage the knowledge of others to help you make a decision. Fortunately, information technologies can help in our quest to use the knowledge of others to help make better decisions.

FOCUSING QUESTIONS:

1. When have you used the knowledge of others to help you make a decision? Briefly describe the decision. Who did you contact to help you? What knowledge were you trying to access?

2. How have you used information technologies to help you connect with others for the purpose of tapping their knowledge? Why did you use those technologies?

| LEARNING ACTIVITY 14.1 | HOW YOU MANAGE KNOWLEDGE |

This chapter helps you understand organizational knowledge management, but individuals also manage their knowledge. The goal of knowledge management is to make sure the right knowledge is available in a useful form to the right people. Personal knowledge management is the process of determining what knowledge you need, and how to find, organize, and use that knowledge. Prepare a one- to two-page paper on how you manage your personal knowledge. What tools do you use? How effective are they? Compare your response with another student's response.

Table 14-1 Characteristics of Data, Information, and Knowledge

Data	Information	Knowledge
Easily structured	Data that has been processed	Hard to structure
Easily captured	Requires unit of analysis	Difficult to capture
Easily transferred	Human involvement necessary	Often tacit
Often quantified		Hard to transfer
Mere facts		

Source: adapted from Pearlson and Saunders, 2006

Knowledge Management

In an earlier chapter we introduced you to the concepts of data, information, and knowledge. You may recall that data are unconnected facts, information is data that has been processed so that it is useful, and knowledge is information that is applied to a decision or action. If you think about these differences, you may see that as we progress from data to information to knowledge, there is a greater level of human contribution and greater value.

However, as we move up the hierarchy towards knowledge, things get harder to manage, in part because of the increased level of human contribution. It is relatively easy to manage data, but managing knowledge is quite difficult. Table 14.1 shows some characteristics of data, information, and knowledge. As you can see from the table, knowledge is hard to structure, transfer, and capture, which leads to knowledge being much harder to manage than data or information.

Knowledge management is a process that allows organizations to generate value from their knowledge-based assets. Knowledge management involves capturing and documenting what employees and other stakeholders know and developing systems that make it easier to share and use that knowledge. Later in this chapter we discuss the process of knowledge management. Before getting into that, however, we help you understand why knowledge management is important.

Why Managing Knowledge Is Important

Knowledge is among the most important resources of any organization. Recall that knowledge is information directed toward action and decision-making. To be successful, organizations must not only effectively manage information, they must also manage knowledge. Unfortunately, knowledge management is often messy and complex.

Organizations have always managed knowledge. More recently, however, organizations have begun using information and communication technologies to help manage knowledge. Organizations that manage knowledge well make better decisions, are generally more innovative, and tend to be more successful overall than those that do not.

Effective knowledge management can bring about big benefits, including:

- better problem solving

- improved customer service

- more effective product management

- increased innovation

- improved processes (more efficient and more effective)

- increased intellectual capital

- better leveraging of intellectual assets

Types of Knowledge

Understanding more about knowledge will help you better understand important aspects of knowledge management systems. We can divide knowledge into two categories: explicit knowledge and tacit knowledge. **Explicit knowledge** can be expressed relatively easily. Examples include operations manuals, books and articles, scientific formulas, and statistical analysis. Because explicit knowledge can be easily expressed, it can be more easily shared, stored, and managed than our other category of knowledge, tacit knowledge. It may be helpful to think of explicit knowledge as "knowing that," while tacit knowledge is more about "knowing how."

Tacit knowledge is not easy to express or communicate. It is internalized and highly individualized. An individual's tacit knowledge is rooted in life experiences, values, and biases. Ask an artist how to create a beautiful piece of art. The chances are that s/he will have trouble expressing exactly how striking art is created. This is an example of tacit knowledge. The artist may be able to create such art, but may not be able to easily communicate that to you. In fact, sometimes the person who possesses the tacit knowledge may not even be aware that s/he has the knowledge.

Tacit knowledge also exists in more mundane contexts. A good salesperson knows when to close a sale and when to back off. A knowledgeable computer programmer can quickly diagnose an error message. There are examples of tacit knowledge in any organization and in any profession. One of the most interesting examples comes from the world of poultry. Determining the sex of a baby chick immediately after hatching is important for commercial egg producers. Egg producers prefer female chicks, since they will be able to lay eggs. Egg producers employ chicken sexers, who have the uncanny ability to discriminate between female and male chicks with a quick glance. What is interesting about this ability is that most expert chicken sexers cannot tell you how they make their decisions, yet they are very accurate. They have the tacit knowledge, but are unable to easily convert this into explicit knowledge. Capturing tacit knowledge and codifying it so that it can be shared is one of the major challenges of knowledge management.

Types of Knowledge Resources

Knowledge is a critical resource for organizations, as we noted earlier. There are different types of knowledge resources in any organization. Understanding these will help you understand knowledge management, which we discuss later. Knowledge resources can be divided into four categories (Nonaka and Takeuchi, 1995).

- **Experiential knowledge** resources consist of tacit knowledge that can be shared through common experiences and interpersonal communication. Examples include skills, know-how, and emotional knowledge.

- **Conceptual knowledge** resources are made up of explicit knowledge that is embodied in language, symbols, and images. Concepts for products, services, and designs are examples.

- **Systemic knowledge** resources consist of explicit knowledge that has been systemized and packaged. Knowledge assets in this category are the easiest to share and manage. Intellectual property, such as patents and licenses, documents and databases are examples.

- **Routine knowledge** resources are made up of the tacit knowledge that is embedded in the organization's practices. Organizational routines for day-to-day activities, and organizational culture are examples of routine knowledge.

Now that you understand more about knowledge and its characteristics, we can turn our attention to how to manage knowledge.

Main Processes for Knowledge Management

A complete knowledge management system should consist of knowledge creation, capture, codification, storage, retrieval, transfer, and application, as shown in Figure 14.1. Knowledge management processes form a cycle. Applying knowledge often leads to

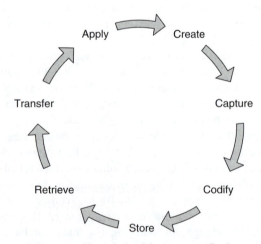

FIGURE 14.1 Knowledge Management Cycle

the creation of new knowledge, which restarts the cycle. While information technology is not required for any of these, as you will see IT can facilitate each process in a knowledge management system. In this section, we discuss each of these processes.

Information technology is critical to modern knowledge management, but technology alone cannot ensure effective knowledge management. Effective knowledge management also requires social and structural mechanisms that support knowledge management. For example, a culture of trust can greatly enhance knowledge sharing within an organization. Poor organizational processes and culture can bring about knowledge management failure.

Creating Knowledge

While knowledge exists in individuals, organizational knowledge can also be created. Nonaka and Takeuchi (1995) proposed the SECI model of organizational knowledge creation. The model is shown in Figure 14.2. According to the model, knowledge creation is a continuous process consisting of interactions between implicit and explicit knowledge. There are four processes by which knowledge is created.

- *Socialization* involves sharing tacit knowledge through direct communication or shared experience. This is tacit knowledge to tacit knowledge communication.

- *Externalization* is tacit to explicit communication. Tacit knowledge is converted to explicit knowledge by developing specific concepts, models, and the like. This conversion allows the knowledge to be understood and interpreted by others. This also serves as a foundation for creating new knowledge.

- *Combination* is the process of combining the externalized explicit knowledge to form broader concepts, models, and theories.

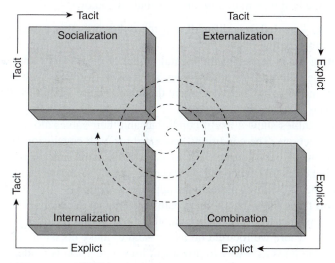

FIGURE 14.2 SECI Model of Organizational Knowledge Creation

- *Internalization* occurs when explicit knowledge transforms to tacit knowledge and becomes internalized by individuals within the organization. This can start a new cycle, beginning with the socialization of the new tacit knowledge.

These four processes form a cycle of increasing knowledge. Completing one cycle can start a new trip through the four processes, but with an ever-increasing amount of knowledge. This is represented by the spiral in the figure.

Knowledge can also be "purchased" by hiring knowledgeable individuals, either as consultants or employees. Knowledge can also be acquired by purchasing reports or even entire companies. Organizations may acquire another company to gain access to the company's knowledge assets.

Capturing and Codifying Knowledge

Once knowledge is created or otherwise acquired, it needs to be captured and codified. There are many techniques for capturing knowledge, including interviewing experts, observing groups as they make decisions, focus groups, "lessons learned" debriefings, and task analysis.

Codifying knowledge means converting tacit and explicit knowledge into a form that organizational members can use. It is representing knowledge so that it can be reused. This also includes documenting knowledge that was previously undocumented. To codify knowledge, organizations should do the following (Davenport & Prusak, 1998):

- Define the strategic intent. (How will the codified knowledge serve the organization?)

- Identify the knowledge necessary to achieve the intent.

- Evaluate existing knowledge's usefulness and ability to be codified.

- Determine the best way to codify and distribute the knowledge.

Codifying knowledge is difficult, but there are tools that can help. Some of these are described below.

Cognitive maps represent the mental model of the expert's knowledge. Key concepts and the relationships among them are shown. Software such as Freemind, MindMeister, and Visio can help document the maps. Figure 14.3 illustrates a cognitive map of Web 2.0 concepts and tools.

Decision tables show a list of conditions and their values along with a list of conclusions or actions. The conditions necessary for each conclusion are indicated. Figure 14.4 shows a decision table for making MBA admission decisions. In each column "Y" indicates that the condition was met, while "N" means that the condition was not met. The "X" entries indicate the appropriate action.

Decision trees show the alternate paths that impact decisions. The tree shows various paths that can lead to certain outcomes. You may remember decision trees from Chapter 6, where we focused on using them to make decisions. Here the idea is to use decision trees as a way to document how a decision is made. Figure 14.5 shows a decision tree version for making MBA admission decisions.

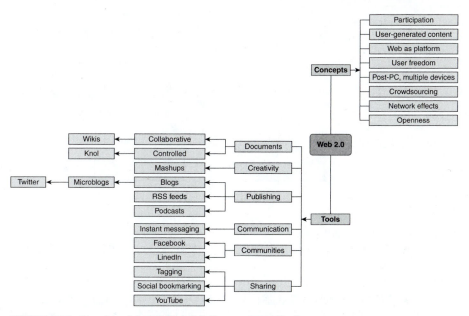

FIGURE 14.3 Cognitive Map of Web 2.0 Concepts and Tools

The purpose of these and other codification tools are to systematically document knowledge that is "stored' in the minds of experts. By working with the experts to create these diagrams and tables, knowledge modelers can help capture and document the expert's knowledge.

Documenting the knowledge allows us to store, organize, and share the knowledge so that others can use it.

	Condition Stub		Condition Entry						
			1	2	3	4	5	6	7
	Applicant has undergraduate degree		Y	Y	Y	Y	Y	Y	N
If	Applicant has > 2 years work experience		Y	Y	Y	Y	N	N	
(condition)	GMAT > 600		Y	Y	N	N	N	Y	
	Undergraduate GPA > 3.0		Y	N	Y	N	N	Y	
Then	Admit		X						
(action)	Conditionally admit			X		X			
	Advise to retake GMAT				X				
	Decline admission						X	X	X

FIGURE 14.4 Decision Table Example

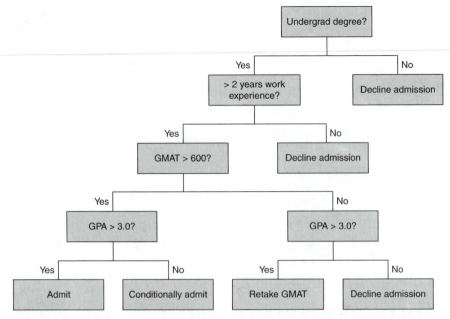

FIGURE 14.5 Decision Tree Example

Managers who want to have good knowledge management systems must work hard to create a culture that rewards rather than punishes knowledge sharing. Knowledge is a critical asset for any business professional. The more useful knowledge you possess, the more valuable you are to the organization. As is the case with any resource, the more rare the knowledge, the more valuable it is. In other words, if you have knowledge that few others have, you are more valuable to the business.

This simple fact can hinder knowledge management. Since sharing knowledge makes it more widespread (less rare), sharing decreases the value of possessing that knowledge. So, if you share your knowledge, you become less valuable to the organization. Because of this, trust is important to knowledge management. Experts who possess knowledge must trust that their organization will not unfairly take advantage of the individual who shares the knowledge. If this trust does not exist, the expert may hoard the knowledge to maintain its value.

Storing and Retrieving Knowledge

Organizing knowledge so that it can be easily accessed is challenging. One reason for this is that knowledge can exist and be documented in many different forms. As a result, there is no single knowledge base for an organization. Knowledge is stored in a variety of forms, including some that you might find surprising. For example, a well-organized corporate directory that lists areas of expertise can be thought of as a knowledge store. Such a directory effectively points to experts, who are repositories of knowledge. Document storage systems are also examples of knowledge stores.

Knowledge storage and retrieval are closely interrelated. Even the most well designed knowledge storage system is ineffective if knowledge consumers cannot retrieve the knowledge. Search technologies are important knowledge retrieval tools. Think about how many times you have used Google, or some other search tool to locate knowledge. Accurate, fast search results are a boon to anyone seeking knowledge.

Transferring and Applying Knowledge

Knowledge needs to be applied to be useful, and application implies that knowledge is available to those who need it. Knowledge maps can facilitate knowledge transfer. Knowledge maps show the location of knowledge within the organization. A knowledge map can identify individual experts, networks of experts or documents and databases.

To manage knowledge transfer you must consider the sources of knowledge. The media used to transfer the knowledge, and the knowledge consumers. Sources of knowledge include experts, knowledge bases (databases for knowledge), and document repositories. Media may include computer networks and other communication media. Consumers are the individuals and groups that apply the knowledge.

You have engaged in knowledge transfer, even though you may not have realized it. Education is a form of knowledge transfer; your professor is transferring some of her/his knowledge to you. Have you ever contacted a friend for help on an assignment or project? If so, you used your social network for transferring knowledge.

While humans have always used their social networks to access knowledge, the emergence of social networking technologies is increasing this sort of knowledge transfer. The use of instant messaging in the Focusing Story is an early example of using software to tap into others' knowledge. New social networking tools make this sort of knowledge transfer even more effective.

LEARNING ACTIVITY 14.2   **WIKIS FOR MANAGING KNOWLEDGE**

A wiki is a website that allows individuals to jointly create and edit Web pages about a chosen topic using a simple Web-based interface. (You learned about wikis in Chapter 7. See the book's website for a link to a video explaining wikis.) Wikipedia, the online collaborative encyclopedia, is the most popular use of a wiki, but many other wikis exist. Prepare a one-page paper that discusses how a wiki can be used for knowledge management.

Knowledge Management Technologies

Information and communication technologies have helped with knowledge management for a long time. Even the telephone can be used to help individuals tap external knowledge. In this section we discuss several knowledge management technologies.

Repositories

The goal of **knowledge repositories** is to make it easy to find and retrieve documents that contain knowledge. According to Pearlson & Saunders (2006), there are three main types of knowledge repositories:

- Externally focused

- Structured internal knowledge, such as research reports and marketing materials

- Informal internal knowledge, such as "lessons learned" reports and discussion databases and frequently asked questions collections.

Communication-based Tools

There are many communication-oriented tools for knowledge management. Email is an example. We often email colleagues when we need knowledge that we do not possess. For example, a sales representative may email another sales rep for advice on how to position a certain offering. While email can be effective, you need to know who has the knowledge you need. You also need access to that individual. Social networks can help overcome these limitations. **Communities of practice** that exist within networks are especially helpful. LinkedIn groups are an example. Some of these groups are effectively communities of practice. For example, the group "Technology-Using Professors" is a network of college faculty who are interested in how technology can enhance learning.

Collaboration tools combine elements of repositories and communication-based knowledge management tools. Systems such as Google Docs and Microsoft Sharepoint allow for document sharing and co-editing. (You may recall that we discussed Google Docs in Chapter 7.)

Some knowledge management experts see a trend from a content-focused view of knowledge management to one that is more connection-focused. This means that rather than being centered around the ideas of collecting knowledge, the focus is shifting to tools that help you manage your connections to those who have helpful knowledge. The social networking tools we mentioned earlier are among the technologies that can help you with this form of knowledge management. For example, the Stats Box in this chapter provides some statistics for groups in LinkedIn. These groups are good examples of how social networking tools can be used for connection-focused knowledge management.

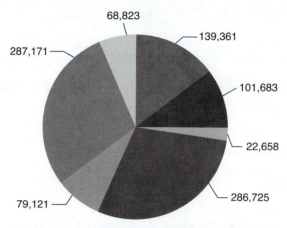

STATS BOX: LINKEDIN GROUPS AS COMMUNITIES OF PRACTICE

As of summer 2011, there were over 980,000 LinkedIn groups. (LinkedIn is a popular profession-oriented social networking site. LinkedIn passed the 100 million user mark in March 2011.) Over 500,000 of these are professional or conference-oriented groups, many of which can be considered communities of practice. Some of these groups are quite large. The Project Management group has over 190,000 members. The Telecom Professionals group has over 160,000 members. Members use these groups to connect with others with similar interests and professions. Most groups allow discussions, which are often used to access the knowledge of group members. The table below shows the distribution of LinkedIn groups by category.

Source: http://www.linkedin.com/myGroups?trk=hb_side_seegrps

Executive Information Systems and Dashboards

Executive information systems help provide high-level managers with the information they need to monitor business activities and make decisions. EIS typically make heavy use of graphical displays of data. They also tend to have easy-to-use interfaces that let executives quickly access the information they need. Both prebuilt reports and tools for custom queries are important components of an EIS. EIS also give executives the ability to "drill down" into information to access more detailed data when necessary. EIS have evolved to make greater use of the dashboard concept. **Digital dashboards** provide graphical views of key data along with graphical warnings when data indicate areas that need attention. Figure 14.6 shows a human resource management dashboard that makes good use of visuals.

Expert Systems

Expert systems help users solve problems or answer questions in a way that mimics an expert's thought processes. An expert system typically has a narrow focus on a

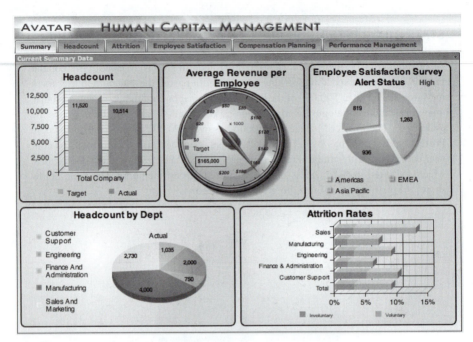

FIGURE 14.6 Executive Dashboard

Source: http://centerview.corda.com/corda/dashboards/HumanCapitalManagement/main
.dashxml#cordaDash=9/.

particular problem domain. For example, an insurance company can use an expert system to guide a salesperson through the process of selecting the most appropriate product for a customer. Many organizations use expert systems to guide nonexpert employees through complex decisions or problems such as technical troubleshooting. There are also systems for medical self-diagnosis, although these systems should be used with caution as they do not make a true diagnosis, but rather provide probabilities of underlying causes for symptoms.

To close this section, we want to make sure that you understand that all organizations need to manage knowledge, even if they do not have formal knowledge management systems. Managing the knowledge resources of an organization is a critically important aspect of organizational success. While knowledge management is seen by some as an esoteric concept favored only by academics, in our opinion organizational leaders are well advised to pay more attention to how they manage knowledge.

Knowledge is typically applied to some decisions; decision-making requires knowledge. While knowledge management technologies are relatively immature, decision support technologies are much more mature in comparison. Decision support systems provide technology tools for helping decision-makers deal with the data and information that are necessary for applying knowledge. The next section discusses these tools.

LEARNING ACTIVITY 14.3	USING A DECISION SUPPORT SYSTEM

Pick one of the following decisions and use the associated decision support system (DSS) to help you analyze the decision. (Your professor may give you a different decision and DSS.)

- What car can you afford?
  DSS: http://www.edmunds.com/calculators/affordability.html

- Should you trade your "gas guzzler" for a more fuel-efficient vehicle?
  DSS: http://www.smartmoney.com/Spending/Deals/Worksheet-Should-You-Trade-in-Your-Gas-Guzzler-23273/

- Should you buy or rent a house?
  DSS: http://www.smartmoney.com/Personal-Finance/RealEstate/To-Rent-or-to-Buy-9687/

Partner with another student and describe your experience using the DSS. Was it useful? Why/why not?

Decision Support Systems and Group Decision Support Systems

Decision support systems (DSS) are computer-based systems that help decision makers use data and models to solve semi-structured or unstructured problems. There are many different types of DSS, so it is convenient to divide them into categories. Our categories are based on Alter's (1977) and Power's (2001) DSS frameworks (http://dssresources.com/).

- **Data-driven DSS** focus on the retrieval and manipulation of data that is stored in an organization's data stores. Data warehouses (which we discuss in the next section) are often important data-driven DSS. While these DSS are useful, they do little to guide the decision maker in making the decision. So, if the decision maker does not use the data properly, a poor decision is likely. However, in the case of unstructured decisions, a data-driven DSS may be particularly useful because of the amount of data retrieval required.

- **Model-driven DSS** focus on providing the decision maker with the ability to access and manipulate analytical models. These models are used to help the decision maker perform sophisticated analysis that would be difficult and time-consuming without the DSS. Model-drive DSS are appropriate for semi-structured decisions. Without some degree of structure it is difficult to build an appropriate model. Model-driven DSS can be applied to decisions in a wide variety of domains, including logistics, portfolio management, demand forecasting, and optimization.

- **Document-driven DSS** focus on managing and retrieving documents that may help with decision-making. The term *documents* should be taken broadly to include chat session transcripts, graphics, and even video and audio files. Document-driven DSS are particularly useful for less structured decisions. Because there is no analytical aspect of document-driven DSS, they draw heavily on the decision-makers analytical ability and cognitive models.

- **Communication-driven DSS** facilitate collaboration and group-based decision-making. According to Power, communication-driven DSS support one or more of the following: communication, information sharing, collaboration, and/or group-based decision-making. Groupware, which we discuss next, is one type of communication-driven DSS. Email, document sharing, and co-editing systems (such as Google Docs) and remote meeting systems are other examples.

Groupware is a network-based system that helps workgroups communicate and collaborate. Time and place are often used to categorize groupware. Synchronous and asynchronous describe whether the users collaborate at the same time (synchronous) or at different times (asynchronous). When group members are in the same physical location, they are co-located. Figure 14.7 uses the dimensions of time and place to categorize common groupware applications, which are described following the figure.

- Group decision support systems
  Group decision support systems (GDSS) facilitate group-based decision-making tasks. GDSS often include applications for brainstorming, anonymous commenting, and voting. The goal of GDSS is to make group decision-making more rational by supporting established group methods that encourage equal participation. Some organizations have "decision rooms," which consist of individual computers that access GDSS software, along with shared devices, such as projection systems. GDSS can also be used remotely.

- Shared whiteboards
  Whiteboards have long been used to help workgroups communicate. You have probably used one yourself. Shared whiteboard systems allow users who are not co-located to share drawings or notes in the same way. Often shared whiteboard systems assign different colors to each user so that you can tell who is drawing each element.

	Same time "synchronous"	Different time "asynchronous"
Same place "co-located"	Group decision support systems (decision room), presentation support	
Different place "distant"	Group decision support systems (remote), video conferencing, chat, remote presentation, shared whiteboards.	Discussion databases, email, email lists, workflow, document co-editing

FIGURE 14.7 Groupware Examples

- Video conferencing
  Video conferencing allows individuals to communicate using both voice and video. Video conferencing systems range from free services such as Skype that you can access through your personal computer to dedicated rooms that have special equipment and software installed. Capability and quality vary widely from the simple "desktop" systems to the dedicated videoconferencing rooms.

- Chat systems
  Online chat systems allow users to write real-time messages in a public space. (Note that we are specifically referring to group-oriented chat systems.) Some systems allow for a moderator to lead the interaction. Many chat systems capture a transcript of a session, which can be useful for documentation purposes.

- Remote presentation
  Remote presentation software allows non-co-located groups to view a presentation remotely. These systems often have a chat window that allows the presenter and remote audience to interact.

- Email and email lists
  Email is one of the simplest groupware applications. Most of us have used email to distribute documents or ideas to a group. Email lists facilitate group communication by making broadcasting emails to the group easier. Some systems allow you to subscribe to an email list. These often let you choose whether you want to see each individual message or periodically receive digests of messages that show all messages sent to the group in a single email message.

- Discussion databases
  Similar to discussion forums, discussion databases store threaded online, asynchronous discussions in a way that allows users to search and retrieve relevant information. These are different from chat session transcripts in that the discussion databases are oriented toward asynchronous discussions. Discussion databases are particularly useful for new group members who need to come up to speed on the group's discussions.

- Workflow
  Workflow systems route documents through a group in a relatively predetermined manner. Workflow systems ensure that documents are routed properly so that the relevant group members are provided with documents in a timely manner. These systems also make sure that the proper authorities within the group review the documents.

- Document co-editing
  Document co-editing systems, which we discussed earlier, help groups with their work by allowing group members to work on documents synchronously, rather than having to email documents back and forth (or otherwise share them). These systems also help with versioning by having all members work on the same version of a document. (If you have ever spent time editing the wrong version of a

document you will appreciate the importance of versioning.) While we list document co-editing in the asynchronous column of Figure 14.7, most systems allow for simultaneous co-editing.

It is important to understand that DSS support decision-making. The decision maker's knowledge is still critical to the decision-making process. The DSS provide tools that help the decision maker operate more efficiently and effectively, but the DSS do not replace the decision maker.

Business Intelligence

Organizations are drowning in a sea of information. A major goal of this book is to help you understand how organizations are trying to cope with the ever-increasing amount of information. Managers know that this information potentially represents a gold mine of value, but are often unsure how to transform the raw material into this information gold. Business intelligence (BI) systems may hold the key to unearthing the value in the information.

Business intelligence is set of applications, technologies, and processes for gathering, storing, analyzing, and accessing data to help users make better business decisions. Often BI combines two sets of technologies, data warehousing and data mining, to help managers leverage the organization's data resources for better decision-making. Figure 14.8 illustrates how data warehousing and data mining combine with transactional systems to enable BI.

The goal of BI is to help managers make sense of data. To get to that level, the data first must be generated. Transactional databases "create" the data. (Data may also come from other sources, such as external systems and databases, but most

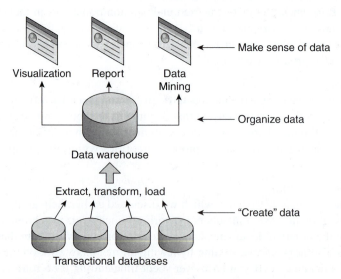

FIGURE 14.8 Business Intelligence Framework

will come from the organization's internal transactional systems.) The data from the transactional databases is put into the data warehouse by a process called extract, transform, and load (E/T/L), which we discuss later. The data warehouse stores and organizes the data in a way that is better suited for supporting decision-making. Analysts and managers use data mining tools make sense of the data stored in the data warehouse.

Business intelligence tools help many different types of organizations reduce spending and increase sales. BI software helped the city of Albuquerque reduce their operating expenses by over $2 million over a three-year period. Toyota used BI tools to save over $800,000 by eliminating double payments to shippers. American Airlines used BI to save $5 million by detecting fraudulent ticket sales. There are many similar examples. (Sources: http://www.cio.com/article/print/40296, http://www.sybase.com/detail?id=210272)

Data Warehousing

Data warehouses support decision-making. Understanding this is a key to understanding the purpose of data warehousing. Supporting transactions requires that databases perform many data additions, deletions, and updates. Decision support, in contrast, is more about data retrieval. Unfortunately, a database that is very efficient for data updates usually does not perform as well for data retrieval. There is another problem: decision-making often requires getting data from multiple transaction databases. Finally, transaction databases usually store data at a very detailed level. Aggregated data are often better for decision-making. So, gathering all of the data necessary for decision-making can be time-consuming and inefficient. Data warehousing addresses these issues. Data warehousing is a process, the goal of which is to gain value from an organization's information through the use of data warehouses. A **data warehouse** is a copy of transactional data (and other data) that is formatted so that it is useful for decision support.

Data warehouses have several characteristics that set them apart from transactional databases:

- Data warehouses are subject-oriented. They are organized around particular subjects such as marketing, human resources, sales, or production.

- Data in data warehouses are integrated from a variety of internal and external sources.

- Data in data warehouses are typically transformed from their original format. Detailed data are often aggregated. For example, a data warehouse for a restaurant chain would aggregate individual sales into total sales from some time period (such as per hour).

- Data in data warehouses typically are nonvolatile, which means that the data do not change. Once data are in the warehouse, they stay in the warehouse and are not changed. (Data that are no longer of value may be deleted from the warehouse.)

Data from various sources are gathered together, prepared, and loaded into the data warehouse through the extract, transform, load process, as we mentioned earlier. The E/T/L process is easy to understand conceptually, but is often very complex and time consuming to perform in practice. Each element is described below.

- *Extract*: Data are pulled from the source systems (such as the transactional databases). Deciding exactly what data to extract is important.

- *Transform*: Data must be changed into a form that is suitable for decision support. Often this involves aggregating detailed data. Data cleansing is also an important part of the transform process. Data in transactional databases is often messy. This problem gets worse when data are extracted from multiple systems. This messy data must be cleaned up before being loaded into the warehouse. Think about all of the ways a company such as AT&T could be represented in different databases: AT&T, ATT, American Telephone and Telegraph, American Tel and Tel, AT and T, and so on. All of these need to be recognized as the same company, otherwise you could make decisions based on faulty data. Data cleansing is often complicated and expensive.

- *Load*: The cleaned data needs to be put into the data warehouse. This must be repeated periodically. Figuring out how often data should be loaded can be difficult. It primarily depends on how up to date the data needs to be in order to support good decision-making. The more time-critical the data, the more frequent the loads.

Once you have the data in the data warehouse, you need to be able to retrieve and analyze in order to gain value from the information. Data mining can help with this.

Data Mining

Data mining is the process of analyzing data to identify trends, patterns, and other useful information. Data mining typically involves applying statistical techniques to identify trends and patterns. Some people consider querying and visualization to be related to data mining. Since we covered those topics in earlier chapters, the focus here is on statistical data mining.

Wouldn't it be nice to be able to predict the future? That is a goal of data mining. Data mining techniques seek to take large amounts of data and form predictions based on the data. There are wide applications of data mining in areas ranging from business to picking players in a pro sports draft. The basic process of data mining is shown in Figure 14.9. Existing data are analyzed using the appropriate data mining technique to build a predictive model. The new model is then applied to new data to make a prediction.

While data mining uses many statistical techniques, it is important to understand the difference between traditional statistical analysis and data mining. In most traditional statistical analyses you create a model (such as a regression equation) and then test that model using data. Essentially, you have a hypothesis, then use data and statistical analysis to test that hypothesis. While this is often effective, it is limited by your knowledge and creativity. You can only test what you can hypothesize. Data

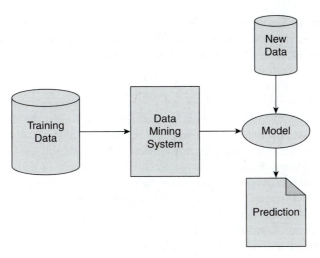

FIGURE 14.9 High-Level View of Data Mining

Source: adapted from: http://www.thearling.com/dmintro/dmintro_2.htm/.

mining can help overcome these limitations. In data mining the emphasis is on discovering the model, then testing the validity of the model. Statistical techniques are used to uncover the relationships in the data that lead to the model. Table 14.2 shows common data mining techniques with descriptions and examples.

Data mining has many applications in business. You may have talked about customer segmentation in a marketing class. Customer groups (segments) can be built through cluster analysis. Cluster analysis divides information into mutually exclusive groups (each member can be in at most one group). The goal is to build the groups so that each member in a group is as close as possible to every other member of the group, and the different groups are as different as possible. For example, a

Table 14.2 Common Data Mining Techniques

Technique	Description	Example
Association detection	Discovering patterns in which multiple events are connected	Customers tend to purchase eggs and butter together
Sequence analysis	Discovering when one event leads to another event	A student graduates from college, then buys a new car
Classification	Dividing data into mutually exclusive groups based on the variable you want to predict	Students are classified according to whether they are likely to drop out
Clustering	Dividing data into mutually exclusive groups using all available data (not just the variable you want to predict)	Hotel guests are grouped according to various preferences
Forecasting	Making predictions using discovered patterns	Past repayment and employment histories predict whether a mortgage applicant will default

hotel chain might use cluster analysis to segment customers into different groups, such as short-stay business customers, vacationers, and long-stay business customers. Advertisements could then be tailored to each of these customers, which should increase the ads' effectiveness. CRM systems can use cluster analysis to customize product or service offerings.

Market basket analysis identifies affinities among customer's product or service offerings. Retailers often use checkout scanner data to identify products that customers tend to buy together. For example, a restaurant might determine that customers who order wine typically buy dessert, while beer drinkers usually buy appetizers. The restaurant could develop special offerings based on this information. Market basket analysis is an example of association detection. Association examines the degree to which variables in a data set are related by considering the frequency with which the variables occur together.

Have you ever played the 20-questions game? If so, you have some familiarity with the concept of decision trees, which is a classification technique. A decision tree makes a prediction based on a series of questions. The next question in the series depends on the answer to the current question. You might have concluded that decision trees are useful devices since we have discussed them twice in this chapter. Earlier we discussed decision trees as a method for knowledge capture. Here the focus is on prediction rather than knowledge capture.

There are many other data mining techniques, including statistical methods such as regression analysis, time series analysis, neural networks, and text analysis. As we mentioned earlier, statistical analysis emphasizes testing preexisting models, while data mining tries to discover the models. Many of the same statistical techniques can be applied to both.

Reporting and data visualization tools (discussed in Chapter 6) are also considered by some to be data mining tools. (There is some debate about this.) These tools help you quickly build different views of your data. In some cases, these views are in the form of visualizations, while in other cases they are built around numbers and text. Spreadsheet pivot tables are an example. Pivot tables allow you to see multidimensional views of a data set. For example, Figure 14.10 shows sales data from a small retail clothing chain. The data in this figure show the total revenue for each store, broken down by state and quarter.

You can quickly modify the dimensions by which you view the data. Suppose you want to add product categories to the analysis. In a matter of seconds, you can modify the pivot table to include the new dimension, as shown in Figure 14.11. (Note that only a portion of the table is shown in the figure.) The flexibility of pivot tables makes them ideal reporting and analysis tools for many common business decisions. You can learn how to build pivot tables in the Spreadsheet In-Depth Guide, which is available on the book's website.

One important point to keep in mind is that you should always assess whether your model and its predictions are reasonable. Many data mining techniques are based on mathematics; they are all about the numbers. The mathematics does not consider whether the underlying associations have any real meaning. That is where human interpretation and judgment comes in.

	A	B	C	D	E	F	G
1							
2							
3	Sum of Sales revenue	Column Labels					
4	Row Labels	Q1	Q2	Q3	Q4	Grand Total	
5	⊟California	1,899,680.30	1,760,147.80	1,930,516.50	1,889,224.70	7,479,569.30	
6	e-Fashion San Francisco	770,502.70	779,742.50	822,383.60	886,011.70	3,258,640.50	
7	e-Fashion San Diego	1,129,177.60	980,405.30	1,108,132.90	1,003,213.00	4,220,928.80	
8	⊟Colorado	525,682.20	500,076.00	510,776.90	523,740.10	2,060,275.20	
9	e-Fashion Dillion	525,682.20	500,076.00	510,776.90	523,740.10	2,060,275.20	
10	⊟DC	766,821.70	706,446.60	692,258.20	796,423.40	2,961,949.90	
11	e-Fashion Washington Midtown	766,821.70	706,446.60	692,258.20	796,423.40	2,961,949.90	
12	⊟Florida	515,687.70	489,997.80	387,809.70	485,663.30	1,879,158.50	
13	e-Fashion Miami Beach	515,687.70	489,997.80	387,809.70	485,663.30	1,879,158.50	
14	⊟Illinois	846,408.40	850,595.00	610,765.20	714,889.80	3,022,658.40	
15	e-Fashion Chicago Loop	846,408.40	850,595.00	610,765.20	714,889.80	3,022,658.40	
16	⊟Massachusetts	312,896.40	291,431.00	249,529.00	429,850.20	1,283,706.60	
17	e-Fashion Boston Newbury	312,896.40	291,431.00	249,529.00	429,850.20	1,283,706.60	
18	⊟New York	1,987,114.70	2,028,090.70	1,672,580.70	1,894,434.50	7,582,220.60	
19	e-Fashion New York 5th	804,084.40	795,193.60	637,277.10	723,811.40	2,960,366.50	
20	e-Fashion New York Midtown	1,183,030.30	1,232,897.10	1,035,303.60	1,170,623.10	4,621,854.10	
21	⊟Texas	2,875,569.20	2,499,276.80	2,146,302.80	2,596,515.50	10,117,664.30	
22	e-Fashion Dallas	555,458.70	450,588.30	467,925.90	496,061.30	1,970,034.20	
23	e-Fashion Houston	614,284.60	560,650.20	465,677.10	662,570.90	2,303,182.80	
24	e-Fashion DFW	775,482.70	667,850.30	581,470.40	674,869.80	2,699,673.20	
25	e-Fashion Houston Downtown	930,343.20	820,188.00	631,229.40	763,013.50	3,144,774.10	
26	Grand Total	9,729,860.60	9,126,061.70	8,200,539.00	9,330,741.50	36,387,202.80	
27							
28							
29							

Sheet1 / Report 1

FIGURE 14.10 Pivot Table Example

	A	B	C	D	E	F
3	Sum of Sales revenue	Column Labels				
4	Row Labels	Q1	Q2	Q3	Q4	Grand Total
5	⊟California	1,899,680.30	1,760,147.80	1,930,516.50	1,889,224.70	7,479,569.30
6	⊟e-Fashion San Francisco	770,502.70	779,742.50	822,383.60	886,011.70	3,258,640.50
7	2 Pocket shirts	27,876.20	33,324.60	30,122.00	31,773.80	123,096.60
8	Belts,bags,wallets	49,517.90	40,896.40	17,621.40	29,908.20	137,943.90
9	Bermudas	994.90		340.30	4,883.40	6,218.60
10	Boatwear	11,091.60	2,065.60	2,040.30	8,949.70	24,147.20
11	Cardigan	36,084.10	22,446.50	14,003.60	1,176.40	73,710.60
12	Casual dresses	4,293.20	4,458.50	12,908.10	5,014.70	26,674.50
13	Day wear	4,344.90	28,676.30	29,980.00		63,001.20
14	Dry wear	1,396.10		6,236.20	10,935.60	18,567.90
15	Evening wear	26,296.00	4,699.80	32,976.70	101,981.50	165,954.00
16	Fancy fabric	4,758.00	3,607.60	3,646.70	4,964.70	16,977.00
17	Full length	1,935.50		4,459.90	15,833.50	22,228.90
18	Hair accessories	4,852.80		3,388.10	7,065.60	15,306.50
19	Hats,gloves,scarves	66,386.40	24,783.20	19,091.00	3,175.00	113,435.60
20	Jackets			6,570.00	381.30	6,951.30
21	Jeans	4,238.70	1,711.80	5,678.80	10,353.60	21,982.90
22	Jewelry	185,083.10	209,951.90	43,683.00	1,815.20	440,533.20
23	Long lounge pants	970.80	424.60	5,234.90	7,961.90	14,592.20
24	Long sleeve	17,300.00	10,490.60	40,848.40	61,425.20	130,064.20
25	Lounge wear	6,423.70	16,771.60	16,017.80	5,639.40	44,852.50
26	Mini city	818.00	3,445.20	5,697.80	1,098.40	11,059.40
27	Night wear			1,837.80	2,846.00	4,683.80
28	Outdoor	3,151.00	3,503.40	7,544.60	6,310.50	20,509.50
29	Pants	572.90		1,831.60	946.20	3,350.70
30	Party pants	8,416.00	14,143.80	59,198.40	4,208.90	85,967.10
31	Samples	1,022.80	10,618.70	12,960.80	7,878.90	32,481.20

Sheet1 / Report 1

FIGURE 14.11 Pivot Table with Additional Dimension

Throughout this chapter we have discussed how information and knowledge can be used to help with decision-making. As is the case with many technologies and methods, they can be used for good or evil. We strongly believe in the importance of making ethical decisions, regardless of the methods or tools used. In the next section we discuss ethical decision-making and provide you with a process that may help you make more ethical decisions.

LEARNING ACTIVITY 14.4	MAKING ETHICAL DECISIONS

The scenarios below describe some decisions that have ethical issues. For each question, state what decision you would make and why you would make that decision. Be prepared to discuss your answers in class.

1. You need some special software for a school project. The software is available in the school's computer labs, but going to the lab is inconvenient. You can purchase the software at the bookstore, but your friend has the software and is willing to loan you the installation CDs. Would you borrow the CDs?

2. One of your coworkers is using his work computer for his part-time business. You become aware of this. Should you report your coworker?

3. You are the Chief Information Officer for your company. As part of your duties, you are in charge of safeguarding data about your customers. The vice president for marketing is interested in trading information about your customers with another company. (Your company will receive information about the other company's customers.) The marketing VP thinks this trade will increase your company's revenue. Should you provide the customer information?

Ethical Decision-Making

"A man without ethics is like a wild beast unleashed on the world." This quote from the French writer Alfred Camus nicely sums up the importance of ethics. While philosophers may argue about the definition of ethics, at its core is the idea of doing the right thing—standards of behavior that tell us how we should act. Since decision-making is choosing among alternatives, ethical decision-making is considering standards of conduct when making choices.

Ethical decision-making requires work, as doing the right thing often does. The work is worth the effort. If you always strive to make ethical choices, you will be a success. Many authors have proposed various procedures for making ethical decisions. One that we like comes from the Ethics Resource Center. It incorporates the PLUS set of questions to keep you on track (http://www.ethics.org/resource/plus-decision-making-model). The PLUS questions whether an alternative:

• [P] is consistent with organizational policies, procedures, and guidelines?

• [L] is acceptable under applicable laws and regulations?

- [U] conforms to universal values such as empathy, integrity, and justice?
- [S] satisfies your personal definition of what is good, right, and fair?

   Keeping the PLUS questions in mind, follow these steps:

1. Define the problem.
   a. Why do you need to make a decision? What outcome do you want from the decision?
   b. Does the current situation violate any PLUS criteria?

2. Identify alternatives.
   a. Try to identify three or more alternatives.

3. Evaluate the alternatives.
   a. What are the positive and negative consequences that flow from each alternative? Consider "positive" and "negative" from the perspective of those impacted by the decision.
   b. How probable is it that those outcomes will occur?
   c. Consider whether each alternative will create or resolve any violations of the PLUS criteria.

4. Make the decision.

5. Implement the decision.
   a. Minimize negative consequences to the extent possible.
   b. Communicate the reasoning behind the decision to those affected by the decision.

6. Evaluate the decision.
   a. Did the decision improve the situation that led to the need for the decision?
   b. Were any new problems created by the solution?
   c. Are any PLUS considerations resolved or introduced by the new situation?

   Source: adapted from http://csweb.cs.bgsu.edu/maner/heuristics/1998EthicsResourceCenter1.htm/.

   If you keep the following in mind throughout the decision-making process, you will be much more likely to make ethical decisions.

- Who are the stakeholders for this decision or its outcomes? Try to think broadly about this. Often stakeholders may not be readily apparent.

- Could someone be damaged by this decision? If so, consider whether there are alternatives that can reduce this harm. Sometimes your decisions will harm people; tough decisions often do. However, by considering the impact on others, and trying to develop ways to minimize the harm, you will often be able to soften the blow.

- What alternatives are available? How do the outcomes from those alternatives impact each stakeholder group? For each alternative, consider which option:
   - Produces the greatest good and the least harm.
   - Best respects stakeholders' rights.
   - Leads you to act as the type of person you want to be.

- How can you implement the decision with the greatest attention to stakeholders' concerns? Decisions often have uncomfortable outcomes. This applies to ethical decisions as well. The way in which you carry out the decision can have a significant impact the level of harm to any individual stakeholder.

While information systems cannot make you an ethical decision maker, they can help reduce some of the extra work that sometimes comes from ethical decision-making. For example, suppose you are tasked with cutting expenses for your company. A spreadsheet can help you analyze various alternatives for doing so. Information systems also contain the data and information you may need for developing and analyzing alternative courses of action.

Ethical decision-making is worth the effort. Leadership requires followers and if you always strive to make ethical decisions, the people you lead will trust you to have their interests in mind, even when making difficult decisions. When those you lead trust you, you can be a great leader.

CHAPTER SUMMARY

In this chapter we discussed knowledge, processes, and tools that help organizations manage knowledge. We also helped you understand technologies that support decision-making and that help organizations gain more value from their information resources. Finally, we presented information that you can use to help you make more ethical decisions.

Here are the main points from the chapter:

- Knowledge management is a process that allows organizations to generate value from their knowledge-based assets.

- Managing knowledge is important because knowledge is among the most valuable resources of any organization.

- Explicit knowledge can be easily expressed. Tacit knowledge is difficult to express and communicate.

- The main processes for knowledge management are create, capture, codify, store, retrieve, transfer, and apply.

- Information and communication technologies that facilitate knowledge management include knowledge repositories, communication and collaboration tools, executive information systems, and dashboards and expert systems.

- Decision support systems are computer-based systems that help decision makers use data and models to solve semi-structured or unstructured problems.

- Business intelligence is a set of applications, technologies, and processes for gathering, storing, analyzing, and accessing data to help decision makers.

- Data warehouses and data mining systems are important business intelligence components.

- Data warehouses store and organize data for decision support.

- Data mining is the process of analyzing data to identify trends, patterns, and other useful information.

- Ethical decision-making considers standards of behavior when making decisions.

REVIEW QUESTIONS

1. Briefly explain how knowledge and information differ in the terms of ease of management and level of human contribution.
2. Why is managing knowledge important to organizations?
3. State five benefits of effective knowledge management.
4. Contrast explicit and tacit knowledge.
5. Give an example of tacit knowledge.
6. Name and briefly describe the four types of knowledge resources described in the chapter.
7. Name the processes in the knowledge management cycle.
8. Briefly describe the four knowledge creation processes in the SECI model.
9. What is knowledge codification? Why is it important to knowledge management?
10. Compare and contrast decision tables and decision trees.
11. Explain why search technologies are important to knowledge management.
12. Give an example of each of the following: knowledge repository, communication-based knowledge management tool.
13. What is a digital dashboard?
14. Name and briefly describe the DSS categories described in the chapter.
15. Compare and contrast synchronous and asynchronous groupware.
16. Name and briefly describe the groupware examples discussed in the chapter.
17. What are the two main components of a business intelligence system? Briefly describe each component.
18. Describe the E/T/L process.
19. What is the purpose of data mining?
20. Name three data mining techniques.
21. Describe the PLUS approach to ethical decision-making.

REFLECTION QUESTIONS

1. What is the most important thing you learned in this chapter? Why is it important?
2. What topics are unclear? What about them is unclear?
3. What relationships do you see between what you learned in this chapter and what you have learned in earlier chapters?

4. The chapter focused on organizational knowledge management, but knowledge management is also important to individuals (this is called personal knowledge management). Why is knowledge management important to your personal and professional development?

5. Have you ever tried to explain to someone how you are able to do something (hit a golf ball, draw, study, etc.)? Was it easy or hard to explain? What about the knowledge you were trying to transfer determined whether it was easy or hard to explain?

6. In Chapter 7 you learned about cloud computing. How can cloud computing facilitate knowledge management?

7. How does data warehousing facilitate data mining?

8. What is the relationship between business intelligence and knowledge management?

9. How is the need for quick decisions related to the need to make ethical decisions?

10. How can information and communication technologies help make ethical decisions?

ADDITIONAL LEARNING ACTIVITIES

1. Describe a situation in which you used technology to access knowledge. Address the following in your description. What knowledge were you seeking? How did you go about finding the knowledge? What technologies did you use? How effective were they?

2. Form groups of two or three.
   - One of you (the *explainer*) answer the following question:
     - Why is knowledge management important to organizational success?
   - When the first person finishes, the other person (the *questioner*) seeks clarification and provides her/his own ideas.
   - Record and be prepared to share your answers.

3. Some music services, including Pandora and iTunes can build smart playlists that use the songs in your library (or playlists) to build playlists that you will like. Research how these services work and prepare a one-page paper on how these services relate to the data mining tools you read about in this chapter.

4. Create a decision table or decision tree to document how you go about making the following decisions:
   - Deciding whether to take a class
   - Deciding which section of a class to take
   - Deciding on a major
   - Deciding whether to join a club

5. Partner with two other students. Create a wiki on how to choose which section of a multisection class to take. You can use Wikispaces (http://www.wikispaces.com/), PK Works (http://pbworks.com/), or any other wiki service to create your wiki. Be prepared to share your wiki with the class.

6. Research how companies are using data mining. Pick one example and prepare a one- to two-page report on how the company used data mining.

7. Think of a time when you had to make a decision that was unclear from an ethical perspective. Apply the PLUS model to the decision. Prepare a two-page reflection paper that comments on
   - why the decision was unclear ethically
   - the effectiveness of the PLUS model

REFERENCES

Alter, S. "Why is Man-Computer Interaction Important for Decision Support Systems?" *Interfaces,* 7(2) (1977): 109–115.

Davenport, T. and L. Prusak. *Working Knowledge: How Organizations Manage What They Know,* Boston, MA: Harvard Business School Press, (1998).

Nonaka, I. and H. Takeuchi. *The Knowledge Creating Company,* New York: Oxford University Press, (1995).

Pearlson, K. and C. Saunders. *Managing and Using Information Systems* (3rd ed.), Hoboken, NJ: John Wiley & Sons, (2006). Pearlson and Saunders (2006)

Power, D. "Supporting Decision-Makers: An Expanded Framework," In Harriger, A. (Ed.), *e-Proceedings Informing Science Conference,* Krakow, Poland, June 19-22, 2001, 431–436.

BIBLIOGRAPHY AND FURTHER READINGS

Courtney, J. "Decision-making and Knowledge Management in Inquiring Organizations: Toward a New Decision-making Paradigm for DSS." *Decision Support Systems* 31 (2001): 17–38.

GLOSSARY

Business intelligence: a set of applications, technologies, and processes for gathering, storing, analyzing, and accessing data to help users make better business decisions.

Codifying knowledge: converting tacit and explicit knowledge into a form that organizational members can use.

Cognitive maps: graphical representation of a mental model of an expert's knowledge.

Communication-driven decision support system: DSS that facilitates collaboration and group-based decision-making.

Community of practice: group of people who share a common interest, usually in a craft or profession, and who interact to share knowledge.

Conceptual knowledge: explicit knowledge that is embodied in language, symbols, and images.

Data mining: process of analyzing data to identify trends, patterns, and other useful information to make predictions.

Data warehouse: a copy of transactional data (and other data) that is formatted so that it is useful for decision support.

Data-driven decision support system: DSS that focuses on the retrieval and manipulation of data that is stored in an organization's data stores.

Decision support systems: computer-based systems that help decision makers use data and models to solve semi-structured or unstructured problems.

Decision tables: a list of conditions and their values along with a list of conclusions or actions.

Decision trees: diagram that shows alternate paths that impact decisions.

Digital dashboards: computer-based systems that provide graphical views of key data along with graphical warnings when data indicate areas that need attention.

Document-driven decision support system: DSS that facilitates the management and retrieval of documents that may help with decision-making.

Executive information systems: information systems that help provide high-level managers with the information they need to monitor business activities and make decisions.

Experiential knowledge: tacit knowledge that can be shared through common experiences and interpersonal communication.

Expert systems: systems that help users solve problems or answer questions in a way that mimics an expert's thought processes.

Explicit knowledge: knowledge that can be expressed relatively easily.

Groupware - network-based system that helps workgroups communicate and collaborate.

Knowledge management: process by which organizations create, capture, store, apply, and protect knowledge to achieve organizational objectives.

Knowledge repositories: tools that make it easy to find and retrieve documents that contain knowledge.

Model-driven decision support system: DSS that provides the decision maker with the ability to access and manipulate analytical models.

Routine knowledge: tacit knowledge that is embedded in the organization's practices.

Systemic knowledge: explicit knowledge that has been systemized and packaged.

Tacit knowledge: knowledge that is difficult to express or communicate. It is internalized and highly individualized.

Index